T0374720

DUMBARTON OAKS
MEDIEVAL LIBRARY

Jan M. Ziolkowski, General Editor

APPENDIX OVIDIANA

DOML 62

Appendix Ovidiana

Latin Poems Ascribed to
Ovid in the Middle Ages

Edited and Translated by

RALPH HEXTER

LAURA PFUNTNER

JUSTIN HAYNES

DUMBARTON OAKS
MEDIEVAL LIBRARY

HARVARD UNIVERSITY PRESS
CAMBRIDGE, MASSACHUSETTS
LONDON, ENGLAND
2020

First Printing

Library of Congress Cataloging-in-Publication Data
Names: Ovid, 43 B.C.–17 A.D. or 18 A.D. | Hexter, Ralph J., 1952– editor,
    translator. | Pfuntner, Laura, editor, translator. | Haynes, Justin
    (Classicist), editor, translator.
Title: Appendix Ovidiana : Latin poems ascribed to Ovid in the Middle
    Ages / edited and translated by Ralph Hexter, Laura Pfuntner, Justin
    Haynes.
Other titles: Dumbarton Oaks medieval library ; 62.
Description: Cambridge, Massachusetts : Harvard University Press, 2020. |
    Series: Dumbarton Oaks medieval library ; 62 | Includes bibliographical
    references and index. | This is a facing-page volume: Latin on the
    versos, and English translation on the rectos.
Identifiers: LCCN 2019037884 | ISBN 9780674238381 (cloth)
Subjects: LCSH: Ovid, 43 B.C.–17 A.D. or 18 A.D.—Spurious and doubtful
    works. | Ovid, 43 B.C.–17 A.D. or 18 A.D.—Influence. | Latin poetry,
    Medieval and modern. | Latin poetry, Medieval and modern—
    Translations into English. | Literature, Medieval—Roman influences.
Classification: LCC PA6520.Z5 2020 | DDC 871/.01—dc23
LC record available at https://lccn.loc.gov/2019037884

Contents

CONTENTS

CONTENTS

Introduction

The present volume brings together virtually all surviving Latin poems that were ascribed to Ovid between roughly 500 and 1500. The majority of these were composed in the Middle Ages, but some are classical in origin. All, however, were at least once attributed to Ovid, even if today's scholarly consensus labels them inauthentic and so designates them as pseudo-Ovidiana. This body of poetry, then, reflects medieval understandings of the greatly admired classical poet, expanding and developing Ovid's legacy—sometimes in disturbing ways, as we will discuss.[1]

This volume marks the first time that an attempt has been made to collect the surviving corpus of pseudo-Ovidiana in one volume, and we have titled it the *Appendix Ovidiana* by analogy with the corpus of pseudo-Vergiliana, commonly known today as the *Appendix Vergiliana*.[2] In contrast to the *Appendix Vergiliana,* many of whose poems tended to travel together through the centuries, the pseudo-Ovidiana composed neither so stable nor so ancient a collection. It is true that a few of the pseudo-Ovidiana circulated as a more-or-less constant grouping in numerous manuscripts from the thirteenth century onward, and that from these manuscripts a select subset of poems made the transition to some early printed editions of Ovid. Nonetheless, virtually every one of the thirty-four poems ascribed to Ovid and printed here has a different provenance. Each calls for its own historical and contextual information, just as each requires its own identification of sources in the textual notes.

Pseudonymity is itself a slippery category. The nature of authorial ascription itself varied when, as in eras before printing and (the even later) establishment of copyright and intellectual property rights, the transmission of texts, and the very availability of a work, depended on the manual preparation of writing surfaces, on copying and recopying by individual scribes, and the transportation of individual manuscripts.[3] Only occasionally does one come across medieval examples of a later author claiming the identity of an earlier *literary* author with the obvious intention of deceiving readers.[4] More often, unattributed texts or those written by lesser-known authors are ascribed to someone better known, all the more so if the latter served as a stylistic model. In the High Middle Ages, when much of the pseudo-Ovidiana was either composed or acquired an Ovidian ascription, so many poets strove to write in the style of Ovid that the period has been described as the "Ovidian age" *(aetas Ovidiana).*[5] When does this kind of "imitation" become "masquerade"? In such a compositional world, it is easy to see how some of these works, not otherwise tethered, could have been drawn into the gravitational field of "planet Ovid," subsequently orbiting under his name.[6]

It may come as a surprise, then, that relatively few of the poems in the *Appendix Ovidiana* are Ovidian in style. A case in point is *On the Old Woman.* Notwithstanding the fact that it is among the least Ovidian in terms of style, it was taken by some, for a time at least, as Ovid's. *On the Old Woman* is of course unique in many ways, not least that it comes with an apparatus of prefatory texts that "establishes" Ovid as the poem's author. What follows is then the first-person narrative of "Ovid." As the scare quotes here indicate, the medieval author of *On the Old Woman* intentionally presented it as authored by the Roman poet. Today we would see this thirteenth-century author's assumption of the persona of Ovid (as well as the provision of prefatory paratexts) as elements of a fictive strategy, not unlike, *mutatis mutandis,* the adoption of Ovid as narrator in some late twentieth-century novels.[7] Furthermore, the tantalizingly anonymous author of *On the Old Woman* seems to have had very specific motivations for making use of precisely this fiction.[8]

While we present texts that were taken (at least once) as Ovid's in the Middle Ages, we are not concerned to categorize pseudo-Ovidiana according to the intentions of the actual authors of the pieces, intentions that in any case can rarely if ever be recovered. Manuscript attribution to Ovid, then, becomes the determining factor for the inclusion of a text in this volume. Many of the poems in the collection were regularly ascribed to Ovid in manuscripts, but, given the great variation in scribal practice as to the inclusion of titles or colophons, many of even these poems also appear in some manuscripts without any authorial attribution. Some of those included are only rarely ascribed to Ovid in the sources, but we have included a poem if it was even once attributed to Ovid and so would have contributed to the perception of Ovid for at least those into whose hands that one manuscript came. Some of the attributions are shared with other authors, for example, *On the Cuckoo,* which is also at times attributed to Virgil.[9]

In light of our reception-oriented principle, we have ordered our collection, as best we can, according to the earliest datable extant manuscript that makes the ascription. The reader, however, should not suppose that the sequence presented here describes in any real sense a "history" of the pseudo-Ovidiana, for the same reasons that any account of an author's reception in eras before print and mass access to published material is at best a grossly generalized summation of what was in fact a myriad of different encounters with the author, ranging from the schoolroom (in some cases) to individual and unique perusals of a single manuscript in a particular library.[10] In the case of the pseudo-Ovidiana, such variability and contingency extend beyond the fact that, as we have described, reception is local and individual to the fact that a given poem's attribution to Ovid is also variable: one and the same work could be received both as Ovidian and as not Ovidian by contemporaries, depending on which manuscript they had before them.[11]

One should understand, further, that though our sequence of presentation maps such chronology of attribution as extant manuscripts permit, the dating of some of the manuscripts is itself uncertain. Moreover, some of the pseudo-Ovidian poems seem inspired not so much by genuine works of Ovid as by other pseudo-Ovidiana—for example, *The Louse* by *The Flea*, *On a Certain Old Woman* by *On the Old Woman*—so that in our introduction, we recognize some of these thematic subgroups within an overarching historically oriented sequence and discuss those poems together.

Our volume begins with the *Summaries of the Books of the Aeneid*, some of the most widely dispersed and frequently copied pseudo-Ovidian poems, although they have almost nothing to do with Ovid at all, if by that is meant his life or his works.[12] The function of attributing the *Summaries* to Ovid was to express and inscribe Ovid's subordinate status in every manuscript of Virgil in which they appear. This schema casts Virgil as the ultimate canonical author, while relegating Ovid to the position of perpetual annotator. These Virgilian paratexts might date from as early as the third or fourth century, although the strict *terminus ante quem* is provided by the famous *Vergilius Romanus* (Vat. lat. 3867) of the fifth century. These and other major versions were also often copied apart from texts of Virgil, most notably in manuscripts of the so-called *Anthologia Latina,* starting with the *Salmasianus* manuscript of the eighth century.[13] We cannot know precisely when these poems were first ascribed to Ovid, because the earliest manuscripts, including the *Vergilius Romanus,* do not contain the prefatory poem, the first couplet of which runs: "Just as Virgil gave precedence to the great Homer, I, the poet Ovid, yield to my Virgil."[14] Since no extant manuscript of these ten introductory verses predates the ninth century, the *Summaries* can be called pseudo-Ovidian with certainty only after that date.[15] The *Quatrains on All of Virgil's Works* do not begin with a comparable proclamation of Ovidian authorship, but they are attributed to Ovid in the manuscript Vat. lat. 1575 of the tenth or eleventh century.[16]

Following come the fragmentary *Verses on Fish and Wild Beasts,* found in a manuscript dating from 785 to 800 (Vienna 277), where they are described as Ovid's. They were not widely read, but they are copied in Paris, Bibliothèque nationale lat. 8071, the *Florilegium Thuaneum.* Centuries later, the Neapolitan humanist and poet Jacopo Sannazaro (1458–

1530) brought them to light and identified them with the *Halieutica* ascribed to Ovid by Pliny. For this reason, this poem appears not infrequently in volumes of Ovid's works as the *Halieutica* or *Halieticon,* but it is important to remember that no reader before Sannazaro likely would have had the linkage with that particular Ovidian title in mind. Next in the collection we have placed the *Words for Pan,* a strange work of the early Middle Ages (the fifth through ninth centuries) — essentially a string of adjectives describing Pan — that was transmitted under Ovid's name as early as the ninth century (noting the date of Paris, Bibliothèque nationale lat. 8094).

There follows *The Walnut Tree,* one of the most noted and widespread of the pseudo-Ovidiana, and stylistically the most Ovidian of the poems in this collection.[17] According to Richard Tarrant, this poem came "to light in several parts of Europe in the decades before and after 1100."[18] Conrad of Hirsau (ca. 1070–ca. 1150) considered it Ovid's and found it worthy of study,[19] and it received a commentary from no less a humanist than Erasmus (1466–1536).[20] Modern scholars vary in their assessment. Tarrant denies Ovid its authorship, while calling it "the most accomplished of pseudo-Ovidian poems."[21] While J. A. Richmond's final stance is agnostic, he admits that there are no insuperable arguments against Ovidian authorship.[22] When the poem was first ascribed to Ovid cannot be said with any certainty, but we have placed it here in our sequence on the basis of two eleventh-century manuscripts (Florence, Laurenziana San Marco 23 and Oxford, Auct. F.2.14).[23]

Just as Virgil was supposed to have written the witty tale of *The Gnat* (*Culex*),[24] so Ovid is assigned a poem — a versified dirty joke, really—which circulated under the title *On the Flea,* composed before 1170.[25] As the gnat "begat" the flea, so to speak, so within the universe of pseudo-Ovidiana the flea ultimately begat *On the Louse,* which dates from around the early thirteenth century and appears later in the volume.[26]

By about this time or shortly before, some older brief poems about other animals were attracted into the Ovidian orbit (which for some readers will have included the *Verses on Fish and Wild Beasts*).[27] Prime examples are *On the Cuckoo*[28] and *On the Nightingale.*[29] Among pseudo-Ovidiana involving animals belongs also *On the Wolf,* but as its alternative title, *On the Monk,* suggests, it might also best be thought of in the context of the antireligious satires discussed below. We offer next the odd case of *On the Wonders of the World,* which most manuscripts designate as Ovid's. The material is bestiary lore, drawn in large measure from Solinus.[30] Its first editor, M. R. James, argues that the seventy-nine sections "were meant to serve as explanations of pictorial representations."[31] The title of Ovid's own *On Medicine for the Female Face* inspired *On Medicine for the Ears,* although an important impulse may have come from a report in Pliny about a recipe Ovid himself versified for a cure for angina.[32] Extending focus on the theme of the body, there is also *On the Four Humors*—in several manuscripts, the two poems are closely connected.[33]

On the Lombard and the Snail, from the late twelfth century, is satiric in spirit.[34] In twenty-six neat elegiac couplets the poet presents a mock-heroic scene in which a Lombard peasant prepares to do battle with the "monster" that is destroying his fields. The monster ultimately turns out to be a

INTRODUCTION

snail. Lenz argues that the point of the joke is not that all
Lombards are stupid. Instead, the poet encourages his fel-
low citizens to recognize that their enemy, Emperor Freder-
ick I, who was in these years campaigning in northern Italy,
was not invincible, as evidenced by his defeat at Legnano
in 1176. Accepting such an interpretation (which is hardly
certain) would make *On the Lombard and the Snail* the only
pseudo-Ovidian poem with a direct political message.

The target of another satirical poem, the mock-
apocalyptic *On the Lamb,* is the legal "school" of Azzo of Bo-
logna (d. ca. 1220). This poem is found in a single manu-
script (Vatican, Chisianus H VI 205, of the thirteenth or
fourteenth century), where it follows Ovid's *Loves (Amores)*
and is attributed to Ovid. Two other allegorical or moraliz-
ing works achieved limited circulation under Ovid's name in
the late thirteenth century (and appear consequently later
in the volume): *On Wine,* a collection of verses usually attrib-
uted to the seventh-century Eugenius of Toledo;[35] and *On
the Grove,* which imagines a debate between Opulence and
Diogenes the Cynic.[36] An allegory of a very different sort
lies behind the pseudo-Ovidian *On the Dream,*[37] from the
late thirteenth century, a poem of thirty-four elegiac cou-
plets that, out of diverse materials and subtexts, some Ovid-
ian, some biblical, presents what is ultimately a dreamer's
apocalyptic vision.[38] The vision itself describes two female
figures, utterly different in appearance and demeanor; in ad-
dition there appears a male figure who explains these women
as allegorical representations of prosperity and scarcity.

One of the most disturbing poems in the collection is *On
the Crafty Messenger,* which Peter Dronke has dated to about
1080, though extant manuscripts attribute it to Ovid no ear-

lier than the thirteenth century.[39] The poem narrates the seduction of a girl *(puella)* for a handsome young man through the offices of a male go-between,[40] though "seduction" is a very misleading term: the poem depicts a rape in which the "crafty messenger" is complicit. (*On Love,* discussed below, includes a comparably odious episode; there the go-between is a woman.) It is important to acknowledge that a significant strain within the pseudo-Ovidiana naturalizes and seeks explicitly to justify the sexual violence men perpetrate upon women. *On the Crafty Messenger* is particularly timely in that, however awkwardly and always from a male perspective, it raises questions of consent. Today what is particularly painful to hear is the way the messenger denies he heard the girl calling for help (although she says she did) and later how, in order to save his own skin, he invents the story that the girl is insane.

It is also important to acknowledge that the misogyny and the crudely, callously, and violently exploitative strains in many of the pseudo-Ovidiana build directly upon views expressed in the canonical poems of Ovid. This is not the place to attempt to characterize the totality of Ovid's views on either women or sexual norms, but it is undeniable that Ovid's narrators, and especially the persona Ovid adopts for himself, often seem to approve and celebrate a view that women wish to be conquered sexually by men. To offer one example only, in the *Amores,* Ovid has an older female go-between, Dipsas, instruct her female charge that "the only girl who is chaste is the one who hasn't been asked" (*casta est quam nemo rogavit, Amores* 1.8.43). This cynicism goes far beyond "mere" misogyny, which is also rampant in the pseudo-Ovidiana—the figure of the hag, which has its ancient roots in a character like Dipsas, underlies the "old woman" that appears in more than one of the pseudo-Ovidiana.[41]

One is forced to conclude, after reviewing the collection as a whole, that the *Appendix Ovidiana* describes a space that not merely perpetuates but gives license to a particularly obnoxious and brutish form of male dominance, especially in the area of sex. Notwithstanding the rich Latin literature created by and for women in the Middle Ages,[42] it is not wrong to point to the extreme gender asymmetry of medieval Latin culture, product of and exaggeration of the grossly asymmetric—along gendered lines—access to literacy and education itself (however limited that may have been for all people compared to modern expectations). That alone, however, does not suffice to explain the extremes of misogyny and sexual violence present and promoted in many of the pseudo-Ovidiana. Though the comparison may seem odd, it is as if the *Appendix Ovidiana* constitutes a diachronic fraternity, many of whose members exhibit behavior that, if it were to come to light, would rightfully get them tried and convicted. It is an uncomfortable realization, yet it is critical to focus light on the problem, since medieval Latin literature and these poems (however small a portion of the former the latter represent) continue to contribute to attitudes that are far from banished even today.

Exhibiting significant misogyny, sexual violence, and, at the risk of deploying anachronistic terminology, ageism and cisgender heterosexism,[43] is a work that, for entirely different reasons, must take a special place in any collection of pseudo-Ovidiana. As noted above, Ovid is not only the inscribed author but the autobiographical subject of the mid-thirteenth-century *On the Old Woman,* by far the longest of the pseudo-Ovidiana. This poem manages to include virtually all the elements of Ovid's life and work as the Middle Ages perceived them—the lover and erotodidact, the student of natural philosophy, the exile—yet it does so in an utterly unique and fantastic fashion. The primary beloved is not Corinna, not even a plausibly Roman woman, but a lady from a somewhat realistically depicted medieval town.[44] The matter descends from high to low (and, ultimately, back again): in a fabliau-like sequence, "Ovid" describes how he became the victim of the aged go-between herself, the "hag," by means of an infamous bed trick even as he sought, with the older woman's help, to force himself sexually on the object of his affection. While "Ovid" and the woman enter into a relationship many years later, after she is widowed and is herself an old woman, the sequence of failures in achieving his erotic dreams with his youthful beloved leads him to transform his life to one of contemplation and philosophical inquiry. (Indeed, some early witnesses extend the title by adding "*or on the Transformation of His Life.*") Specifically, the author of *On the Old Woman* sets himself the task of imagining how a pagan natural philosopher might, through pure reason, infer the incarnation of Christ, the resurrection of Christ, and the potential for human redemption.[45] The narrator, under the guise of Ovid, even theorizes the necessity of the immaculate conception of Christ's mother, her freedom from sin, and her assumption before the end of time.[46] This strange poetic fiction includes, via the typical schoolroom preface *(accessus)* confected to accompany it, a description of how the book was found, a feature of popular fiction in many cultures and periods.[47]

Continuing the theme of the body from *On Medicine for*

the Ears and *On the Four Humors,* though with a less medical focus, is *On the Stomach,* also called the *Dispute between the Stomach and Limbs.* Ascribed to Ovid beginning in the fourteenth century, this poem describes the debate among the body's parts for precedence, a rhetorical set piece from Livy (*Ab urbe condita,* 2.32.8 and following) to John of Salisbury.[48]

Ovid was of course a noted naturalist, not only in the *Halieutica* that Pliny ascribes to him (whether or not it is identified with the *Verses on Fish and Wild Beasts* printed here) but throughout the *Metamorphoses.*[49] Given the prominence of the latter, it might at first blush seem surprising that Ovid's greatest work, often simply referred to as "the Greater Ovid" *(Ovidius maior),* did not inspire more pseudo-Ovidian epics, but it would not be easy to create a multibook pseudo-Ovidian *Metamorphoses.* Nevertheless, the *Metamorphosis of a Priest into a Rooster,* published first by W. S. Anderson from the margins of a fourteenth-century Vatican manuscript of the *Metamorphoses,* indeed describes, as Anderson notes, a metamorphic episode.[50] Following upon what might best be described as a liturgical "malfunction," a priest *(flamen)* and several priestesses ("vestals") are metamorphosed into a cock and hens. As W. D. Lebek argued four years after Anderson, however, beneath what seemed to Anderson a pathetically ignorant attempt to write about an ancient Roman rite there lies a scandalous tale, whether an actual event (or rumors thereof) or just a fabliau.[51] Marginal notes claim that this poem was found in an especially ancient manuscript of the *Metamorphoses* and was meant to appear just after the tale of Baucis and Philemon (*Metamorphoses* 8.679–724).[52]

Next come two short poems on similar amatory themes, also found in a single manuscript of the late fourteenth century (Vat. lat. 1602), where they are interspersed with other Ovidian and pseudo-Ovidian works (including *On the Crafty Messenger*). While *On the Distribution of Women* is a light-hearted satire of the clergy's relations with the opposite sex, *Against Women,* as might be guessed from the title, is explic-itly misogynistic. Its mention of Eve and Adam may seem un-Ovidian to us, though it is clear that in this poetic space a Christian (or biblical) reference was no bar to an attribu-tion to Ovid, even absent the kind of elaborate explanatory schema *On the Old Woman* provides. Later in the volume comes an even more extravagant example of the crudely mi-sogynistic strain characteristic of a number of the pseudo-Ovidiana, *On a Certain Old Woman,* which one might see as riffing on the cursing hurled at the old nurse at *On the Old Woman* 2.526–49; it is found in a single fifteenth-century manuscript (Venice, Marciana lat. XII 192).

On Love and *On the Remedy for Love* are in fact excerpts drawn from the anonymous *Art of Courtly Living (Facetus: "Moribus et vita"),* probably composed about 1130 to 1140.[53] The *Art of Courtly Living* is Ovidian in its disposition, and Ovid himself was called "courtly" *(facetus)* by Hugh of Trim-berg, but the *Art of Courtly Living* was not attributed in its entirety to Ovid.[54] Two segments, however, circulated sepa-rately from the *Art of Courtly Living* (and with no reference to it); these were attributed to Ovid and hence are included here as *On Love* and *On the Remedy for Love,* respectively.[55] In twentieth-century scholarship these poems were commonly referred to as the *Pseudo–Ars amatoria* and *Pseudo–Remedia amoris,* but we have retitled them to better reflect the titles found in the manuscript tradition.[56] These poems are any-thing but "courtly" and partake of the misogyny all too common among the pseudo-Ovidiana, the first, as noted above, virtually recommending rape.

The Rule of the Table, a seventy-line poem in elegiacs nominally addressed to Christ in its opening verse, probably dates to the thirteenth century but certainly no later than the first half of the fourteenth and extends Ovid's profile as a teacher of the art of manners.[57] *On the Game of Chess* may well have been inspired by Ovid's own mention of instruction manuals for dice and other games,[58] though a more proximate impulse may have been the extensive treatment of games in *On the Old Woman.*

In the fifteenth century, several older poems (or composites and sections of these poems) on a wide range of themes gained manuscript attribution to Ovid. In addition to the excerpts from the *Art of Courtly Living (Facetus)* that circulated as *On Love* and *On the Remedy for Love,* these "late" pseudo-Ovidiana include a number of variants on the moralizing *On Money,* best known from the *Carmina Burana. Another Poem on the Nightingale,* which combines *seriatim* verses from four works attributed to Eugenius of Toledo, was attributed to Ovid at this point. Likewise, *On the Rustic* appeared as a work of Ovid in this period; it combines four verses of a late antique poem (*Anthologia Latina* 26) that was at points attributed variously to Martial, Cato, and Avienus with the *Words for Pan* (albeit with some variations from the version of that earlier poem we print). One of the latest pseudo-Ovidian works is *On the Three Girls,* a long poem, recalling the amatory and allegorical themes of *On the Crafty Messenger* and *On the Dream,* though it did not achieve wide circulation.[59]

We conclude our survey of late pseudo-Ovidiana with the *Poem of Consolation for Livia,* whose style and subject (the grief of the Roman empress Livia upon the death of her son Drusus) suggest a date of composition in the mid-first century CE (although the "dramatic date" is somewhat earlier). The ascription of the poem, which appears only in manuscripts of the fifteenth century, to Ovid seems to be based on the growing sensitivity to Latin style and especially to the historical nature of style and metrical habits that we associate with humanism and with the scholarly discipline of philology that developed from it. Also philological is Sannazaro's identification (as noted above) of the *Verses on Fish and Wild Beasts* as the *Halieutica,* hitherto known only as the title of a work by Ovid; here the philological work has less to do with style than with the matching of a title of a work by Ovid mentioned by Pliny with a text marked as Ovid's in its ninth-century manuscript.

The contents of extant (and reported) manuscripts provide precious evidence not only of the availability of pseudo-Ovidiana but also of the degree to which they were grouped together with other works of Ovid or traveled independently of them. The number of manuscripts that contain at least one of the works in the pseudo-Ovidian family is roughly four hundred. In the following, we can highlight only some of the general trends that can shed light on medieval reception of the pseudo-Ovidiana. We must register two important caveats. First, our review relies on a variety of sources for the dates of these manuscripts, many of which are ranges rather than dates, and should not be pressed overmuch. Second, a manuscript often contains sections of different dates.

Until the very end of the twelfth century, extant manuscripts contain one pseudo-Ovidian poem apiece (most frequently, either *On the Cuckoo* or *On the Nightingale*).[60] In the thirteenth century, larger groupings of pseudo-Ovidiana become common. The most significant thirteenth-century manuscript containing several pseudo-Ovidian poems is Frankfurt, Stadt und Universitätsbibliothek, Barth. 110. The manuscript contains *The Walnut Tree, On the Nightingale, On the Cuckoo, On Medicine for the Ears, On the Dream, On Wine, On the Four Humors, On the Flea,* and *On the Grove,* as well as Ovid's *Metamorphoses, The Art of Love, The Remedies for Love, The Loves* (including 3.5), *Ibis,* sections of the *Heroides* (including the *Letter of Sappho* [*Heroides* 15]),[61] *Fasti, Black Sea Letters,* and *Lamentations (Tristia).* Of the pseudo-Ovidiana, only *On Wine* is in a section of the manuscript written, according to Richmond, "towards the end of the twelfth century; the others [are] not earlier than the late thirteenth."[62] Indeed, *On the Flea* may even be a fifteenth-century addition.

From the thirteenth century onward, the trend seems only to accelerate, with extensive collections in fourteenth- and fifteenth-century books often comprising notable subsets of the poems in this volume. Throughout this time, the pseudo-Ovidian poems tend to appear in collections containing multiple authentic works of Ovid as well.

None of the early printed editions of Ovid incorporates as many of the pseudo-Ovidiana as the most compendious of the composite pseudo-Ovidiana manuscripts. Indeed, there are but two or three poems—usually *On the Flea, On the Nightingale,* and *The Walnut Tree*—that are part of the printed Ovidian vulgate that emerged in the 1470s.[63] Pseudo-Ovidian poems are rarely printed with true works of Ovid after 1500;

however, a few editions do present groups of these poems separately, and still under the name of Ovid.[64]

In addition to the contents of manuscripts themselves, it is worth noting that some *testimonia* give a sense of how scholars fitted some of these works into the context of Ovid's poetic career. In the early fifteenth century, Sicco Polenton (1375/76–1447/48) assigned a number of the works now considered pseudo-Ovidian to the first part of Ovid's life.[65] These included *On Medicine for the Ears, On the Cuckoo, The Walnut Tree, On the Nightingale, On the Game of Chess, On the Old Woman, On the Three Girls,* and *On Wine.* In positing this, Polenton may have been influenced by the tradition that the poems in the *Appendix Vergiliana* were juvenilia, works of the young Virgil prior to his composition of the *Eclogues.* In contrast, at least one of Ovid's medieval biographies (Milan, Ambros. H 64 sup., fourteenth century) sets *The Walnut Tree, On the Cuckoo, On the Flea,* and *On the Three Girls* after the *Heroides* and the *Loves (Amores).*[66]

Although we discuss our editorial approach in notes to the individual poems, we offer a word here about our overarching principles. Except in the case of *On the Lamb,* where we offer the first printed text of the poem, we have chosen as our base either the most recently published critical edition or the one widely recognized as the best, noting departures from that text in our notes. We depart from a published text in many cases where we have examined manuscripts not known to, or not taken into account by, its editor. Many of these poems exhibit a level of variation, at least in some sections, hardly ever seen in the texts of canonical authors. In other cases, we have made selections with an eye specifically to variants that occur in those manuscripts of the work that in fact attribute the poem to Ovid. (We cannot, however, claim to be entirely consistent in this regard, since we have not seen every witness.) Put simply, we seek to offer our readers the opportunity to read what was read as Ovid's in the medieval period, though of course there was a great deal of variation in manuscripts, with some exhibiting verses that are not much better than gibberish. Modern critical editions, in part by design, generally obscure the messiness that medieval readers, with one manuscript in front of them, actually confronted. We have not set out to give our readers that experience, but rather to present a text that is as readable as it can be, with consistently recognizable (in other words, generally classicizing) spellings and modern punctuation.

The work that undergirds this collection goes back many years, so there are many individuals and institutions to thank. During the laying of the foundation on which the present edifice rests, the assistance of Dr. Uwe Vagelpohl was as indispensable as it was enormous. We are deeply grateful to Dr. Luca Villani for reaching out to us, helping us with great goodwill and generosity, pointing us to manuscript resources and the most recent scholarly bibliography, and sharing the fruits of his own research. We are grateful to, among others, Professors Richard Tarrant, Edan Dekel, and Andrew Hicks for responding to specific questions we had, and of course the editors of DOML for accepting so unconventional a project and assisting it so materially. The

DOML interns made many helpful suggestions. Above all, we must thank the efforts of those editors who directed their attention to the entire text in its penultimate form; Michael Roberts and David Townsend expended extraordinary efforts on improving the accuracy and fluency of the translations throughout. In a few places their questions and suggestions pointed the way to a better Latin text. We also thank the institutions that have supported the research over many years: University of California, Berkeley; Hampshire College; and University of California, Davis. In particular, we thank the many staff at University of California, Davis, without whose assistance parts of the project would have been much more difficult. Finally, Ralph Hexter wants to record a debt of gratitude to the individual who first suggested to him, so many years ago, that he should work on the "medieval Ovid": the late Professor Peter Ganz.

Notes

1 Preparatory to the work of this volume was a book chapter by R. J. Hexter, "Shades of Ovid: *Pseudo-* (and *para-*) *Ovidiana* in the Middle Ages," in Clark, Coulson, and McKinley, *Ovid in the Middle Ages,* 284–309; that chapter offers a more extensive prolegomenon to the pseudo-Ovidiana, and portions of this introduction perforce cover the same territory. We signal the verbatim correspondences in the notes. This has permitted us to limit references to secondary sources here, since more abundant documentation is available in the corresponding portion of "Shades." However, this volume updates that 2011 survey, correcting details in not a few places.

2 G. P. Goold offers a fresh introduction to the *Appendix Vergiliana* in the revised edition of the second volume of the Loeb *Aeneid,* and M. Putnam and J. Ziolkowski treat it briefly in *The Virgilian Tradition: The First Fifteen Hundred Years* (New Haven, 2008), 25–27. On issues of transmission, see Reeve, "Appendix Vergiliana," 437–40, with further bibliography. The term

appendix seems to go back to J. J. Scaliger and the title of his Lyon 1573 edition.

3 These related points are surveyed more expansively in Hexter, "Shades," 286–92, with further bibliography.

4 Note the word "literary," which we use understanding the complexity of its application to premodern periods. The creation and circulation of pseudepigrapha were more common in other traditions, for example, those of religion, politics, and sometimes even medicine, both in the Middle Ages and in prior periods. Examples range from the so-called "Deutero-Pauline" epistles and works ascribed to Galen to the "Donation of Constantine."

5 This now-popular phrase was originally coined by Ludwig Traube in his account of the successive poetic models for medieval Latin poets. According to his scheme, the *aetas Vergiliana* (age of Virgil) of the eighth to ninth centuries is succeeded by an *aetas Horatiana* (age of Horace) in the tenth to eleventh centuries, which in turn gives way to the *aetas Ovidiana* of the twelfth and thirteenth centuries; L. Traube, *Vorlesungen und Abhandlungen* 2, *Einleitung in die lateinische Philologie des Mittelalters* (Munich, 1965), 113.

6 Hexter, "Shades," 285. An example of works "otherwise tethered" might be the Ovidian poems of Baudri of Bourgeuil; of course, since all of Baudri's poems are extant in one manuscript only, these did not have the opportunity for retransmission.

7 To name two, David Malouf's *An Imaginary Life: A Novel* (Sydney, 1978) and Christoph Ransmayr's *Die letzte Welt* (Nördlingen, 1988; English, *The Last World,* London, 1990).

8 The poem was deemed anonymous by both of its modern editors, but it is still often assigned to Richard Fournival by other scholars. On the question of authorship, see Klopsch, *"De vetula,"* 78–99; Robathan, *"De vetula,"* 1–10. In an article currently under review, Justin Haynes has proposed Roger Bacon as the author. Although Bacon has long been recognized as the earliest extant author to quote from *On the Old Woman,* his authorship has not previously been seriously considered. Haynes, in the view of his two coeditors, presents convincing evidence to establish Bacon as the author. Nonetheless, we chose not to attribute the poem to him in this volume; that should await the formation of a broader scholarly consensus.

9 We do not, however, include interpolations in otherwise authentic

INTRODUCTION

texts by Ovid, such as the *Heroides,* and sections of works by Ovid himself that were excerpted and then reattached to Ovid as if each were a separate and distinct minor work; for example, *Amores* 1.5 circulated under the title *De meridie* (Walther no. 632; Schaller and Könsgen no. 406), *Amores* 2.15 as *De anulo* (Walther no. 1345; Schaller and Könsgen no. 919), and *Amores* 3.5 as either *De somno* or *De rustico* (Walther no. 12342; Schaller and Könsgen no. 10626). We also include only Latin poems, though a small number of texts might be considered vernacular pseudo-Ovidiana; Hexter, "Ovid in Translation," 1317.

10 On this line of thought, see further R. J. Hexter, "Literary History as a Provocation to Reception Studies," in *Classics and the Uses of Reception,* ed. Charles Martindale and Richard Thomas (Oxford, 2006), 23–31.

11 Even our collection of thirty-four poems cannot be said to fully exhaust the possibility of what poetry was taken as Ovidian at some point. For example, in his survey of some 2,500 English sermons from the fourteenth and fifteenth centuries, Siegfried Wenzel noted, among many references to and citations from Ovid, references to two otherwise unknown pseudo-Ovidian poems, "De fallaciis fortune" and "De Iano"; from at least the latter some number of (very un-Ovidian) hexameters are transmitted, but clearly as a quotation from some work, not as a separate poem; S. Wenzel, "Ovid from the Pulpit," in Clark, Coulson, and McKinley, *Ovid in the Middle Ages,* 160–76, here 161–62.

12 This paragraph corresponds closely to a paragraph in Hexter, "Shades," 295–96.

13 The three major sets are printed as Shackleton Bailey, *Anthologia Latina,* vol. 1.1, nos. 1–2a; and Buecheler and Riese, vol. 1.1, nos. 1–2 and 654.

14 Shackleton Bailey, *Anthologia Latina,* vol. 1.1, no. 1, lines 1–2; Putnam and Ziolkowski, *Virgilian Tradition,* 22. As Marpicati points out, no extant manuscript of these ten introductory verses predates the ninth century; P. Marpicati, "Gli Argumenta Aeneidos pseudo-ovidiani (AL 1–2 Sh.): Un esempio di paratestualità didattica [part 2]," *Schol(i)a* 2 (2000): 147–64, at 150–51.

15 It would certainly make sense if this gesture of bringing Ovid on the scene but relegating him to a subordinate status is datable to the *aetas Vergiliana,* that is, the eighth and ninth centuries according to Traube's scheme; see note 5, above.

16 Shackleton Bailey, *Anthologia Latina,* vol. 1.1, pp. 11 and x. Given the

characteristics the *Quatrains* share with the *Summaries,* we group the two cycles in this volume together despite the fact that the first attestable Ovidian attribution of the latter comes somewhat later than the first Ovidian attribution of the former.

17 Schaller and Könsgen no. 10797; the best edition is Lenz, *P. Ovidii Nasonis Halieutica,* though Tarrant, "Pseudo-Ovid" is less than enthusiastic about his apparatus and use thereof. See also, more recently, Villani, "Le tre nuces." This paragraph mirrors one from Hexter, "Shades," 294–95.

18 Tarrant, "Pseudo-Ovid," 285.

19 R. B. C. Huygens, ed., *Dialogus super auctores,* in *Accessus ad auctores: Bernard d'Utrecht; Conrad d'Hirsau: Dialogus super auctores* (Leiden, 1970), lines 1331–35.

20 The year 1524 saw two printings: Johannes Frobenius in Basel and Joannes Soter in Cologne. It was reprinted frequently through the following forty years and well past Erasmus's death (1536).

21 Tarrant, "Pseudo-Ovid," 285.

22 Richmond, "Manuscript Traditions," 468–69, and "Doubtful Works," 2765–67.

23 Richmond also raises the question: if it is by Ovid, where does it fall in his sequence of compositions? (Compare Hexter, "Shades," 295n43.) If it is Ovidian, the argument that it, like the *Ibis,* is also a product of his years in Tomis has attractions. Another work that seems best dated to this period, the *Elegiae in Maecenatem,* we do not include, since it was not associated with the Ovidian corpus prior to the sixteenth century and then very rarely.

24 *Culex* belongs to the canonical *Appendix Vergiliana;* see above, note 2. (This paragraph corresponds closely to part of one in Hexter, "Shades," 299.)

25 Munk Olsen, *L'étude des auteurs classiques,* 262. An Italian translation of the pseudo-Ovidian *On the Flea (De pulice)* is found in multiple manuscripts; see Hexter, "Ovid in Translation," 1321, with further references.

26 Lenz dates the poem before 1250 and argues that the louse is a teacher and monk who was particularly nasty in the way he forced his students to write Latin hexameters and who was further excessively carnal. This interpretation, though possible, is hardly an obvious construction of the poem's modest seven elegiac couplets. As Jan Ziolkowski observes, "from

another vantage, the ring poem begat both the flea and the louse" (personal communication); both poems appear in translation in Ziolkowski, *Talking Animals*, 289–90, 293.

27 This paragraph draws on material in Hexter, "Shades," 299 and 301–2.

28 These verses (Schaller and Könsgen no. 2750; Walther no. 3288) have also been attributed to Alcuin or a member of his circle; the text has been frequently printed (*MGH* 270; Buecheler and Riese 687); see further, Castillo, "La composición," 53–61.

29 See Klopsch, "Carmen de philomela," 174–75, who regards it as most likely a tenth-century product on the basis of metrical peculiarities.

30 The *Collectanea rerum memorabilium* of the third-century, which circulated widely and was itself a compendium of, primarily, Pliny and Pomponius Mela.

31 See James, "Ovidius," 288. James hazarded no guesses as to date or provenance. Préaux, "Thierry de Saint-Trond," 353–66, proposed Thierry, abbot of Saint-Trond (fl. 1075–1100), as the author.

32 This same poem appears under yet other titles, for example *De speculo medicinae/medicaminis* and *De herbarum virtutibus*. For Pliny's testimony, see *Natural History* 30.4.12.

33 Lenz, "*De medicamine aurium*," 533–36, discusses the close relation between *On Medicine for the Ears* and *On the Four Humors* and identifies an additional verse at the end of the former and attested by two manuscripts as a transition added by a redactor to create a link between the poems.

34 This paragraph corresponds closely to one in Hexter, "Shades," 301.

35 See Lenz, "Einführende Bemerkungen," 176–77; Ghisalberti, "Medieval Biographies," 37.

36 Compare Lehmann, *Pseudo-antike Literatur*, 95n42; Walther no. 10440; Winter, *Die europäischen Handschriften*, 15. Villani has recently examined this poem's relationship to other pseudo-Ovidian works: "*Pseudo Ovidius imitator sui*," 139–45; "Paride," 67–76.

37 This poem begins "It was night and I was sleeping peacefully" (*Nox erat, et placido capiebam pectore sompnum*) and is to be distinguished from *Amores* 3.5, "It was night and sleep . . ." (*Nox erat et somnus . . .*), which, though printed in all standard editions of the *Amores,* is regularly doubted to be Ovid's own poem. As noted above (n. 9), it also appears in medieval manuscripts with the title *De somno* (= *De rustico*), often along with authen-

tic Ovidian poems unmoored from their original context (for example, *Amores* 1.5 and 2.15). (The last two sentences of this paragraph correspond closely to one in Hexter, "Shades," 301.)

38 Ovidian passages include *Amores* 3.1 and 3.5 (see immediately above), *Metamorphoses* 8.788–808; biblical passages include Genesis 41:1–7 (Pharaoh's dream) and Revelations 6–7; non-Ovidian nonbiblical sources include Boethius's *Consolatio philosophiae* and the anonymous *Carmen de ventis* (in several versions); Smolak, "*De sompnio,*" especially 199–205.

39 Dronke, "A Note on Pamphilus," 230.

40 Though, as noted, we do not know of a manuscript attribution of the poem to Ovid before the thirteenth century, indirect evidence that it was taken as Ovid's as early as the last quarter of the twelfth century comes from the Tegernsee love letters (Munich, Bayerische Staatsbibliothek, MS Clm 19411); Dronke, "Pseudo-Ovid, Facetus," 130n10.

41 On the topic of medieval misogyny, foundational is Walther, *Carmina misogynica*. See also R. H. Bloch, *Medieval Misogyny and the Invention of Western Romantic Love* (Chicago, 1991); P. G. Walsh, "Antifeminism in the High Middle Ages," in *Satiric Advice on Women and Marriage,* ed. W. Smith (Ann Arbor, 2005); G. García Teruel, "Les opinions sur la femme dans quelques récits des xiie et xiiie siècles," *Moyen Âge,* vol. 101, no. 1 (1995): 23–39.

42 By no means the only source, but indispensable is P. Dronke, *Women Writers of the Middle Ages: A Critical Study of Texts from Perpetua (†203) to Marguerite Porete (†1310)* (Cambridge, 1984).

43 And potentially homophobia. These attitudes—offensive from a modern perspective—underlie the extensive tirade on "eunuchs" at the beginning of the second book (2.8–196).

44 References to a recognizably Augustan Rome are few and far between: for example, 2.585–86.

45 While Ovid was not as associated with Christianity as Virgil, one medieval biography places Tomis sufficiently near to Patmos for Ovid to meet Saint John; Bischoff, "Eine mittelalterliche Ovid-Legende," 268–73.

46 Siegfried Wenzel observes that the English sermons of the thirteenth and fourteenth centuries he has studied "were particularly attracted to this poem's praise of the Blessed Virgin and the astronomical predictions of the birth of Jesus," noting as well that "in this context *De vetula* [*On the*

Old Woman] cites Albumasar, whose prediction that a virgin would give birth at the conjunction of Jupiter and Venus occurs separately elsewhere in late medieval sermons" ("Ovid from the Pulpit," 161).

47 On Ovidian biographies, see Ghisalberti, "Medieval Biographies." On the topos of *Buch im Grab* ("the book in the grave"), see Klopsch, *"De vetula,"* 22–34. On the fictional circumstances of finding the poem, see W. Speyer, *Bücherfunde in der Glaubenswerbung der Antike,* vol. 24, *Hypomnemata* (Göttingen, 1970). Note that *On the Old Woman* was among the relatively few pseudo-Ovidian works translated into vernaculars: on Jean Le Fèvre's mid-fourteenth-century translation (with additions), see Hexter, "Ovid in Translation," 1316; on Bernat Metge's late fourteenth-century partial Catalan prose rendering entitled *Ovidi enamorat,* see Hexter, "Ovid in Translation," 1318.

48 Indeed, Lenz believes John knew this poem before penning his version in the *Policraticus* (6.24). Compare Hexter, "Shades," 302.

49 Compare S. Viarre, *La survie d'Ovide,* 8. This paragraph corresponds closely to portions of one in Hexter, "Shades," 300.

50 Anderson, "A New Pseudo-Ovidian Passage." The subtitle of *On the Old Woman* noted above, "or on the Transformation [*mutatio*] of His Life," can be seen as casting that entire narrative into the frame of the *Metamorphoses.*

51 Lebek, "Love in the Cloister," especially 113. Lebek dates the poem to the eleventh century or later (120) and points to the conclusion of the Philemon and Baucis story (*Metamorphoses* 8.698–720) as the Ovidian passage most likely to be in the anonymous poet's mind (122).

52 Anderson, "A New Pseudo-Ovidian Passage," 7–8.

53 Dronke, "Pseudo-Ovid, Facetus," and (for the date), "A Note on Pamphilus." For further discussion and bibliography, see Hexter, "Shades," 297–98.

54 The final line in some of its many manuscripts suggests that the author may be an otherwise unidentifiable "Aurigena." On *facetus* as "courtly," see Elliott, "The *Facetus,*" 27.

55 These sections are fairly stable; the earliest manuscript identified by E. J. Thiel is from the fourteenth century. They are edited together in Thiel, "Mittellateinische Nachdichtungen," with further commentary in Thiel, "Beiträge zu den Ovid-Nachdichtungen," and Schnell, *"Facetus,* Pseudo-*Ars amatoria.*" They were also known as distinct poems to

Lehmann, *Pseudo-antike Literatur,* 11. Notice that they in fact make up portions of another larger and preexisting work was provided by Dronke ("Pseudo-Ovid, Facetus," 126–27).

56 For discussion of the titles appearing in the manuscripts, see Thiel, "Mittellateinische Nachdichtungen," 157–59.

57 Edited on the basis of seven manuscripts in Klein, "Anonymi 'Doctrina mense'"; for the date, see especially 185.

58 *Tristia* 2.471–82.

59 Pittaluga, "De tribus puellis."

60 For more information on this topic as well as the contents of several important manuscripts containing pseudo-Ovidiana, see Hexter, *Shades,* 303–4.

61 Well known as the single medieval manuscript witness to this work; see W. Engelbrecht, "Der Francofortanus und die *Epistula Sapphus,*" *Mittellateinisches Jahrbuch* 28 (1993): 51–57.

62 Richmond, "Manuscript Traditions," 453.

63 For example, Baldassare Azzoguidi's 1471 Bologna edition contains the *Heroides, Epistula Sapphus, Amores, Ars amatoria, Metamorphoses, Ibis, Fasti, Tristia, Epistulae ex Ponto, De pulice (On the Flea), De philomela (On the Nightingale), De medicamine faciei,* and *Nux (The Walnut Tree).*

64 Gaspard Philippe's 1500 Paris edition presents *De nuce (The Walnut Tree), De philomena (On the Nightingale),* and *De pulice (On the Flea);* his 1502 edition of *On the Flea* is subtitled *non putatur a quibusdam Ovidii opus* ("not considered by some to be a work of Ovid"). Kornelius von Zierikzee's 1500 Cologne edition includes *On the Three Girls, On the Crafty Messenger, On the Flea, Pamphilus, On Money, On the Cuckoo,* and *On the Stomach;* his 1508 edition adds *On the Nightingale* (titled *De cuculo* [*On the Cuckoo*]).

65 Ullman, *Scriptorum Illustrium,* 66. Polenton seems to suggest these are genuine, although by saying *edidisse fertur* ("he is said to have published") he hedges his bet. On Polenton on Virgil see Putnam and Ziolkowski, *Virgilian Tradition,* 321 and 369–70.

66 Ghisalberti, "Medieval Biographies," 64.

APPENDIX OVIDIANA

Argumenta *Aeneidis*

Praefatio

Vergilius magno quantum concessit Homero,
    tantum ego Vergilio, Naso poeta, meo.
Nec me praelatum cupio tibi ferre, poeta;
    ingenio si te subsequor, hoc satis est.
5 Argumenta quidem librorum priva notavi,
    errorem ignarus ne quis habere queat.
Bis quinos feci legerent quos carmine versus
    Aeneidos totum corpus ut esse putent.
Adfirmo gravitate mea, me crimine nullo
10   livoris titulo praeposuisse tibi.

1. Aeneas primo Libyae depellitur oras.

Vir magnus bello, nulli pietate secundus
Aeneas odiis Iunonis pressus iniquae
Italiam quaerens Siculis erravit in undis,
naufragus et tandem Libyae est advectus ad oras
5 ignarusque loci, fido comitatus Achate,
indicio matris regnum cognovit Elissae.
Quin etiam nebula saeptus pervenit in urbem,
abreptos socios undis cum classe recepit
hospitioque usus Didus per cuncta benignae
10 excidium Troiae iussus narrare parabat.

Summaries of the Books of the *Aeneid*

Preface

Just as Virgil gave precedence to the great Homer, I, the poet Ovid, yield to my Virgil. In no way do I desire to present myself as placed before you, poet; if I follow not far behind you in talent, it is enough. Nevertheless, I have written 5 individual summaries of the books, so that no inexperienced reader can remain ignorant. I have made ten verses of poetry which they may read, so that they may come to know the whole body of the *Aeneid*. I declare in all seriousness that it was in no envious spirit that I have placed myself in 10 front of you through these prefaces.

1. In the first book, Aeneas is driven to the shores of Libya.

A man great in war and second to none in piety, Aeneas, oppressed by the hatred of unjust Juno, wandered in Sicilian waters while searching for Italy; and was finally borne, shipwrecked, to the coast of Libya. Not knowing his location, 5 and accompanied by faithful Achates, he came to learn of the kingdom of Elissa with his mother's guidance. Enveloped in a cloud, he went into the city, recovered his comrades, who had been snatched by the waves along with his fleet, and—taking advantage of the hospitality of Dido, who was obliging in all respects—at her bidding, prepared to tell 10 of the fall of Troy.

2. Funera Dardaniae narrat defletque secundo.

Conticuere omnes. Tum sic fortissimus heros
fata recensebat patriae casusque suorum:
fallaces Graecos simulataque dona Minervae,
Laucontis poenam et laxantem claustra Sinonem,
5 somnum, quo monitus acceperat Hectoris atri,
iam flammas, caedes Troum patriaeque ruinas
et regis Priami fatum miserabile semper
impositumque patrem collo dextraque prehensum
Ascanium, frustra a tergo comitante Creusa,
10 ereptam hanc fato, socios in monte repertos.

3. Tertius errores pelagi terraeque requirit.

Post eversa Phrygum regna ut fuga coepta moveri
utque sit in Thracen prima devectus ibique
moenia condiderit Polydori caede piata,
regis Ani hospitium et Phoebi responsa canentis,
5 coeptum iter in Cretam, rursus nova fata reperta,
naufragus utque foret Strophadas compulsus ab undis,
inde fugam et dirae praecepta horrenda Celaenus,
liquerit utque Helenum perceptis ordine fatis,
supplicem Achaemeniden Polyphemo urgente receptum
10 amissumque patrem Drepani. Sic deinde quievit.

2. In the second book, he narrates and bewails the destruction of Troy.

All fell silent. Then the bravest of heroes recounted the fate of his homeland and the sufferings of his people in this way: the deceitful Greeks and the feigned offering to Minerva, the punishment of Laocoon and Sinon weakening the defenses, the dream in which he received the warnings of black ₅ Hector, then the fires, the slaughter of the Trojans and the destruction of the city and the ever-pitiful fate of King Priam, the father carried on his back and Ascanius held by his hand while Creusa following behind in vain was taken ₁₀ away by fate, and his reunion with his comrades on the mountain.

3. The third book investigates his wanderings on sea and land.

After the kingdoms of Phrygia were overthrown, he recounted how he began to take flight, and how he was first carried into Thrace and how there he built a mound when the slaughter of Polydorus had been expiated. He spoke of the hospitality of king Anius and the responses of singing Apollo, the journey begun to Crete, how again a new fate ₅ was revealed, and, shipwrecked, he had been forced from the sea to the Strophades. He described his escape from there and the terrible commands of fearful Celaeno, and how he left Helenus once he had learned the due course of his fate. He also mentioned his reception of the supplicant Achaemenides while Polyphemus was looming, and the loss ₁₀ of his father at Drepanum. After that, he fell silent.

4. Uritur in quarto Dido flammisque crematur.

At regina gravi Veneris iam carpitur igni.
Consulitur soror Anna; placet succumbere amori.
Fiunt sacra deis, onerantur numina donis.
Itur venatum; Veneris clam foedera iungunt.
5 Factum fama notat. Monitus tum numine divum
Aeneas classemque fugae sociosque parabat.
Sensit amans Dido; precibus conata morari,
postquam fata videt nec iam datur ulla facultas,
conscenditque pyram dixitque novissima verba
10 et vitam infelix multo cum sanguine fudit.

5. Quintus habet ludos quos concelebrabat Acestes.

Navigat Aeneas. Siculas defertur ad oras.
Hic Manes celebrat patrios una hospes Acestes.
Ludos ad tumulum faciunt, certamina ponunt.
Prodigium est cunctis ardens adlapsa sagitta.
5 Iris tum Beroen habitu mentita senili
incendit naves, subitus quas vindicat imber.
In somnis pater Anchises quae bella gerenda
quoque duce ad Manes possit descendere monstrat.
Transcribit matres urbi populumque volentem
10 et placida Aeneas Palinurum quaerit in unda.

4. In the fourth book, Dido is inflamed with love and is consumed by flames.

But the queen is now being devoured by the intense fire of Venus. She consults her sister Anna and decides to surrender to love. Sacrifices are made to the gods, and the divinities are showered with offerings. They go hunting and secretly unite in the bond of Venus. Rumor takes note of the deed. Then, warned by the divine power of the gods, Aeneas was preparing his fleet and his comrades for flight. His lover Dido learned of this. She tried to delay him with entreaties, but after seeing what was fated, and with no other opportunity left for her, she climbed onto the pyre and spoke her last words. Then, the unfortunate woman poured out her life with a great quantity of blood.

5. The fifth book contains the games that Acestes celebrated with them.

Aeneas sets sail, and is carried to the shores of Sicily, where he honors the spirit of his deceased father together with his host, Acestes. They institute games at the tomb, and hold competitions. An arrow burning in flight is a portent to everyone. Then Iris, in the feigned appearance of old Beroë, sets fire to the ships, which a sudden rainstorm spares. In a dream, father Anchises shows the wars that must be waged and the guide with whom Aeneas can descend to the underworld. He assigns to a city the Trojan matrons and those who wish to remain, and looks for Palinurus in the calm sea.

6. Quaeruntur sexto Manes et Tartara Ditis.

Cumas deinde venit; fert hinc responsa Sibyllae.
Misenum sepelit; mons servat nomen humati.
Ramum etiam divum placato numine portat
ad vatis tecta atque una descendit Avernum.
5 Agnoscit Palinuron ibi, solatur Elissam
Deiphobumque videt lacerum crudeliter ora.
Umbrarum poenas audit narrante Sibylla.
Convenit Anchisen penitus convalle virenti
cognoscitque suam prolem monstrante parente.
10 Haec ubi percepit, graditur classemque revisit.

7. Septimus Aenean reddit fatalibus arvis.

Hic quoque Caietam tumulo dat; deinde profectus
Laurentum venit, hanc verbis cognoscit Iuli
fatalem terram; "mensis iam vescimur" inquit.
Centum oratores pacem veniamque petentes
5 ad regem mittit Latii tunc forte Latinum,
qui cum pace etiam natae conubia pactus.
Haec furia Allecto Iunonis distrahit ira.
Rex cedit fatis, quamvis pia vota repugnent.
Belli causa fuit violatus vulnere cervus.
10 Arma ferunt gentes sociae, flat bella iuventus.

8. Praeparat octavo bellum quosque armet in hostes.

Dat belli signum Laurenti Turnus ab arce
mittitur et magni Venulus Diomedis ad urbem,

6. In the sixth book, the spirits of the dead and Pluto's realm of Tartarus are sought out.

Next he comes to Cumae, where he carries out the commands of the Sibyl. He buries Misenus where the cape preserves the name of the buried man. After appeasing the divinity, he also carries the sacred bough to the cave of the oracle and with her he descends to Avernus. There he recognizes Palinurus, consoles Elissa, and sees Deiphobus with his face cruelly mutilated. He hears of the punishments of the shades from the Sibyl's narration. He comes upon Anchises deep in a verdant glade and from his father he learns of his progeny. When he has understood these things, he leaves and returns to his fleet. 10

7. The seventh book delivers Aeneas to his destined land.

Here he also buries Caieta, and then sets sail and comes to Laurentum, which he recognizes as his destined land from the words of Iulus, who says "now we are eating our tables." He sends a hundred spokesmen seeking peace and favor to the king of Latium—Latinus, as it happened, at the time—who, along with peace, also pledged the marriage of his daughter. All this the fury Allecto rips apart on account of the anger of Juno. Latinus yields to destiny, though his pious vows oppose it. The cause of the war was the dishonorable wounding of a stag. The allied peoples bear arms, the youth trumpet war. 10

8. In the eighth book he prepares the war and seeks troops to arm against the enemy.

Turnus gives the signal of war from the citadel of Laurentum and Venulus is sent to the city of great Diomedes to seek

qui petat auxilium et doceat quae causa petendi.
Aeneas divum monitis adit Arcada regem,
5 Evandrum Arcadia profugum nova regna tenentem.
Accipit auxilia et natus socia agmina iungens
Evandri Pallas fatis comes ibat iniquis.
Iamque habilis bello et maternis laetus in armis
fataque fortunasque ducum casusque suorum
10 miratur clipeo divinam intentus in artem.

9. Nonus habet pugnam nec adest rex ipse tumultu.

Atque ea diversa penitus dum parte geruntur,
Iunonis monitu festinat Turnus in hostem.
Teucrorum naves Rutulis iaculantibus ignem
nympharum in speciem divino numine versae.
5 Euryali et Nisi coeptis fuit exitus impar.
Pugnatur: castra Aeneadae vallumque tuentur.
Audacem Remulum leto dat pulcher Iulus.
Fit via vi. Turnus Bitian et Pandaron altum
deicit et totis victor dat funera castris,
10 iamque fatigatus recipit se in tuta suorum.

10. Occidit Aeneae decimo Mezentius ira.

Concilium divis hominum de rebus habetur.
Interea Rutuli portis circum omnibus instant.
Advenit Aeneas multis cum milibus inde.
Mars vocat et totis in pugnam viribus itur.
5 Interimit Pallanta potens in proelia Turnus

assistance and explain the reason for his request. Aeneas, on
the advice of the gods, goes to the Arcadian king Evander, 5
who fled from Arcadia and acquired a new kingdom. He
accepts assistance, and Pallas, the ill-fated son of Evander,
unites his forces as allies and goes with Aeneas as a comrade.
And now, primed for war and delighting in the weapons
from his mother, Aeneas, gazing at the divine art on his 10
shield, marvels at the lots and fortunes of the generals and
future events of his people.

9. The ninth book contains a battle, but the king himself is
not present in the clash.

While these things were happening in a completely differ-
ent part of the battlefield, on the advice of Juno, Turnus has-
tens against the enemy. When the Rutulians hurl fire at the
Trojan fleet, the ships take on the appearance of nymphs by
divine power. Euryalus's and Nisus's end fell short of their 5
intentions. The battle rages, while Aeneas's men defend the
camp and the fortifications. Handsome Iulus sends haughty
Remulus to his death. A path is made by sheer force. Turnus
brings low Bitias and tall Pandarus and, as victor, deals death
to the whole camp. Finally, when he is worn out, he returns 10
to the safety of his own troops.

10. In the tenth book, Mezentius dies by the wrath of
Aeneas.

A council of the gods is held about the affairs of men. Mean-
while the Rutulians are pressing around all the gates. Aeneas
arrives with many thousands of men. Mars calls and battle is
joined with every ounce of strength. Mighty Turnus slays 5
Pallas in battle and leaders are killed, while the nameless

caedunturque duces, cadit et sine nomine vulgus.
Subtrahitur pugnae Iunonis numine Turnus.
Aeneas instat Mezenti caede piata;
Lausus fata patris praesenti morte redemit.
10 Mox ultor nati Mezentius occidit ipse.

11. Undecimo victa est non aequo Marte Camilla.

Constituit Marti spoliato ex hoste tropaeum
exanimemque patri feretro Pallanta remittit.
Iura sepulturae tribuit tempusque Latinis.
Evander patrios affectus edit in urbe.
5 Corpora caesa virum passim disiecta cremantur.
Legati referunt Diomeden arma negasse.
Drances et Turnus leges aequante Latino
concurrunt dictis. Aeneas imminet urbi.
Pugnatur. Vincunt Troes. Cadit ipsa Camilla.
10 Dein reduces castris nocti cessere monenti.

12. Duodecimo Turnus divinis occidit armis.

Turnus iam fractis adverso Marte Latinis
semet in arma parat pacem cupiente Latino.
Foedus percutitur passuros omnia victos.
Hoc Turni Iuturna soror confundit et ambos
5 in pugnam populos agit ementita Camertem.
Aenean volucri tardatum membra sagitta
anxia pro nato servavit cura parentis.
Urbs capitur. Vitam laqueo sibi finit Amata.
Aeneas Turnum campo progressus utrimque
10 circumfusa acie vita spoliavit et armis.

masses also fall. Turnus is removed from the battle through the divine power of Juno. Aeneas pursues the justified slaughter of Mezentius; Lausus forestalled the destiny of his father with his own sudden death. Soon after Mezentius, attempting to avenge his son, is himself killed.

11. In the eleventh book, Camilla is vanquished in an unequal fight.

Aeneas sets up a trophy to Mars from the enemy spoils and sends the lifeless Pallas back to his father on a bier. He grants a truce and time for burial to the Latins. Evander shows fatherly affection in his city. The slain bodies scattered all around are cremated. Envoys report that Diomedes has refused to take up arms. Drances and Turnus spar with words as Latinus weighs their propositions. Aeneas threatens the city. There is a battle, which the Trojans win. The famous Camilla falls. Then, returning to their camps, they yield to night's insistence.

12. In the twelfth book, Turnus dies by divine arms.

Now Turnus, with the Latins broken by the opposition of Mars, dons his armor, though Latinus desires peace. A treaty is struck: the vanquished will have to submit to everything. Turnus's sister Juturna overturns this and, disguised as Camers, incites both peoples to battle. The concern of a parent anxious for her son saved Aeneas, who was hobbled by a flying arrow. The city is captured. Amata ends her life with a noose. Aeneas advanced to the battlefield and, in the midst of the soldiers crowded around on both sides, deprived Turnus of his life and weapons.

Tetrasticha in cunctis libris Vergilii

Praefatio

Qualis Bucolicis, quantus tellure domanda
vitibus arboribusque satis pecorique apibusque,
Aeneadum fuerit vates, tetrasticha dicent:
contineat quae quisque liber, lege munere nostro.

Bucolica

Tityrus agresti modulatur carmen avena;
formosum pastor Corydon dilexit Alexin;
Silenumque senem sertisque meroque ligavit,
pastorumque melos faciles duxere cicutae.

Georgica

Sidera deinde canit, segetes et dona Lyaei
et pecorum cultus, Hyblaei mella saporis.
Principio breviter ventura volumina dixit.
Intercidit opus coepitque referre secundo.

1

Quid faciat laetas segetes, quae sidera servet
agricola, ut facilem terram proscindat aratro,
semina quo iacienda modo cultusque locorum,
edocet et messes magno cum faenore reddi.

2

Hactenus arvorum cultus et sidera caeli,
pampineas canit inde comas collisque virentis
discriptasque locis vites et dona Lyaei,
atque oleae ramos pomorum et condere fetus.

Quatrains on All of Virgil's Works

Preface

These quatrains will speak to the quality of the poet of the *Aeneid* in his *Bucolics* and his greatness in thoroughly taming the earth with vines and trees, flocks and bees: through our gift, read what each book contains.

Eclogues

Tityrus accompanies his song with a rustic shepherd's pipe; the shepherd Corydon loved handsome Alexis; and he bound old Silenus with garlands and undiluted wine, and pleasant pipes produced the song of shepherds.

Georgics

Then he sings of stars, of crops, and of the gifts of Lyaeus; of the keeping of flocks, and of honey that can match Hybla's in taste. In the beginning he spoke briefly of the books to come. He interrupted the work and began his narration a second time.

1. What makes for thriving crops; what stars the farmer should watch, in order to cleave the friable earth with his plow; how seeds should be sown, and the cultivation of different locations—he teaches these things, and the production of very profitable harvests.

2. Up till now he sings of the cultivation of fields and of the stars of the sky, and then of budding vine shoots and the hills they make green, of vines and their positioning, and of the gifts of Lyaeus, as well as how to establish the branches of olive trees and the produce of fruit trees.

3

Teque, Pales, et te, pastor memorande per orbem,
et pecorum cultus et gramine pascua laeta,
quis habitent armenta locis stabulentur et agni,
omnia divino monstravit carmine vates.

4

Protinus aerii mellis redolentia regna
Hyblaeas et opes alveorum et cerea texta
quique apti flores examina quaeque legenda
indicat humentisque favos, caelestia dona.

Aeneis

1

Arma virumque canit mira virtute potentem
Iunonisque odio disiectas aequore puppes
hospitium Didus, classem sociosque receptos,
utque epulas inter casus regina requirat.

2

Conticuere omnes. Infandos ille labores
deceptamque dolis Troiam patriaeque ruinas
et casus Priami dolet et flagrantia regna
ignibus et mediis raptum deque hoste parentem.

3

Postquam res Asiae deceptaque Pergama dixit,
tum, Polydore, tuos tumulos, tum Gnosia regna,
Andromachen Helenumque et vasta mole Cyclopas
amissumque patrem Siculis narravit in oris.

3. The poet in his divine song treats of all things: of you, Pales, and you, world-renowned shepherd, as well as the keeping of flocks and pastures thriving with grass, and where herds should be kept and lambs should be penned.

4. Next he describes the kingdoms scented by air-given honey, the Hyblaean wealth of beehives, and their weaving with wax; he tells which blossoms are suitable and which swarms should be collected; and describes the moist honey-combs, the gifts of the gods.

Aeneid

1. He sings of arms and the man, strong with marvelous courage, and of the ships scattered over the sea because of Juno's hatred, the hospitality of Dido, his fleet and com-rades recovered, and how the queen, at the banquet, asks about his misfortunes.

2. Everyone fell silent. He laments the unspeakable travails, and Troy deceived by trickery, the destruction of his home-land, the fall of Priam, the kingdom on fire, and how in the midst of the fires he carried his father away from the enemy.

3. After he related the events in Asia and the deception of Troy, he told of your tomb, Polydorus, then of the kingdom of Knossos, of Andromache and Helenus, and of the Cyclo-pes with their huge bulk, and of the loss of his father on the shores of Sicily.

4

At regina gravi Veneris iam carpitur igni
venatusque petit. Capitur venatibus ipsa
et taedas, Hymenaee, tuas ad funera vertit,
postquam Anchisiades fatorum est iussa secutus.

5

Interea Aeneas pelagus iam classe tenebat
ludorumque patris tumulum celebrabat honore.
Puppibus ambustis fundavit moenia Acestae
destituitque ratem media Palinurus in unda.

6

Sic lacrimans tandem Cumarum adlabitur oris
descenditque domus Ditis comitante Sibylla.
Agnoscit Troas caesos, agnoscit Achivos,
et docet Anchises venturam ad sidera prolem.

7

Tu quoque litoribus famam, Caieta, dedisti,
intrat et Aeneas Latium regnumque Latini
foedus agens. Saevit Juno bellumque lacessit
finitimosque viros Turnumque in proelia mittit.

8

Dat belli signum Turnus Mezentiaque arma
concivitque duces. Tum moenia Pallantea
Aeneas adit Evandri socia agmina quaerens.
Arma Venus portat proprio Vulcania nato.

9

Atque ea diversa dum parte, hic diva Cybebe
puppes esse suas nympharum numina iussit.

4. But now the queen is tormented by the painful fire of Venus and desires a hunt. She herself is captured in the hunt and applies your torches, Hymen, to a funeral pyre after the son of Anchises has followed the commands of fate.

5. Meanwhile Aeneas was now sailing the sea with his fleet and was honoring the tomb of his father with funeral games. After the ships were set on fire, Aeneas founded the walls of Acesta, and Palinurus fell from his vessel in the middle of the sea.

6. Still mourning, eventually Aeneas puts in at the shore of Cumae and descends to the home of Dis, accompanied by the Sibyl. He recognizes fallen Trojans as well as Greeks, and Anchises tells him of his offspring who will advance to the stars.

7. You, Caieta, also gave your legend to those shores; and Aeneas, seeking a treaty, enters Latium and the kingdom of Latinus. Juno rages, provokes war, and impels Turnus and the neighboring peoples into battle.

8. Turnus gives the signal for war and rouses Mezentius's martial valor and generals. Then Aeneas approaches the walls of Pallanteum, seeking Evander's troops as allies. Venus brings arms crafted by Vulcan to her son.

9. While this was going on in a distant part of the country, here divine Cybele ordered the ships dear to her to be

Euryali et Nisi caedes et fata canuntur
fecit et inclusus castris quae funera Turnus.

10

Panditur interea caelum coetusque deorum.
Iam redit Aeneas et Pallas sternitur acer.
Eripuit Iuno Turnum Lausoque parentem
adiecit comitem mortis Cythereia proles.

11

Oceano interea surgens Aurora videbat
Mezenti ducis exuvias caesosque sodales
et Latium proceres Diomedis dicta referre,
tum qualis pugnae succedat Volsca Camilla.

12

Turnus, ut infractos vidisset et undique caesos,
ultro Anchisiaden bello per foedera poscit,
quae Iuturna parat convellere. Sed tamen armis
occidit et pactum liquit cum coniuge regnum.

Versus de piscibus et feris

. . . accepit mundus legem; dedit arma per omnes,
admonuitque sui. Vitulus sic †manuque† minatur,
qui nondum gerit in tenera iam cornua fronte,
sic dammae fugiunt, pugnant virtute leones,
5   et morsu canis, et caudae sic scorpius ictu,

turned into divine nymphs. The slaughter of Euryalus and Nisus and the fate they met are described, as are the deaths that Turnus caused when inside the camp.

10. Meanwhile heaven is revealed and there is a council of the gods. Soon Aeneas returns, and fierce Pallas is struck down. Juno snatched away Turnus, and the son of Venus made Lausus and his father companions in death.

11. In the meantime, Dawn, rising from the Ocean, saw the spoils stripped from general Mezentius, and Aeneas's fallen comrades, and the envoys bringing back Diomedes's reply to Latium, then how Volscian Camilla entered the fray.

12. Turnus, when he saw his forces broken and lying dead all around, on his own challenged the son of Anchises to combat under a truce that Juturna was preparing to break. But nonetheless he dies in the fight and relinquished both promised wife and kingdom.

Verses on Fish and Wild Beasts

. . . the world observed this law; it distributed weapons to all of the wild beasts and reminded each of its defense. So the bull calf menaces †even with his hoof†, which does not yet bear horns on his still-tender forehead; deer make their escape, lions battle with courage, the dog with his bite, and 5

concussisque levis pinnis sic evolat ales.
Omnibus ignotae mortis timor, omnibus hostem
praesidiumque datum sentire, et noscere teli
vimque modumque sui—sic et scarus arte sub undis
10 si n . . .
decidit, adsumptaque dolos tandem pavet esca,
non audet radiis obnixa occurrere fronte:
aversus crebro vimen sub verbere caudae
laxans subsequitur, tutumque evadit in aequor.
15   Quin etiam si forte aliquis, dum praenatat, arcto
mitis luctantem scarus hunc in vimine vidit,
aversi caudam morsu tenet, atque †litat† . . .
liber servato quem texit cive resultat.
    Sepia tarda fugae, tenui cum forte sub unda
20 deprensa est, iamiamque manus timet illa rapacis,
inficiens aequor nigrum vomit illa cruorem
avertitque vias, oculos frustrata sequentis.
    Clausus rete lupus, quamvis inmitis et acer,
dimotis cauda submissus sidit arenis,
25 .... in auras
emicat, atque dolos saltu deludit inultus.
    Et murena ferox, teretis sibi conscia tergi,
ad laxata magis conixa foramina retis,
tandem per multos evadit lubrica flexus,
30 exemploque nocet: cunctis iter invenit una.
    At contra scopulis crinali corpore segnis
polypus haeret, et hac eludit retia fraude;
et sub lege loci sumit mutatque colorem,

the scorpion with the sting of his tail, so the bird takes flight raised up by the beating of its wings. All of these fear unknown death; to all of them the ability is given to recognize a foe and to defend themselves, and to understand both the power and the extent of their particular weapon. So even the scar under the waves through craft, if . . . falls, and only when the bait is eaten finally fears the trap, and does not dare to dash against the rods with a stubborn forehead: facing backward and loosening the wicker with repeated blows of its tail, it shoots out and escapes to the safety of the sea.

Moreover if, perhaps, another kindly scar, while swimming by, has seen it struggling in the narrow wicker, grips with its teeth the tail of the other from behind, and †devotes† . . . once the comrade whom it had protected has been saved, it freely darts away.

The cuttlefish, slow to flee, when it happens to be discovered in shallow water, at the moment it fears grasping hands, discharges black blood, staining the sea, and changes its course, deceiving the eyes of its pursuer.

When the wolffish is enclosed by a net, though savage and fierce, it settles quietly in the sands dispersed with its tail, . . . it springs into the air, and unharmed eludes the traps with a leap.

Also the wild lamprey, in full knowledge of the smoothness of its back, pushing especially against the loose meshes of the net, finally, with many a turn, the slippery creature escapes, setting a damaging example: alone, it finds a path for the rest.

By contrast, the immobile octopus clings to the rocks with its tentacled body, and with this trick evades the nets; and according to where it is, it assumes and changes color,

semper ei similis quem contegit; atque ubi praedam
35 pendentem saetis avidus rapit, hic quoque fallit,
elato calamo cum demum emersus in auras
brachia dissolvit, populatumque expuit hamum.
    At mugil cauda pendentem everberat escam,
excussamque legit. Lupus acri concitus ira
40 discursu fertur vario fluctusque furentem
prosequitur, quassatque caput, dum vulnere saevus
laxato cadat hamus, et ora patentia linquat.
    Nec proprias vires nescit murena nocendi
auxiliiique sui morsu nec comminus acri
45 deficit, aut animos ponit captiva minacis.
Anthias in tergo, quae non videt, utitur armis,
vim spinae novitque suae, versoque supinus
corpore lina secat, fixumque intercipit hamum.
    Cetera, quae densas habitant animalia silvas,
50 aut vani quatiunt semper lymphata timores,
aut trahit in praeceps non sana ferocia mentis.
Ipsa sequi natura monet vel comminus ire.
    Inpiger ecce leo venantum sternere pergit
agmina, et adversis infert sua pectora telis!
55 Quoque venit fidens magis et sublatior ardet
(concussitque toros et viribus addidit iram) . . .
prodidit atque suo properat sibi robore letum.
    Foedus Lucanis provolvitur ursus ab antris,
quid nisi pondus iners, stolidique . . .
60 actus aper saetis iram denuntiat hirtis,

always similar to what it rests on. And when it greedily 35
snatches the hanging bait with its tentacles, in this too it
cheats; when the fishing rod is lifted up, finally emerging
into the air, it loosens its arms and ejects the plundered fish-
hook.

Now the mullet strikes the hanging bait with its tail, and
gathers what has been shaken off. The wolffish, roused with
fierce anger, is borne this way and that, and it leaves a wake 40
behind it in its rage, and it shakes its head until the wound
opens up and the cruel hook falls out, leaving its gaping
mouth.

Nor is the lamprey unaware of its own powers of doing
harm and not even close up does it abandon its sharp bite as
a defensive measure, or, once captive, give up its threatening 45
spirit. The *anthias* uses the weapons on its back, though it
does not see them, and knows the power of its own spine;
when turned over on its back, it cuts fishing lines, and severs
the affixed hook.

As for the other animals, which dwell in dense forests, ei- 50
ther groundless fears always terrify them into panic, or an
unsound ferocity of mind drives them headlong. Nature
herself prompts them to pursue or come to close quarters.

Behold, the energetic lion advances to strike down the
ranks of hunters, and offers its breast to their hostile spears!
Wherever it comes, it is all the more confident, and roused 55
into fiery passion (it has shaken its mane and bolstered its
strength with anger), . . . it betrayed and by its very strength
hastens its death.

The ugly bear shambles out from Lucanian caves, noth-
ing but an ill-formed mass, and of slow . . . the wild boar, 60
once stirred, announces its anger with its shaggy bristles,

se ruit oppositi nitens in vulnera ferri,
pressus et emisso moritur per viscera telo.
    Altera pars fidens pedibus dat terga sequenti,
ut pavidi lepores, ut fulvo tergore dammae,
65 et capto fugiens cervus sine fine timore.
    Hic generosus honos et gloria maior equorum:
nam cupiunt animis palmam gaudentque triumpho,
seu septem spatiis circo meruere coronam
(nonne vides victor quanto sublimius altum
70 adtollat caput, et vulgi se venditet aurae?)
celsave cum caeso decorantur terga leone.
Quam tumidus, quantoque venit spectabilis actu,
conpescitque solum generoso concita pulsu
ungula sub spoliis graviter redeuntis opimis!
75   Quin laus prima canum, quibus est audacia praeceps,
venandique sagax virtus, viresque sequendi.
Quae nunc elatis rimantur naribus auram,
et nunc demisso quaerunt vestigia rostro,
et produnt clamore feram dominumque vocando
80 increpitant, quam, si conlatis effugit armis,
insequitur tumulosque canis camposque per omnis . . .
    Noster in arte labor positus, spes omnis in illa . . .
Nec tamen in medias pelagi te pergere sedes
admoneam, vastique maris temptare profundum:
85 inter utrumque loci melius moderabere finem . . .
aspera num saxis loca sint: nam talia lentos
deposcunt calamos, at purum retia litus;
num mons horrentes demittat celsior umbras

rushes forward, hurling itself on the wounding blades that meet it, and dies, overcome by the spear sent through its entrails.

Another part of the animal kingdom, trusting in its feet, turns its back to its pursuer, such as timid hares, and tawny-skinned deer, and the stag, endlessly fleeing when it has 65 taken fright.

Here is the noble renown and superior glory of horses: for they long for victory in their souls and rejoice in triumph, whether they have earned the crown in the seven laps of the racetrack (don't you see how much higher the victor raises his head, and pays court to the favor of the common 70 people?), or their tall backs are decorated with a dead lion's hide. How spiritedly, how ostentatiously it advances in its gait, and its hoof, moving with a noble stride, paws the ground as it returns heavily laden with the weight of the rich spoils!

But the glory of dogs is foremost; they possess reckless 75 courage, a keen hunting sense, and powers of pursuit. First they explore the air with raised nostrils, and then, lowering their snouts, they seek tracks, and drive out the wild beast with their barking, and they urge on their master with their call; if the beast escapes from the weapons brought against 80 it, the dog pursues it through all the hills and plains . . .

Our work depends on craft, all our hope is in that . . . Yet I would warn you not to venture into the middle of the sea, or to test the depths of the vast ocean: you will better mod- 85 erate your course between the two extremes . . . whether places are rough and rocky: for such places demand pliant fishing rods, but an unobstructed coast allows the use of nets; or whether a lofty mountain casts down flickering

in mare: nam varie quidam fugiuntque petuntque;
90   num vada subnatis imo viridentur ab herbis ...
obiectetque moras, et molli serviat algae.
    Discripsit sedes varie natura profundi,
nec cunctos una voluit consistere pisces:
nam gaudent pelago quales scombrique, bovesque,
95   hippuri celeres, et nigro tergore milvi,
et pretiosus helops, nostris incognitus undis,
ac durus xiphias, ictu non mitior ensis,
et pavidi magno fugientes agmine thynni,
parva echenais (at est, mirum, mora puppibus ingens),
100   tuque, comes ratium tractique per aequora sulci,
qui semper spumas sequeris, pompile, nitentes.
    ... cercyrosque ferox scopulorum fine moratur,
cantharus ingratus suco, tum concolor illi
orphus, caeruleaque rubens erythinus in unda,
105   insignis sargusque notis, insignis iulis,
et super aurata sparulus cervice refulgens,
et rutilus phager, et fulvi synodontes, et ex se
concipiens channe, gemino non functa parente,
tum viridis squamis parvo saxatilis ore,
110   et rarus faber, et pictae mormyres, et auri
chrysophrys imitata decus, tum corporis umbrae
liventis, rapidique lupi, percaeque, tragique,
quin laude insignis caudae melanurus, et ardens
auratis murena notis, merulaeque virentes,
115   inmitisque suae cancer per vulnera genti,
et capitis duro nociturus scorpios ictu,
ac numquam aestivo conspectus sidere glaucus.
    At contra herbosa pisces luxantur arena,

shadows onto the sea: for some fish seek the shade, others
avoid it; or whether the sea bed is made green by underwa-   90
ter seaweed . . . sets obstacles, and accommodates the soft
seaweed.

Nature has apportioned the habitats of the sea variously
and did not want all of the fish to be in the same place: for
the fish that take pleasure in the deep sea include mackerel,
the ox fish, the swift *hippurus,* and the dark-skinned gurnard,   95
as well as the precious *helops* (unknown to our waters), the
harsh swordfish (no gentler in its strike than the blow of a
sword), the timid tuna which flee in a great shoal, the little
remora (but, surprisingly, a big delay to ships), and you, the   100
companion of ships and of the wake drawn through the wa-
ters, you, *pompilus,* who always follow the glistening foam . . .

. . . and the fierce *cercyrus* lingers at the edge of the rocks,
the *cantharus* with an unpleasant flavor, then the similarly
colored *orphus,* the sea mullet bright red in the sky-blue wa-
ters, the *sargus* and rockfish, each distinguished by their   105
markings, moreover the bream resplendent with its golden
neck, the red *phager,* the tawny *synodons,* the hermaphroditic
channe (not making use of a second parent), then the rock-
fish with its green scales and small mouth, and the hard-   110
to-find dory, the painted mormyrs, the *chrysophrys* which
imitates the splendor of gold, then the umbers with
shadowy-blue bodies, the quick wolffish, perches, and *tragi,*
as well as the blacktail (notable for the glory of its tail), the
lamprey shining with its gold markings, the powerful black-
bird fish, the crab savage in wounding its own kind, the scor-   115
pion fish (which will harm with a savage blow of the head),
and the bluefish, which is never seen in summer.

On the other hand there are fish that revel in the weedy

ut scarus, epastas solus qui ruminat escas,
120   fecundumque genus menae, lamirosque, smarisque,
atque inmunda chromis, merito vilissima salpa,
atque avium dulces nidos imitata sub undis . . .
et squamas tenui suffusus sanguine mullus,
fulgentes soleae candore, et concolor illis
125   passer, et Adriaco mirandus litore rhombus,
tum lepores lati, tum molles tergore ranae,
extremi †pareuc† . . .
. . .
130   lubricus, et spina nocuus non gobius ulla,
et nigrum niveo portans in corpore virus
lolligo, durique sues, sinuosaque caris,
et tam deformi non dignus nomine asellus,
tuque, peregrinis, acipenser, nobilis undis.

Versus Panos

Rustice, lustrivage, capripes, cornute, bimembris,
Cinyphie, hirpigena, pernix, caudite, petulce,
saetiger, indocilis, agrestis, barbare, dure,
semicaper, villose, fugax, periure, biformis,
5   audax, brute, ferox, pellite, incondite, mute,
silvicola, instabilis, saltator, perdite, mendax,
lubrice, ventisonax, inflator, stridule, anhele,
hirce, hirsute, biceps, niger, hispidissime, fallax, sime.

sands, like the scar, the only fish that chews its cud, and the 120
fruitful race of *maenae,* and the *lamirus, smaris,* the foul
chromis, the deservedly most-despised stockfish, and the one
that imitates the soft nests of birds under the waves . . . and
the red mullet, whose scales are suffused with subtle blood,
the soles that radiate whiteness, the similarly colored spar- 125
row fish, the flatfish (the wonder of the Adriatic coast), as
well as the broad sea hares, and the fleshy-tailed frogfish,
the strange †pareuc†, . . . the slippery goby whose spine does 130
no harm, the cuttlefish that carries black poison in its white
body, the rough pigfish, the sinuous prawn, the ass fish (un-
worthy of such a shameful name), and you, *acipenser,* cele-
brated in foreign waters.

Words for Pan

Rustic, wandering-in-the-woods, goat-footed, horned, half-
beast, Cinyphian, goat-born, swift, tailed, frisky, bristly,
unteachable, wild, uncivilized, hardy, half-goat, shaggy, fleet,
false, two-formed, bold, irrational, fierce, skin-clad, un- 5
couth, dumb, forest-dwelling, changeable, a dancer, incorri-
gible, deceitful, slippery, braggart, puffed-up-with-pride,
harsh-sounding, panting, billy goat, hirsute, double-natured,
black, hairiest, deceptive, snub-nosed.

Nux

Nux ego iuncta viae cum sim sine crimine vitae,
    a populo saxis praetereunte petor.
Obruere ista solet manifestos poena nocentes,
    publica cum lentam non capit ira moram.
5 Nil ego peccavi nisi si peccare docetur
    annua cultori poma referre suo.
At prius arboribus tum, cum meliora fuerunt
    tempora, certamen fertilitatis erat.
Tum domini memores sertis ornare solebant
10   agricolas fructu proveniente deos.
Saepe tuas igitur, Liber, miratus es uvas,
    mirata est oleas saepe Minerva suas,
pomaque laesissent matrem, nisi subdita ramo
    longa laboranti furca tulisset opem.
15 Quin etiam exemplo pariebat femina nostro,
    nullaque non illo tempore mater erat.
At postquam platanis sterilem praebentibus umbram
    uberior quavis arbore venit honor,
nos quoque frugiferae (si nux modo ponor in illis)
20   coepimus in patulas luxuriare comas.
Nunc neque continuos nascuntur poma per annos,
    uvaque laesa domum laesaque baca venit;
nunc uterum vitiat quae vult formosa videri,
    raraque in hoc aevo est quae velit esse parens.
25 Certe ego, si nunquam peperissem, tutior essem:
    ista Clytaemestra digna querela fuit!
Si sciat hoc vitis, nascentes supprimet uvas,
    orbaque, si sciat hoc, Palladis arbor erit.

The Walnut Tree

I am a roadside walnut tree, and though my life is blameless, I am pelted with stones by passersby. Such a punishment tends to strike down convicted criminals, when the people's wrath doesn't tolerate lengthy delay. I have committed no sin, unless it is taught that rendering yearly fruit to one's planter is a sin. But back then, when times were better, there was competition among trees in fruitfulness. Then, mindful masters were accustomed to decorate the farmer-gods with wreaths as the fruit ripened. Often, therefore, Liber, you marveled at your grapes, often Minerva marveled at her olives, and the apples would have damaged their mother tree, if a long fork placed under the struggling branch had not provided support. Indeed, following our example, women gave birth, and in those times no woman was not a mother. But since more abundant honor has come to plane trees offering a sterile shade than to any other tree, we fruit trees (if I, a walnut tree, am counted among them) also have begun to abound in spreading foliage.

Now fruit does not grow every year, and damaged grapes and bruised berries come into the home; now women who want to seem beautiful harm their wombs, and in this age it is rare that anyone wants to be a mother. Certainly I would have been safer had I never given birth: that would be a complaint worthy of Clytemnestra! If the vine should ever know this, it will suppress its grapes at birth, and if it should know this, the tree of Pallas will be barren. Should this come

Hoc in notitiam veniat maloque piroque,
30   destituent silvas utraque poma suas.
Audiat hoc cerasus, bacas exire vetabit:
     audiat hoc ficus, stipes inanis erit.
Non equidem invideo, nunquam tamen ulla feritur,
     quae sterilis sola est conspicienda coma.
35   Cernite sinceros omnes ex ordine truncos,
     qui modo nil quare percutiantur habent.
At mihi saeva nocent mutilatis vulnera ramis,
     nudaque deiecto cortice ligna patent.
Non odium facit hoc, sed spes inducta rapinae:
40   sustineant aliae poma, querentur idem.
Sic reus ille fere est, de quo victoria lucro
     esse potest; inopis vindice facta carent.
Sic timet insidias qui se scit ferre viator
     cur timeat: tutum carpit inanis iter.
45   Sic ego sola petor, solam quia causa petendi est;
     frondibus intactis cetera turba viret.
Nam quod habent frutices aliquando proxima nostris
     fragmina, quod laeso vimine multa iacent,
non istis sua facta nocent, vicinia damno est:
50   excipiunt ictu saxa repulsa meo;
idque fide careat, si non, quae longius absunt,
     nativum retinent inviolata decus.
Ergo si sapiant et mentem verba sequantur,
     devoveant umbras proxima quaeque meas.
55   Quam miserum est odium damnis accedere nostris
     meque ream nimiae proximitatis agi!
Sed, puto, magna mea est operoso cura colono:
     inveniat, dederit quid mihi praeter humum.

to the notice of the apple and the pear, both fruits will for- 30
sake their orchards. Should the cherry hear this, it will for-
bid its fruits to come forth; should the fig hear this, its
branch will be empty.

I'm certainly not envious, yet no tree is ever struck that is
sterile and admired for its leaves alone. Look at all of those 35
uninjured trunks in a row that now have no reason why they
should be pelted. But cruel wounds hurt my mutilated
branches, and my wood lies bare where the bark has been
stripped away. Hatred doesn't do this, but the inducement
of plunder: should others bear fruit, they will make the same 40
complaint. Thus, a person brought to court is usually one
whose conviction brings gain; the pauper's deeds escape the
prosecutor. Similarly, the traveler who knows that he is car-
rying something for which he should fear is afraid of an am-
bush; the empty-handed one enjoys a safe journey. So it is 45
that I alone am assaulted, because I alone give cause for as-
sault; the rest flourish, with their leaves intact. For although
sometimes trees have broken pieces nearby my trunk, and
many of these branches lie on the ground with snapped
twigs, it is not their deeds that harm them—their proximity
is the source of their damage: they receive the stones that 50
strike me and rebound; and this would not be believable if
those that are further away did not retain, unharmed, their
original glory. So, if they were sentient and words could fol-
low their thought, all of the nearest trees would curse my
shade. How wretched it is that hate should accompany my 55
injuries, and that I should be charged with being too close!

But I'm very important, I suppose, to the industrious
farmer. I challenge him to find anything he has given me,

Sponte mea facilis contempto nascor in agro,
60   parsque loci, qua sto, publica paene via est.
Me, sata ne laedam (quoniam et sata laedere dicor),
     imus in extremo margine fundus habet.
Non mihi falx nimias Saturnia deputat umbras,
     duratam renovat non mihi fossor humum.
65   Sole licet siccaque siti peritura laborem,
     irriguae dabitur non mihi sulcus aquae.
At cum maturas fisso nova cortice rimas
     nux agit, ad partes pertica saeva venit.
Pertica dat plenis immitia vulnera ramis,
70   ne possim lapidum verbera sola queri.
Poma cadunt mensis non interdicta secundis,
     et condit lectas parca colona nuces.
Has puer aut certo rectas dilaminat ictu
     aut pronas digito bisve semelve petit.
75   Quattuor in nucibus, non amplius, alea tota est,
     cum sibi suppositis additur una tribus.
Per tabulae clivum labi iubet alter et optat
     tangat ut e multis quaelibet una suam.
Est etiam par sit numerus qui dicat an impar
80   ut divinatas auferat augur opes.
Fit quoque de creta, qualem caeleste figuram
     sidus et in Graecis littera quarta gerit.
Haec ubi distincta est gradibus, quae constitit intus
     quot tetigit virgas, tot capit ipsa nuces.
85   Vas quoque saepe cavum spatio distante locatur,
     in quod missa levi nux cadat una manu.
Felix secreto quae nata est arbor in arvo
     et soli domino ferre tributa potest.
Non hominum strepitus audit, non illa rotarum,
90   non a vicina pulverulenta via est.

besides earth. I grow willingly and easily on unvalued land, and part of the place where I stand is almost a public road. 60 So that I do not harm the crops (for I am even said to harm crops), I occupy the furthest border of the most distant part of the estate. Saturn's sickle does not prune my excessive shade; no digger refreshes my compacted soil. Although I 65 toil close to death from the sun and from parching thirst, no trench of water will be given to me for irrigation. But when the new nut shows ripening cracks in its splitting shell, the harsh rod comes to play its role. The rod gives cruel wounds to full branches, so that I cannot complain only of being 70 stoned. Down falls the fruit that is no stranger to desserts, and the frugal farmwife pickles the collected nuts.

A boy splits these with a precise strike as they stand upright, or, as they lie on their side, he thrusts at them with a finger once or twice. In four nuts, no more, is his entire haz- 75 ard, when one is added to the three underneath it. A different boy causes them to roll down a sloping board and hopes that out of the many nuts at least one will touch his. There is also the one who declares whether the number is odd or even, so that the diviner may carry away the prophesied 80 wealth. Then there is drawn in chalk the sort of shape that a heavenly constellation or the fourth Greek letter bears. When this has been divided into bands, the nut that stops within it wins as many nuts as it has touched lines. Often 85 too a hollow vessel is placed at a distance, into which a nut thrown by a nimble hand is to fall.

Happy is the tree that grows in a hidden field and can pay its taxes to its master alone. It does not hear the clamor of men or of wheels, nor is it dusty from the neighboring road. 90

Illa suo, quaecumque tulit, dare dona colono
et plenos fructus adnumerare potest.
At mihi maturos numquam licet edere fetus,
ante diemque meae decutiuntur opes.
95 Lamina mollis adhuc tenero est in lacte, quod intra est,
nec mala sunt ulli nostra futura bono:
iam tamen invenio qui me iaculentur et ictu
praefestinato munus inane petant.
Si fiat rapti, fiat mensura relicti,
100 maiorem domini parte, viator, habes.
Saepe aliquis, foliis ubi nuda cacumina vidit,
esse putat boreae triste furentis opus;
aestibus hic, hic me spoliatam frigore credit,
est quoque qui crimen grandinis esse putet.
105 At mihi nec grando, duris invisa colonis,
nec ventus fraudi solve geluve fuit:
fructus obest, peperisse nocet, nocet esse feracem,
quaeque fuit multis, ei mihi, praeda malo est.
Praeda malo, Polydore, fuit tibi, praeda nefandae
110 coniugis Aonium misit in arma virum.
Hesperii regis pomaria tuta fuissent,
una sed immensas arbor habebat opes.
At rubus et sentes tantummodo laedere natae
spinaque vindicta cetera tuta sua est.
115 Me, quia nec noceo nec obuncis vindicor hamis,
missa petunt avida saxa proterva manu.
Quid si non aptas solem mutantibus umbras,
finditur Icario cum cane terra, darem?
Quid nisi suffugium nimbos vitantibus essem,
120 non expectata cum venit imber aqua?

It can give whatever it bears as gifts to its farmer and provide a full quota. But I'm never allowed to give birth to fruit that are ripe, and my bounty is knocked off before its proper time. The husk of my nuts is still soft with the young milk that is within, and my misfortunes will not be to anyone's benefit: yet I already find men pelting me and seeking a useless reward with a premature blow. If what has been stolen and what is left behind were calculated, you, traveler, would have a greater share than my master. Often someone, when he sees my top bare of leaves, thinks that it is the cruel work of the raging northerly wind; another thinks that I am robbed because of the heat, another blames the cold, and another thinks that hail is to blame. But neither hail, hated by hardy farmers, nor wind, nor sun, nor frost was injurious to me: my fruit does me harm, it injures me to have produced it, it is harmful to be fruitful; as it has done to many, woe is me, plunder brings misfortune to me. Plundered treasure was the source of your misfortune, Polydorus; the treasure of a wicked wife sent her Aonian husband to war. The orchards of the Hesperian king might have been safe, but one tree held boundless wealth.

But brambles and briars, born only to hurt, and other thorny plants are safe because of their defense. But because I neither harm nor am protected by hooked thorns, violent stones thrown by greedy hands attack me. What if I did not give suitable shade to those who shun the sun, when the earth is cleaved by the Icarian dog? What if I were not a refuge for those avoiding the thunderclouds, when a storm brings unexpected rain? Though I do all these things,

Omnia cum faciam, cum praestem sedula cunctis
   officium, saxis officiosa petor.
Haec mihi perpessae domini patienda querela est:
   causa habeor, quare sit lapidosus ager.
125 Dumque repurgat humum collectaque saxa remittit,
   semper habent in me tela parata viae.
Ergo invisa aliis uni mihi frigora prosunt:
   illo me tutam tempore praestat hiems.
Nuda quidem tunc sum, nudam tamen expedit esse,
130   non spolium de me quod petat hostis habet.
At simul induimus nostris sua munera ramis,
   saxa novos fructus grandine plura petunt.
Forsitan hoc aliquis dicat "quae publica tangunt,
   carpere concessum est: hoc via iuris habet."
135 Si licet hoc, oleas destringite, caedite messes,
   improbe, vicinum carpe, viator, holus.
Intret et urbanas eadem petulantia portas,
   sitque tuis muris, Romule, iuris idem:
quilibet argentum prima de fronte tabernae
140   tollat et ad gemmas quilibet alter eat.
Auferat hic aurum, peregrinos ille lapillos
   et, quascumque potest tangere, tollat opes.
Sed neque tolluntur nec, dum regit omnia Caesar,
   incolumis tanto praeside raptor erit.
145 At non ille deus pacem intra moenia finit:
   auxilium toto spargit in orbe suum.
Quid tamen hoc prodest, media si luce palamque
   verberor et tutae non licet esse nuci?
Ergo nec nidos foliis haerere nec ullam
150   sedibus in nostris stare videtis avem.
At lapis in ramo sedit quicumque bifurco,
   haeret ut et capta victor in arce sua.

though I provide untiring service to all, despite being ever
dutiful I am pelted with stones. And after putting up with
this, I must endure the complaint of my master: I am con-
sidered the cause of the field's stoniness. And while he clears   125
the ground again and throws away the stones he has col-
lected, the road always has weapons ready against me.
Therefore, the cold that is hated by others benefits me
alone: in that season winter keeps me safe. Then indeed I
am naked, but it is advantageous to be naked, since I have   130
no spoils for an enemy to seek. But as soon as I put the de-
sired prizes on my branches, stones more numerous than
hail assail the new fruit.

Perhaps someone might say here: "Whatever touches
public land may be picked: the road possesses this right." If   135
this is lawful, strip off the olives, cut down the crops, pick
nearby vegetables, shameless traveler. Let the same impu-
dence even enter the gates of Rome, and let this same right
be granted within your walls, Romulus: let anyone who
wants take silver from a shop front, and some other person   140
go for the jewels. Let one steal gold, another foreign gems,
and take whatever riches he is able to touch. But these
things are not stolen, and, while Caesar rules the world, no
thief will be safe under so powerful a protector. But that god   145
does not limit peace to within city walls: he extends his aid
throughout the entire world. Yet what good is this, if I am
struck openly in broad daylight and if a walnut tree can't be
safe?

For this reason, you see neither nests entwined in my foli-
age nor any bird sitting perched on me. But whatever stone   150
settles in the fork of a branch holds fast like a conqueror in a

Cetera saepe tamen potuere admissa negari,
    et crimen noxa est infitiata suum:
155 nostra notat fusco digitos iniuria suco
    cortice contactas inficiente manus.
Ille cruor meus est, illo maculata cruore
    non profectura dextra lavatur aqua.
O, ego, cum longae venerunt taedia vitae,
160   optavi quotiens arida facta mori!
Optavi quotiens aut caeco turbine verti
    aut valido missi fulminis igne peti!
Atque utinam subitae raperent mea poma procellae,
    vel possem fructus excutere ipsa meos!
165 Sic, ubi detracta est a te tibi causa pericli,
    quod superest, tutum, Pontice castor, habes.
Quid mihi tunc animi est, ubi sumit tela viator
    atque oculis plagae destinat ante locum?
Nec vitare licet moto fera vulnera trunco,
170   quem sub humo radix curvaque vincla tenent.
Corpora praebemus plagis, ut saepe sagittis,
    quem populus manicas deposuisse vetat,
utve gravem candens ubi tolli vacca securim
    aut stringi cultros in sua colla videt.
175 Saepe meas vento frondes tremuisse putastis,
    sed metus in nobis causa tremoris erat.
Si merui videorque nocens, excidite ferro
    nostraque fumosis urite membra focis,
si merui videorque nocens, imponite flammae,
180   et liceat miserae dedecus esse semel.
Si nec cur urar nec cur excidar habetis,
    parcite: sic coeptum perficiatis iter.

citadel he's captured. Although other crimes are often able
to be denied, and the criminal has disavowed the very accu-
sation, the injuries that I have suffered mark the fingers   155
with dark juice, dyeing the hands that have touched the
husk. That is my blood; the hand tainted with that blood
cannot be cleaned by being washed with water. Alas, when I
have grown weary with my long life, how often have I wished   160
to dry up and die! How often have I wished either to be up-
rooted by an unseen gust of wind or to be struck by the pow-
erful fire of a hurled thunderbolt! Indeed, I wish that a sud-
den gale would snatch away my fruit, or that I myself could
shake off my nuts! Just as, once you have removed the source   165
of your peril, Pontic beaver, you keep safe what remains.
Imagine my state of mind, when the traveler picks up his
weapons and with his eyes predetermines the spot for his
blow. I cannot avoid the fierce strike by moving my trunk,
which the root's curved bonds hold beneath the ground. I   170
proffer my body to the blows, just as one whom the people
forbid to remove his manacles often proffers his body to the
arrows, or as when the white cow sees the heavy ax raised up
or the knife pressed to her neck.

Often you thought that my leaves had been trembling in   175
the wind, but fear was the cause of my trembling. If I have
deserved it and am judged guilty, cut me down with an ax
and burn my limbs on smoky hearths; if I have deserved it,
and am judged guilty, set me on fire, and let disgrace come to   180
wretched me once and for all. But if you have no cause to
burn me or cut me down, spare me: so may you finish the
journey you have begun.

De pulice

Parve pulex, sed amara lues inimica puellis,
　　carmine quo fungar in tua facta, ferox?
Tu laceras corpus tenerum, durissime, morsu,
　　cuius cum fuerit plena cruore cutis,
5　emittis maculas nigro de corpore fuscas,
　　levia membra quibus conmaculata rigent.
Cumque tuum lateri rostrum defigis acutum,
　　cogitur e somno surgere virgo gravi;
perque sinus erras, tibi pervia cetera membra;
10　　is quocumque placet: nil tibi, saeve, latet.
A piget et dicam: cum strata puella recumbit,
　　tu femur avellis cruraque aperta subis.
Ausus es interdum per membra libidinis ire
　　et turbare locis gaudia nata suis.
15　Dispeream, nisi iam cupiam fieri meus hostis,
　　promptior ut fieret ad mea vota via.
Si sineret natura mihi, quod verterer in te
　　et, quod sum natus, posse redire daret,
vel si carminibus possem mutarier ullis,
20　　carminibus fierem ad mea vota pulex,
aut medicaminibus, si plus medicamina possunt,
　　vellem naturae iura novare meae.
Carmina Medeae vel quid medicamina Circes
　　contulerunt, res est notificata satis.
25　His ego mutatus, si sic mutabilis essem,
　　haererem tunicae margine virgineae.
Inde means per crura meae sub veste puellae
　　ad loca quae vellem me cito subriperem,

On the Flea

Tiny flea, but a bitter plague, harmful to girls, what chant shall I perform against your deeds, vicious one? You wound a tender body, cruelest one, with your bite, and because her skin is full of blood, you produce dark stains from your black 5 body, and when her smooth limbs have been stained, they stiffen. And when you fix your pointed beak into her side, the maiden is forced to rise from deep sleep; you wander all over her breast and the other parts accessible to you; you 10 go wherever you please: nothing is hidden from you, you savage.

Ah, I'm ashamed, but I'll say it anyway: when the girl lies back down on the bed, you part her thighs and insinuate yourself between her open legs. Sometimes you have dared to go through her private parts and stir up the joys native to those places. I'll be damned if I don't wish now to become 15 my enemy, so the way to my desires may be closer at hand. If nature allowed that I be turned into you and granted that I could return to the form of my birth, or if I could be changed by some sort of incantation, by such an incantation in accor- 20 dance with my desires I would become a flea. Or by means of drugs, if drugs are more potent, I would wish to reform the conditions of my nature. What the spells of Medea or the potions of Circe brought about is very well known.

Changed by these (if I could be thus changed), I would 25 cling to the hem of the girl's dress. From there, passing along the legs and under the gown of my girl I would steal my way quickly to the places that I desired, and, just as I wished,

sicut et optarem, nil laedens ipse cubarem,
30 donec de pulice rursus homo fierem.
Sed si forte novis virgo perterrita monstris
exigeret famulos ad mea vincla suos,
aut temptata meis precibus subcumberet illa,
aut mox ex homine verterer in pulicem.
35 Rursus mutatus fundens humilisque precatus
afferrem cunctos in mea vota deos,
dum bona, vel precibus vel vi, sperata tenerem
et iam nil mallet quam sibi me socium.

De cuculo

Conveniunt cuncti subito de montibus altis
pastores pecudum vernali luce sub umbra
arborea, pariter laetas celebrare Camenas.
Adfuit et iuvenis Daphnis seniorque Palaemon.
5 Omnes hi cuculo laudes cantare parabant.
Ver quoque florigero succinctum stemmate venit;
frigida venit Hiems, rigidis hirsuta capillis.
His certamen erat cuculi de carmine grande.
    Ver prius allusit ternos modulamine versus:
10 "Opto meus veniat cuculus clarissimus ales.
Omnibus iste solet fieri gratissimus hospes
in silvis, modulans ritu bona carmina rostro."
    Tum glacialis Hiems respondit voce serena:
"Non veniat cuculus, nigris sed dormiat antris.
15 Iste famem secum semper portare suevit."

harming nothing, I would lie there, until I changed back 30
from a flea to a man. But if by chance the maiden, fright-
ened by this strange prodigy, were to order her attendants to
throw me in chains, either she would be induced by my
prayers to yield, or I would immediately be changed from a
man into a flea. Changed back again and pouring out hum- 35
ble prayers, I would call on all the gods to further my wishes,
until I obtained the longed-for prize, either by prayers or by
force, and then she would want nothing more than for me to
be her companion.

On the Cuckoo

Suddenly all of the shepherds of flocks gathered together
from the high mountains, in the spring light beneath the
shade of trees, to honor the happy Muses in concert. Young
Daphnis also attended, as did his elder Palaemon. All of 5
them were preparing to sing the praises of the cuckoo.
Spring also came, girded with a flowery garland; frigid Win-
ter came, bristling with stiff hair. There was a great contest
between them about the song of the cuckoo.

First Spring sported in a song with three verses: "I wish 10
that my cuckoo would come—the most famous of birds! He
is always the most welcome guest in all of the woods, when
he gives voice to fine songs from his beak, as is his practice."

Then icy Winter responded in a calm voice: "May the
cuckoo not come—may he sleep in dark caves instead. He 15
always is accustomed to bring hunger with him."

    [*Ver*] "Opto meus veniat cuculus cum germine laeto,
frigora depellat, Phoebo comes almus in aevum.
Phoebus amat cuculum cantantem voce serena."

    [*Hiems*] "Non veniat cuculus, generat quia forte labores,

20   omnia disturbat: pelagi terraeque laborant;
proelia continuat, requiem disiungit amicam."

    [*Ver*] "Quid tu, segnis Hiems, cuculo convicia captas,
corpore quae gravido tenebrosis dormit in antris
post epulas Veneris, post stulti pocula Bacchi?"

25   [*Hiems*] "Sunt mihi divitiae, sunt et convivia laeta,
est requies dulcis, calidus est ignis in aede.
Haec cuculus nescit, sed perfidus ille laborat."

    [*Ver*] "Ore feret flores cuculus et mella ministrat,
aedificatque domus, placidas et navigat undas,

30   et generat soboles, laetos et vestiet agros."

    [*Hiems*] "Haec inimica mihi sunt, quae tibi laeta videntur.
Sed placeat gazas optatas semper habere
et gaudere cibis simul et requiescere semper."

    [*Ver*] "Quis tibi, tarda Hiems, semper dormire parata,

35   divitias cumulat gazas vel congregat ullas,
si ver aut aestas primo tibi nulla laborant?"

    [*Hiems*] "Vera refers: multi, quoniam tibi multa laborant,
sunt etiam servi nostra ditione subacti,
nam mihi servantes domino, quaecumque laborant."

40   [*Ver*] "Non illis dominus, sed pauper inopsque superbus,
nec te iam poteris prece ulla pascere cantu
ni cuculus tibi quae venient alimonia praebet."

Spring: "I wish that my cuckoo would come, along with the lush growth of vegetation, and drive out the chill, as Apollo's benign attendant forever. Apollo loves the cuckoo, who sings in a calm voice."

Winter: "May the cuckoo not come, because he habitu- 20 ally gives rise to hardship; he disturbs everything: the seas and the lands suffer; he prolongs wars, and he disrupts welcome repose."

Spring: "Why do you, sluggish Winter, strive to censure the cuckoo, you who, with a heavy body, sleep in shadowy caves after the feasts of Venus, and after the cups of foolish Bacchus?"

Winter: "I have riches, I also have pleasant feasts, in my 25 house there is sweet repose, there is a warm fire. The cuckoo knows nothing of these things, but that betrayer only toils."

Spring: "The cuckoo will bring flowers with its song and provide honey; it constructs houses, navigates calm seas, gives birth to offspring, and will clothe the fertile fields." 30

Winter: "The things that seem pleasant to you are distasteful to me. Rather, may I have the pleasure of always possessing the wealth that I want, of enjoying good food, too, and of continual repose."

Spring: "Sluggish Winter, always ready to sleep, who ac- 35 cumulates wealth or collects any treasure for you, if spring or summer do not first toil for you?"

Winter: "You tell the truth: many, inasmuch as they perform many labors for you, are also servants under my rule, for in whatever they labor at, they serve me as their master."

Spring: "You are not their master, but rather a wretched, 40 haughty beggar, and you won't be able to feed yourself by means of any prayer, unless the cuckoo by its song provides you with the nourishment to come."

Tum respondit ovans sublimi e sede Palaemon
et Daphnis pariter, pastorum et turba piorum:
45 "Desine plura, Hiems, rerum tu prodigus, atrox.
Et veniat cuculus, pastorum dulcis amicus.
Collibus in nostris erumpant germina laeta,
pascua sint pecori, requies et dulcis in arvis,
et virides rami praestent umbracula fessis,
50 uberibus plenis veniantque ad mulctra capellae,
et volucres Phoebum varia sub voce salutent.
Quapropter cuculus citius nunc ecce venito!
Tu iam dulcis amor, cunctis carissimus ales.
Omnia te expectant: pelagus tellusque polusque.
55 Dulce decus cucule salve per saecula salve!"

De philomela

Dulcis amica, veni noctis solatia praestans,
    inter aves etenim nulla tui similis.
Tu, philomela, potes vocum discrimina mille,
    mille vales varios rite referre modos;
5 nam quamvis aliae volucres modulamina temptent,
    nulla potest modulos aequiperare tuos.
Insuper est avium spatiis garrire diurnis:
    tu cantare simul nocte dieque potes.
Parus enim quamquam per noctem tinnipet omnem,
10   sed sua vox nulli iure placere potest.
Dulce pelora sonat, dicunt quam nomine droscam;
    sed fugiente die illa quieta silet.

Then Palaemon joyfully replied, rising from his lofty seat, together with Daphnis and the throng of pious shepherds: "Say no more, harsh Winter, waster of wealth. And let the 45 cuckoo come, the sweet friend of shepherds. Let thriving vegetation burst out in our hills, let there be grazing for the flocks, and sweet repose in the fields, and let the greening branches offer shade to the weary, let the she-goats come to 50 the milk pails with full teats, and let the birds greet Apollo with diverse calls. Therefore, cuckoo, come, come quickly now! You are already our sweet beloved—the dearest bird to all. Everything awaits you: the sea and the earth and the heavens. Hail, cuckoo, our sweet glory—hail through the 55 ages!"

On the Nightingale

Sweet mistress, come offering the solace of night, for there is none like you among birds. You, nightingale, can produce a thousand distinct voices, and you can duly make a thousand different tunes; for although other birds attempt 5 songs, none can equal your melodies. Moreover it is the habit of birds to chirp in the daytime hours: but you can sing day and night alike.

For the titmouse peter-peter-peters all night long, but its 10 voice cannot rightly give pleasure to anyone. The thrush, which they call by the name throstle, sings sweetly; but when the day is done it rests quietly. And the blackbird

Et merulus modulans tam pulchris zinzitat odis,
    nocte ruente tamen cantica nulla canit.
15 Vere calente novo componit acredula cantus
    matutinali tempore rurirulans.
Dum turdus trucilat, sturnus tunc pusitat ore,
    sed quod mane canunt, vespere non recolunt.
Caccabat hinc perdix et graccitat improbus anser,
20   et castus turtur atque columba gemunt.
Pausitat arborea clamans de fronde palumbes,
    in fluviisque natans sorte tetrinnit anas.
Grus gruit in gronnis, cycni prope flumina drensant,
    accipitres pipant, milvus hiansque lipit.
25 Cucurrire solet gallus, gallina cacillat,
    pulpulat et pavo, trissat hirundo vaga.
Dum clangunt aquilae, vultur pulpare probatur,
    et crocitat corvus, fringulit et graculus.
Glottorat immenso merens ciconia rostro,
30   pessimus et passer sons titiare solet.
Psittacus humanas depromit voce loquelas
    atque suo domino "chaere" sonat vel "ave."
Pica loquax varias concinnat gutture voces,
    scurili strepitu omne quod audit ait.
35 Et cuculi cuculant, et rauca cicada fritinit,
    bombilat ore legens munera mellis apes.
Bubilat horrendum ferali murmure bubo
    humano generi tristia fata ferens.
Strix nocturna sonans et vespertilio stridunt,
40   noctua lucifuga cucubat in tenebris.
Ast ululant ululae lugubri voce canentes,
    inque paludiferis butio butit aquis.
Regulus atque merops et rubro pectore procnes
    consimili modulo zinzizulare sciunt.

check-check-checks, piping with such sweet tunes, yet when night comes it sings no more songs. The finch composes its songs in the new spring warmth, trilling roo-ree-roo in the morning. While the fieldfare chuckles, the starling rattles with its mouth, but what they sing in the morning, they do not repeat in the evening.

Next the partridge cackles, the rude goose honks, and the pure turtledove and dove lament. The woodpigeon coos, calling from the foliage of trees, and it's the duck's lot to quack as it swims in its streams. The crane crunkles in its quagmires, the swans trumpet by the rivers, the hawks pipe, and the predatory kite whistles. The rooster goes cock-a-doodle-do, the hen clucks, the peacock screeches, and the wandering swallow twitters. While the eagles scream, the vulture is found to screech, the raven croaks, and the jackdaw chatters.

The worthy stork makes a clattering with its huge beak, and the criminal sparrow, the worst of all, likes to chatter. The parrot produces human speech with its voice and sings to its master "hello" or "goodbye." The talkative magpie produces different voices in its throat—with a mocking cry it repeats everything that it hears. The cuckoos cuckoo, the noisy cicada clicks, and the bee buzzes as it gathers with its mouth its gifts of honey.

The horned owl howls a frightening noise with a cry announcing death, bringing sad fate to the human race. The nocturnal wood owl and the bat shriek, and the night owl, who shuns daylight, hoots in the darkness. The screech owls wail, singing with mournful voice, and the bittern booms in swampy waters. The wren, the bee-eater, and the red-breasted swallows know how to whistle in a completely similar rhythm.

45 Scribere me voces avium philomela coegit,
        quae cantu cunctas exuperat volucres;
    sed iam quadrupedum fari discrimina vocum
        nemine cogente nunc ego sponte sequar:
    Tigrides indomitae rancant, rugiuntque leones,
50   panther caurit amans, pardus hiando felit.
    Dum lynces urcando fremunt, ursus ferus uncat,
        atque lupus ululat, frendit agrestis aper.
    Et barrus barrit, cervi crocitant et onagri,
        ac taurus mugit, et celer hinnit equus,
55 quirritat et verres saetosus, et oncat asellus,
        bratterat hinc aries et pia balat ovis.
    Sordida sus subiens ruris per gramina grunnit,
        at miccere caprae, hirce petulce, soles.
    Rite canes latrant, fallax vulpecula gannit,
60   glaucitat et catulus, ac lepores vagiunt.
    Mus avidus mintrit, velox mustelaque drindrit,
        et grillus grillat, desticat inde sorex.
    Ecce venenosus serpendo sibilat anguis,
        garrula limosis rana coaxat aquis.
65 Has volucrum voces describens quadrupedumque
        paucas discrimen cuique suum dederam,
    sed cunctas species animantum nemo notavit,
        atque ideo sonitus dicere quis poterit?
    Cuncta tamen Domino depromunt munera laudis,
70   seu semper sileant sive sonare queant.
    Tu valeas felix ceu longo tempore phoenix,
        te foveat veluti cum pelle vitellus!

The nightingale, who surpasses all winged creatures in 45
song, compels me to describe the calls of birds; but now I'll
proceed willingly, with no one compelling me, to speak of
the differences in the sounds made by four-legged creatures:
untamed tigers growl, and lions roar, the rutting panther 50
caterwauls, the leopard makes a yawning meow.

While lynxes make a loud yowl, the wild bear growls, the
wolf howls, and the wild boar gnashes its teeth. The ele-
phant trumpets, deer and onagers caw, the bull bellows, the
swift horse whinnies, the bristly feral pig grunts, the donkey 55
brays, the ram bleats and the loyal ewe baas. The filthy pig
oinks as it roots through the countryside grass, but you,
frisky he-goat, like to bleat urgently after the she-goat. Dogs
properly bark, the sly little fox gabbles, the puppy yelps, and 60
hares wail. The greedy mouse peeps, the swift weasel chat-
ters, the cricket chirps, and the shrew squeaks. Behold, the
venomous serpent hisses as it snakes along, and the garru-
lous frog croaks in slimy waters.

By describing these few voices of winged and four-legged 65
creatures, I have assigned to each its own distinctive sound,
but no one knows every species of living thing, and so who
will be able to name their sounds? Yet all offer their gifts of
praise to the Lord, whether they are perpetually voiceless or 70
are able to sing. May you thrive for a long time, like the for-
tunate phoenix, and may the calf nourish you, so to speak,
with its hide!

De lupo

Saepe lupus quidam per pascua lata vagantes
    arripuit multas opilionis oves.
Laedere raptorem postquam virtute nequivit,
    illaqueare dolo pastor eum studuit.
5 Nam rigidam flectit tanto conamine quercum,
    ut caput illius tangere possit humum,
et capiti flexo laqueus sic nectitur unus,
    mobilis ut laqueum detineat baculus,
sed laqueum terrae baculus sic applicat ille,
10   ut laqueo pereat, qui baculum moveat.
Et medio laquei sic inseritur caput agni,
    ut baculum moveat, qui caput arripiat.
Tunc abit opilio. Lupus ingenium petit illud,
    et rapit agninum protinus ore caput,
15 sed baculo moto laqueus ligat ilico collum,
    atque rigor quercus tollit in alta lupum.
Ut videt opilio captum pendere latronem,
    mittit in hunc lapides accelerando necem;
vulnera mille facit, lupus ut pereat lapidatus,
20   sed nequit expelli spiritus ille malus.
Ut magis hunc cruciet, tandem deponit ab alto,
    atque levans fustem protulit ista lupo:
"Nil faciunt lapides, cerebrum iam fuste relidam,
    atque meis agnis inferias faciam."
25 Mox lupus exclamat: "Miserere, piissime pastor,
    et tibi quae referam percipe pauca precor.
Si mihi dignatus fueris concedere vitam,
    omnia, quae rapui, quadrupla restituam.

On the Wolf

Often a certain wolf snatched many of a shepherd's sheep as they wandered through the wide pastures. After he failed to thwart the thief by force, the shepherd strove to ensnare him in a trap. For he bent a rigid oak with so much effort 5 that its top could touch the ground, and he fastened a snare to the bent top, in such a way that a pliant stick held back the snare, but the stick kept the snare on the ground in such a way that whoever moved the stick would perish in the 10 snare, and he placed a lamb's head in the middle of the snare, so that whoever snatched the head would move the stick. As soon as the shepherd departs, the wolf rushes to that contrivance, and grabs the lamb's head immediately in its mouth, but since the stick has been moved, the snare in- 15 stantly binds the wolf's neck, and the oak's rigidity lifts the wolf up high.

When the shepherd sees the captured thief hanging, he throws rocks at him to hasten his death; he wounds him a thousand times, so that the wolf should perish from being stoned, but that wicked spirit cannot be dislodged. In order 20 to torture him even more, at length the shepherd takes him down, and raising a cudgel, says this to the wolf:

"Stones have accomplished nothing—now I'll strike your skull with a cudgel, and make a sacrifice in honor of my dead lambs."

Immediately the wolf exclaims: "Take pity, most pious 25 shepherd, and learn a little about what I can repay you, I beg you. If you deign to grant me life, I will restore fourfold

57

Sed nihil hic habeo. Si me patiaris abire,
30   ne tibi sim fallax, utile pignus habe.
Congruus obses erit lupulus meus, hunc tibi tradam,
      ut veniente die, quam dederis, redeam.
Ut redeam nunquam, minimum dampnum tibi restat,
      pro sene confecto si iuvenis pereat.
35 Ille nocere potest, ego nec vivendo nocebo,
      et tibi, si perimar, commoda nulla dabo.
Tolle meam pellem: tibi non erit apta coturno;
      tolle meam carnem: non erit apta cibo.
Nescio, cur miserum corpus disperdere quaeras,
40   cum tibi de neutra parte sit utilitas.”
Ut breviter narrem, quantocius obside sumpto
      dat remeare lupum credulus opilio.
Ille parans artem, qua falleret opilionem,
      dum remeat, monachum repperit et famulum.
45 “Mi pater,” inquit, “ave, ne despice verba precantis,
      nec quia peccavi, me reprobare velis.
Paenitet erroris, bona mundi sumere taedet,
      innocuumque pecus me iugulasse pudet.
Iugibus illecebris nil prodest membra fovere,
50   si sit habenda mihi nulla salus animae.
Percute me virga, vel quovis tunde flagello,
      hanc animam tantum, vir pie, redde deo.
Caesariem tondens latam, rogo, rade coronam,
      et mihi converso da monachi tunicam.
55 Neve putes frustra tantum perferre laborem,
      cum mihi nunc data sit, do tibi munus ovem.
Si tibi non placeant data fercula carnis ovinae,
      da famulo carnem, tu tibi vellus habe.”

everything that I have stolen. But I have nothing here. If you'll allow me to depart, so that I don't deceive you, receive a suitable pledge. My little brother-wolf will be a suitable hostage; I'll surrender him to you, so that when the day comes that you have appointed, I will return. Even if I never return, there is practically no cost for you, if a youth perishes in place of a worn-out old creature. He can still do a lot of harm if he lives, but I will do no harm even if I keep on living, and if I am killed, I will bring you no benefit. Take my pelt: it will not make a good boot for you; take my flesh: it will not make good food for you. I don't know why you seek to destroy my wretched body, when neither part of me is useful to you."

To tell it briefly, as soon as the hostage was received, the credulous shepherd allows the wolf to go back home. On his way home, while strategizing how to deceive the shepherd, he meets with a monk and his servant.

"Hail, my father," he says, "don't disdain the words of a petitioner, and don't reproach me because I have sinned. I regret my error, I am sick of taking worldly possessions, and I am ashamed to have slain innocent sheep. There is no profit in nurturing my body with continual enticements, if there is to be no salvation for my soul. Strike me with a rod, or beat me with any kind of scourge—only restore this soul, my pious fellow, to God. Shear my full hair, I beg, shave me a tonsure, and when I have been made a brother, give me a monk's tunic. And do not think that you carry out such a great task in vain—once you have given the tunic to me, I will give you the gift of a sheep. If gifts of mutton dishes do not please you, give the meat to your servant and keep the fleece for yourself."

Ut recipit monachus nimis acceptabile donum,
60   forpicibus sumptis ilico tondet eum,
atque caput radens tantam studet esse coronam,
      ut sit ab auricula circus ad auriculam,
et docet ulterius, qualis foret ordo tenendus,
      inde cucullatum precipit ire lupum.
65 Gaudens intravit lupus in cellam monachorum,
      et simplex vultu constitit ante chorum.
Denudansque caput dixit: "Benedicite, fratres,
      vobiscum dominus perpetuo maneat."
Accedens melius stetit in medio monachorum,
70   dicens: "Vos dominus pace sua repleat.
Horribilem vultum nostrum nolite timere,
      quadrupedes monachos patria nostra tenet."
Hoc dicto monachi surgunt ex ordine cuncti,
      dantes devoti basia multa sibi.
75 Tunc ait ille: "Mihi dominum monstrate priorem,
      debeo namque sibi verbula pauca loqui."
Tunc omnes currunt, dominum vocitantque priorem,
      si monstrum cupiat cernere, quod veniat.
Dum prior advenit, hunc laeta voce recepit,
80   et dixit: "Frater, quid petis, unde venis?"
Raptor cum fletu: "Miserere mei, pater," inquit,
      "sum pauper monachus, de patria profugus.
Exul, inops terram perlustravi peregrinam,
      nec reperire scio, qui det opem misero.
85 In claustrum nostrum subierunt vispiliones
      atque redegerunt in cinerem penitus,
quae fuerant nostra, rapuere manu violenta.
      Haec est tristitiae causa viaeque meae."

As soon as the monk accepts the very welcome gift, he takes up the shears and shaves the wolf on the spot, and in shaving his head, aims to make the tonsure so big that its circle extends from ear to ear; and furthermore, the monk teaches him what order he is to uphold, and then, once the wolf is hooded, the monk orders him to go.

The wolf happily entered a monastery and, with an open countenance, stood before the choir. Uncovering his head, he said: "Bless you, brothers, may the Lord be with you always."

Advancing further, he stood in the midst of the monks, saying: "May the Lord fill you with his peace. Do not fear my terrible countenance—my homeland has four-footed monks."

With this speech, the monks all rise in order, and devotedly give many kisses to him. Then the wolf says: "Show me the lord prior, for I ought to exchange a few words with him."

Then they all run off and summon the lord prior, if he wishes to see the marvel that has come. When the prior arrived, he received the wolf with a cheerful voice, and said: "Brother, what do you seek? Where are you from?"

The thief tearfully replies, "Take pity on me, father—I am a poor monk, a fugitive from my homeland. As a destitute exile I have wandered through foreign lands but cannot find anyone to help me in my misery. Bandits snuck into our cloister, and reduced it utterly to ash; they violently seized our possessions. This is the reason for my sadness and my journey."

Tunc prior auditis huius sermonibus inquit:
90   "Frater, tristitias, te rogo, pone tuas.
Esto gavisus, hic fletus erit tibi risus,
   noster, si quaeris, ammodo frater eris."
Post haec conventus hunc supplice voce rogavit
   totus, ut ipsorum claviger esse velit.
95 Ex istis verbis lupus est bene laetificatus,
   et magnas grates omnibus inde refert.
Tunc velut invitus fuit hic ad vota paratus,
   suscipiens pactum protinus officium.
Sedulus, intentus, vigilans, discretus et aptus
100   extat in officio tempore non modico.
Sollerti cura semper cavit nocitura;
   solus disposuit omnia, quae voluit.
Sed quia Natura quemvis trahit ad sua iura,
   vobis de lupulo pauca referre volo.
105 Fratres indicta ieiunia tempore quodam
   servabant. Abbas intulit ista sibi:
"Frater, conventus ieiunans est quoque lentus,
   illi pisciculos te dare mando bonos."
Assumpsit monachum pergens ad flumina secum,
110   et cernens asinum carpere gramen ait:
"Crede mihi, frater, quod sum, tibi conqueror, aeger,
   estque genus cancri sanior esca mihi.
En video cancrum, quem ni rapiam, subit antrum.
   Hic optatus adest." Rettulit ista comes:
115 "Non est tam magnus cancer. Puto, quod sit asellus."
   "Me fraudas," inquit raptor, eumque vorat.
Sed monachus celat factum, culpam quoque velat,
   nec visum sociis rettulit iste suis.
Inde lupus modicum vel nil in luce comedit,
120   fingens se modicum semper habere cibum.

When he has heard the wolf's speech, the prior replies: "Brother, I beg you, put aside your grief. Be joyful—here your tears will turn to laughter; if you desire, from now on you will be our brother." 90

After this, the whole assembly beseeched him with entreaties to agree to be their key holder. The wolf is extremely delighted by these words, and so gives his profound thanks to them all. Then, as if reluctant, he was prepared for his vows, immediately assuming his agreed duty. Diligent, attentive, vigilant, discrete, and ready, he remains in the post for quite a long time. With artful care, he always avoided anything that could do harm; he alone arranged everything as wished. 95 100

But because Nature draws everyone to her laws, I wish to tell you a little more about this wolf. One time, the brothers were observing the appointed fasts. The abbot said these words to him: "Brother, in fasting the community has become idle; I command you to provide it some good little fish." 105

The wolf took a monk with him when he went to the river, and seeing a donkey eating the grass, says: "Believe me, brother, I am ill, I'm sorry to tell you, and crab is the healthiest food for me. Look—I see a crab; unless I grab it, it will go into its cave. Here is just what I wanted." 110

His comrade made the following reply: "A crab isn't that big. I think that's a donkey." 115

"You're fooling me," says the thief, and eats it.

But the monk conceals the deed, and also hides his fault, and did not report what he saw to his colleagues. From then on, the wolf ate little or nothing during the daytime, pretending that he always had only a little food. But when night 120

Sed cum nox venit, veteri de more voravit,
    et furtim rapuit omnia, quae potuit,
carnes, lac, capras et oves, farcimina, pullos,
    porcellos, agnos et simul anserulos.
125   Abbas ipsorum dum cerneret altile nullum,
    ut consuetus erat, sic ait ipse lupo:
"Dic, frater, nostri quo venerunt modo pulli
    cunctaque quae fuerant hactenus altilia?"
Iratus raptor abbati taliter inquit:
130   "De vestris porcis quae mihi cura fuit?
Numquid porcorum custos ego? Sum dominorum.
    Absit, ut istius dicar agaso domus."
Abbas respondit: "Non sic, non sic, bone frater.
    Omnia tradidimus nostra tuis manibus.
135   Tu debes super his rationem reddere nobis.
    Dic, dic absque mora, sint ubi nostra bona."
Post haec per pullam lupulum traxere cucullam,
    iniecere suis bracchia saeva pilis,
illius et dorsum caedentes verbere multo
140   dixerunt: "Frater, debita redde cito."
"Parcite" clamavit lupus et veniam rogitavit,
    ut salvet vitam sub nece iam positam.
Et pedibus tremulis stans indutias petiebat,
    ut post quinque dies omnia restituat.
145   Abbas, aetate lupuli motus, pietate
    sic ait: "Accipias, quas petis, inducias."
Raptor gavisus abiit, non postmodo visus,
    nam fugiens nemora quaeritat absque mora.
Venerat illa dies, qua reddi debuit obses,
150   qua lupus ut redeat pollicitus fuerat,
tunc redit. At pastor cognoscere vix valet illum,
    nam modo fulvus erat, quem videt esse nigrum.

came, he ate as he'd always been accustomed to and secretly stole everything that he could: meat, milk, goats and sheep, sausage, chicken, pork, lamb, and even goslings.

When the abbot saw no livestock, as he had been accustomed, he addresses the wolf himself in this way: "Tell me, brother, where have our chickens gone now and the rest of our animals, which until now had been here?" 125

The thief, enraged, replies to the abbot in this way: "What concern are your pigs to me? Am I the guardian of the pigs? I am the guardian of their masters. God forbid that I should be called the animal keeper of this household." 130

The abbot responds: "Not so, not so, my good brother. We have entrusted all we own to your hands. You ought to render an account to us regarding these possessions. Tell, tell us without delay, where our possessions are." 135

After this, they dragged the poor wolf by his dark cowl, laid violent hands on his coat, and striking his back with a great blow, said: "Brother, return what you owe at once!" 140

"Be merciful!" shouted the wolf, and asked for forgiveness in order to save his life now in peril of death. And, with trembling feet, he sought a truce on the terms that after five days he would return everything.

The abbot, moved by the poor wolf's age, mercifully speaks thus: "You can have the truce that you seek." The thief departs joyfully, never to be seen again, for in flight, he heads for the woods without delay. 145

The day had come on which the hostage was to be returned, on which the wolf had promised to come back, so then he reappears. But the shepherd can scarcely recognize him, for he had once been tawny, but now appears black. He 150

"Qualis eras," inquit, "nimis es mutatus ab illo,
    qui pecudum raptor captus eras laqueo."
155 Ille caput flectens postquam "Benedicite" dixit,
    ora rigans lacrimis talia verba dedit:
"Vulneribus lapidum, mihi quae dederas, maceratus
    nuper eram languens, affuit et medicus.
Ille premens venam pulsum male currere sensit
160   et mihi 'Non vives, sed morieris' ait.
Interea monachus venit, ut me visitet aegrum,
    et monet, ut tandem peniteat scelerum,
spemque docet sanctam, quia nullus perditus esset,
    cui mala vita fuit, si bona mors fieret.
165 Denique persuasit penitus contemnere mundum,
    et mihi sic raso tradidit hunc habitum.
Ut veteres mores alimentaque prisca reliqui,
    qui fueram languens, ilico convalui.
Nunc quia debebat meus obses perdere vitam,
170   ne pereat frater, ponere quaero meam.
At rediens, sicut me constitui rediturum,
    quod tibi restituam, nil habeo proprium.
Fallere nolo fidem. Si vis mihi parcere, parce,
    si placet, ut peream, me citius perime."
175 "Haec mea," pastor ait, "te laedet dextera nunquam,
    sed quoniam laesit, postulo, da veniam.
Interimens monachum fierem duplex homicida,
    obses eat liber, tuque domum remea."
Tunc remeant hilares, tutique morantur in agro,
180   cum lupus esuriens protulit haec lupulo:
"Crede mihi, frater, nimis est caro dulcis ovina,
    et cibus asper erit caseus atque faba.

says, "You have been greatly changed from what you were, the thief of livestock who was captured by a snare."

The wolf, bending his head after he said, "Bless the Lord," 155 his face moist with tears, made this reply: "Debilitated by the stoning that you had given me, not long ago I was languishing, and a doctor came to me. Pressing my vein, he felt the weak pulse, and said to me, 'You won't live—rather, 160 you'll die.' Meanwhile a monk came to visit me in my illness, and advised me to finally repent my wickedness, and taught me holy hope, because no one who led a bad life would be lost, if he had a good death. At length he persuaded me thor- 165 oughly to despise the world, and, once I was shorn in this way, he bestowed this habit upon me. When I relinquished my old ways and former diet, I who had been languishing immediately recovered. Now, since my pledge must lose his life, I ask to offer my own life so that my brother might not 170 perish. I have returned, as I agreed to return, but I have nothing of my own to restore to you. I don't wish to break my word. If you are willing to spare me, then spare me; if you want me to die, then kill me quickly."

"This hand of mine," the shepherd says, "will never again 175 hurt you, but since it once struck you, I ask for your forgiveness. In killing a monk, I would become a double murderer; let the hostage go free, and you go home."

Then they go away happy and spend their time in safety in the field, when the wolf, being hungry, said this to the 180 younger wolf: "Believe me, brother, sheep's meat is exceedingly sweet, and cheese and beans will be a disagreeable

67

Non onus assumam, quod non possim tolerare."
   Dixit, et ut dudum coepit oves rapere.
185 Sed breve post tempus, dum rapto vescitur agno,
   aspicit hunc, et sic arguit opilio:
"Sanus es et monachus, non debes carne cibari.
   Non ita sancta iubet regula Basilii."
Inde lupus "non est simplex," ait, "ordo bonorum,
190 et modo sum monachus, canonicus modo sum."
Et simul in silvas lupus ivit tramite recto,
   se male delusum comperit opilio.

De mirabilibus mundi

1. Iaculus

Hic serpens ventis pernicior atque sagittis
transfigit quosque iaculatus ab arbore sese.

2. Herba Sardonia

Huic fera tam saevum tribuit Natura venenum
ut quicumque bibat vitam ridendo relinquat.

3. Pelorium stagnum

5 Corpus in hac unda tinctum tabescit ad ossa.

meal. I'm not going to undertake a burden that I can't endure."

He spoke, and as before, he began to steal sheep. But after a short time, while he was eating a stolen lamb, the shepherd sees him and reproaches him in this way: "You are a healthy monk; you ought not to eat meat. The holy rule of Basil does not prescribe this." 185

Then the wolf says, "There is not just one order of good men—sometimes I am a monk, sometimes a canon." And as soon as the wolf went straight into the woods, the shepherd learned that he had been thoroughly deceived. 190

On the Wonders of the World

1. THE TREE SNAKE

This serpent is swifter than winds or arrows, and transfixes its prey by hurling itself out of a tree.

2. THE SARDONIC PLANT

Savage Nature gave this so harsh a poison that whoever consumes it ends his life by laughing.

3. THE PELORIAN SWAMP

A body dipped in its waters dissolves to the bone. 5

4. Lynx

Lyncis in eximium durescit urina lapillum;
hanc tegit in fossis velut usibus invida nostris.

5. Tragopan

Vervecis specie frons est cornuta tragopae.

6. Albanus

Nascitur hic canus, niger est aetate gravatus;
10   luce videt modicum, sed noctis tempore mirum.

7. Amphisibaena

Parte caput gemina vergens rotat amphisibaena.

8. Bucephalus

Hoc provectus equo magnus fuit ille Macedo.

9. Tigris

Saltibus est agilis et morsibus aspera tigris.

10. Gymnosophista

Ne coquat extrema vestigia fervor harena,
15   dum quaerit mathesim suspendit crura vicissim.

4. THE LYNX

The lynx's urine hardens into a remarkable jewel; it hides this in holes as if hostile to our using it.

5. THE TRAGOPAN

The forehead of the tragopan is horned, like a ram's.

6. THE ALBANIAN

He is born with white hair, which darkens with age; he sees   10
little in the daylight but marvelously at night.

7. THE AMPHISBAENA

The amphisbaena turns in a circle, bending a head at each
end.

8. BUCEPHALUS

The great Macedonian was borne by this horse.

9. THE TIGER

The tiger is agile in its leap and fierce in its bite.

10. THE GYMNOSOPHIST

So that the burning-hot sand does not roast the soles of his
feet, as he seeks knowledge, he lifts one leg, then the other.   15

11. HIMANTOPUS

Hoc genus ire nequit, sed flexo poplite repit.

12. ANTHROPOPHAGUS

Hunc habet hic morem, fert hunc in mente furorem,
carne sui generis pro summis utitur escis.

13. BOS TRICORNIS

Hunc opulenta bovem finxit Natura tricornem.

14. SCYTHA HOSTIS

20 Haec gens hostilem gaudet sorbere cruorem.

15. HAEMORRHOIS

Corpus ab hoc hydro morsum rubet imbre cruento;
egreditur sanguis per mille foramina carnis.

16. LEUCROCOTA

Haec currens nimium superat genus omne ferinum.

17. BOS UNICORNIS

Venerat hic lentus ad cornua danda iuvencus.

11. THE HIMANTOPOD

This race cannot walk, but creeps on bent knee.

12. THE ANTHROPOPHAGUS

He has this custom, he bears this madness in his mind: he uses the flesh of his own species as his principal food.

13. THE THREE-HORNED OX

Bountiful Nature fashioned this ox as three horned.

14. THE HOSTILE SCYTHIAN

This race enjoys drinking enemy blood.   20

15. THE HAEMORRHOIS

A body bitten by this serpent reddens with a shower of blood; blood comes out through a thousand holes in the flesh.

16. THE LEUCROCOTA

This, when it runs, is much superior to every other species of wild animal.

17. THE ONE-HORNED OX

This bullock was slow to produce horns.

18. Elephas, draco

25 Hic draco frigentem bibit ex elephante cruorem.
Ast elephas fortem dum labitur opprimit hostem.
Hinc fit cinnabarum, confuso sanguine mixtum.

19. Taurus Indicus

Omnibus his fauces geminae scinduntur in aures.

20. Fur, fons Sardinius

Huic fonti tanta vis est ad furta probanda
30 ut si latro bibat caecus post pocula fiat.

21. Mantichora

Haec facie nostra, leo corpore, scorpio cauda.

22. Ladas

Hic dum currebat tanta levitate vigebat
ut minime laesam pede pervolitaret harenam.

23. Cinnamolgos

Haec avis ad nidum convectat cinnama tantum.

74

18. An Elephant and a Dragon

This dragon drinks the chill blood of an elephant. But the   25
elephant, as it sinks down, crushes its strong enemy. Cinna-
bar arises from this, made up of the mingling of blood.

19. The Indian Bull

In all of these, their jaws are split to the ears.

20. A Thief and the Sardinian Fountain

Such is the power of this fountain at revealing theft that if a   30
thief takes a drink, he goes blind afterward.

21. The Manticore

This has a face like ours, a lion's body, and a scorpion's tail.

22. Ladas

When he ran, he so excelled in nimbleness that he flew
across the sand, which was hardly disturbed by his foot.

23. The Cinnamolgos

This bird only carries cinnamon to its nest.

24. NILUS

35 Ignorat physicus quae me producat abyssus.

25. HIPPOPUS

Hic sibi dissimilis pedibus fulcitur equinis.

26. RHINOCEROS, VIRGO

Hic rhinocerotem demulcet virgo ferocem.

27. HYENA, TUGURIUM, PASTOR

Hunc vocat a cavea noctu per nomen hyena,
accitumque rapit et saevo vulnere carpit.

28. ASTOMOS

40 Indicus hoc more pomorum vivit odore.

29. TIBICEN, FONS HALAESINUS

Hic fons pauper aquis cum perflat tibia flabris
admirans odas transcendit litoris oras.

24. THE NILE

The natural philosopher does not know the abyss from 35
which I come forth.

25. THE HIPPOPOD

With a feature unlike the rest of himself, he is supported by
horses' hooves.

26. A RHINOCEROS AND A MAIDEN

Here the maiden soothes the fierce rhinoceros.

27. A HYENA, A HUT, AND A SHEPHERD

The hyena calls the shepherd by name from his enclosure
at night, seizes him once summoned, and wounds him sav-
agely.

28. THE ASTOMOS

This Indian lives in this way off the scent of fruit.   40

29. A FLUTE PLAYER AND THE HALAESAN FOUNTAIN

This fountain is poor in water, but when a flute blows a tune,
the fountain overflows its banks, in admiration of the music.

30. Troglodyta

Vescitur hic colubris, nec defit vita salubris:
non timet inde mori cum mortem porrigat ori.

31. Visontis

45 Esse bovi similem iussit Natura visontem.

32. Camelus Bactrianus; camelus Arabicus

Singula de vestris procedunt tubera tergis;
vos Arabum duplis vectatis corpora strumis.

33. Cynocephalus

Hic deformis homo latrat stridore canino.

34. Satyrus

Aethiopes, vobis haec vivit bestia solis.

35. Phoenix, sol

50 Hic specifex atomum sic vitae terminat aevum.

36. Hae feminae vocantur Bitiae apud Scythiam.

Haec mulier quadrupla visum praebente pupilla
mortificat visu quem respicit aspera vultu.

30. The Troglodyte

He feeds on snakes, and he always has a healthy life: because of this he does not fear death, since he puts death in his mouth.

31. The Bison

Nature ordered the bison to resemble an ox.   45

32. The Bactrian Camel; the Arabian Camel

Single humps protrude from your backs; you carry the bodies of Arabs on double humps.

33. The Cynocephalus

This misformed man barks with the yelp of a dog.

34. The Satyr

Ethiopians, this creature lives among you alone.

35. The Phoenix and the Sun

This spice builder ends its indivisible lifetime in this way.   50

36. These Women Are Called Bitiae in Scythia.

This woman, who sees through four pupils, kills with her gaze whomever she looks at, fierce in expression.

37. Crocodrillus

Tergus huic monstro nulli penetrabile ferro.

38. Apis, homo quilibet; Iulius C., Apis

Nil erit huic triste cuius gustantur aristae;
55 hunc aversatur cui sors adversa minatur.

39. Balsamum

Arboris ex nodis rorant opobalsama nobis.

40. Fons gelonius

Exstat huic liquido diversa potentia rivo;
nam steriles gravidat, fecundas germine privat.

41. Leaena, catulus, leo

Exanimem biduo catulum lea servat in antro,
60 quem leo vivificat cum vasto murmure clamat.

42. Cerastes

Decepturus aves corpus tegit omne cerastes;
cornua denudat, miserumque volatile captat.

37. The Crocodile

The back of this monster cannot be penetrated by any weapon.

38. Apis and Some Man; Julius Caesar and Apis

He whose grain is tasted will not have a sad future; the man 55
that Apis rejects is threatened by a hostile fate.

39. The Balsam

Balsam juice trickles to us out of the knots of a tree.

40. The Frosty Fountain

This stream possesses opposite powers; for it makes pregnant the barren, and deprives the fertile of seed.

41. A Lioness, a Cub, and a Lion

The lioness keeps its lifeless cub in a cave for two days; the 60
lion brings it to life by howling with a great roar.

42. The Horned Viper

The horned viper conceals its entire body in order to catch birds; it uncovers its horns, and captures an unfortunate bird.

43. Vipera

Conceptos morte parit aequa vipera sorte.

44. Scytalis

Cum serpens scytalis toto sit corpore segnis,
65   splendet tantarum varius fulgore notarum
ut stolidos homines capiat sua membra stupentes.

45. Caesar, quattuor scribae

Caesar maiores transcendens atque minores
nutibus alternis dictat scribenda quaternis.

46. Delphinus

Transilit hic piscis pendentia carbasa puppis.

47. Alce

70   Huic tanta mole labrum dependat ab ore
ut pasci nequeat nisi retro crura reducat.

48. Bufomon vel enhydros vel suillus

Hic probat in cena si sint admixta venena.

43. THE VIPER

The viper bears her young, conceived with the father's death, suffering the same fate herself.

44. THE SCYTALIS

Though the entire body of the scytalis snake is slow moving, it is glossy and colorful, with so many brilliant markings that 65 it captures foolish men who are astounded by its body.

45. CAESAR AND FOUR SCRIBES

Caesar, surpassing all men who preceded and followed him, dictates what is to be written with alternating commands to four men at a time.

46. THE DOLPHIN

This fish jumps over the sails hanging from boats.

47. THE ELK

Such a massive lip hangs down from its mouth that it cannot 70 feed without drawing its legs backward.

48. THE BUFOMON OR ENHYDROS OR SUILLUS

This can tell if poisons have been mixed into a meal.

49. Seps

Fert speciem leti species miranda veneni;
viscera tabescunt, caro, nervus et ossa liquescunt.

50. Antipus

75 Cum digitis octo surgit pede planta retorto.

51. Castor

Ut redimat sese truncat genitalia dente,
hoc quoniam purum medicina requirit ad usum.

52. Equus Iulii C.

Caesar in hac belua gessit civilia bella.

53. Apis taurus

Quaeritat eventus a tauro bruta iuventus.

54. Hypnale

80 Haec stirps serpentis quem laedit acumine dentis
illi dulce mori, quia mors est mixta sopori.

49. THE SEPS

A remarkable type of poison brings a remarkable type of death; the innards dissolve, and the flesh, nerves, and bone liquefy.

50. THE ANTIPOD

He has eight toes and the foot rises up from the sole facing 75
backward.

51. THE BEAVER

To save itself, it bites off its genitals because medicine requires it unharmed for its purposes.

52. JULIUS CAESAR'S HORSE

Caesar waged civil wars mounted on this animal.

53. THE APIS BULL

Irrational youth seeks to find out what will happen from the bull.

54. THE HYPNALE

This type of serpent gives a sweet death to whomever it 80
strikes with its fangs, because the death is mingled with sleep.

55. Chameleon, corvus, laurus

Extimuere meum volucresque feraeque venenum,
sed corvo soli cessit victoria nostri,
cui contra virus praestat medicamina laurus.

56. Sciapus

85 Hic pedis obiectu sese defendit ab aestu.

57. Monoceros

Dum cornu pugnat transverberat omne quod obstat.

58. Eale

Cornua fronte duo gerit haec, sed pugnat ab uno,
et tamen alterutro per proelia prima retuso
alterius tandem pugnae succedit acumen.

59. Hippopotamus

90 Dum segetem pascit retro vestigia ducit;
retia tendenti sic deficit ordo sequendi.

55. A Chameleon, a Raven, and a Laurel Tree

Both birds and beasts fear my poison, but victory over me goes to the raven alone, to whom the laurel provides an antidote against my venom.

56. The Sciapod

This one defends himself from the heat by blocking it with 85 his foot.

57. The Monoceros

When it fights with its horn, it transfixes everything that stands in its way.

58. The Two-Horned Rhinoceros

It bears two horns on its forehead, but fights with one, and though one may be dulled in its first battles, eventually the sharp point of the other takes over the fight.

59. The Hippopotamus

As it feeds on crops, it leaves a trail in the reverse direction; 90 in this way it cannot be tracked.

60. Leo, leontophona

Membra leontophonae leo solo lancinat ungue;
hac solet ex carne quoniam deceptus obire.

61. Arimaspus

Omnis in hac gente fert unica lumina fronte.

62. Ibis

95 Ore parit nidis vivitque volucribus hydris.

63. Aquila, aethites lapis

Temperat hoc lapide ne decoquat ova calore.

64. Polymestor

Hic poterat facile leporem currendo praeire.

65. Fons Epiri

Mersa sub hoc amne pereunt incendia flammae,
at iuxta flumen repetit fax mortua lumen.

60. A Lion and a Leontophone

The lion lacerates the limbs of the leontophone only with its claw; since, if deceived, it commonly dies from eating the meat.

61. The Arimaspian

Everyone in this race bears a single eye on his forehead.

62. The Ibis

It gives birth in its nest from its mouth and lives on winged water snakes.

95

63. An Eagle and Eaglestone

It regulates the temperature with this stone so that it doesn't cook its eggs in the heat.

64. Polymnestor

He could easily outstrip a hare in a race.

65. The Fountain of Epirus

Burning flames die away when they are submerged in this stream, but an extinguished torch when brought close to the river reignites.

66. Psittacus

100 Hi volucres rostris dant verba simillima nostris.

67. Pegasus

Huic Natura duas aures adiecit equinas.

68. Blemmyas

Dum caput abscidit, sensus Natura reliquit:
fert humeris visum, discernit pectore gustum.

69. Puerpera plebeia

Clam pia merentem fovet ubere nata parentem
105 cum vigil observet nequis fomenta ministret.

70. Leo

Parcere prostratis scit nobilis ira leonis;
tu quoque fac simile quisquis dominaris in orbe.

71. Chameleon

Hoc animal miserum cum nil sibi quaerit ad esum
ore patet semper, quia pascitur aere venter.

66. THE PARROT

These birds utter with their beaks words very like ours.   100

67. THE PEGASUS

To it Nature has attached two horse's ears.

68. THE BLEMMYAE

Though it deprived him of a head, Nature left him with senses: his sight is in his shoulders, and he tastes with his chest.

69. A PEASANT WOMAN

Secretly the pious daughter nurtures a deserving parent at her breast, though a watchman makes sure that no one pro-   105 vides relief.

70. THE LION

The noble wrath of the lion knows to spare the fallen; you who rule in the world should also do likewise.

71. THE CHAMELEON

This unfortunate animal, though it seeks nothing to eat for itself, always has its mouth open, because its stomach feeds on air.

72. Phanesius

110 Omnis in hoc genere pro vestibus utitur aure;
hinc corpus nudum fit contra frigora tutum.

73. Diomedea avis, sepulchrum eius

Pugnaces socii Diomedis in aera rapti,
contra naturam volucrum sumpsere figuram,
imbrificantque ducis tumulum rorantibus alis.

74. Dypsas

115 Ardens poscit aquas quem laedit vulnere dypsas:
continuat potus, sed eo magis uritur intus,
et nisi per mortem nescit finire calorem.

75. Prester

Laesus ab hoc angue distendit membra tumore
et caro cuncta suam perdit tumefacta figuram.

76. Arimphaeus, laurus

120 Non petit hic magnum donis cerealibus annum,
fructifera totum quia ponit in arbore votum.

77. Karthago, Strabo, Lilybaeana specula

Providus hic Strabo de culmine Lilybaeano
per numerum classem notat ad Carthaginis arcem.

72. The Phanesian

Everyone of this race uses his ear for clothing; in this man-   110
ner his naked body is made safe against the cold.

73. The Diomedean Bird and the Tomb of Diomedes

The combative comrades of Diomedes were snatched into
the air, and assumed the shape of birds, contrary to nature;
they moisten the tomb of their leader with dripping wings.

74. The Dipsas

Whomever the dipsas strikes is on fire and demands water: 115
he keeps on drinking, but all the more he burns within, and
he cannot stop the burning except through death.

75. The Prester

The limbs of whatever is struck by this snake distend with
swelling, and all its flesh is inflated and loses its shape.

76. An Arimphaean and a Laurel

He does not seek a year rich with gifts of grain, because he   120
puts all of his hopes in fruit-bearing trees.

77. Carthage, Strabo, and the Lilybaean Lookout

Here prudent Strabo, from the Lilybaean promontory, as-
sesses the size of the fleet at the stronghold of Carthage.

78. Hyrcinia avis

Huius avis plumae sparsim per compita fusae,
125 luce sua multum dant nocte viantibus usum.

79. Gryppes, equus

Hanc quasi permodicam gryppes vehit ungue rapinam.

De medicamine aurium

Ne tibi displiceam, quia sic sum corpore parvus:
    hortulus iste brevis mitia poma gerit.
Plurima doctorum sunt hic experta priorum,
    hinc, lector, sumas quae meliora putas.
5 Materies monstrat tibi quae medicamina constant,
    teque quid amplecti quidve cavere decet.
Si fueris dives, quae sunt pretiosa require;
    si nummis careas, elige quod valeas.
Ne nos contemnas, viles cum videris herbas:
10   quod bene compones, gratius esse solet.
Caelestis medicus, cuius manus omnia pensat,
    mirandum prodit, quod tibi vile fuit.
Hoc medicamentum surdis est auribus aptum:
    de sempervivae suco coclearia bina,
15   tantundem sumas olei quod praebet oliva,

78. The Hyrcinian Bird

The feathers of this bird, spread here and there through the crossroads, are very useful to travelers at night because of their light. 125

79. A Griffin and a Horse

The griffin carries this plunder in its claws as if it were very small.

On Medicine for the Ears

Do not be displeased because I am so small in size: this small garden bears pleasant fruit. Here are many remedies of earlier doctors; from here, reader, you may select what you think are better. The subject matter shows you what things 5 constitute medicines: what you should embrace and what you should avoid. If you're rich, seek out the ones that are expensive; if you lack money, choose what you can afford. But do not scorn us when you see cheap herbs: what you put 10 together well is likely to be more agreeable. The heavenly physician, whose hand weighs everything, produces a marvel that was cheap for you.

This remedy is good for deaf ears: take two spoonfuls of houseleek juice, and just as much oil as an olive provides; 15

hinc ovi testa porrorum collige sucum,
lactentis pueri tantundem sumito lactis.
Haec tribus ad solem vitro suspende diebus,
noctibus et totidem sub aperto desine caelo.
20 Ex hoc auriculae studeas infundere surdi,
ut solis radium patiens assumat in aurem.
Auris sic morbum dimisit denique totum.

De quattuor humoribus

Auctor apud Graecos medicinae primus Apollo.
Hic docuit Thamyran, propriae qui crimine natae
perdidit auditum. Cui mox oracla petenti,
si sibi iam possit reparari cura salutis,
5 Themis ait posse, sceleris si membra recidat
terque caput liniat totum medicamine tali.
Quod mox ut fecit, medicinae dona recepit.
    Hinc Aesculapius, generis successor et artis,
in multis famam sibi contulit experimentis.
10 Nam variis artem et pulchris novitatibus auxit.
Sed postquam periit iaculatus fulminis ictu,
ars pariter latuit quingentos fere per annos.
Mox Asclepiades Hypocras post tempora tanta
claruit, artis honor et mundi publica cura.
15 Hic docuit gentes humani corporis esse
quattuor humores, vario moderamine quorum
nunc dolor obrepit, nunc vero cura salutis.

then thicken the juice of leeks with eggshell, and take as much milk as a nursing child. Hang these in a glass, facing the sun, for three days, and leave for the same number of nights under the open sky. Some of this you should take care 20
to pour into the outer ear of a deaf person, so that the patient may take a ray of sunlight into his ear. In this manner, finally he will have relieved all of the affliction of the ear.

On the Four Humors

The first founder of medicine among the Greeks was Apollo. He taught Thamyras, who, because of the crime against his daughter, lost his hearing. Soon afterward, as he was asking oracles whether good health could now be restored to him, Themis said that it could, if he cut off the 5
faulty parts, and thrice anoint his entire head with a special ointment. As soon as he did this, he received the gift of medicine.

Next Aesculapius, his follower in birth and in the art of medicine, brought fame to himself with many experiments, for he enhanced the art with various fine innovations. But 10
after he died, struck down by a lightning bolt, the art also languished for almost fifty years. Then, after all that time, Hippocrates, of Aesculapius's line, became famous—the glory of the art and the world's universal healer. He taught 15
everyone that the human body has four humors and by the various proportions of these sometimes pain comes upon one, but at other times good health.

Ex quibus est sanguis "vitae substantia" dictus,
unde etiam "sanguis" nostro sonat ore "suavis."
20 Suntque homines blandi, quibus hic humor dominatur.
Hunc sequitur cholen, medici quod cholera dicunt.
"Cholera" dicta sonat, quod sit diffusio fellis.
Nam "cholen" graece, "fel" dicitur esse latine.
Tertius est humor melancholia vocatus,
25 quod sit felle simul nigro quoque sanguine mixtus.
Nam "melan" "nigrum," "cholen" "fel" traditur esse.
Post hos phlegma latet spumoso frigore torpens,
corporibus fundens naturam frigiditatis.
Graeci "phlegmonen" dixerunt esse "rigorem."
30 Quattuor hi mixti modo dant adimuntque salutem.
Nam si iungantur Naturae lege volentis
nec super exundent nec se per mutua vincant,
crescit mira salus, rutilat color et caro gaudet.
At si confusi naturae iura refrenent,
35 morbus et anxietas non cessat laedere corpus.
Sanguinis humorem superat si copia fellis,
aut si fel rarum suffocat sanguinis aestus,
passio concipitur, quae dicitur "oxea" vulgo,
"oxea" quippe sonat "velox" vel "acuta" latine.
40 Quae cito, quem rapuit, necat aut cito deserit aegrum.
Vel si phlegma frequens melancholia subibit,
aut melancholicos fundet phlegmatis humor,
passio fiet item, quam nomine "chronia" dicunt.
Est autem morbus, qui longo tempore durat.
45 Nam "chronos" graece, nos "tempus" dicimus esse.
Quattuor hos mundi perhibent elementa notare.
Aera sanguis habet, fel vero contrahit ignis,
terra melancholien aqua phlegma notare probatur.

Among these, blood was so called as "the substance of life," and also because "blood" sounds like "sweet" in our language, and the men whom this humor governs are pleas- 20 ant. After this follows *chole,* which physicians call cholera. The term "cholera" means there is an excess of bile, for the Greek word *chole* means "bile" in Latin. The third humor is called black bile, which is composed of bile mixed with 25 black blood. For *melan* is translated as "black," and *chole* as "bile." After these, phlegm resides inside, stiffening with its frothy chill, spreading the essence of cold in bodies. The Greeks said that *phlegmone* is "stiffness."

These four, when mixed, bestow and take away health. 30 For if they are mixed according to the will of Nature's law and they neither are overabundant nor cancel each other out, marvelous health arises, the color takes on a reddish glow, and the flesh rejoices. But if, in confusion, they go against the laws of Nature, illness and anxiety won't cease 35 harming the body. If an abundance of bile overcomes the sanguine humor, or if the heat of the blood stifles the insufficient bile, a disease arises which is commonly called *oxea,* for *oxea* signifies "quick" or "sharp" in Latin. This quickly 40 kills the person it has seized or quickly quits the patient. Or if a large amount of black bile surpasses the phlegm, or if the phlegmatic humor overwhelms the melancholic, in either case a disease arises which goes by the name *chronia.* For 45 what the Greeks called *chronos,* we call "time."

They say that these correspond to the four elements of the universe. Blood gets the air, fire is tied to bile, earth and water are judged to represent black bile and phlegm, respectively.

De Lombardo et lumaca

Venerat ad segetes Lombardus, circuit illas,
    circuit et gaudet quod sata laeta videt.
Dum laetus laetas sic admiratur aristas,
    huic praeter solitum visa lumaca fuit.
5 Quid sit miratur; stupet, horret et exanimatur;
    mens abit atque color, deserit ossa calor.
Ut tandem rediit ad se, procul adstat et inquit:
    "Quod video scelus est: haec mihi summa dies.
Non lupus hoc, ursus, vel vipera: nescio quid sit;
10   sed scio, quicquid sit, quod mihi bella parat.
Est clipeus signum, signum sunt cornua belli:
    Hem, pugnare negem? Non ego: malo mori.
Si superare queam monstrum talis speciei
    et decus et famam perpetuam merui.
15 Quid dixi? Non est probitas occurrere monstro;
    cetera non desunt bella timenda minus.
Quae dabitur laus, si furor haec, non pugna vocetur?
    Humanum non est hoc periisse modo.
Hoc mea si coniunx et proles tota videret
20   pro solo visu iam sibi terga darent.
Insuper haec pugna non aequa videbitur ulli;
    nam meus armatus hostis, inermis ego."
Sic dubitat, metus atque pudor pugnant in eodem.
    Dat pugnare pudor, sed metus ista fugit.
25 Denique, consilio fieri quod iudicat aequum,
    consulit uxorem consulit atque deos.
Di sibi respondent quod sit palma fruiturus
    cum vix auderet credere numinibus.

On the Lombard and the Snail

A Lombard had come to his fields and was walking around them, and as he circled them he rejoiced at the sight of the abundant crops. As he happily admired the flourishing ears of grain in this way, unexpectedly a snail appeared to him. He wondered what it was; he was stunned, he shuddered and was paralyzed with fear; he lost his mind and his color, the warmth left his bones. When he finally regained his composure, he kept his distance and said: "What I see is ter-rible—my last day has come. This isn't a wolf, or a bear, or a snake: I don't know what it is; but I know that whatever it is, it's preparing to do battle with me. Its shield is a sign of war, as are its horns: well, should I refuse to fight? Not I: I'd rather die. If I'm able to defeat a monster of this sort, I will win honor and lasting fame. What have I said? There's no sense in meeting a monster in battle; after all, there's no shortage of other less fearsome wars. What praise will I get, if this is called madness, not a battle? It's inhuman to die in this way. If my wife and all my children saw this, at the sight alone they would turn their backs. Besides, this battle won't seem fair to anyone; for my enemy is armed, and I'm de-fenseless."

In this way he hesitated, and fear and shame wrestled within him. Shame spurred him to fight, but fear fled such things. Finally, according to the plan that he determined to be right, he consulted his wife and consulted the gods. The gods responded to him that he would be victorious, though he scarcely dared to believe them. But his timid wife, fearing

At coniunx timida, metuens, ut casta, marito,
30   exclamat lacrimans: "Quid, furibunde, paras?
Quae tibi bella placent? Tandem sine monstra perire!
     Pone tuos animos! Parce mihi misere,
parce tuis natis, si non tibi parcere curas!
     Pro dolor, externos viderit ista dies!
35 Non audax Hector, non hoc auderet Achilles,
     Herculis hic virtus ardua deficeret."
"Pone modum precibus"—inquit—"carissima coniunx,
     non prece mens audax flectitur aut lacrimis;
di mihi sunt hodie nomen sine fine daturi.
40   Iam precor ut valeas et valeant pueri."
Ut stetit in campo, velox huc tendit et illuc
     circumdatque feram magna satis minitans:
"O fera cui numquam similem natura creavit,
     monstrum monstrorum, perniciosa lues,
45 quae mihi nunc pandis non me tua cornua terrent,
     testaque sub cuius tegmine tuta manes.
Hac hodie dextra forti moriere nec ultra
     te patiar segetes commaculare meas."
Et vibrans telum quae sint loca proxima morti
50   prospicit et palmam strenuus exequitur.
Pro tanto facto quae premia digna dabuntur?
     Non est res parva: causidici veniant.

for her husband as befits a chaste wife, tearfully exclaimed, 30
"What are you plotting, you madman? What wars do you
desire? Just let the monsters perish! Set aside your animos-
ity! Spare me in my misery, spare your children, if you don't
care to spare yourself! For pity's sake, this day will see us
separated! Neither brave Hector, nor even Achilles would 35
attempt this, the mighty courage of Hercules would fail
here."

"Put an end to your prayers, dearest wife," he said, "A dar-
ing mind is not swayed by prayer or by tears; today the gods
are going to give me fame without end. Now I pray for you 40
and the boys to fare well."

When he returned to the field, he moved quickly to and
fro and circled the beast, threatening very menacingly: "Oh
beast whose equal nature has never created, monster of
monsters, ruinous plague, the horns that you brandish now 45
don't frighten me, nor does the shell under whose cover you
keep safe. Today you'll die by this strong right hand, and
no longer will I endure you contaminating my fields." And
balancing his spear, he looked for the most vulnerable points
and vigorously pursued the victory. What prizes worthy of 50
such a deed will be given? It's not a small matter: let the law-
yers come forward.

De agno

Quos libertatis docet Azzo fideliter armis
valde mirandos sibi dant ter quattuor agnos.
Primus dum ballat mel ab eius gutture manat.
Omnia consultus dividat furta secundus.
5   Tertius est pinguis membris vescendo lupinis.
Cauda potest totam ter quarti cingere ramam.
Cornibus a quinti summum pulsatur Olympi.
Cur sol deficiat sexti prudentia narrat.
Septimus incendit pedibus solum modo bonis,
10 ast niger octavus totus extat simul et albet.
Iam constat nonus plures lacerasse leonum.
Podice de decimi fluunt saepissime nummi.
Undecimus rite viget omni parte sophiae.
Mille duodenus parit ova quibusque diebus.
15 Aula magistralis resonat balantibus agnis.

De pediculo

In cute sudanti sub veste pediculus haesit
    atque cutem rupit, suxit et intumuit.
Quem postquam sensi—nam me sentire coegit—
    admovi digitum qui cito cepit eum.
5   In lucem ductus, metuens, puto, pollicis ictus,
    de digito cecidit lubricus et latuit
inter nodorum iuncturas articulorum.
    Sed fuga nil valuit: cura secuta fuit.

On the Lamb

Those whom Azzo faithfully teaches with freedom's weapons present him with twelve especially wondrous lambs. The first, while it bleats, drips honey from its throat. The second wisely apportions all of the stolen goods. The third is   5
fat from feeding on wolves' limbs. The tail of the fourth can encircle a whole branch three times. The summit of Olympus is struck by the horns of the fifth. The wisdom of the sixth tells why the sun goes dark. The seventh now lights the ground on fire with his excellent feet, but the eighth is black   10
all over and yet at the same time white. The ninth is already known to have torn apart many lions. Coins flow very often from the ass of the tenth. The eleventh thrives duly with every kind of wisdom. The twelfth lays a thousand eggs every day. The master's lecture hall resounds with bleating lambs.   15

On the Louse

A louse clung to the sweating skin under my shirt and broke the skin, sucked, and swelled up. After I felt him—for he forced me to take notice—I moved my finger close, which quickly caught him. Brought into the light, fearing, I sup-   5
pose, being squished by my thumb, he craftily slipped from my finger and hid between the joints of my knuckles. But flight availed him naught: my diligence pursued him. He is

Inventus rapitur, raptus reus esse probatur
10 et pro supplicio traditur exitio.
Hunc omnes lendes deflent nigraeque sorores
  et faciunt tumulum, cum tumulo titulum:
CUM SENIS PEDIBUS CAPUT ET SINE
    PECTORE CORPUS
  HOC IACET IN TUMULO, CARNE CREATA
  CARO.

De nuntio sagaci

Summi victoris fierem cum victor Amoris,
sperabam curis finem fecisse futuris.
Rursus ad arma vocor, me quaerit et ecce Cupido.
Dic, Amor, unde venis pharetris sic undique plenis?
5 Cuius castra petis? In cuius vulnera tendis?
Perdere quem quaeris? Certamina velle videris.
  Hinc procul, hinc absis, quia mecum nulla movebis.
Tot tibi sunt Parides, tibi tot sunt et Ganymedes,
qui vix expectant, tua dum certamina discant:
10 his precor insistas optataque vulnera mittas;
nil facies mecum, quia non mihi gratia tecum.
  Dum tibi miles eram, tua solus signa ferebam.
undique processi, pro te tua proelia gessi

found and seized, and, once seized, proved guilty, and for 10
punishment he is handed over to death.

All his fellows mourn him, and his black sisters too, and
they make him a tomb, and with the tomb the inscription:

A HEAD WITH SIX FEET AND A BODY
WITHOUT A SPIRIT LIES IN THIS TOMB,
FLESH BEGOTTEN OF FLESH.

On the Crafty Messenger

When I became the conqueror of Love, the greatest of all
conquerors, I hoped to make an end of future worries. *But I
am called back to arms,* and lo, Cupid seeks me out. Tell me,
Love, where do you come from with your quiver so full?
Whose fortress do you attack? Whom do you aim to wound? 5
Whom do you seek to destroy? You look like you're spoiling
for a fight.

Begone, and away with you, because you won't get any-
where with me. You have so many Parises, so many Gany-
medes, too, who can scarcely wait to be instructed in your
battles: go after them, I beg you, and wound those who de- 10
sire it; you'll get nowhere with me, because I'm not well dis-
posed toward you.

When I was your soldier, I bore your standards all alone.
Wherever I went, I waged your battles for you; and if it

et nisi forma mea, tua laus foret annihilata.
15 Nam mea forma placens ad amorem traxerat omnes.
Ecce puellarum sequitur me turba tuarum:
Daphnis et Europa, cum Phyllide Deianira;
profuga cessat Io; me vult cum Pallade Iuno.
Telis succincta sequitur lasciva Diana,
20 promittens mortem, per me nisi vincat Amorem.
Instat et ipsa Venus sibi mecum iungere foedus,
nec curat Paridem, quia me videt Helena talem.
Respice quod Stigiis Proserpina fertur in undis
nec vult salva fore, nisi me sibi iungat amore.
25   Has omnes vici subiectas et tibi feci.
Sed quid tu contra? Quae sunt tua praemia monstra.
Sic tu me serva, per quam modo iuro, Minerva;
O Venus, o Iuno, per vos etiam bene iuro
quod nemo iuvenum tam dulciter arsit in illum.
30 Aptus sicut ego iuvenum fuerat sibi nemo,
fidus sicut ego iuvenum fuerat sibi nemo,
omnia sicut ego iuvenum fuerat sibi nemo.
Omnia nil prosunt, meritis quia praemia desunt.
Conqueror hoc vobis et do mea munera vobis,
35 ut bene servetis quem sic servire videtis.
Cernite quid feci pro factis quidve recepi.
   Splendidior stella fuerat mihi visa puella,
nobilis et talis, non hoc in tempore qualis:
corpus ei gracile, sua candidior caro lacte,
40 purpureus vultus, mirabilis undique cultus;
nigra supercilia fuerant sibi, lumina clara.
Oscula quae cuperes, os eius habere putares.
Et cum ridebat, tunc dentes lactis habebat.
Caesaries flava volitat per eburnea colla;

weren't for my beauty, your fame would be no more. For 15
my pleasing appearance drew everyone into love. Look—a
throng of your girls follows me: Daphnis and Europa, Dei-
anira and Phyllis; the runaway Io stops in her tracks; Juno
wants me, as does Pallas. Lusty Diana, girded with weapons,
follows me, threatening death if she does not get the better 20
of Love through me. Even Venus herself insists on making a
bond with me, and Helen cares not for Paris, when she sees
how handsome I am. Look how Proserpina is carried off
upon the Stygian waters, and doesn't want to be saved, un-
less she joins me to herself in love.

I conquered all of them and made them your subjects. 25
But what did you give me in return? Show me your rewards.
So save me, Minerva, in whose name I now swear; O Venus,
O Juno, by you too I solemnly swear that no youth burned
so sweetly for Love. No youth was as well suited to him as I, 30
no youth was as faithful to him as I, no youth was all the
things I was to him. But all of this was worthless, since there
were no rewards for my merits. I bring this complaint to you
and dedicate my gifts to you, so that you may be of service to 35
the one you see offering service to you. Consider what I did
and what I received in return.

I once saw a girl more splendid than a star, fine and of a
beauty this age hasn't seen: she had a graceful body, her flesh
was whiter than milk, a shining countenance, and of won- 40
drous refinement in every respect; her eyebrows were black,
her eyes bright. You would think her mouth had all the
kisses that you desire. When she laughed, she had milky-
white teeth. Long blond locks flutter upon her ivory neck;

45 Auro vestita, fuit auro pulchrior ipsa;
     pulchra manus superat quod gemma decoris habebat.
     Quid referam multa? Multum fuit undique culta:
     molliter incessit, apte satis omnia gessit.
       Hanc miser ut vidi! Cum vidi, saepe revidi.
50 Admirans multum me talem cernere vultum,
     mox nimis ardebam: fuit et plus quod cupiebam,
     sed non audebam sibi dicere quid cupiebam.
     Nam pudor hoc vetuit quod Amor me dicere iussit.
     Tandem quid feci? Mea munera mittere coepi,
55 mandans quaeque bona, me, si placet, et mea dona.
       Suscepit, vidit, miratur, clam quoque risit,
     fit rubor in facie, mox coepit pallor inesse.
     Quid faciat nescit, verbum proferre nequivit
     et tremulis manibus missum cecidit sibi munus.
60 Illico respexit, suspirans haec quoque dixit:
     "Quis puer est ille, qui dat sua dona puellae?
     Quando me novit? Dic. Novit? Nescio quis sit.
     Dic mihi: quis puer est? Taceas, mihi conscia mens est.
     Fama volat mundo quod non sit pulchrior illo,
65 nobilior nemo vel in omnibus aptior illo.
     Nescio si sic sit." "Sic est," sibi nuntius inquit,
     "Et, si scire cupis, restat quod carius audis."
     "Cur dicis 'restat'? Quid restat?" quaerit et instat.
       Hic tacet, haec instat: hoc "restat" scire laborat.
70 Hic negat ut dicat, quia scit quod sic magis instat.
     Quaerit et illa magis quid sit "quod carius audis."
     His simul auditis negat hic "quod carius audis."
     Haec magis admirans et adhuc perquirere temptans,

dressed in gold, she was lovelier than gold; the beauty of her 45
hand exceeded that of a gem. Why say any more? She was
refined in every respect: she walked with grace, she did ev-
erything in perfect measure.

But woe was I, who saw her! When I saw her once, I had
to see her again. Amazed that I saw so lovely a face, at once I 50
was inflamed; and there was something more that I desired,
but I did not dare tell her what I desired. For modesty pre-
vented me from saying what Love commanded me to say. So
what did I finally do? I began to send gifts, offering all my 55
goods and, if she wanted, myself, along with my gifts.

She took them, looked at them, admired them, laughed
to herself, grew red in the face, then began to grow pale. She
knew not what to do, she couldn't say a word; and the gift I
had sent her fell from her trembling hands. Suddenly she 60
looked up, sighing, and spoke these words: "What boy is
this who gives his gifts to a girl? When did he meet me? Tell
me—did he meet me? I don't know who he is. Tell me: who
is this boy? But be silent, my mind knows something of him.
Rumor has it that no man on earth is more handsome than
he, no one more noble or more accomplished in every way. I 65
do not know if it is so." "It is," the messenger replies, "And, if
you want to know, something dearer remains for you to
hear." "Why do you say 'remains'? What remains?" she asks
and insists.

He stays silent, she persists: she strives to learn what "re-
mains." He refuses to say, because he knows that that way, 70
she'll insist all the more. And she asks all the more what
"something dearer for you to hear" means. In reply, he de-
nies that there is "something dearer for you to hear." At this
her wonder only increased; what wonderful promises she

quam bene promisit quam dulciter et sibi risit
75   dicens: "Cur iste mittit sua dona puellae?
Dic mihi, dic, care; nisi dicas, nescio quare."
     [*Nuntius*] "Dicam, si locus est et si mihi dicere prodest."
     [*Puella*] "Aptus ad hoc locus est et fortassis bene prodest."
His ita concessis, fit laxa licentia verbis.
80   [*Nuntius*] "Accipe mandata, quae postulo sint tibi grata.
Munus mittens amans, 'sit vita, salus tibi' mandans;
noscere te quaerit, quod quaerere laus tua fecit.
Si laudem quaeris, pulcherrima virgo videris.
Pulchrior est nulla nec carior omnibus ulla.
85   Nullius mores fore dicuntur meliores:
es bene nutrita, mansueta, iocosa, pudica;
ut res ostendit, tibi nil natura negavit.
Ergo vides quid sis. Ne perdas praemia laudis.
Quaere parem laudi; quis par sit taliter, audi.
90   Huc qui me misit, omni sine crimine vivit;
vivit, ad omne valet, iuvenili corpore floret,
et facie pulchra posset satis esse puella.
Nobilis ac humilis, prudens nimiumque fidelis,
est dives, largus, verax et ad omnia cautus.
95   Ultra quid dicam? Puer hic te quaerit amicam,
quaerit, habere cupit; sic me tibi dicere iussit."
     [*Puella*] "Iussit? Quid iussit? Sibi me retinere cupivit?
Absit quod dicis! O laxa licentia verbis!
Es sane mentis, quod me non afore sentis?
100 Vere nil sentis: da talia frivola ventis!

made, and how sweetly she laughed to herself as she tried to sound him out, saying: "Why does he send his gifts to a girl? Tell me, dear, tell me; if you don't tell me, I won't know why." 75

Messenger: "I will tell you, if it is the place for it and if I would profit from telling."

Girl: "This place is appropriate for it and perhaps you will be well rewarded."

When this agreement had been made, their words became more uninhibited:

Messenger: "Hear my message, which I ask you to find pleasing. Your lover sends you this gift, adding 'may you have long life and good health.' He seeks to know you, because your reputation has inspired his search. If you want to know your reputation, it's that you're the most beautiful maid, and that there is no other more lovely or dearer to everyone. No one's manners are said to be finer; you are well brought up, gentle, playful, chaste; as reality shows, nature denied you nothing. So you see what you are. Don't lose the rewards of your fame. Seek a match for that fame; hear who such a match is. He who sent me here lives a faultless life; he is full of life, has strength for anything, has a young and vigorous body, and with his beautiful face, he could pass for a girl. He is noble and humble, wise and very faithful; he is wealthy, generous, truthful, and prudent in all matters. What more can I say? This boy seeks you as a girlfriend, seeks and desires to have you; this he ordered me to tell you." 80 85 90 95

Girl: "Ordered? What did he order? He wished to have me for himself? I want nothing of what you say! How uninhibited are his words! Are you in your right mind that you think I will not stay away? Indeed, you perceive nothing: 100

Ut tam magna petas, nondum mea sufficit aetas.

Iungi posse thoris nimius labor esset Amoris.

Tolle, precor, tolle; bene scis me talia nolle."

    [*Nuntius*] "Parcius, o virgo! Nullum tibi dedecus opto.

105 Fac puerum videas et secum verba reponas.

Si tunc sit dignus, facias secum tibi pignus."

    [*Puella*] "Pignus? Quid pignus? Quis nostro pignore dignus?

Regi sufficeret, si mecum pignus haberet."

    [*Nuntius*] "Reges qui vivunt non omnes omnia possunt;

110 pauper iam fecit quod rex fecisse nequivit.

Rex ubi terga dabit, pauper per proelia vadit.

Pauper, si probus est, plus regno vivere prodest

quam cum divitiis rex prosit vivere vilis."

    [*Puella*] "Ah, nimis astute, mihi reddis singula caute!

115 Dic ubi nunc ille qui dat sua dona puellae;

fac saltem videam quod laudem postea dicam.

Quid? Dixi 'videam'? Si dixi, paenitet unquam."

    [*Nuntius*] "Audivit quisnam pro certo 'paenitet unquam'?"

    [*Puella*] "Nescio quid dixi. Si dixi, mortua dixi."

120 [*Nuntius*] "Tu bene dixisses, si factis dicta probasses.

Dixisti vere puerum te velle videre.

Ecce negas dictum! Laudares, si foret actum."

    [*Puella*] "Laudarem factum? Quod factum? Nescio
       'factum.'

Dic quid sit 'factum.' Puto quod non sit bene dictum."

125 [*Nuntius*] "Et bene stat dictum, melius quoque si foret
       actum."

cast such nonsense to the wind! I am not old enough for you to seek things so great. To get me into bed would be a feat too great for Love. Go away, I beg you, go away; you know well that I don't want such things."

Messenger: "Be calm, maiden! I desire nothing shameful to you—only that you see the boy and talk to him. If then he seems worthy, give him your pledge." 105

Girl: "Pledge? What pledge? Who is worthy of my pledge? It would suffice for a king, if he were to have my pledge."

Messenger: "No king in the world can do everything; pau- 110 pers have done what a king was unable to do. When a king turns tail, a pauper charges into battle. A pauper's life, if he is honest, is of more use to a realm than the life of a worthless king, despite all his riches."

Girl: "Ah, you sly fellow, all your replies are too clever! So 115 tell me where the one now is, who gives his gifts to a girl; let me see him at least so that I can hereafter sing his praises. What? Did I say 'Let me see him'? If I said that, I regret it forever."

Messenger: "Who heard for certain 'regret it forever'?"

Girl: "I don't know what I said. If I said it, I said it dead."

Messenger: "You would have spoken well, if you had 120 proved your words with deeds. You really did say that you wish to see the boy. But look—you deny that you said it! You would commend it, if it were to be done."

Girl: "I would commend the deed? What deed? I don't know what you mean by 'deed.' Tell me what this deed is. I don't think it's a nice thing to say."

Messenger: "It is a nice thing to say, and even better for it 125 to be done."

[*Puella*] "Quid vocat hoc 'factum'? Quoddam fortasse
    profanum.
Nescio quid dicit. Sua me sententia vicit.
Factum quod dicis, dic notum si sit amicis."
    [*Nuntius*] "Vix vivunt aliqui quicumque vocantur amici,
130 qui possint vere firmum sibi foedus habere,
quin Veneris pactum primum ducatur ad actum.
Est illud factum quod vult Veneris sibi pactum."
    [*Puella*] "Sentio quid quaeris: me fallere velle videris.
Vere discedam tua nec vestigia laedam.
135 Expedit hinc ire. Tu me vis sponte perire."
    [*Nuntius*] "Si tu sic ibis, fortasse sponte redibis."
    [*Puella*] "Ut redeam sponte, quis cogit? Cogor ab hoste?"
    [*Nuntius*] "Hostis non cogit, sed amicus stare rogabit.
Audi quid dicam: cupio te vivere sanam,
140 et mihi si credis, fit quod placuisse videbis."
    [*Puella*] "Quid placet ut credam? Puerum quod visere
    pergam?
Hoc esset durum: bene certa quid inde futurum."
    [*Nuntius*] "Non tibi sit cura: tibi sunt bona quaeque
    futura.
Me cape ductorem; venias, postpone timorem.
145 Ignoras illum qui se promittit amicum;
si bene cognosses, velut agnum tangere posses.
Quid sit amor nescit: pudor est ubi femina tangit."
    [*Puella*] "Tu laudas quod amas, sed non erit omne quod
    optas.
Lascivus puer est et tela Cupidinis infert:

Girl: "What does 'deed' refer to? Perhaps it's something indecent. I don't know what it means. Its meaning has confounded me. This deed you speak of—tell me, is it common among friends?"

Messenger: "There are hardly any among those considered friends who can really maintain strong bonds of friendship, unless the pact of Venus is first brought to the deed. That is the deed that the pact of Venus demands." 130

Girl: "I understand what you're after: you seem to want to trick me. So I'll go away and I won't disturb your tracks. It's best that I go away from here—you want me to destroy myself of my own accord." 135

Messenger: "If you go in this manner, perhaps you'll return willingly."

Girl: "Who is going to compel me? Am I compelled by an enemy?"

Messenger: "It's not an enemy who compels you, but a friend will ask you to stay. Listen to what I am saying: I want you to live in good health, and if you believe me, something will happen to please you." 140

Girl: "What is this pleasure that I should believe you? That I go and see the boy? This would be a hard thing: I know well what would come from that."

Messenger: "Don't worry yourself; whatever comes about will be good for you. Take me as a guide; come, and put aside your fear. You don't know the boy who offers himself as your boyfriend; if you really knew him, you would treat him like a lamb. He doesn't know what love is: he blushes when a woman touches him." 145

Girl: "You praise what you love, but you won't get everything you desire. The boy is frisky and shoots Cupid's

150 non esset tutum secreto ludere secum."
     [*Nuntius*] "Tu mihi coniuncta postpone pericula cuncta.
     Presens esse volo, solam dimittere nolo."
     [*Puella*] "Quam cito dimittis si forte fores mihi claudis;
     et mox sum victa, postquam sum sola relicta."
155 [*Nuntius*] "Si vulpes stares, catulos fortasse fugares;
     nam multis verbis tibi diverticula quaeris."
     [*Puella*] "Si vulpes starem, te fallere posse probarem:
     mel portas ore, sed fel latitat tibi corde."
     [*Nuntius*] "Iam cessent verba, satis esse videntur acerba.
160 Est mihi parva mora, redeamus ad illa priora."
     [*Puella*] "Laudo quid dicis: nam convenit illud amicis,
     aspera quod celent et dulcia quaeque revelent.
     Ergo tu repetas eadem quae nuper agebas."
     [*Nuntius*] "Quid iuvat ut repetam, quia spem mihi nescio
         certam?"
165 [*Puella*] "Est grave quod quaeris; me perdere velle videris.
     Si mater sciret, manibus lacerata perirem
     nec non cognatos timeo mihi perdere gratos."
     [*Nuntius*] "Tu mihi si credis, nil perdes, salva manebis."
     [*Puella*] "Quid faciam? Credam? Vix te ductore recedam.
170 Primum mitte fidem mecum venias ut ibidem,
     et postquam venias, non me post terga relinquas."

arrows: it wouldn't be safe to fool around in secret with 150 him."

Messenger: "I'll be with you; set aside all thoughts of danger. I want to be present—I don't want to leave you alone."

Girl: "How quickly you'll abandon me, once you've shut me in! And as soon as I'm left alone I'll be overcome."

Messenger: "If you were a fox, perhaps you would flee a 155 pack of dogs; for you seek an escape for yourself with many words."

Girl: "If I were a fox, I would show that I can outwit you: your words are honeyed, but bile is concealed deep in your heart."

Messenger: "Enough of words—I think they're becoming very hostile. I have only a little time—let's return to what 160 we were speaking of before."

Girl: "I approve of what you say: for it befits friends to conceal the unpleasant and show all that is pleasant. So go ahead and repeat what you were proposing a little while ago."

Messenger: "What use is it to repeat, since I don't know if I have any real hope?"

Girl: "What you ask for is a serious matter; you seem to 165 want to ruin me. If my mother knew, she would tear me apart with her own hands; also, I'm afraid to ruin my dear parents."

Messenger: "If you trust me, you won't ruin anything, and you'll remain safe."

Girl: "What shall I do? Should I believe you? It will be difficult to turn back again with you leading the way. First 170 give me your word that you will go there with me, and that you won't turn your back on me and leave once you arrive."

[*Nuntius*] "Sit velut ipsa petis et adhuc si plurima quaeris.
His ita concessis, volo finem ponere verbis."
    Dicens "Surgamus," sibi nuntius inquit "Eamus."
175 Sic vadunt ambo, sic multa locuntur eundo.
    Hanc ego cum vidi, talem venisse cupivi;
cum prope plus fuerat, tanto plus ipsa placebat.
Protinus ardebam; bene scitis quid cupiebam,
sed non audebam sibi dicere quid cupiebam.
180 Molliter accessi, sibi dulciter oscula gessi.
Quod cum cernebat, mihi multa referre volebat
et rogat audire, sed nuntius innuit ire.
Tandem quid feci? Festinans pergere coepi
et mox intravi loca quae secreta probavi.
185 Iam sibi virgo timet quaerens quo nuntius iret;
dixi misisse, promisi semper adesse.
    Mox ut persensit quod nuntius ille recessit,
exclamat virgo: "Pacem, carissime, quaero.
Non ego sic veni, per vim me nolo teneri.
190 Cur mihi non credis? Hic nuntius est mihi testis.
Dic ubi sis, care. Puer hic me quaerit amare.
Audis clamare? Debes hic tu prope stare.
Quo tu venisti? Numquid fantasma fuisti?
Facta fides fuerat, sed eam quis nunc mihi servat?
195 O maledicta Fides, aliis te taliter offers?
Nulla fides certe: cunctis hoc testor aperte.
Nam modo si qua foret, etiam malus ille teneret.
Sponte fides mille periurus fecerat ille.
Me male decepit; si vixero, non bene fecit.

Messenger: "It shall be as you ask, and even more if you desire. Now that I have made these concessions, I'd like to end this conversation."

The messenger says to her, "Let's get up," and then, "Let's go." So they both go, and as they go they speak of many things. 175

As soon as I saw her, I longed for such a beauty to be by my side; the closer she got, the more pleasing she was. At once I was aflame; you know well what I desired, but I dared not tell her what I desired. Softly I approached, sweetly I 180 kissed her. When she perceived this, she had much she wanted to say to me and asked me to listen, but the messenger signaled to me to go in. What did I do then? I quickly stepped forward and soon entered into what I knew was a secluded place. Already the maiden was afraid and asked 185 where the messenger was going; I said that I had sent him away but promised that he would always be near.

As soon as she understood that the messenger had gone away, the maiden exclaimed: "I demand my freedom, dear sir. I didn't come here on these terms, and I don't wish to be kept here by force. Why don't you believe me? This messen- 190 ger is my witness. Tell me where you are, dear sir. The boy wants to rape me here. Do you hear my shouts? You ought to stay nearby. Where have you gone? Were you some sort of ghost? You gave me your word, but who keeps faith now? Oh 195 cursed Faith, do you treat others this way? For sure, there is no such thing as faith: I openly declare this before all. For if there were any now, even that scoundrel would respect it. That oath breaker of his own accord made a thousand promises to me. He wickedly deceived me; even if I live, his ac-

200 Quo fugit ille canis mendax, lecator inanis?
Si presens esset, a me cito mortuus esset."
    Talia cum loquitur, lecto prope stante locatur.
Cetera quae restant, Venus associata ministrat.
His ita finitis, ludus novus accidit illis.
205   Nuntius accessit dicens: "Quis talia iussit?
Non fuerat pactum quod taliter hoc foret actum.
Ah, quod nescivi noviter cum nuntius ivi;
nam si praescissem, non sic deceptus abissem.
Sentio, deliqui, quod te post terga reliqui.
210 Cur oculos tergis? Dic quae sit causa doloris.
Laesit te quisquam? Mox accipiet sibi poenam."
    [*Puella*] "Luctus saepe gravis risu contingit inani.
Nam modo si gaudes quod fecisti mihi fraudes,
fit, cum ridebis, quod gaudia dura tenebis."
215   [*Nuntius*] "Aspera cur loqueris? Irasci velle videris.
Sed mihi tu soli culpas imponere noli:
nam cum venisti sine me tu clausa fuisti.
Ante fores stabam, me velle vocare putabam.
Sed nihil audivi: mirabar, solus abivi.
220 Postea quid fieret quis Iupiter hoc modo sciret.
Custodem puerum feci consistere tecum,
qui te servaret, et contra quosque iuvaret.
Nescio si fecit, bene te puer ille recepit."
    [*Puella*] "Sum male decepta, puero custode recepta,
225 et male tractata, te deceptore vocata.
Numquid eram surda, quod non sensi tua verba?
Cauta satis fueram; cur tunc non ipsa timebam?
Si praedixisses, pro me recitasset Ulixes.

tions were evil. Where has that lying dog fled to—that
worthless sycophant? If he were here, I would swiftly kill
him."

While she was saying these things, she was placed on a
nearby bed. All that followed Venus prompted as an accom-
plice. When this was finished, it was time for a new game.

The messenger came up, saying: "Who gave these com-
mands? It wasn't our agreement that something like this
should happen. If only I'd known it just now, when, being
only a messenger, I went away; for if I had known it before, I
wouldn't have been deceived in this way and gone away. I un-
derstand, I was wrong to turn my back and leave you. Why
do you wipe your eyes? Tell me why you are sad. Has some-
one harmed you? He'll be punished right away."

Girl: "Often idle laughter occasions great sorrow. For if
presently you rejoice because you have deceived me, re-
member, when you laugh, that you will find your rejoicing
brings pain."

Messenger: "Why do you speak so harshly? It seems you
want to get angry. But don't cast the blame on me alone: for
when you came here, you were shut in away from me. I stood
before the door, thinking that you would call me, but I heard
nothing; I was surprised, but I went away on my own. What
happened afterward only Jupiter could know. I arranged for
the boy to stand guard over you, to protect you and to come
to your aid against anyone. I don't know if the boy did it, but
he received you well."

Girl: "I was wickedly deceived, taken into the boy's cus-
tody, and roughly treated, but it was your deceit that brought
me to this. Was I deaf in that I didn't understand your
words? I had been very cautious; so why wasn't I then afraid?
If you had warned me in advance, Ulysses would have

Pessimus es certe, cunctis hoc testor aperte.

230 Nulla fides tecum; non hoc etiam foret aequum,
nam servus nequam numquam rem diligit aequam."

    [*Nuntius*] "Aspera verba tenes; aliquid, rogo, parcere
       debes.

Nil merui tale mihi quin bene sit veniale.

Nubere tempus erat; iuveni tua forma placebat:

235 ille laboravit, donec sibi te sociavit.

Ne ducas aegre, nam vult sibi talia quisque;

talia ne cures, fecerunt talia plures;

est et semper erit iuveni quod virgo placebit.

Non ita sis maesta, fit quod fueris bene laeta."

240   [*Puella*] "Sum merito maesta: res est mihi facta molesta;
fas est plorare: sum perdita, nescio quare."

    [*Nuntius*] "Hoc non est sapere quod vis bene facta dolere:
nescis fortasse grave pondus te superasse.

Scis quid fecisti. Fortunam sola tulisti.

245 Respice quis puer est: merito rex vivere posset.

Nobilis et prudens, in forma praevalet omnes,

aptus et est agilis, merito placet ipse puellis.

Dum modo sis praesens, sibi cur non oscula praebes?

Femina si starem, vellet vel nollet, amarem.

250 Tolle moras longas, et te melius sibi iungas.

Curque sedes? Surgas, accedes, postulo, tangas.

Nil pudeat tactus, quoniam pervenit ad actus;

ut res est gesta, mihi iam satis est manifesta.

Nil ultra cures, noverunt talia plures.

255 Mos est antiquus, ut amicam quaerat amicus.

Quis non laudabit, si pulchram pulcher amabit?"

spoken for me. You're definitely the worst—I declare this openly before all. You're completely dishonest; but there's no way this could be just, for a bad servant like you never has any respect for justice." 230

Messenger: "Your words are harsh; but I ask that you go easy on me. I haven't committed any unpardonable crime. It was time for you to marry; the youth liked the look of you: he worked hard to get to know you. Don't take it hard, for everyone wants such things for themselves; and don't worry—lots of people have done such things. It is the case, and always will be, that young men find maidens pleasing. So don't be sad—there is reason to be very happy instead." 235

Girl: "I have good reason to be sad: a horrible thing has been done to me. I have every right to cry: I'm ruined, and I don't know why." 240

Messenger: "It doesn't make sense that you want to mourn a happy outcome: perhaps you don't know the heavy weight you've thrown off. You know what you did. You alone have won this good fortune. Look at what sort of boy he is: he could deservedly be a king. Noble and wise, the most handsome of all men, he is able and active, and a favorite of the girls for good reason. While you're still here, why don't you give him a kiss? If I were a woman, I would love him whether he liked it or not. Don't delay any longer, and make yourself his partner. Why are you still sitting? Get up, go to him, I beg you, and caress him. A caress is not shameful, now that the deed has been done; it's already quite clear to me that it's happened. Don't worry any more, many people have experienced such things. It's an old custom that a lover should seek his beloved. Who would disapprove of a handsome young man loving a pretty girl?" 245 250 255

[*Puella*] "Tu dicis vera. Quid prodest magna querela?
Ut res est dicam: puer hic me quaerit amicam.
Talia qui faciunt non omnes inde peribunt;
260 multi salvantur, qui plus peccasse probantur.
Non ego sum sola quae sit maledicta vocanda:
Iupiter et Iuno lecto sociantur in uno,
Mars duxit Venerem, Vulcanus amavit eandem.
Quis dicit contra? Nusquam scelus, omnia iusta.
265 Non curo verba mihi si dicantur acerba;
saepe quod optavi feliciter ipsa probavi.
Nunc velit aut nolit, sibi me puer iste tenebit.
Si placet, hunc teneo, si non, tamen ipsa tenebo.
Fas est ut surgam, sibi collo brachia iungam."
270   Surgit et accessit, amplectitur, oscula gessit,
dicens: "O care, quis te non posset amare?
Ipsius Veneris tu filius esse videris.
Ut fateor certe non diligo clam, sed aperte:
non timeo factum, satis est quia taliter actum.
275 Gaudeo te puero, non altera gaudia quaero;
est mihi vita salus, poteris dum vivere sanus.
Hic tibi legatus meruit quod sit tibi gratus:
donum regale tibi duxit nescio quale.
Si regina forem, facerem quod haberet honorem,
280 et merito facerem, quia nescio vivere talem.
Est bene nutritus, bene cautus, ad omne peritus,
nobilis est, aptus, nostro stat munere dignus."
    [*Puer*] "Quod dicis laudo: gemmis donetur et auro.
Plurima si qua velit, dabitur quodcumque placebit."
285   Inquit legatus dono primum decoratus:
"Adsit parva mora, quia lucis adimminet hora.

Girl: "You speak the truth. What's the point of complaining too much? I'll tell you how it is: this boy wants me as his lover. Not everyone who does such things will be ruined because of it; many are saved, who are known to have sinned 260 even more. I'm not the only one who deserves to be called accursed: Jupiter and Juno are united in one bed, Mars wed Venus, and Vulcan loved her too. Who can deny it? There's nothing wrong—all is right. I don't care if I'm reproached; I 265 am happy to have experienced what I have so often desired. Now like it or not, that boy will keep me with him. If he agrees, I'll keep him; if not, I'll stick with him nonetheless. It's right that I should get up and wrap my arms around his neck."

She gets up and goes to me, embraces me, and gives me 270 kisses, saying: "Oh my dear, who couldn't fall in love with you? You look like the son of Venus herself. I certainly admit it: I love you, and not in secret, but openly; I do not fear the deed—it's fine that it happened in this way. I rejoice in you, 275 my boy, and I do not seek other pleasures. My life is happy, as long as you live in good health. This messenger has earned your gratitude: he brought a regal gift to you like no other. If I were a queen, I would see to it that he was honored, and I 280 would do this with good reason, for I know no one like him. He is well brought up, very prudent, expert in everything. He is noble, capable, and worthy of our reward."

Boy: "I approve of what you say: he shall be given jewels and gold. And if he wants more, he will be given whatever he desires."

Says the messenger, when first he received the gift: 285 "There's not a moment to lose, because dawn approaches.

Per loca secreta redeas sub nocte quieta,
ne manifestetur, si quisquam forte vagetur."
    [*Puella*] "Vera mones, care, rogo mecum te remeare."
290   [*Nuntius*] "Tu mihi coniuncta postpone pericula cuncta.
Hector et Achilles, Aiax, fortissimus Hercles,
si presto starent, non me pugnando fugarent."
    His verbis tuta fuit illum virgo secuta.
Mox ut pergebant et mutua verba ferebant,
295 nuntius astutus fuerat cum virgine captus.
Hos qui ceperunt laeti satis inde fuerunt
illico dicentes se virginis esse parentes.
Et dicunt pariter: "Non convenit ire latenter,"
et cupiunt scire quo vellent taliter ire
300 horis nocturnis, cum sit fas ire diurnis.
    [*Parentes*] "Dic, bone vir, quis sis, aut quo vestigia tendis?
Miramur multum te sic abscondere vultum.
Virgo venit tecum; dic quae tibi gratia secum.
Dic cito quid quaeris: nisi dicas, morte peribis.
305 Hostis venisti nobis, hanc et rapuisti?
Quid stamus? Reus est: illum suspendere fas est."
    Nuntius, ut vidit captus quod abire nequivit,
dissimulat fugere, sperans sic posse cavere
ne sentiretur si secretum quod habetur.
310 Quid fecit? Risit, astantibus oscula misit,
dicens: "Salvete, vobis haec dona tenete,
et, dum vivatis, mihi grates ut referatis,
est vestrum facere, per me quia vita puellae
est prolongata: nam turpi morte parata
315 suspendi laqueo voluit pulcherrima virgo.

Go home by secret byways in the quiet of night, so that you won't be seen, if anyone happens to be about."

Girl: "You make a good warning, my dear, but—I beg you—come back with me."

Messenger: "Have no fear when you're with me. Hector   290
and Achilles, Ajax, mighty Hercules—if they were here now, they couldn't drive me away in a fight."

Reassured by these words, the maiden followed him. But then, as they were walking and exchanging conversation, the clever messenger was caught along with the maiden.   295
Those who caught them were quite delighted, at once explaining that they were the maiden's parents. And together they said, "It's not proper to take secret walks," and they wanted to know where they intended to go in such a way in   300
the nocturnal hours, since it is proper to travel in the daytime.

Parents: "Tell, good sir, who you are, and where are you going? We're quite astonished that you conceal your face like that. There's a maiden with you; tell what your motives are with her. Tell us at once what you're after: if you don't tell, consider yourself dead. Have you come as our enemy   305
and have you stolen her away? Why are we just standing here? He's guilty: we should string him up."

The messenger, when he saw that he was caught and that escape was impossible, disguised his desire to flee, hoping that in this way he might prevent their noticing whether he had a secret. So what did he do? He laughed, blowing kisses   310
to the bystanders, saying: "Greetings! Receive from me this gift; your part, as long as you live, is to show me your gratitude, because it's owing to me that the girl still lives; for she had prepared a terrible death for herself—she wished to   315

Quod cum cernebam, festinans arripiebam
et mox incidi laqueum quem gutture vidi.
Quaesivi quare se vellet mortificare.
Mox velut insana coepit clamare profana,
320 dicens: 'Care, veni, venias, pro te quia veni!'
Saepius hoc dixit, sed nescio dicere quis sit,
quem sic optavit et semper adesse rogavit.
Ignoro nomen et miror nominis omen,
quod nullum vidit, tamen ipsa venire cupivit.
325 Quid fecit tandem? Fugit ipsa, sequebar eandem,
si sic aufugeret, metuens ne forte periret.
Mox insensata, male me lacerare parata,
per crines cepit vestesque meas ita fregit.
Hinc poenas ferret, nisi pro nobis remearet."
330   [*Parentes*] "Nunc grates habeas, quod male non faciebas,
vir bone, vir care, quem nos bene constat amare.
Nescivit certe quod vita fuit sibi per te.
Nunc ignoramus de tali re quid agamus,
quod caret ingenio nobis carissima virgo
335 et tam formosa fertur quod sit furiosa.
O Pallas, Pallas, scelus hoc nisi forte repellas,
dedecus est nostrum, cum sit mirabile monstrum,
nobis cognata quod debet stare ligata,
ne laceret manibus quae demonstrat sibi visus.
340 Dic, bone vir, nobis: licet illam tangere nobis
saltem per vestes, ne nos trahat illa per ungues,
aut opus est, care, per cetera membra ligare?"
        [*Nuntius*] "Si plus torquetur, magis illa furore repletur.
Corpori nam tenero plus proficiet, bene spero,
345 blandiri verbis quam vincula ponere membris.

hang herself, and such a lovely maiden! When I saw this, I hurried to get to her, and at once cut the noose I saw on her neck. I asked her why she wished to take her own life. Then, like a maniac, she began to shout unholy things, saying: 'My dear, I have come, you come too, because I have come for you!' She said this again and again, but I can't say who it was she so desired and constantly asked to join her. I don't know the name, and I wonder about its omen, since she saw no one, but still she wanted someone to come. So what did she do in the end? She fled and I followed her, fearing that if she escaped, she would perhaps end up dead. But soon she had lost her mind, and, all set on savagely wounding me, she grabbed me by my hair and tore my clothes in this way. She would be punished for this, if she were not returning through my efforts."

Parents: "Now receive our thanks for doing her no harm, good sir, dear sir, whom we have good reason to love. Clearly, she doesn't know that she owes her life to you. But now we don't know what to do about this matter, because our dearest maiden has lost her senses, and it seems that one so lovely has gone mad. Oh Pallas, Pallas, if you don't drive away this evil, it will bring disgrace on us, since it's a remarkable wonder that our daughter should have to be tied up so that she doesn't wound with her hands what her sight presents to her. Tell us, good sir: can we touch her, at least, by her clothes, without her scratching us with her fingernails, or, dear sir, must we tie her up by her other limbs too?"

Messenger: "If she's constrained even more, it will only make her more ferocious. Her body is so delicate that it would be more helpful, I believe, to speak soft words to her than to bind her limbs. And so that this doesn't become

320

325

330

335

340

345

Est etiam melius, ne clamet talia vulgus,
quod sit clausa domo quam languida vadat aperto."
   [*Parentes*] "O quam turpe scelus quod non celare valemus!
Si fuerit clausa, fertur quod non sine causa
350 hoc fecissemus, sed si causam reticemus,
undique clamatur: 'Bona femina cur cruciatur?'
O virgo misera, de te quam magna querela
fit cognatorum, cum te per templa deorum
sic insensatam cernent transire ligatam!
355 Dic saltem nobis quae sit tibi causa doloris.
Est aliquis medicus tali nunc arte peritus
qui vellet censum, dare quod posset tibi sensum?
Si censum quaerit, pro censu non remanebit
quin teneat sensum, si forte dabit tibi sensum."
360   [*Puella*] "Cognati cari, dimittite me cruciari;
ut laqueo peream, placet hanc mihi sumere poenam.
Quin mihi clamorem compescatis per amorem?"
   [*Parentes*] "Virgo, quid pateris, quod amorem velle fateris?
Si tibi clamorem vis compesci per amorem,
365 nos promittemus super omne te quod amemus."
   [*Puella*] "Non est vester amor pro quo cesset mihi
      clamor."
   [*Parentes*] "Dic nobis quis sit. Semper faciemus ut adsit."
   [*Puella*] "Est alius quidam qui si mihi dat medicinam,
plus non laedit amor et cessat postea clamor."
370   Ut virgo vidit quod amicos fallere possit,
dissimulat velle medicum quem postulat ante,
velle mori dicens, statim per devia currens
semper clamando: "Moriar, quia vincor amando!

common talk, it would be better for her to be confined at home rather than to wander about listlessly in public."

Parents: "What a shameful calamity—and one we cannot hide! If she is kept inside, they'll say that we have done this not without cause, but if we keep silent about the reason, everyone will say: 'Why do they torture a good woman?' Oh you poor maiden, what great grief you will cause your family, when they see you pass among the temples of the gods crazed and tied up in this way! At least tell us the cause of your distress. Is there some doctor experienced in this skill who wishes to earn a reward for restoring you to your senses? If he seeks a reward, he will not remain for the reward, unless he is sensible, if by chance he succeeds in restoring your senses."

Girl: "Dear parents, stop tormenting me; dying by the noose is the punishment I want. Why not end my wailing with love?"

Parents: "Poor girl, what is the matter, why declare that you want love? If you want your wailing to end with love, we will promise that we love you above all else."

Girl: "It's not for your love that I want my wailing to stop."

Parents: "Tell us who it is then. We'll see to it that he's always present."

Girl: "There is another person. If he gives me medicine, love will no longer wound me and my wailing will then cease."

When the maiden saw that she could deceive her friends, she ignored her previous wish for a doctor, saying she wanted to die. Immediately she started running off the path, shouting all the time: "Let me die, for love has conquered

Et iam mors esset, nisi vir malus iste fuisset.
375 Adduxit vinctam, mihi debet solvere poenam."
    [*Parentes*] "Fas est arripere. Sed quid iuvat hunc retinere?"
    [*Puella*] "Cognati cari, per vos precor hunc cruciari."
    Nuntius astutus de tali re bene tutus
coepit abire fuga clamans: "Retinete puellam!
380 Pro vobis feci quod eam per vincula cepi.
Si cito non capitis, de vita stat mihi finis."
    Qui tunc adstabant, postquam bene percipiebant
quae Davus dixit, credunt quod seria res sit,
festinant capere, ne vitam perderet ille.
385 Illa reluctatur, Davus retinere precatur.
Illa ferit pugno, Davus ferit inde secundo . . .

De vetula

Introitus in librum Ovidii Nasonis Paelignensis "De vetula"
promulgatum a Leone protonotario sacri palatii Byzantei,
qui tunc erat scriniarius Vathachii et eius a commentariis.
Quando videlicet rex Colchorum dictum librum invenit in
quodam sepulcro extracto de coemeterio publico sito in su-
burbio Dioscori civitatis, quae caput est sui regni, misit
Constantinopolim, ubi erat copia Latinorum, pro eo quod
Armenici nec Latinam linguam intelligunt nec apud se in-
terpretes huius tunc habebant.

me! I would be dead already, if not for that evil man. He ³⁷⁵
brought me here in chains, so he ought to be punished for
what he did to me."

Parents: "He should be arrested. But what good will it do
to imprison him?"

Girl: "Dear parents, I beg you to have him tortured."

The crafty messenger, well prepared for such an event,
began to flee, shouting: "Keep hold of the girl! It was for ³⁸⁰
your good that I put her in chains. If you don't catch her at
once, my life will be over."

When the bystanders comprehended what Davus said,
they believed that the matter was serious, and they hastened
to catch her, so that he would not lose his life. She resisted, ³⁸⁵
but Davus begged them to hold her back. She gave him a
blow with her fist, then Davus struck back at her . . .

On the Old Woman

Introduction to the work of Ovidius Naso of the Paeligni,
"On the Old Woman," published by Leo, protonotary of the
holy palace of Byzantium, who was then the keeper of the
letter case of Vatatzes and his record keeper. Now when the
king of Colchis found the said work in a certain coffin that
had been removed from the public cemetery located in a
suburb of the city of Dioscurias, the capital of his kingdom,
he sent it to Constantinople, where there was an abundance
of Latin speakers, because the Armenians neither under-
stand the Latin language nor had translators among them at
that time.

PRAEFATIO SIVE ARGUMENTUM LEONIS
PROTONOTARII SACRI PALATII BIZANTEI
SUB VATHACHIO PRINCIPE IN LIBRUM
OVIDII NASONIS PELIGNENSIS "DE VETULA"

Ovidius Naso, Peligni ruris alumnus,
certus ab exilio se iam non posse reverti
et quaerens utcumque sibi solacia librum
edidit hunc, in eo describens, quis modus ipsi
5   vivendi fuerat tunc, quando vacabat amori,
qua re mutavit et quo modo postea vixit
quidve intendebat, simul ac ab amore vacavit;
imposuitque suo titulum nomenque libello
"De vetula," pro qua fuerat mutatio facta,
10 inque suo secum iussit condire sepulcro,
ut, sua si saltem contingeret ossa referri,
corredeunte libro redivivum nomen haberet.
Sed quia nullus eis curavit de referendis,
nec fuit authentim lectus nec habetur in usu.

ITEM PRAEFATIO IPSIUS AUCTORIS

Quaeritur, unde mihi quod opus processerit istud
versibus hexametris solum nec subduplicarim
more meo pentimemerin, cum nullus herorum
hic describatur; sed qui perlegerit ipsum
5   sedulus, inveniet serviti semper amoris
amodo me debere iugo subducere sicque
respondere sibi poterit, cur evacuata
causa debuerit causatus et evacuari
versus amatorum proprius Venerique dicatus.

The Preface or Argument of Leo, Protonotary of the Holy Palace of Byzantium under King Vatatzes, on the Work of Ovidius Naso of the Paeligni, "On the Old Woman"

Ovidius Naso, raised in the Paelignian countryside, certain that he wouldn't be able to return from exile and seeking some kind of solace for himself, produced this work, in which he describes the manner of his life when he was de- 5
voted to love, why he changed and how he lived afterward, or what he turned to once he was free from love. He gave to his book the title and name "On the Old Woman" after the woman who had caused his change. He gave instructions 10
that it be buried with him in his coffin, so that, if at least it happened that his bones were returned, his name would be restored to life because of the accompanying book. But, since no one took care to have them returned, it was neither read as one of his authentic works nor kept in circulation.

Also, the Preface of the Author Himself

One might wonder why this work of mine runs along entirely in hexameters and why I did not split them up with pentameters in my usual manner, since no hero is described here; but whoever reads it carefully will discover that hence- 5
forth I must forever free my neck from the yoke of slavery to love. And thus my reader will be able to answer for himself why, once love had been abandoned, the verse inspired by it would also have to be abandoned, since it is character-istic of lovers and dedicated to Venus.

Liber primus

O quam carus erat mihi quamque optabilis ille
femineus sexus, sine quo nec vivere posse
credebam quemcumque virum, sed et inferiorem
me certe quocumque viro quoad hoc reputabam,
5   qui procul a cara me vivere posse negassem
omnes sollicite venerans unius odore,
esse mihi malens unam, cuius modus esset
commodus et concors, quam multiplicare puellas,
ex quibus importuna foret mihi forsitan una.
10   Nam sicut vulgare solet paradigma tenere,
sicut habens centum nullam reputatur habere
sic et habens unam pro centum computat illam,
nam nullius eris, dum te non vendicet una,
unaque sufficiet quasi centum solus haberes.
15   Unusquisque sibi quod mavult eligit, et quod
non placet, hoc renuit. De me scio, quod magis unam
vellem quam nullam, quod concordem magis unam
quam multas, quarum mihi contradiceret una.
Unam propterea cribraram e milibus, unam
20   perfectam, quam si citius fortuna dedisset,
inter felices merito numerabilis essem.
     O quantum laetabar ea quantumque iuvabat
esse sui memorem! Quanta dulcedine curis
expulsis pectusque meum mulcere solebat
25   postpositosque iocos modulis revocare sonoris!
Vestibus ornari nitidis faciebat, alutae
castigare pedes circumplexu sinuosos.
Nil erat incultum, facies nisi sola; puellis
esse videbatur solis pars illa colenda.

Book One

Oh, how dear to me and how desirable was the female sex! I used to believe that no man could live without it and yet I reckoned that I was inferior to every man in this respect. I would have said that I could not live far from my beloved, anxiously worshiping all women through the fragrance of just one, preferring to have one whose manner was pleasant and agreeable, rather than to have a large number of girls among whom might be one troublesome to me. For, as the common saying goes, having a hundred girls counts as having none, and having one girl counts as having a hundred, since you will be no one's, as long as not one girl claims you as her own, but one girl will be as sufficient as if you alone had a hundred girls. Every man chooses what he wants and refuses what displeases him. As for myself, I know that I would rather have one girl than none. I would rather have one agreeable girl than many girls, one of whom might gainsay me. Therefore, I had sifted one out of the thousands, one perfect girl, and if fortune had granted her more quickly to me, I would have rightly been counted among the fortunate.

How much I rejoiced in her, and how I delighted in thinking of her! How sweetly she used to soothe my heart, banishing my cares, and revive our neglected delights with sweet-sounding melodies! It was because of her that I dressed in elegant garments and enclosed my arched feet in the embrace of soft leather. Nothing was unadorned, except for my face alone; it is seemly only for girls to embellish that

30 Nec facies neglecta tamen, quin providus essem,
   ne circumstarent fluxi vestigia puris
   seu lacrimalia seu cuiusque foramina sensus!
      Et iuvenescebam, quotiens mento reparato
   barbalem radebat acuta novacula silvam.
35 Cuius cum spolium nullam ferat utilitatem,
   carior ulla tamen non est, nec debitus ulli
   tantus honor silvae. Multum placet asperitas haec,
   —non pro se, sed pro signato: silva viriles
   indicat haec animos, vires quoque partis amicae
40 per quam salvatur species divina, licet sit
   ex individuis mortalibus. Ipsa dat, unde
   non in se rediens, licet in se visa reflecti,
   sed processive generatio continuetur.
   Ipsa receptricem fecundat tempore certo
45 sponte refusuram dulcissima pignora natos,
   quo nihil est homini coniunctius. Ipsa ministrat,
   unde superba tori consors se grata libensque
   supponat maris imperio,—subiectio mira,
   nam famulamur eis! Tanta inclinatio nostra
50 naturaliter est ad sexum femineum, qui
   prae cunctis laetum me fecerat esse coaevis.
      Me refici laute clara faciebat in aula,
   cuius campus erat stratus pro tempore, prati
   nunc spoliis, iunco, Cereris nunc stipite flavo.
55 Invitare bonos mea larga manus satagebat
   et propriis rebus tamquam communibus uti,
   multiplicare dapes, effundere sanguinis uvae
   mille modos et, ubi rigor exigeret glacialis,
   ignibus accensis truncosque vorante camino
60 aestatem revocare novo quasi sole creato.

body part. Yet my face was not neglected, but rather I was 30
careful that no traces of flowing mucus surrounded either
my tear ducts or the orifices of each sense!

I grew young again, whenever a sharp razor shaved the
forest of my beard so my chin was revealed. Although the 35
cuttings have no use, nonetheless, no forest is more pre-
cious or due as much honor. This roughness is greatly pleas-
ing—not for its own sake, but for what it signifies: this for-
est indicates a manly spirit, as well as the vigor of the sex
organ through which the immortal species is preserved, al- 40
though composed of mortal individuals. This part enables
generation to continue forward, never returning into itself
even if it has seemed to be reflected in itself. It impregnates
the female receiver, who after a fixed time of her own accord 45
will bring forth children as her sweetest pledges, than which
nothing is more agreeable to humankind. This same organ is
the cause of the proud partner of his bed gladly and willingly
placing herself under the authority of her husband—an
amazing submission, for we are their servants! So great is
our natural inclination towards the female sex, which made 50
me happier than all of my contemporaries.

My desire caused me to feast sumptuously in a noble
court whose open space, depending on the season, was cov-
ered sometimes with rushes, the spoils of the meadow, at
other times with the golden stalks of Ceres. My bountiful 55
hand was busy offering entertainment to gentlemen and
sharing my own goods for the benefit of all, hosting many
feasts, pouring out a thousand measures of bloodred wine,
and, whenever icy cold demanded it, bringing back summer
warmth as if a new sun had been created by lighting fires and 60

Utque meis posset de nocte diescere mensis,
sidereas aptare faces, quas mellis alebat
sponsa, sed ipsius sponsi divortia passa.
His immiscebam, quicquid poterat modulari,
65 concentus varios, licet in diversa trahentes,
concordare tamen visos, vel voce vel usu
instrumentorum, quicquid vel musica scribit
vel didicere manus auditu, indice, tactu,
pulsu vel tractu vel flatu. Cimbala pulsum
70 dura volunt tractumque fides et fistula flatum.
     Intrabam thalamos etiam, si quando libebat,
secretos, ubi lux, si vellem, multa vigeret
nullaque, si vellem, vel, si mallem, mediocris,
inde videre potens silvas agrosque feraces,
75 hortos et vites, fluvios et prata lacusque.
Si tamen aspectus horum quoscumque iuvaret,
quantumcumque iuvet aspectus longus eorum,
aspectum credas et delectabiliorem
inclusum mecum satis et mirabiliorem;
80 nam, si dives erat, qui visum pascere posset,
ditior alonge, qui pascere sufficiebat
sensibus intellectum multo nobiliorem;
sicut enim virtus intellectiva superstat
sensibili, sic et, nisi sit proportio mendax,
85 obiectum obiectum superabit, et interiori
luci doctrinae, quae illuminat intellectum,
numquam praesumet conferre foranea se lux.
Quodsi contulerit temere, ridebitur inde,
tamquam si candela velit contendere soli.
90 Haec lux doctrinae mecum conclusa nitebat,
plusque fovebar ea quam quoquam materiali.

having a stove burn logs. And to make day out of night at my
tables, I had lights as bright as stars prepared, which honey's
bride nourished, though it had suffered divorce from its
partner. I added to these all forms of music, various musi- 65
cians that, though sounding different notes, yet seemed har-
monious, whether using the voice or instruments, whatever
the music dictates or the hands have learned by hearing, by
pointing, by touching, by striking, by plucking, or by blow-
ing. The harsh cymbals want striking, the strings plucking, 70
and the pipe blowing.

I also used to enter my secluded bedchamber, whenever I
liked, where the light was exceedingly bright or entirely
lacking, depending on my whim, or, if I preferred, of mid-
dling brightness, so I could see the woods and the fertile
fields, the gardens and the vines, the rivers, meadows, and 75
lakes. Now if the sight of these things is pleasing to every-
one, however much pleasure the sight of them gives when
viewed from afar, yet still more agreeable and quite wonder-
ful, believe me, was the sight enclosed in my chamber. For, if 80
he would be a rich man who could feast his sight in this way,
richer by far is the person who is capable of feasting his in-
tellect, so much nobler than his senses. For, just as the power
of the intellect is superior to that of the senses, just so, un-
less the analogy is deceptive, the one object will surpass the 85
other object, and the exterior light of day will never pre-
sume to compare itself to the interior light of learning,
which illuminates the intellect. But if it rashly made the
comparison, it would be ridiculed for it, as if a candle wished
to vie with the sun. Enclosed in my chamber, this light of 90

Eleganter erat paries vestitus amenis
undique picturis diversicoloribus, auro
clarus, imaginibus tacitis praeconia clamans
95 artificis, non historiam sed mystica quaedam
demonstrans illis, quorum descriptio plus est
huius quam libri capiat sententia tota.
    Illic lectus erat caro pretiosus amictu,
quo posset se velle premi quaecumque puella.
100 Si virgo vim sponte pati captaret in illo,
quae nihil amittens amisso flore notatur,
audacterque tori foedus dirrumperet uxor,
quae fructum faciens sobolem turbare timetur,
orba viro refocillari gauderet ibidem,
105 dum non conciperet, eremi frondentis amica.
Hic flos virgineus, fructusque uxorius illic,
hic viduus ramus foliis facientibus umbram
gratus, sed postquam desertum deserit, illi
fertilitas metuenda, nisi transegerit annos.
110 Eligit hic flores, hic fructus, illeque frondes.
    Sed quia crudelis qui famam negligit, illam
vir prudens cupiat, quam suggillatio famae
non sequitur. Sane virgo manet integra fama,
donec prodat eam partus vel prodiga linguae
115 divulget secreta minus fidis sociabus.
Vel si fors experta virum desiderat ultra
quam sit opus, nec iam scit dissimulare, sed ignem
nunc gestu, nunc ornatu confessa profundum
circuit et quaerit oculis quem diligit. Et iam

learning shone brightly, and I was nurtured by it more than by any other artifice. The wall was elegantly covered all over with beautiful paintings in various colors, bright with gold, proclaiming the message of the artist with silent images, and depicting with these not a narrative but certain myster- 95 ies, whose description not even the entire content of this book could accommodate.

In that place there was a bed, valuable because of its expensive covering, where any girl could wish herself to be bedded. If a maiden willingly aspired to submit to force in it, 100 though losing nothing she was said to have lost her flower. If a married woman rashly broke the pact of her marital bed in it, she was feared to be confounding the family tree by producing fruit. If a widow rejoiced to be revived in that place, as long as she did not conceive, as a lover she was like a bur- 105 geoning desert. In the first case, a virgin's flower won favor, in the second, a wife's fruitfulness, and in the third, the widow's branch with its shade-making foliage, though after she gave up her solitude, she had to fear her fertility, if she had not passed childbearing years. Some men prefer flowers, 110 some, fruit, and others, foliage.

Now since it's a heartless man who neglects a woman's reputation, the wise man should desire a woman to whom no whisper of scandal clings. Indeed, a maiden's reputation remains unblemished until childbirth betrays her, or 115 else, with a careless tongue, she divulges her secrets to untrustworthy companions. Or perhaps she has had experience and feels extreme longing for a man. Not knowing how to dissemble but betraying her intense passion now with a gesture, now with her elaborate dress, she prowls about, seeking with her eyes the one whom she loves. Now

120 gaudia differri non sustinet. Intrat et exit,
inconsulta quidem, quia, dum sibi non cavet, illi
nemo cavere potest, caecoque furore vagatur.
    Verum nupta quoad quaedam minus est onerosa
atque quoad quaedam maiora pericula subdit.
125 Nupta potest ubi vult et quando et qualiter ire.
Si iuvenis trahit unanimes trahiturve per illas,
seque theatrales simulat ludos adituram.
Si matura, forum pro multis rebus emendis
esse frequentandum praetendit deque minutis
130 intromittit se maiora gerente marito.
Quodsi iam non sit humili de plebe nec ipsam
his operam dare conveniat, delubra deorum
circuit et modicum censet vicina valere,
plusque remota placent. Gaudet novitate viarum
135 cotidieque deos creat et miracula fingit
votis digna novis, quo se promittat ituram.
Nec vadit quia voverit. Immo vovet quia vadat,
cum votum non causa viae sit, sed via voti.
Ergo vovet vel se dudum vovisse fatetur,
140 forsitan in partu vel pro valitudine vera
seu commenticia, causasque perennat eundi.
Religione quidem lucrata fidem, sed eadem
est sibi peccandi captata licentia. Quo fit,
ut peccatricis excusativa fides et
145 audax peccandi fiducia sint ab eodem.
    Porro, si coitum furtivum, ut saepe, sequatur
fetus, semper eum tibi sponsus alet, quia semper

she cannot bear to have her joy delayed. She goes in and out 120
of her house, unadvisedly so, because, as long as she does
not take heed for herself, no one else can take heed for her,
as she wanders about in a blind frenzy.

A married woman is in certain respects less burdensome,
and yet in other respects presents greater dangers. A mar- 125
ried woman can move where, when, and however she wants.
If she is young, she influences like-minded young women, or
is influenced by them, and pretends that she is going to the-
atrical performances. If she is older, she pretends that she
must go to the marketplace to make many purchases, and
starting with trifles, progresses to bigger things, with her 130
husband footing the bill. But if she is not from humble cir-
cumstances, and it is not appropriate for her to concern her-
self with such things, she visits the shrines of the gods, set-
ting little store by the nearby ones, but preferring the more
distant. She delights in new journeys, and every day invents 135
gods and feigns miracles deserving of new devotion, where
she declares she will go. She does not go because she has
made a vow. Rather she makes a vow because she is going
there. The vow is not the cause of her excursion, but rather
the excursion is the cause of her vow. Therefore, she makes a
vow or says that she previously made a vow, perhaps in child- 140
birth or for an actual or feigned illness, and she continually
invents the reasons for her trips. Having acquired credibil-
ity by religious devotion, by that same devotion she has ob-
tained a license for sinning. So it happens that the credible
excuse of the sinner and her rash confidence in sinning 145
come from the same source.

Furthermore, if a child results from a secret affair, as is
often the case, her spouse will always raise it for you, be-

filius uxoris praesumitur esse mariti.
Econtra durum est sollemnizare quod ille
150 conculcat, sed et ex nupta poterit quis habere
maiores inimicitias, quia paelice laesa
non tantum dolet haec quam rivali magis ille.
Aegra sed indemnis iniuria provocat ipsum
armaque iusta movet. Qui, si praepossit, amanti
155 forte superveniens deprensoque et mutilato
purget adulterium, fiet commotio, risus
in populo, nec erit, qui compatiatur eidem
damna sui passo, nec iudex audiet ipsum.
    Ad viduam venio. Quae si tantum timeat, ne
160 concipiat, parat, unde sibi procuret aborsum,
immemorabilibus se potatura quibusdam,
ut nondum nati fiat miserabile bustum.
Vel si iam natus clamore repleverit auras
accusans matrem, subito perplexa stupore
165 et furiis agitata novis improvida stringit
aversis oculis teneri puerilia nati
guttura. Nec spirare licet, sed deficiente
aere non reperit, quid cordi pulmo ministret,
et moritur nondum gustato lacte parentis.
170 Pro scelus, o superi, fit, ut insons sentiat hostem
cuius pars uteri nuper fuit, ut prius inter
manes quam vivos habitet, prius experiatur
mortem quam vitam vix natus tempora complens
et matris peccata luens! Illi, hercule, quae sic
175 tractat inhumane sua viscera, me male credam,
quin irata mihi dando sit prona veneno!
    Di bene, pro foribus si quorumcumque deorum

cause the son of the wife is always presumed to be the son of the husband. On the other hand, it is hard to acknowledge something a husband despises, and a person will likely incur 150 greater hostility from sleeping with a married woman, because a woman does not lament the harm done by a mistress as much as a man deplores a rival lover. The painful but unavenged injury provokes him and moves him to wage just warfare. If he prevails, perhaps coming upon the lover, 155 whom he catches and mutilates, and so avenges the adultery, then there will be anger and ridicule from the people, nor will anyone feel compassion for him and the mutilation he has suffered nor will any judge listen to his case.

I come now to the widow. If she is so afraid that she might 160 conceive, she will prepare a means to procure an abortion by planning to dose herself with ingredients not to be mentioned, so that she may become a wretched tomb for the not yet born. Or perhaps a child has already filled the air with its cries, indicting its mother. If so, suddenly perplexed with astonishment and impelled by new fury, recklessly she averts 165 her eyes and chokes the delicate infant's young throat. It cannot breathe, and, since air is lacking, it finds nothing for the lungs to supply to the heart, and it dies without ever tasting its mother's milk. Alas, O gods, what villainy, that an 170 innocent should find her an enemy when it had just been a part of her womb, and that it should dwell among the dead before the living, experiencing death before life! Scarcely born, it ends its life, and pays for the sins of its mother! By Hercules, I'd hardly trust that a lover who treats her internal 175 organs so cruelly wouldn't be likely to give me poison when she is angry!

Gods willing, if the child had been crying, left at the

proiectus flesset, elemosina publica saltem
nutrivisset eum nullius et omnis alumnum!
180 Dic mihi crudelis, dic mater cruda, tyrannus
quid plus fecisset? Deeratne pater? Modo desit!
Numquid mater eras? Ubi tu? Non corpore deeras,
ut mater deeras! Utinam tu defueris! Nam
si sibi fatorum series utrumque parentem
185 subtraxisset, adhuc hodie superesset! At una,
quam natura sibi debebat ad omnia totam,
quae merito speranda fores sic tota futura
plus sua quam tua, quod materno foedere velles
nutricis gerulaeque vices supplere, fuisti
190 una inimica sibi confundens omnia iura.
   Felix, qui posset vitare pericula, sed qui
scandala vitaret, longe felicior esset.
Nam sicut melius mortali corpore nomen,
quod manet aeternum, sic sunt peiora periclis
195 scandala corporeis, cum sint contraria famae.
Felicissimus est igitur, qui vitat utrumque,
dum tamen optata possit quandoque potiri.
Ha, quantis voluit rationibus insinuare
naturae pater et dominus se velle, quod usque
200 propagarentur animalia! Nam quis amaret,
quis tantum appeteret nisi bruto ductus amore
tam foedum coitum, nisi delectatio tanta
tamque patens esset genitalibus indita membris!
Sed potuit, scivit, voluit tantam indere, nosque
205 o utinam cupiamus eam iuxta quod oportet!
   Legem naturae fixam ponamus, et illam
circumscribamus modo, quae positiva vocatur.
In qua peccabo, si fecero, quod prohibetur,

doors of any of the gods, at least the public almshouse would
have nurtured it, everyone's nursling and no one's! Tell me,   180
merciless and cruel mother, tell, what more would a tyrant
have done? Was the father absent? Let's say that's the case!
Were you not the mother? Where were you? You were not
absent in body but you were absent as a mother! If only you
had been absent! For if the course of fate had removed both
of its parents, it would still survive today! But you, the very   185
person whom nature bound to it in all respects, and who
rightly should be looking out for its future more than your
own since you should want to fulfill the roles of both wet
nurse and nanny because of the maternal bond, you alone   190
were hostile to it, confounding every law.

Fortunate is the man who can avoid dangers, yet the man
who can avoid scandals is much more fortunate. For just as
one's good name is better than the mortal body, because it
lasts forever, so scandals are worse than physical dangers,
because they destroy one's reputation. Most fortunate,   195
therefore, is the man who avoids both of these, while still
sometimes getting what he wants. Ha! With what excellent
reasons did the father and lord of nature choose to make
known his desire that living creatures should always repro-   200
duce! For who would make love, who would desire so filthy a
coupling, unless impelled by brute passion, and if a pleasure
so great and so manifest had not been planted in the genera-
tive organs! But he had the ability, the knowledge, and the
will to endow them with so much pleasure; and we—oh, if   205
only we could desire that pleasure as we should!

Let us posit that the law of nature is unchanging, and let
us now define that law which is called "positive." In such a
law, I will sin if I do what is forbidden, not because it is a sin,

non quia peccatum sit, sed quoniam prohibetur.
210 Rursum: praeceptum si negligo, non quia iustum,
sed quia praeceptum. Circumscripta modo tali
lege loquor, ne multa loquens immiscuerim quid,
quod contra legem possim dixisse videri.
    In votis tunc esse meis plerumque fatebar
215 felicem, si quis cognoscere posset amicam.
Dum laevum capiti submitteret ipse lacertum,
ipsa suum laevo lateri dextrum daret atque
molle femur, sed et una manus restaret utrique
libera, secretis tractatibus apta quibusdam,
220 pectora sic essent sibi iuncta, quod ubera pressam
cordis amatoris circumstarent regionem,
fomentum stimulans stimulumque datura foventem
ad meditativam coitu super evigilandam.
Oscula densa darent sibi colluctantibus inter
225 denticulos linguis dulcem sugente salivam
alterutro. Leni cum murmure, membraque membris
aptarent multisque modis multisque figuris
iuncti vagirent circumvolvendo sibi se
illecebrasque suas verbis augendo iocosis.
230 Seque observarent, ut neuter praeveniendus
a consorte foret vel praeventurus eundem,
quin simul ad Veneris lacrimas, quas motus amicus
elicit, adducti quasi commoriendo iacerent.
Iam velut exanimes facti cessare coactis
235 motibus et tanta victis dulcedine, quantam
tantorum completio dat desideriorum.
Iamque viderentur animas efflare vicissim
alter in alterius faciem virtute sepulta,
et tandem sensim redeunte resurgere vita

but because it is forbidden. Then again, I will also sin if I 210
disregard a rule, not because it is right, but because it is a
rule. I speak now of this law as I have defined it, so that I do
not say too much and so include something that I could
seem to have said contrary to this law.

Back then, I often used to declare in my vows that any-
one who was able to know a lover was lucky. When he places 215
his left arm under her head, she would set her right arm and
soft thigh against his left side, but both of them would keep
one hand free, ready for secret caresses, their chests would 220
be brought together in such a way that her breasts envelope
and press upon the place of her lover's heart, arousing a
warm response and soon to produce a warm arousal in him
to wake up his desire for intercourse. They would give each
other a forest of kisses, exchanging sweet saliva as their 225
tongues wrestle between their teeth. With a soft moaning,
limbs would adjust to limbs, and, entwining in many ways
and in many positions, they would cry out while wrapping
themselves around each other, increasing their arousal with
amorous talk. They would take care that neither could be 230
outstripped by the partner, or outstrip the partner; but
rather, being brought simultaneously to the tears of Venus,
which the pleasing motion produces, they would lie there as
if dying together. Now as if lifeless, they would be forced to 235
desist from their movements which had been urged on and
now overcome by as much ecstasy as the fulfillment of such
enormous desire gives. Then, they would seem to exhale
their last breath face to face in turn, their strength ex-
hausted, but at last, as life gradually returned, to rise up,

240 quamvis inviti mallentque fuisse morosam.
      Delicias istas et gaudia tanta docere
      nullus inexpertus posset nullusque doceri.
      Sed quia nulli sunt adeo consortia cara,
      quin aliquando velit consorte carere, iuvabat
245 nonnumquam solum spatioso me dare lecto.
         Et quia non semper domibus delectat inesse,
      mos erat interdum turba comitante meorum
      conspicuos phaleris in equos conscendere, fontes
      visere cum saltu de montis ventre scatentes
250 praecipiti rivo modo subvertente lapillum.
      Fructiferis et odoriferis versabar in hortis,
      olfactuque vagos florum venabar odores
      tempore vernali. Processu temporis undas
      fluminis intrabam; cumque essem plus gravis illis,
255 alterno motu me reddebam leviorem
      bracchia sic iactare sciens et crura movere,
      quod, quamvis gravior, quamvis undae leviores,
      lucrabar levibus graviorem me superesse.
      Et modo silvarum latebrae modo prata placebant,
260 nunc Bacchi Cererisve nemus, meditabar ubique,
      qualiter hic vel ibi iucunde vivere possem.
         Nam curis plerumque urgentibus ut relevarer,
      nunc volucrum turmis mihi mos erat insidiari,
      ventilabro moto passim sabulone ligato,
265 fila supertracturus eis, si forsitan illic
      oblectarentur; per equum deducere quasdam,
      donec in alatas caligas et pyramidales
      intrassent minime rediturae gesticulando;
      quasdam sicut agunt pastores cum ioculantur,

although unwillingly, and they would prefer that life's return 240
had been delayed. No one without experience of these plea-
sures and great joys could teach them, or be taught them.
But because no one's partners are so dear that he does not
sometimes wish to be without them, I occasionally took 245
pleasure in giving myself, alone, to my spacious bed.

And because I did not always want to stay at home, some-
times it was my custom to mount one of my horses fitted
with fine trappings in the company of my men, and to visit
the springs bubbling and leaping up from the belly of the
mountain, where the water flowing with headlong force 250
overturns the pebbles. In the springtime, I used to linger in
fragrant, fruit-bearing gardens and with my sense of smell
hunt the wafting perfume of flowers. With the advance of
the seasons, I would enter the water of the river, and al-
though I was heavier than it, I rendered myself lighter with 255
an alternating motion. I knew just how to throw forward my
arms and move my legs so that, although I was heavier and
the waters lighter, I managed to keep my heavier self above
its light waves. Sometimes I took pleasure in shaded forests,
sometimes in meadows, at other times in the groves of Bac- 260
chus and Ceres; wherever I was, I would contemplate how I
could live happily there.

For often in order to find relief from pressing concerns, it
was my habit at such times to set traps for flocks of birds.
With a winnowing fork put in place and sandy gravel scat-
tered about, I would be ready to draw nets over the birds, if 265
they happened to be attracted there. On horseback, I would
flush out some birds until they entered into wing nets and
pyramid traps and could not get out with their struggles.
Others I would flush out by moving around, as shepherds do

270   sicut et ad sistrum saltat lasciva puella,
      sicut multotiens agitur furiis agitatus,
      sicut iectigat is, cuius nervi resoluti;
      nunc quasdam laqueis, quasdam visco retinere,
      quarundam visus obtundere noctibus igne
275   ac improvisas involvere retibus illas;
      nunc avidis avibus pavidas terrere vel illas,
      quas fluvius vel quas ager aut nemus educat, hasque
      prendere, quas nec penna celer sublimat in altum
      nec nemus occultat nec aquae submersio salvat.
280   O quicumque pias furtiva fraude columbas
      talibus ingeniis aliisve quibusque fatigas,
      cultrices Veneris fecundas prole, gemellos
      omni mense fere sibi multiplicare potentes,
      questu viventes, vastare domestica parcas,
285   divitias mensae, quarum nec simplicitati
      parcis nec domini, cuius sunt, utilitati.
      Defers ovantes comedens, quarum cibus ori
      non sapit et stomachum male nutrit, durus utrique.
      Omnibus in templis anathemate percutiaris,
290   in quibus alma Venus colitur seu filius eius!
        Nunc mihi mos etiam venatum per nemus ire
      et strepitu cornuque cavo et mordacibus omnes
      sollicitare feras canibus vestigia doctis
      certa sequi et numquam mutaturis semel actam;
295   nunc illis arcere lupos, ut simplicitati
      parcatur timidarum ovium, vulpisque dolosae
      cautelas urgere vicemque rependere fraudi;
      armatosque metu lepores retrovertere, dammas

at play, as a wanton girl dances to the sistrum, as a man who 270
is frequently gripped by seizures of madness is agitated, or
as one who has lost control of his muscles flails about. Then
again I would catch some with nooses, others with birdlime.
At night, I would impede the vision of some with fire and 275
ensnare them unawares in nets. Using birds of prey, I would
frighten the timid birds that river, field, or grove breeds, and
would capture those that swift wings did not raise into the
air, or the grove did not hide, or diving into water did not
save.

O all of you who stealthily harass pious doves by such de- 280
vices or any others, birds who are Venus's devotees, prolific
of offspring and able to multiply themselves twofold nearly
every month, and living with a plaintive call—do not ravage
these domestic animals, the wealth of the table, for in doing 285
so you have no regard either for their innocence or the
profit of the lord who owns them. You carry them off and
eat them while they sing cheerfully, though a meal made of
these stolen birds does not taste good in the mouth and
does not properly nourish the stomach, being harsh to both
these parts. May you be struck down with a curse in every
temple in which holy Venus or her son is worshipped! 290

At another time, it was also my custom to go hunting
through the woods, and to rouse all of the wild beasts with
shouting, with the hollow horn, and with biting dogs trained
to follow definite tracks and once in chase never to let up.
Sometimes with these dogs I used to ward off wolves to 295
spare the innocence of timid sheep, and to challenge the
trickery of the crafty fox and to pay him back for his cun-
ning. I used to make the hares, whose defense was their fear,
turn tail, or I might quickly fatigue the cowardly deer or

ignavas lassare cito, capreasque fugaces
300 prendere, dum caput occultant nullumque videntes
arbitrantur et a nullo se posse videri;
nunc ad cuniculum foveae munimine tutum
mittere furonem, qui dente lacessiat ipsum,
donec in insidias praetensas retiolorum
305 se stimulatus agat male cautus ab obsidione;
nunc baculis brevibus clavellosae capitatis
confisos levitate sua promptosque salire
de ramo in ramum cyrogrillos diiaculare;
nunc quoque praecipites inconsulteque ruentes
310 exspectare sues, quos in venabula torrens
impetus atque furor agit et temerarius ausus;
nunc cervum celerem succinctum cruribus altis
per densos veprium ramos ramosa ferentem
cornua et, auditum quod terruerat, repetentem
315 vel morsu retinere canum, vel aquas adeuntem.
      Cum longo cursu iam deficit alitus oris
speque renascendi seque ut refrigeret, haurit,
non quod eum reparetve fuge reparetve labori,
sed quod sic fauces sitibundas impleat, ut non
320 confortetur eo sua virtus, immo voluntas
inconsulta quidem, nam quod sorbetur ab illo,
torporem generat, cum quaerere debeat illa,
quae faciant agilem, tunc mos violenter adire,
ut vel se reddat ripae canibus lacerandum
325 vel mediis mersus succumbat aquis redimendo
morte metum mortis, gravior qui morte quibusdam;
vel certe, postquam nuper per opaca repertum
excivere canes, vestitum fronde latere,
qua sperabat eum venator praeteriturum,

catch the fleeing wild goats as they hid their heads and 300
thought that they could be seen by no one because they saw
no one. Sometimes I would set a ferret on a rabbit, other-
wise safely protected in its hole, to snap at it with its teeth,
until the tormented rabbit, unaware of a trap, was driven 305
into the net I had previously set across the opening. At
other times I used to hurl short cudgels whose heads were
studded with little nails at squirrels which, trusting in their
own agility, were quick to jump from branch to branch.
Sometimes, I would lie in wait for boars' headlong and rash
charge whose rushing attack, rage, and reckless daring 310
drives them upon the hunting spears. Sometimes, I would
catch with biting dogs the swift, high-stepping stag, carry-
ing its branching horns through branches and thickets, ei-
ther as it tried to run away, alerted by some sound, or as it 315
approached the water.

For, when a stag loses its breath after a long chase, it
drinks in the hope of refreshing and restoring itself, not to
recover itself for more flight and struggle, but to fill its
parched throat, with the result that its strength is not forti- 320
fied by it. On the contrary, its desire to drink is unwise in-
deed, for what it drinks produces sluggishness, when it
should be seeking what makes it agile. At that precise mo-
ment, it is my custom to strike with such fury that it either
returns to the bank to be torn apart by the dogs or succumbs 325
to drowning in the midst of the waters, purchasing with
death escape from the fear of death, which for certain crea-
tures is worse than death itself. Or at least, soon after the
dogs had found it in the shadows and roused it out, I might
hide, concealed in the foliage where the hunter expected it

330 exspectareque, dum veniat, certaque sagitta
figere moxque canis gustato sanguine naso
credere, sicque sequi, quoadusque cubilia tandem
intraret fessus, quibus inventus caperetur,
ne moreretur inutilis in lustris sed in aula.
335 Praeterita iam morte nihil sensurus adesset
festivus, quia iam tutus, quia mors semel usa
iure suo non plus in idem fungetur eodem.
    Nunc et erat mihi mos pisces captare marinos,
retibus hos, illos hamis, illosque sagena,
340 alatis quosdam caligis in pyramidalem
conum protensis. Etiam nunc ad fluviales
me convertebam connexis vimine quosdam
decipiens calathis, ubi cederet ingredienti
virgula flexibilis pisci reditumque paranti
345 mordax eiusdem cuspis praeacuta negaret,
quosdam decipiens aliquando tenacibus hamis
vermibus allicitos, quosdam per linea fila
nodosis connexa modis involvere gnarus,
dum lignumque supernatat et plumbum petit ima,
350 neve vel aeriam saliens approximet oram
vel fodiens in visceribus limi peregrinet
illudens nobis alienis ex elementis;
et nunc anguillas tonitru terrente minaci
attonitas et aquae se praecipitantis in arcam
355 cursum sectantes servare manu capiendas,
nunc et dentato transfigere pectine visas
cum face succensa nitidis de nocte sub undis.
    Sontibus a curis per talia me relevabam
solos evitans decios, quibus alliciuntur
360 multimode multi, de quo super omnia miror.

to pass by, and I would wait for it to come, then shoot it with 330
an unerring arrow. Then I rely on the dog's nose soon smell-
ing blood, so I can follow until the exhausted deer finally
enters its den, where it can be found and taken, so that it
does not die uselessly in the wild but in the banquet hall.
Once death has passed, with nothing left to feel, it would be 335
happy, because now it is safe, since death, having taken its
due once, will never claim it again.

It was also my custom, at times, to capture sea fish, some
with nets, some with hooks, and some with a seine; others I 340
caught with winged leather extended into a pyramidal cone.
At other times, I also turned my attention to river fish,
tricking some with baskets woven from wicker, in which a
pliant withe gives way to the fish as it enters, while its 345
sharply pointed tip prevents the fish from leaving when it
tries to leave. Others I sometimes tricked by luring them
with worms set on barbed hooks; still others I was good at
reeling in by means of linen threads tied with knots, while
the wooden float bobs on the water and the lead sinker
plumbs the depths, so that the fish do not approach air level 350
by leaping or disappear in the depths of the mud by digging,
and so mock us from foreign elements. I also sometimes
used to track eels that, when stunned and terrified by threat-
ening thunder, follow the course of the water driving them 355
headlong into a box so that they might be caught by hand.
At other times, I transfixed with a toothed fishing spear the
ones I saw at night with a burning torch under the gleaming
waves.

Through such activities I relieved myself of my sinful
concerns, avoiding only dice games to which many men are
variously attracted; I marvel at this above all things. What 360

Quis furor est homines exponere sic sua sorti,
cum solus casus in talibus inveniatur!
Unde venire potest, hominem quod taliter urat
tantus amor ludi tamque irrefragabilis ardor?
365 Quid tibi cum numeris? Quid habet numerus numero plus?
Quid curas, prior alteruter veniat numerorum?
Mirari non sufficio; quaero undique causam,
non tamen invenio, nisi quod praetendo sequaces
ludi lucrandi solius odore moveri
370 in summo cupidos aliterque acquirere segnes
et demum fures, si possit adesse facultas.

    Vidi multotiens ego de patre paupere natum
multiplicasse sibi nummismata, multiplicasse
divitias alias et agros agris cumulasse
375 atque domos domibus. Vidi contraria: nam cui
predecessores acquisierant bona multa,
omnia dispergens lusor temulentus adulter
omnia paulatim vendebat et omnibus usus
tandem ad egestatem supremam deveniebat.
380 Vidi nonnullum, cuius possessio multa,
nec dispergebat vendendo taliter illam,
sed minus incaute faciebat deteriorem:
Forsitan in domibus plumbo tectis habitabat,
ostia de ferro sibi, de ferroque fenestrae,
385 pro plumbo lateres mutabat, ferrea vendi
atque saligna loco poni faciebat eorum;
expensurus erat, quod de pretio remanebat.

    Quem consuetudo mala difficilisque relinqui
vini potandi maturos duxit ad annos
390 et bona dispergit pro consuetudine tali,
quod delectat, habet, aliquatenus excusatur.

madness it is that men thus entrust their fortunes to chance, when only misfortune is to be found in such games! How is it that so great a love of gambling and so irresistible a passion can consume a man in such a way? Why concern yourself with numbers? How can one number be worth more than another? Why do you care which of two numbers comes first? I am not content just to marvel; I seek an explanation everywhere, yet I do not find it except that I allege that devotees of gaming are excited by the scent only of winning, greedy in the extreme, too lazy to earn money in any other fashion, and ultimately would be thieves, if they ever had the chance.

I myself often have seen the son of an impoverished father multiply his cash holdings, multiply his other sources of wealth, and accumulate fields upon fields and houses upon houses. I also have seen the opposite: a man whose ancestors had acquired great wealth losing it all—a drunken, lecherous gambler—selling his possessions piece by piece, and finally, having used up all his resources, sinking to the ultimate poverty. I have seen quite a few men who had considerable property not dispersing it entirely by selling it in such a way, but, by being too heedless, still diminishing it. If such men happened to be living in houses with lead roofs and iron doors and windows, they would substitute tile for the lead and have the ironwork sold and replaced with osier, planning to spend the resulting profit.

If someone has reached old age accompanied by the bad but hard-to-quit habit of drinking wine and wastes his possessions to satisfy such a habit, then at least he has something that gives him pleasure and so he is to some extent

Qui vero facit hoc, optatum ut pascat amorem,
ut, cui forma deest desuntque moventia verba,
saltem muneribus cara potiatur amica,
395 quod delectat, habet, aliquatenus excusatur.
Sed qui pro ludo sua dispergit, nihil unde
excusetur habet, nihil est insanius ipso.
Mercator prudens non semper, non ubicumque
vel vendit vel emit merces quascumque, sed illas
400 vendit tunc vel ibi, quando carae vel ubi sunt,
et, quando vel ubi viles, emit has ibi vel tunc
cognoscitque bonas, et inest industria multa;
sed locus et tempus desunt lusoribus et res,
quae fieri possit modo vilis vel modo cara.
405   Forte tamen dices quosdam praestare quibusdam
ex numeris, quibus est lusoribus usus, eo quod,
cum decius sit sex laterum sex et numerorum
simplicium, tribus in deciis sunt octo decemque,
quorum non nisi tres possunt deciis superesse.
410 Hi diversimode variantur, et inde bis octo
compositi numeri nascuntur, non tamen aequae
virtutis, quoniam maiores atque minores
ipsorum raro veniunt mediique frequenter
et reliqui, quanto mediis quavis propiores
415 tanto praestantes et saepius advenientes;
his punctatura tantum venientibus una,
illis sex, aliis mediocriter inter utrosque,
sic ut sint duo maiores totidemque minores,
una quibus sit punctatura duoque sequentes,
420 hic maior, minor ille, quibus sit bina duobus,
rursum post istos sit terna, deinde quaterna

excused. Moreover, if someone does the same to satisfy his
sexual desire so that, although he lacks beauty and seductive
words, he may at least win over his desired girlfriend with
gifts, then he has something that gives him pleasure and so   395
he is to some extent excused. But if someone wastes his pos-
sessions on gambling, for this he has no excuse, and nothing
is crazier than that. The prudent merchant does not sell
goods at any time or anywhere or buy just any goods, but
rather sells those goods at the time or place when or where   400
they are in demand. He buys them at the time or place when
or where they are cheap, recognizing their worth, and he
practices great diligence. But gamblers have no such place
and time and capital, since it can sometimes turn out worth-
less and sometimes valuable.

Yet perhaps you will say that certain of the numbers used   405
by players are superior to others, since, although a die con-
sists of six sides and just six numbers, on three dice there are
eighteen, of which only three can be on top of the dice.
These vary in different ways, and from these sixteen num-   410
bers different compound numbers arise, but not of equal
worth, because the higher and lower combinations happen
rarely, the middle ones frequently, and as for the rest, the
closer they are in any way to the middle ones, the better   415
they are and the more frequently they occur. The higher and
lower numbers occur only with one configuration of the
dice, the middle ones happen with six, and the rest happen
with configurations between these two, such that there are
two larger compound numbers and exactly as many smaller
ones that have a single configuration of dice. The two com-
pound numbers that follow—one larger, one smaller—each   420
have two configurations of dice. Again, after these, there are

165

quinaque, sicut eis succedunt appropiando
quattuor ad medios, quibus est punctatio sena;
quae reddet leviora tibi subiecta tabella:

```
18 666  —    631 622 541 532 442 433 10
17 665  —    621 531 522 441 432 333  9
16 664 655   —   611 521 431 422 332  8
15 663 654 555   —   511 421 331 223  7
14 662 653 644 554   —   411 321 222  6
13 661 652 643 553   —    —  311 221  5
12 651 642 633 552 543 444  —  211    4
11 641 632 551 542 632 443  —  111    3
```

425   Hi sunt sex et quinquaginta modi veniendi,
nec numerus minor esse potest vel maior eorum;
nam quando similes fuerint sibi tres numeri, qui
iactum componunt, quia sex componibiles sunt,
et punctaturae sunt sex, pro quolibet una;
430   sed cum dissimilis aliis est unus eorum
atque duo similes, triginta potest variari
punctatura modis, quia si duplicaveris ex sex
quemlibet adiuncto reliquorum quolibet, inde
produces triginta quasi sex quintuplicatis;
435   quodsi dissimiles fuerint omnino sibi tres,
tunc punctaturas viginti connumerabis,
hoc ideo, quia continui possunt numeri tres
quattuor esse modis, discontinui totidem, sed
si duo continui fuerint discontinuusque
440   tertius, invenies hinc tres bis et inde duos ter,
quod tibi declarat oculis subiecta figura:

compound numbers with three, then four, then five configurations, as they follow them in succession, approaching the four compound numbers in the middle, which have six configurations. The following table will demonstrate this to you more easily:

18	666	—	631	622	541	532	442	433	10
17	665	—	621	531	522	441	432	333	9
16	664	655	—	611	521	431	422	332	8
15	663	654	555	—	511	421	331	223	7
14	662	653	644	554	—	411	321	222	6
13	661	652	643	553	—	—	311	221	5
12	651	642	633	552	543	444	—	211	4
11	641	632	551	542	632	443	—	111	3

These are the fifty-six ways for the numbers to fall, and there can be neither a lower nor a higher number of them; for whenever the three numbers that make up the throw are the same (since there are six numbers that can be put together) there are six configurations, one for each number. But when one is not the same as the others, and two are the same, the configuration can vary in thirty ways, because, if you double any of the six numbers, and add any of the numbers that remain, then you will come up with thirty, as if you multiply six by five. But if all three numbers are different, then you will count twenty configurations for this reason: because three numbers can be successive in four ways, and nonsuccessive in four ways, but if two numbers are successive and a third is nonsuccessive, you will find from the one side six ways and from the other side also six, as the figure set before your eyes demonstrates:

425

430

435

440

666	555	444	333	222	111	665
664	663	662	661	556	554	553
552	551	446	445	443	442	441
336	335	334	332	331	226	225
224	223	221	116	115	114	113
112	654	543	432	321	642	641
631	531	653	652	651	621	521
421	542	541	643	631	632	532

Rursum sunt quaedam subtilius inspicienti
de punctaturis, quibus una cadentia tantum est,
suntque, quibus sunt tres aut sex, quia schema cadendi
445 tunc differre nequit, quando similes fuerint tres
praedicti numeri. Si vero sit unus eorum
dissimilis similesque duo, tria schemata surgunt
dissimili cuicumque superposito deciorum.
Sed si dissimiles sunt omnes, invenies sex
450 verti posse modis, quia quaelibet ex tribus uni
cum dederis, reliqui duo permutant loca, sicut
punctaturarum docet alternatio, sicque
quinquaginta modis et sex diversificantur
in punctaturis, punctaturaeque ducentis
455 atque bis octo cadendi schematibus. Quibus inter
compositos numeros, quibus est lusoribus usus,
divisis, prout inter eos sunt distribuenda,
plene cognosces, quantae virtutis eorum
quilibet esse potest seu quantae debilitatis,
460 quod subscripta potest tibi declarare figura.

666 555 444 333 222 111 665
664 663 662 661 556 554 553
552 551 446 445 443 442 441
336 335 334 332 331 226 225
224 223 221 116 115 114 113
112 654 543 432 321 642 641
631 531 653 652 651 621 521
421 542 541 643 631 632 532

Again, there are some—upon closer inspection of the configurations—which have only one way of falling, and some which have three or six, because the ways of falling cannot be different when the three numbers concerned are the same. But if one of them is different and the other two are the same, three ways of falling arise when a different number turns up on top of any of the dice. But if they are all unalike, you will discover that they can turn out in six ways, because when you give any position to one of the three, the other two change positions, just as the alternation of the configurations shows. And so the numbers are varied in fifty-six configurations of the dice, and the configurations are varied in 216 ways of falling. When these have been divided among the compound numbers that gamblers need—inasmuch as they must be distributed among them—you will learn fully how great a gain or how great a loss any of them is able to be. The figure below can make this clear to you.

445

450

455

460

Quot punctaturas et quot cadentias habeat quilibet
numerorum compositorum:

3	18	punctatura	1	cadentia	1
4	17	punctatura	1	cadentiae	3
5	16	punctaturae	2	cadentiae	6
6	15	punctaturae	3	cadentiae	10
7	14	punctaturae	4	cadentiae	15
8	13	punctaturae	5	cadentiae	21
9	12	punctaturae	6	cadentiae	25
10	11	punctaturae	6	cadentiae	37

Non igitur solus ibi casus inest; ego vero
dico tibi brevibus casu non posse carere,
quod tibi vel socio concedat sors meliorem.
Respondes, quod inest ludo ingenium iaciendi
465 excludens casum, sed ad hoc etiam tibi dico:
Si recte iacias, modicum valet, ac aliter quam
recte si iacias, furtum committis, eo quod
a ludi socio comperto probra sequuntur:
iuratur temere, blasphemia multiplicatur.
470 Post probra percutitur cum pugno, dilaniantur
crines, cultelli sequitur temerarius ictus.
Solus inest casus, quem non sequitur nisi stultus!
    Quodsi fortunam dicas, fortuna coaequa
non erit erga omnes individuos, quia, si tu
475 fortunatus es, est te fortunatior alter,
nec potes ante omnes fortunatissimus esse
nec scis fortunas hominum. Concluditur ergo,
quod redit ad casum, quem non sequitur nisi stultus.
Adde, quod in multis ludis quicumque lucratur
480 non solus sua lucra refert—dabit undique, si non

An enumeration of the configurations and ways of falling any of the compound numbers can have:

3,	18:	1 configuration,	1	way of falling
4,	17:	1 configuration,	3	ways of falling
5,	16:	2 configurations,	6	ways of falling
6,	15:	3 configurations,	10	ways of falling
7,	14:	4 configurations,	15	ways of falling
8,	13:	5 configurations,	21	ways of falling
9,	12:	6 configurations,	25	ways of falling
10,	11:	6 configurations,	37	ways of falling

Therefore, not chance alone is involved; but, I tell you, briefly, that it is not possible to abolish chance, because the lot may grant better fortune to you or to a fellow player. You will reply that in the game there is an inherent skill to throwing that excludes chance, but to this I also say to you: if you 465 throw legitimately, it is of little value, and if you throw in any way other than legitimately, you commit fraud and, once it has been discovered by a fellow player of the game, insults follow: rash oaths are sworn, and slanders multiply. After the 470 insults, punches are thrown, hair is torn out, and the reckless thrust of a dagger follows. It's all a matter of chance, which none but an idiot pursues.

But if you call it fortune, not all will enjoy equal fortune, because, if you are fortunate, there is another more fortu- 475 nate than you, and you cannot be the most fortunate of all or know the fortunes of men. The inescapable conclusion is that it goes back to chance, which none but a fool pursues. Also consider that in many games, whoever wins does not 480 keep his profits to himself—he will announce them in every

dyscolus est, et ei circumstans quisque nocebit;
quodsi perdiderit, non inveniet relevantem.
Unde fit, ut si non plures fortuna sequatur
ludos, non poterit ludorum evadere damna.
485 Addeque, quod lusor se continuare lucrando
nescit, perdendo nescit dimittere ludum.
Si fatum ponas, fatui, qui fata sequuntur;
nam posito fato libertas arbitrii non
esset, sed libertas est aliquid, nihil ergo
490 est fatum fatuum; fatui, qui fata sequuntur—
solus inest casus, quem non sequitur nisi stultus.
Non dico me non lusisse, sed omnia libres,
quae vel lucratus fuerim casuve sinistro
perdiderim, summam si de maiore minorem
495 diminuas, non invenies solidum remanere.
   Excusare tamen speciem ludi deciorum
nituntur, cum qua deducitur alea pernix,
ipsam dicentes pauco discrimine rerum
pasci posse diu—tanta est dilatio ludi,
500 tanta lucri damnive mora est. Successio cuius
tot parit eventus, quot iactus continet in se
fine tenus ludus. Nec sola sorte, sed arte
procedunt acies et inest industria mira,
praesertim cum multimode mutatio ludi
505 quolibet in iactu disponi possit, eo quod,
sicut praecessit iactus, diversificantur
in punctatura propriae, quia schema cadendi
nil operatur in hoc, sed punctatura docet, quid
lusoris faciat viso sollertia iactu.
510 Quomodo militiam disponat, ibi legit, unde
transferat et qua quam vel quas ter quinque suarum,

direction, unless he is ill tempered, and everyone around will do him harm. But if he loses his winnings, he will find no one to relieve him. So it happens that if he does not enjoy good fortune in a number of games, he will not be able to escape losses from his gaming. Consider too that the gam- 485 bler does not know how to maintain his luck when winning and does not know how to abandon a game when losing. If you assume fate exists, only fools rely on fate; for if there were fate, there would be no free will, but there is free will to some extent, therefore foolish fate is nothing. Only fools 490 rely on fate—chance alone is involved, which none but an idiot pursues. I'm not saying that I have never played, but you could weigh evenly everything that I have won or lost through bad luck; if you were to subtract the lesser sum from the greater, you won't find a single penny remaining. 495

Yet some strive to excuse a kind of dice game in which the swift throw of the dice is prolonged, saying that it can be sustained for a long time with little risk to resources; for as long as the game lasts, profit or loss is postponed. The prog- 500 ress of the game produces as many outcomes as the throws of which the game is comprised from start to finish. Engagements proceed not through chance alone, but through skill, and there is wondrous scheming involved—especially since a change in the course of the game can be brought about in 505 many ways on any throw, because, at each successive throw, each player's possibilities are diversified in accordance with the configuration of the dice, because the way that they fall has no effect in this situation; rather, the configuration shows what the skill of the player can accomplish once he has seen the throw. In that configuration the player reads 510 how he should arrange his army, from where and in what

et combinat eas, ne si capiantur ab hoste
solivagae, cogantur, ut ad sua castra recurrant
et numeros perdant impensos, solivagasque
515 hostiles capit ad sua castra recurrere cogens
damnificansque hostem numeris quibus egerat illas.
    Districtusque praeoccupat angustatque meatus,
ut pateat via tuta suis ad circueundum
atque negetur eis, quibus adversarius uti
520 debet; sed postquam praecluserit omnia neve
descendat series sua praecipitantius aequo,
exponit quasdam capiendas sponte suarum,
ut renovet sursumque reciprocet obsidionem
restauretque suam, si rupta est forte, catenam,
525 donec tot teneat captivas quot recipi vix
possent in castris, etiamsi castra vacarent,
vel donec, quae transierant, ita praecipitatae
sint vel dissutae, quod non possent retinere
si quam captivam regredi contingeret illuc.
530   Non tamen ad votum numeri succedere iacti
saepe solent, sed destruitur series magis uno
perverso iactu, quam multis restituatur.
Unde fit, ut dubio casu victoria nutet
et confundantur spes et metus ac subigatur
535 qui quasi victor erat, desperatusque resurgat.
Permutentque vices faciles hinc inde triumphi
spe sterili vanoque metu, dum concutiuntur
seque subalternant modo victores modo victi.
Verum quantumcumque iuvet deducere pulchre

direction he should transfer which checker or checkers (of the fifteen he has), and how he should combine them so that they are not caught by the enemy wandering singly and forced to return to their camp with considerable losses. The 515 player too captures enemy pieces wandering singly, forcing them to return to their camp and penalizing the enemy by as many pieces as he has taken.

He is intent on being first to occupy and limit the passages, so that a safe route for encircling is open to his checkers and is denied to those which his opponent must use. But 520 as soon as he has blocked off everything, and so that his chain does not fall away more quickly than it should, he voluntarily exposes certain of his checkers to be captured, so that he can recover and repeat the blockade from below and restore his barrier, if it happens to have been broken, until 525 he holds as many captives as could scarcely be received in the camp, even if the camp were empty; or until those that had already gone across have been so reduced or scattered that they could not hold fast if it were to happen that some captive returned there.

Yet the rolled numbers do not usually follow as desired, 530 and the chain is ruined by one bad throw more completely than it is restored by many throws. Hence it happens that victory is in the balance, subject to the uncertainty of chance, hope and fear are confused, and the one who was on 535 the cusp of winning is overthrown, while the player who had given up hope rises again. Victory readily reverses itself from one to another, making hope futile and fear groundless, as long as the players are liable to shocks and alternate with each other, sometimes as winners and sometimes as losers. However gratifying it is to skillfully advance

540 militiam ludi vel quantum succubuisse
ludendo pudeat, quantum quoque pascere ludum
pro modico liceat vel fortuitu sine damno,
quantum se recreent quantove levamine curas
tempus inutiliter ducendo fallere possint,
545 finalis tamen est lusorum intentio lucrum.
Cuius habe signum, quod ad infortunia nullus
sic debacchatur lusor tantove furore
torquetur, quin mox sua defervesceret ira,
si, qui lucra tulit, sibi perdita reddere vellet;
550 nec minus immodici quam multi perditione
rixant inter se, sed iurant turpiter, immo
nomina blasphemant, quae non meruere, deorum.
    O mortale genus, quae te vesania pulsat!
Compellesne deos contraria velle? Quod optat
555 alter lusorum, reliquo non posse placere
constat, et alterutrum, si curant talia, laedent
atque ita non poterunt evadere turpia verba
alterutrius eorum, cum nulla ratione
possit utrique satisfieri. Tu, qui modo perdis,
560 dic mihi: Quid debent tibi di plus quam socio? Dic:
Si tibi fortunam ludi dare noluerint di,
quid de iure tuo minuunt? Iniuria nulla est
non dare. Debueras potius sibi grata negare
tura pari poena purgando negata negatis!
565 Si tamen ex aequo cum dis contendere fas est,
at, quasi sis laesus, laedis quantum potes armis,
si posses laesurus eos: Dic, improbe, linguam
quis docuit formare sonos, quibus egrederetur
mens tua cum velles? Numquid ratio? Rationem

one's men to victory in the game, or shameful to concede 540
defeat in playing, and however much one can delight in the
game for a small wager or with luck without a loss, however
much players enjoy the recreation or however great the re-
lief they can find in escaping their worries by whiling away
their time in idle pursuits, nonetheless, the ultimate aim of 545
gamblers is profit. Here is evidence of this: no gambler is so
enraged by his misfortunes or tormented by so much fury
that his anger is not soon assuaged if the person who carried
away the prize wishes to return his losses to him. Nor are 550
they less extravagant than the many who quarrel among
themselves at their ruin, and swear viciously, even cursing
the names of the gods, who don't deserve it!

O human race, what madness assails you! Will you drive
the gods to favor contradictory things? What one of the
gamblers wants clearly cannot please the other, and if the 555
gods concern themselves with such things, they will offend
one of the two players, and so won't be able to avoid the foul
words of the other one, since in no way is it possible for both
to be satisfied. You—the one who is losing now—tell me: 560
why are the gods obliged to you, rather than your compan-
ion? Tell me: if the gods don't wish to give you success in the
game, in what way do they infringe on your rights? There is
no injustice in not giving. You ought rather to deny them the
incense they value, with an equal penalty paying back denial
with denial! If, however, it is right to contend with the gods 565
on an equal footing, well then, do as much harm as you can
with your weapons, as if you were harmed, if you could
indeed harm them. Tell me, you rogue, who taught your
tongue to form the sounds by which you give expression to
your thoughts whenever you wish? Was it not reason? Who

570 quis dedit absque deo? Quisquis fuit ille deorum,
tu vero nullum excipiens, ingrate, lacessis
igne venenato linguae communiter omnes,
tu brutis miserabilior, quia bruta datorem
laudarent, si posse loqui deus ille dedisset!
575 Sicque tibi non posse loqui melius fuit. Ergo
vel tu blasphemare deos vel ludere cessa!

    Est alius ludus scaccorum ludus, Ulixis
ludus, Troiana quem fecit in obsidione,
ne vel taederet proceres in tempore treugae
580 vel belli, si qui pro vulneribus remanerent
in castris; ludus, qui castris assimulatur.
Inventor cuius mire laudandus in illo est,
sed causam laudis non advertunt nisi pauci.
Quam subtile fuit species sex praemeditari
585 saltus in campis, quos tantum multiplicare
possemus, quod ab initio nulli duo ludi
omnino similes fuerint. Advertite pauci,
quod sicut vultus hominum sibi dissimilantur
hactenus in tantum, quod non fuerint duo, qui non
590 distingui possent, cum tantae disparitatis
causa sit in caelo, quia caeli nulla figura
est alii similis: tanta alternatio motus,
quem septem faciunt per bis sex signa planetae.
Et tamen est numerus finitus motibus ipsis,
595 sicut et astrorum domini scripsisse leguntur.
Sic ludus factus motus caelestis ad instar
est ex finitis saltus speciebus in agris,
infinita tamen est multiplicatio ludi.

    Sex species saltus exercent sex quoque scacci,
600 miles et alphinus, roccus, rex, virgo pedesque.

gave you reason, if not a god? Whichever god it was, you make an exception of none of them but, ingrate, you attack all of them together with the poisonous fire of your tongue! You are more wretched than the dumb beasts, because they would praise the giver, if that god had given them the ability to speak! And so, it would be better if you did not have the ability to speak! Therefore, either stop blaspheming the gods or stop gambling! 570 575

There is another game, the game of chess, Ulysses's game, which he invented during the siege of Troy, so that the nobles would not grow bored in the period of truce, or in wartime, if they were remaining in the camp on account of wounds—the game is itself similar to a military camp. Its inventor should be praised highly for it, but only a few perceive the real reason it should be praised. How exquisite it was to come up with the six types of move on the board, which we can multiply to such an extent that, right from the start, no two games are similar at all. You enlightened few, observe that, similarly, the faces of men are so very different from each other that there are no two that cannot be distinguished, for the cause of such disparity lies in the heavens because no configuration of the heavens is similar to any other. So great is the variation of movement which the seven planets produce through the twelve signs of the zodiac! And yet those movements have a finite number, as can be read in the writings of the authorities on the stars. Thus, the game was made in imitation of heavenly motion with limited possibilities of moves on the board, yet the game's variety is infinite. 580 585 590 595

Six pieces make the six types of move: knight, *aufin,* rook, king, maiden, and pawn. Into the first space move three of 600

In campum primum de sex istis saliunt tres:
rex, pedes et virgo; pedes in rectum salit atque
virgo per obliquum, rex saltu gaudet utroque.
Ante retroque tamen tam rex quam virgo moventur,
605 ante pedes solum capiens obliquus in ante,
cum tamen ad metam stadii percurrerit, ex tunc
sicut virgo salit. In campum vero secundum
tres alii saliunt: in rectum roccus, eique
soli concessum est ultra citraque salire,
610 oblique salit alphinus, sed miles utroque
saltum componit. Caeli veniamus ad instar!
    Campos, signa, modos saliendi, scito, planetas:
rex est Sol, pedes est Saturnus, Mars quoque miles,
regia virgo Venus, alphinus episcopus ipse est
615 Iuppiter, et roccus discurrens Luna. Quid ergo
Mercurius? Numquid non omnibus omnia? Certe
omnia Mercurius, cuius complexio semper
est convertibilis ad eum, cui iungitur ipse,
sicut et astrorum domini scripsisse leguntur;
620 aut quia Mercurii complexio frigida sicca
sicut Saturni, licet intense minus, ex quo
pervenit ad metam pedes, extunc Mercurii fit,
praesertim quia tunc salit ut virgo. Venerisque
Mercuriique locus doctrina quaeritur una,
625 et medius cursus est idem semper eorum,
sicut et astrorum domini scripsisse leguntur.
Nobilis hic ludus nulli suspectus et omni
personae licitus, moderate dummodo ludat,
dummodo quaeratur victoria sola per ipsam,

the six: king, pawn, and maiden; the pawn moves in a straight line, the maiden on the diagonal, and the king enjoys both types of move. While both the king and the maiden are moved both forward and backward, the pawn is 605 moved only forward, capturing along the forward diagonal. However, as soon as the pawn reaches the end of the board, from then on, he moves like the maiden. But the three others move into the second space. The rook moves in a straight line and it alone is allowed to move a greater or a shorter distance, the *aufin* moves on the diagonal, while the knight 610 combines both moves. Let us go on to the game's resemblance to the heavens.

Know, then, that the board, the pieces, and the ways of moving are the planets: the king is the Sun, the pawn is Saturn, Mars is the knight, the royal maiden is Venus, the *aufin*, himself a bishop, is Jupiter, and the roaming rook is the 615 Moon. What is Mercury, if not all things for everyone? Certainly, Mercury is everything. Its constitution is always changeable to the one to which it is joined, as is read in the writings of the authorities on the stars. Or, since the consti- 620 tution of Mercury is cold and dry, like that of Saturn, although less intensely so, for this reason, when the pawn comes to the end of the board, it becomes "mercurial," particularly because then it moves like the maiden. The position of Venus and of Mercury is ascertained by a single principle, and they always follow the same middle course, as 625 again is read in the writings of the authorities on the stars. This noble game is viewed with alarm by no one and is permitted to all, provided they play with moderation, and so long as victory is obtained only for its own sake,

630 non lucrum, ne cum praedictis annumeretur.
Cum deciis autem qui primus lusit in illo,
foedavit ludum; languebit namque satelles
immotus, nisi sors deciorum moverit ipsum,
nec fuit hoc factum nisi vel, quia non nisi pauci
635 ludere noverunt tractim, vel amore lucrandi!
     Sunt alii ludi parvi, quos scire puellas
esse decens dixi, sed parva monere pudebat,
nuncque magis quam tunc pudet illa minora referre.
Quare praetereo ludos, ubi parva lapillos
640 nunc bis sex, nunc vero novem capit una tabella.
Ac ubi sunt bis sex, capit ex hostilibus illum,
ultra quem salit alteruter, nec ibi deciorum
exigitur iactus. Ubi vero novem, bene ludunt
cum deciis et eis sine quando volunt, capit autem
645 unum quem mavult ex hostibus iste vel ille,
quandocumque potest tres continuare suorum.
Istos et similes, nec enim modo prosequar omnes,
praetereo ludos veniens ad nobiliores.
     O utinam ludus sciretur rithmimachiae,
650 ludus arithmeticae folium, flos, fructus et eius
gloria, laus et honor, quia totam colligit in se!
Ludus, ubi bellum disponitur ordine miro,
campis in geminis congressio fit numerorum
quattuor imparium, qui sunt in limite primo,
655 cum totidem paribus, qui limite sunt in eodem.
Principio numeri numeris non connumerato
octoque sunt isti patres utriusque cohortis
auxiliatoris, nam parti dantur utrique
prima multiplices, quia ducto quolibet in se

not for profit, so that it is not reckoned among the games I   630
spoke of before. But, whoever first involved dice in this
game corrupted it; for his chess piece will languish un-
moved, unless the lot of the dice moves it. And this only
happened either because just a few knew how to play at   635
length, or because of the love of gambling!

There are other minor games, which I have said are ap-
propriate for girls to know, though I was ashamed to teach
such unimportant things, and now, even more than then, I
am ashamed to bring up those trivial things. Therefore, I am
omitting the games where a small board holds twelve or nine   640
pebbles. When there are twelve, a player captures one of his
opponent's pieces, when his pebble jumps over it, and in this
game the throw of the dice is not required. But when there
are nine pieces, people play it equally well with and without
dice as they wish, and one or the other player captures the   645
one of his opponent's pebbles that he prefers, whenever he
manages to connect three of his own in a row. These and
similar games—for I will not describe all of them now—I
omit, moving on to more noble ones.

Oh, if only the game of rithmomachia were better known,
a game that is the leaf, flower, and fruit of arithmetic, and its   650
glory, praise, and honor, because it encompasses the entirety
of that art in it! The game, when the battle is arranged in its
marvelous order, takes place on a checkerboard as a conflict
of four odd numbers, which are in the first line, with just as   655
many even numbers, which are in the same line. The root of
the number is not counted among the other numbers, and
there are eight such "fathers" for each auxiliary cohort,
because multiples of the first number are distributed to each
side, for, after one of them has been multiplied by itself,

660 quadrati subduntur eis, quibus ordine bino
subsunt supraparticulares adicientes
toti particulam dictam patris a quotitate.
His alii subsunt, qui particulas superaddunt
dictas a numero vincente patris quotitatem,
665 uno sed numero patris equales quotitati,
ordoque binus eis. Numeros hinc inde tabellae
seu scacci portant, et sunt acies bicolores
ad discernendum, praesertim cum paritas et
imparitas mixtae sibi sunt in utraque cohorte.
670 Distinguntur item scacci tabulaeve figuris,
hi trigonis, hi tetragonis illique rotundis.
Scilicet ut scacci numeros utrimque rotundi
primos octo ferant. Trigoni sunt octo sequentes,
tetragoni reliqui, nisi quod duo sunt ibi reges
675 pyramidalibus ex numeris. Ideo quoque scacci
pyramidales sunt, et habet pars utraque regem.
In castris parium nonusdecimus locus unam
perfectam dat pyramidem. Senarius in se
ductus pyramidi basim producit eidem,
680 totaque pyramis est nonagenarius unus.
Ac locus imparium decimus bis pyramidem dat
ter curtam, cuius basim octonarius in se
ductus producit, quam pyramidem coadunat
centenarius et nonagenarius una.
685 Istae pyramides sunt reges his aciebus
et sunt ex numeris quadratis omnibus ambae,
quod potes ex tabula subiecta noscere plane:

the squares are placed under those. Behind these, in turn, 660
are the superparticulars in a double row adding to the sum
the aforesaid fractional part from the quotity of the father.
Others are behind these, which add besides the aforesaid
fractional parts from the number surpassing the quotity of
the father but equal to the quotity of the father plus one 665
number, and these have a double row. On both sides, the to-
kens and pieces bear numbers, and the battle lines are two
colors in order to tell them apart, especially necessary since
the odd and the even numbers are mixed together in each
cohort. The pieces and tokens can also be distinguished by 670
their shapes: some are triangular, some are square, and oth-
ers are round. The round pieces bear the first eight numbers
on both sides. The triangles are the next eight, and the
squares are the remainder, except that there are two kings
made out of number pyramids. And so there are also pyra- 675
mid pieces, and each side has a king. On the side of the even
numbers, the nineteenth position yields one complete pyra-
mid. The number six multiplied by itself produces the base
of this pyramid, and the sum of the pyramid is ninety-one. 680
Also, the twentieth position of the odds yields a pyramid
truncated by three, whose base is produced by eight multi-
plied by itself, and one hundred and ninety is the total sum
of this pyramid.

These pyramids are kings for their respective sides, and 685
they are both made up entirely of squared numbers, as you
can clearly understand from the following table:

acies parium
2 4 6 8
multiplices
4 16 36 64
superparticulares
6 20 42 72
superparticulares
9 25 49 81
superpartientes
15 45 91 153
superpartientes
25 81 169 249
pyramis perfecta

1
4
9
16
25
36

basis cuius 6 est radix

acies imparium
3 5 7 9
multiplices
9 25 49 81
superparticulares
12 30 56 90
superparticulares
16 36 64 100
superpartientes
28 66 130 190
superpartientes
49 121 215 361
pyramis ter curta
desunt enim 1, 4, 9

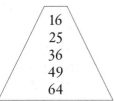

16
25
36
49
64

basis cuius 8 est radix

O utinam multis numerorum pugna placeret!
Quae si sciretur, placidam se redderet ultro.
690 Sed mathesis vix inveniet, qui iam velit ipsam.
Omnes declinant ad eas, quae lucra ministrant,
utque sciant discunt pauci, plures, ut abundent.
Sic te prostituunt, o virgo Scientia! Sic te
venalem faciunt castis amplexibus aptam
695 non te propter te quaerentes, sed lucra per te!

lineup of the evens	lineup of the odds
2 4 6 8	3 5 7 9
multiplexes	multiplexes
4 16 36 64	9 25 49 81
superparticulars	superparticulars
6 20 42 72	12 30 56 90
superparticulars	superparticulars
9 25 49 81	16 36 64 100
superpartients	superpartients
15 45 91 153	28 66 130 190
superpartients	superpartients
25 81 169 249	49 121 215 361
complete pyramid	pyramid truncated by three (because it lacks 1, 4, and 9)

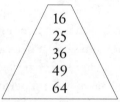

1
4
9
16
25
36

16
25
36
49
64

its base is the root 6   its base is the root 8

Oh, if only many people took pleasure in the battle of numbers! If it were known, it would win approval of its own accord. But mathematics will scarcely find anyone who pre- 690
fers it now. Everyone avoids it in favor of those games that offer gains, and few learn so that they may know, while many learn so that they may be prosperous. In this way, they pros-titute you, O maiden Knowledge! Thus, they put you up for sale, though you are best suited for chaste embraces. They 695
do not seek you for your own sake, but seek profit through

Ditarique volunt potius quam philosophari,
cum sit eis operae pretium plus quam esse videri;
garrit enim, *qui necdum nomina novit equorum.*
    Tempus erat, cum philosophos res publica quondam
700 quaerebat magnis in sumptibus utilitati
communi vigilans et eos tractabat honeste,
ut sibi consulerent summis in rebus agendis.
Tunc visum senioribus est in qualibet urbe,
ut pueros dociles ex patribus ingeniosis
705 eligerent mittendos ad gymnasia causa
discendi, quibus ad victum stipendia grata
praestarent, urbs quaeque suis, et ibi faciebant
discerni per iudicium physiognomicorum,
quae quibus ars discenda foret. Sic ars sua cuique
710 assignabatur, sic iussae quilibet arti
semper adhaerebat, et in una quemlibet esse
perfectum sat erat nec eam mutare licebat.
Tunc viguere artes, perfecte cognita quaeque
tunc erat et poterat perfecte posteritati
715 tradi, scribendisque libris pars magna vacabat;
tunc matheses solae doctrinae nomine dignae
scitores habuere suos, tunc utilitatis
quaeque quid afferret clarebat apud studiosos:
Qualiter in magno regnat mensura, sciebant,
720 qualiter in multo numerus, per quae duo motus
demonstrabilis est; proportio consona circa
haec tria versatur, quae quattuor ulteriores
ad disciplinas sunt introductio certa,
utpote quae claves portant ad eas reserandas
725 declarantque vias causarum et principiorum.
Sed nunc vix modicum de qualibet arte moderni

you! They want to get rich more than to study philosophy, since it is more worthwhile for them to seem than to really be; for he who *does not yet know the names of the horses* talks nonsense.

There was once a time when the state, watching out for the common welfare, used to seek out philosophers at great 700 expense and treat them well, so that they could consult with them on matters of the greatest importance. At that time, the elders in every city saw fit to select bright boys from clever fathers to be sent to colleges to be educated. Each city 705 supplied their own boys with stipends sufficient to support themselves and then had the assessment of physiognomists determine which art ought to be learned by each boy. In this manner each boy was assigned to his own art, and so everyone always adhered to his assigned art. It was enough for 710 each one to be accomplished in that art alone, nor was he permitted to change it. At that time, the arts flourished, and each one was thoroughly understood and could be passed on to posterity in its entirety, and a great portion had time for 715 writing books. Back then, mathematics, the only field of learning worthy of the name, had its own investigators, and anything that was beneficial was clearly understood by the learned. They used to know how measure governs magnitude, and how number governs degree. Through these two 720 things, motion is determined. Harmonious proportion depends on these three things. These, in turn, are a firm introduction to the four higher disciplines, inasmuch as they carry the keys to unlocking them, and reveal the paths of 725 their causes and principles. But now the moderns sample scarcely a tidbit of each liberal art and barely touch upon it;

degustant et vix a limine quamque salutant,
sed vacui veniunt ad eas vacuique recedunt.
    Philosophis quoad hoc prudentior est laicorum
730 cura ministerium coeptum unoquoque sequente;
et sua connumerant inter proverbia, quod, qui
pluribus intendit, numquam ditabitur inde.
Nonne magisterio deberent ergo vacare
uni, maiores operas ubi reddere oportet
735 quam multis in mechanicis? Sed philosophia
exilium patitur, et philopecunia regnat!
Restitit una tamen natarum philosophiae,
libera sed non est, quoniam captiva tenetur.
Iustitia vivente solet florere pudicum
740 rhetoricae studium; nunc ad praetoria prostat,
quo rudis adveniens de rure vocatus ad urbem
cogitur ad linguam proclamatoris emendam,
ne sit in emenda; tamen emptam non habet, immo
nullus ei damnosior adversarius illo est,
745 quem reputat causae tutorem sive patronum.
    O miserande, tuam plus diligit ille monetam
quam causam! Non curat enim, quantum tibi constet,
dummodo lucretur, nec te fore succubiturum
in causa metuit. Proponit frivola multa
750 iuraque subvertens causam protelat in annos
ac immortalem litem facit, ut tua carpat,
qui pacem pro dimidio sumptus habuisses.
Rustice stulte, tibi multum est sua cara camena,
aequivoceque sibi multum est tua cara crumena!
755 Rustice, componas, de componendo suum ne
quaeras consilium, quia non est pacis amicus!
Sic te prostituunt, olim iustissima virgo,

indeed, they come to the arts empty-handed and leave empty-handed.

The practice of laymen is wiser in this respect than philosophers since each one continues to pursue the occupation he started out with; and they count among their proverbs that he who focuses on many things will never be enriched by them. Shouldn't people therefore devote themselves to a single field of study, where they must exert greater effort than in many mechanical arts? But philosophy suffers exile, and the love of money reigns! Yet one of the daughters of philosophy remains, but she is not free, for she is held captive. When justice is living, the study of rhetoric tends to flourish and be chaste; now she prostitutes herself at the courthouses, where an uneducated person, called to the city from the countryside, is forced to buy the speech of a lawyer, so that he not be fined. However, he does not keep what he has purchased; on the contrary, no adversary is more injurious to him than the one whom he reckons to be the advocate or the defender of his case.

O you pitiful fellow, he has more love for your money than your case! For he does not care how much it will cost you, so long as he profits, nor does he fear that you will lose the case. He puts forward many trifling matters and, undermining the law, drags the case out for years and makes the suit immortal, so that he can fleece you of your goods, even though you could have had a resolution for half the expenditure. You foolish peasant, his muse is very costly for you, and likewise, your purse is very dear to him! You peasant, you should come to terms, not seek his counsel about coming to terms, because he is no friend of peace! In this way they prostitute you, once most just of maidens, who should not

quae non debueras exponi taliter istis
captivis, qui te captivant, non modo captant,
760 et, quia non captant, captivari meruissent!
O quam ferventer tales hodie sequerentur
Alchimiam, cuius fructus ditatio tanta,
sed praecellit in hoc aliis, quod nullus in ipsa
hactenus obtinuit, qui propter habere studeret.
765 Sic dedignatur cupidos largissima virgo.
    Culpa tamen magna est magnatum, quos hodiernis
temporibus populus in qualibet eligit urbe.
Quodsi non fuerint populi concordia vota,
assumuntur de populo quidam seniores,
770 qui populi vice praeficiunt concorditer unum.
Vel, si discordes sint inter se, quia pro se
quilibet aspirat nec se bene compatiuntur
livor et ambitio, quamvis in utroque duorum
esse simul possint, tandem discordia concors
775 fit, quia concordant discorditer, et fit ab illis
tertius electus, qui forte est peior utroque.
Sic indignorum creat indignatio quendam
forte minus dignum. Sic se collidere possunt
a se collisi, placeat cum neuter utrique.
780 Sicque vides, quod, ubi corregnant ambitiosus
livor et ambitio livens, non ambitioni
succumbit livor, sed inebriat ambitionem.
    Ille, putas, qui sic adipiscitur hoc anabathrum,
cuius habet turpem promotio reproba causam,
785 qui non pro meritis, sed ut invidiae satagatur
praeficitur populo, bene sit facturus et urbi?
Absit, sed similes factoribus et sibi, ductus
irrationali quadam simili ratione,

have been so exposed to those captives who capture you but are not now captivated by you and, because they are not captivated, deserve to be captured! Oh, how fervently such men today follow Alchemy, whose fruit is great wealth; but she is superior to the others in this respect: that no one who studies her for the sake of gain so far has been successful in it. Thus, the most bountiful maiden scorns the greedy.

Yet the magnates whom the people these days elect in every city are greatly at fault. But if the wishes of the people are not in agreement, certain elders are selected from the populace, who, as representatives of the people, by agreement put one in command. Or, if they disagree with each other because each one harbors aspirations for himself, and because malice and ambition do not make them very mutually compatible, although they can be present in each of two rival candidates at the same time, in the end, there is coincidence in disagreement because they agree to disagree. And so it happens that a third candidate is elected by them, who is worse than either one. Thus, the indignation of the unworthy produces someone perhaps less worthy. After the rivals have contended with one another, they are able to beat each other, since neither pleases the other. And so you see that when ambitious envy and envious ambition are corulers, envy does not succumb to ambition, but rather intoxicates ambition.

Do you think that a person will do well for the city who achieves elevation in this way, whose illegitimate promotion arises from a foul cause, who was placed in command of the people not because of his merits but as a result of envy? Not in the least! Rather, since he was appointed by unworthy people and is inspired by a similarly irrational reasoning, he

factus ab indignis indignos promovet et non
790 attendit meritum, patriae nec pensat honorem,
indigenas ut amet et honoret praecipue, quos
exornant mores, ditat sapientia, dotat
eloquium, sed eos sublimat, quos sibi iungit
linea sanguinis aut contractus amicitiarum
795 aut spes obsequii. Sane promotor amici
est laudandus, sed plerumque pecunia talem
nectit amicitiam, quae nec meruisse videtur
nomen amicitiae, nisi detur ei per abusum.
Quodsi rem dominus tali committit amico,
800 furtum in re domini talis committit amicus;
ultio digna quidem, nec enim decreta deorum
sic immutari possunt, quod sordida praeda
procedat vel sit laudabilis exitus eius.
Istos indignos indignus promovet iste
805 indignisque suis postponit amabiliores
indignosque suos ditando praeordinat illos
ordine perverso, qui palpant blandius ipsum.
Culpaque sic magna est magnatum, quod perierunt
artes, nam quoniam sublimant deteriores,
810 desperant multi nec scire student, sed habere.
      Sed quia de ludis fiebat sermo, quid illo
pulchrius esse potest exercitio numerorum,
quo divinantur numeri plerique per unum
ignoti notum, sicut ludunt apud Indos
815 ludum dicentes "algebrae almucgrabalaeque"?
Inter arithmeticos ludus pulcherrimus hic est
ludus arithmeticae, praxis descriptio cuius
plus caperet, quam sufficiat totus liber iste.

promotes unworthy men similar to his appointers and to himself. He pays no attention to merit and does not show 790 regard for his homeland's honor by especially cherishing and honoring those of his fellow countrymen who are adorned with good character, enriched by wisdom, and endowed with eloquence. Instead, he elevates those that are joined to him by bloodline, bonds of friendship, or hope of allegiance. 795 Certainly, the promoter of a friend should be praised, but often money attaches to such friendship, and so it seems not to merit the name of friendship, unless it is given to it through misuse of the term. But if a lord entrusts property to such a friend for safekeeping, such a friend will commit a 800 theft of the lord's property. This is a fitting payback indeed, for the decrees of the gods cannot be so altered that his sordid profit would continue or that his life would end happily. That unworthy leader promotes those worthless men and 805 prefers unworthy men to more agreeable ones. Enriching his own unworthy men, perversely he advances those who flatter him more ingratiatingly. And thus it is in great part the fault of the magnates that the arts have vanished, for since they elevate ever-worse men, many despair and study 810 not in order to know, but to possess.

But seeing as my discussion was about games, what can be finer than that numerical exercise in which many unknown numbers are deduced by means of one that is known? It's a game that they play in India, calling it the game of "al- 815 gebra and *almucabola*." Scholars of arithmetic consider this to be the finest arithmetical game, but a description of its practice would take up more space than this whole book could supply.

Liber secundus

Talibus atque aliis ludo excepto deciorum
sontibus a curis cum me relevare pararem,
non tamen a cura carae relevabar amicae.
Solum felicem super omnes esse putabam,
5 qui, quotiens vellet, cognoscere posset amicam.
Solum laudabam, cui vim natura dedisset,
ut, quotiens vellet, cognoscere posset amicam.
At nunc semiviros laudo, quibus has modo vires
componentibus a primis natura negavit,
10 sive quibus solitis thalamos violare pudicos
deprensis in adulterio genitalia membra
iracunda manus sponsi violenter ademit,
sive quibus ruptura siphac ita magnificari
coepisset, quod non prohiberet in oscea casum
15 intestinorum, vel tantus ad ova veniret
fluxus aquae putris stomacho mandante, quod ultra
herniam patiens non posset onus tolerare,
aut aliis causis ita computresceret ovum,
ne fieri posset, quin crudeli medicina
20 ova recidisset medici reprobabilis usus.
    Istos semiviros nunc laudo, si licet "istos"
dicere, nam dubium, an sit semivir iste vel ista.
Ista quidem non est, quia vulvam non habet; iste
non est, quem talis defectus devirat; ergo
25 sit neutrum. Tamen hoc nihil ex animalibus umquam
esse potest, nisi sit hic aut haec; si nihil horum
est spado, iam non est animal, nec enim sine sexu
esse potest animal,—igitur non est animal. Sed
non est non vivens,—ergo sit planta. Quis umquam

BOOK TWO

Although I resolved to relieve myself of my sinful concerns with these and other games (dice games excepted), still I was not relieved of anxiety over my beloved girlfriend. I believed he alone was fortunate above all others who could 5 know his girlfriend as often as he wished. I used to praise only the man to whom nature had given the stamina to know his beloved as often as he wanted. But now I praise half-men, to whom nature denied such abilities from their very creation; or those who had been accustomed to violate 10 chaste beds and so had their genitals violently cut off by the hand of an angry husband after they were caught in adultery; or those for whom a rupture of the abdominal membrane had begun to enlarge so much that it did not prevent the falling of the intestines into the scrotum, either so that such 15 a great flood of putrid water came into the testicles from the discharging stomach that the person suffering from the hernia could not bear the weight; or so that the testicle was so putrefied from other causes that there was no other recourse except for the dreadful practice of the physician cut- 20 ting off the testicles through a cruel kind of healing.

Now I praise those half-men, if I can call them "men," for there is doubt whether a half-man is masculine or feminine. Indeed, feminine is incorrect, because there is no vagina— but you can't describe one whom such a serious defect unmans as masculine; therefore let it be neuter. Yet no animal 25 can be a neuter noun—only masculine or feminine; if a eunuch is neither of these, then it is not an animal, for there cannot be an animal without a gender—therefore it is not an animal. But it is a living creature—therefore it must be a

30   vidit frustratam fructu vel semine plantam?
Quod plus est, quis eam vidit radice carentem?
Quod radice caret, etiam frondescere nescit.
Sperma foret semen, et fructus filius atque
radix testiculi, frondes circumdata silva

35   mento, qua quicumque caret suspectus habetur,
ne sit castratus vel frigidus; est honor ergo
barba viro, testis virtutis testiculorum,
spermatis augmenti signum, fiducia fructus.
Econtra, si testiculi desunt, generandi

40   spes periit, quia sperma deest, barbaque caret vel
est cariturus ea, folium quia defluet eius.
Eunuchus porro, cum non sit femina, non vir,
non animal, non planta, quid est? Non est sine vita;
ergo quid esse potest? Nihil esse potest nisi monstrum!

45   Monstrum grammaticae, quia, declinabile cum sit
cum casu, nullus sibi congruit articulorum,
cum sibi praeponi nullus per se queat, ut sit
hic aut haec aut hoc nec sit commune nec omne.
Nec modicum miror, cum non habeat genitivum,

50   cui sua congreget et quare placeat sibi tantum
ablativus casus displiceatque dativus.
Et quia nullius fieri constructio partis
hac cum parte potest, non est oratio, quae sit
huic parti totum, sed pars est et sine toto

55   absque relativo sibi respondente relata.
     Ut non solius sit monstrum grammaticae, sed
inveniat dialectica, quid miretur in ipso:
non solum, quod abest alterna relatio, sed quod
sic est mirivocum, quod non cadit in genus et quod

60   non cadit in speciem, cui non individuorum

plant. Whoever saw a plant deprived of fruit or seed? What's $_{30}$ more, who has seen one that lacks a root? Whatever lacks a root also cannot put forth leaves. Seed can be understood as sperm, the fruit as the son, the root as the testicles, and the leaves as the forest covering the chin, and whoever lacks $_{35}$ this last is under suspicion of being castrated or feeble. Therefore, a man's beard is his honor, the witness to the potency of his testicles, the symbol of the proliferation of his sperm, and assurance of his fertility. On the other hand, if the testicles are missing, any hope of begetting has been $_{40}$ lost, because there is no sperm, and he has no beard or soon will have none because its foliage will fall off. So since a eunuch is neither woman nor man, neither animal nor plant, what is it? It is not without life, therefore what can it be? It can be nothing other than a monstrosity!

It is a monstrosity of grammar, because, though it is de- $_{45}$ clinable with a case, no pronoun can agree with it, since none can be attributed to it, whether it be masculine or feminine or neuter, nor would it be common gender, or all gender. And I wonder not a little for whom it accumulates its $_{50}$ possessions, since it does not have a genitive case, and why the ablative case so pleases and the dative displeases it. And because there can be no combination of any part of speech with this part, there is no expression that makes up a whole statement with this part, but it is a part without a whole, without a relative pronoun referring to it. $_{55}$

As a result, not only is it a grammatical monstrosity, but dialectic also finds something astonishing in it: not only that it has no external referent, but also that it is so unique that it falls into neither a genus nor a species, since it is predicate $_{60}$

quicquam subicitur, cui carnem dividat, et quod
nec species speciosa genusve sibi generosum.
Degener immo genus specie sine dividit ipsum
a cunctis, quibus est cordi generatio, cuius
65 et genus et species sunt monstra, magis quoque monstrum
est individuum, digito monstrabile monstrum!
    Monstrum rhetoricae, qui iudicis officio si
fungatur, crudelis erit, si rhetoris utens
themate truncato, causam non instruet et sic
70 non persuadebit; nec enim facundia grata
eius, qui standi personam iudice coram
non habet, esse potest, quocumque sit usa lepore,
ac infecundi est omnis facundia pauper.
    Rursus apud matheses indemonstrabile monstrum,
75 cui de subiecto concludi passio per se
nulla potest, nec diffinitio ponitur eius
in medio, quia deficit in medio neque novit
credere supposito vel consentire petito
et nulla dignitatis virtute iuvatur.
80 Et quia bis duo sunt, ubi demonstratio regnat
precipue: motus, numerus, mensura sonusque,
invenies in eo, quo sit per singula monstrum.
Deficiente sibi numero pare cum pare se non
mensurare potest motumque perhorret amicum;
85 quem si temptarit, tandem lyra murmurat ani.
    Monstrum naturae rerum mutabiliumque,
cum sit principium motus, mutabilitatem
tantam non novit nec tantam prodigiosam,
sicut in eunuchum si mutatus fuerit vir.
90 Solo in quo natura potest vacuum reperire
aut infinitum, primum propter spoliatos
folles et reliquum propter fines mutilatos.

to no individual to which it apportions flesh, neither a special species nor a generous genus. On the contrary, a degenerate genus, without a species, distinguishes it from all of those for whom begetting is pleasing; both its genus and its species are monstrosities, and more monstrous is the individual, a monstrosity demonstrable with a finger! 65

He is a monstrosity of rhetoric. If he discharges the duty of a judge, he will be cruel. If by using a mutilated rhetorical theme, he will not make his case and so will not be persuasive. For the eloquence of someone who is not a person of standing before a judge cannot be pleasing, whatever charm she may use, and all of the eloquence of an infertile man is unavailing. 70

Furthermore, in mathematics, the eunuch is an incalculable monstrosity, for whom no attribute *per se* can be deduced from the subject, nor is his definition located in the middle term, because he is deficient in the middle and does not know how to believe a supposition or assent to a postulate, and he is aided by no virtue of dignity. And since there are four areas where the proof particularly holds sway—motion, number, measure, and sound—you will find that he is a monstrosity in each case. Since he lacks an even number, he cannot measure himself with an even number, and he has a great horror of the motion of sex; if he should attempt this, in the end there sounds the lyre of the ass. 75 80 85

He is a monstrosity of nature and all inconstant things. Although its beginning is motion, nature does not know such great and prodigious mutability as when a man has been changed into a eunuch. In him alone can nature find a void or the infinite, the first on account of his empty sack, and the other on account of his mutilated extremities. 90

Monstrum naturae, sed praecipue quoad illam
partem, quae corpus regit humanum, quia sanus
95 non est aut aeger impossibilisque reduci
ad medium, quia deficit in medio neque supplet
defectum medicina suum; complexio cuius
est sine complexu nec iam complexio dici
digna, per antiphrasim nisi sit complexio dicta.

100 Est etiam monstrum morale, nisi quia mores
dicendi non sunt, ubi tam perversa voluntas
regnat, tam nequam tamque invida; nam status eius
tam vilis nequit invidiae livore carere,
nec bene velle potest, qui nequior est super omnes;
105 nam mansuetudo morum est specialis alumna.
Et quia cum mulis id habent commune spadones,
quod steriles sunt ambo, sic homines spado vincit
nequitia sicut animalia cetera mulus.
Et dicunt etiam, quod naturaliter omnis
110 est piger eunuchus et quod timidusque rapaxque,
quod piger et timidus praesumentes ideo, quod
vultus rugosus vetulaeque simillimus et vox
exilis perhibent animum non esse virilem,
quodque rapax per idem, quia, qui timidusque pigerque
115 sit, in egestatem labi timet, ut latro fiat
porro rapax timidus nequam piger invidus. In se
virtutem quod habere queat, non est leve credi,
praesertim, sicut scribunt ethici, quia virtus
nulla potest, si non omnes habeantur, haberi
120 nec cum tot vitiis habitare vel unica posset.
Sane sunt aliqui, qui castos esse spadones
propterea reputant, quod non sunt luxuriosi;
sed non sunt, quoniam casti sunt, qui patiuntur

A monstrosity of nature, but particularly with respect to that part which governs the human body, since the eunuch is neither healthy nor unwell, and is unable to be restored to 95 the mean, because he is missing something in the middle, a defect medicine cannot remedy. His temperament is devoid of sexual union, nor does it deserve the name "temperament," unless it is so called by antiphrasis.

He is also a moral monstrosity, unless it's the case that we 100 should not speak of moral character where a will that is so perverted, wicked, and malign holds sway, for his condition is so base that it cannot rid itself of envious malice. Nor can one who is more wicked than everyone show benevolence, for gentleness of character takes a special upbringing. And 105 since eunuchs have in common with mules that both are sterile, so the eunuch exceeds men in vileness, as the mule does other animals. They also say that every eunuch is by nature indolent, and that he is cowardly and grasping, suppos- 110 ing that he is lazy and cowardly because his wrinkled face, very like an old woman's, and his feeble voice show that his spirit is not manly. And they assume that he is rapacious for the same reason, since one who is cowardly and indolent fears slipping into poverty, so that he becomes a thief, and 115 even more grasping, cowardly, vile, indolent, and envious. It is hard to believe that he can have any virtue within himself, especially because, as the moral philosophers write, no single virtue can be possessed unless all are possessed, nor can 120 even a single one dwell with so many vices.

There are certainly some who reckon that eunuchs are chaste for the reason that they are not wanton. But they are not, since those who are chaste suffer from desire but are

nec deducuntur; qui vero non patiuntur,
125   sunt insensibiles multum a virtute remoti;
quodsi de studiis, quod plus reputatur inesse
non insit, nec inest, quod inesse minus reputatur.
    Amplius est metaphysicum monstrum spado, nam non
solum impossibile est, quod perducatur ad actum,
130   sed nec adest ipsi quaecumque potentia sive
longinque praecedens actum sive propinque;
praeterea subiectum non habet, esse vel in quo
vel de quo dici possit, nec taliter unum
esse potest, quod multiplicatio surgat ab ipso.
135   Postremo monstrum nihilominus est apud illos,
a quibus investigatur natura deorum,
quos imitatores dicunt legis positivae,
qui ritus ac historias veterum venerantur,
arbitrio gens quaeque suo diversa secuti.
140   Monstrum fastorum, quia si spado forte sacerdos
efficiatur, erit sic iste vel ista sacerdos,
ut dici possit ita neutrum sicut utrumque.
O quicumque deus, cuius templo dominatur
tam deforme pecus cuiusque effeminat aras,
145   si deus esse potest infortunatus, eorum
infortunatissimus es, pro quo reperiri
non potuit de tot modo milibus integer unus!
Rictus ei, non risus inest, et sacrificari
deberet certe potius quam sacrificare.
150   Cui tamen ex superis holocaustum tale placeret,
turpe pecus mutilum, quod porca foedius, hirco
fetidius, nisi forte, suas ut liberet aras,
quas miserabiliter ementulus occupat iste,
compensare velit clavumque retundere clavo,
155   turpe ministerium redimit dum victima turpis.

not led astray, while those who do not suffer from desire are insensible and far removed from virtue. But, with regard 125 to desire, if what is thought more likely innate is not so, then neither is that which is thought less likely to be present.

Furthermore, a eunuch is a metaphysical monstrosity, for not only is it impossible for him to be brought to action, but 130 there is also not present in him any sort of capacity, that either closely or distantly precedes an action. Moreover, he does not have a subject either in which, or about which, existence can be posited; nor can he be a single being in such a way that multiplication arises from him.

Finally, the eunuch is just as much a monstrosity to those 135 men by whom the nature of the gods is investigated, who are called followers of positive law, who revere the rites and stories of the ancients, each group following different traditions according to its own choice.

The eunuch is a monstrosity of sacred rites, because if he 140 should happen to be made a priest, the priest will be either masculine or feminine, and as easily be called neither as both. O whatever god you are, whose temple such a base flock controls and whose altars it emasculates, if a god can 145 be unfortunate, you are the most unfortunate of all, for whom not a single intact man can be found among the now many thousands! He has gaping jaws, not a smile, and certainly ought to be sacrificed rather than perform the sacrifice. Yet which of the gods would such a burnt offering 150 please—a foul, mutilated animal, filthier than swine, ranker than a billy goat—unless, by chance, in order to free his altars (which that dickless wonder occupies miserably), he wanted to exact retribution and hit a nail with a nail, as that 155 foul victim atones for his base ministry.

Monstrum fastorum, quem cum fas pontificare
nusquam sit, minus esse potest ibi fas, ubi rerum
summa gerendarum residet cum pontificatu.
Quod legisse potes in quodam codice, cuius
160   omnia supponens nihil omnino probat auctor,
ac ipsum pro lege tenet gens credula quaedam,
exemplar quibus est vivendi vita priorum
estque fides sua, quod sequitur primogenituram
ius benedicendi; benedictus et a patre tali
165   fit dominus fratrum talesque vocant patriarchas.
Nec falluntur in hoc, veram probat esse fidem res;
nam plerumque vident dominari fratribus illos,
quos aliis praefert patrum benedictio terrae
semper abundantes pinguedine roreque caeli.
170   Imbenedicibilem lex innuit illa spadonem
exemplo quodam famoso; nam spado cum sit
voce Iacob manibus, non est Esau, neque tutus
comparere potest coram patre, ne pater eius
colli nuda manu pertractet et, absque pilosis
175   pellibus inveniens, putet illudi sibi velle.
Ac indignatus maledictum pro benedicto
inducat, quoscumque cibos praesentet eidem,
iratusque repellat eum passique repulsam
et desperantis facies ignara rubere
180   palleat, et demum desit benedictio tantum
exoptata, diu tanto conamine tamque
ferventi desiderio quaesita (licet non
quaeratur pro se, sed caecus amor dominandi
concomitatur eam, quam qui sic acriter ambit,
185   intendit prodesse parum multumque praeesse).

He is a monstrosity of sacred rites. Although nowhere is it lawful for him to be a high priest, it can never be less lawful than where supreme power resides in the office of the high priest. You can read this in a certain book, whose author, in making all sorts of suppositions, proves nothing at all, but which a certain credulous people, for whom the life of their ancestors is their model for living, takes as their law. And it is their belief that the rite of receiving a blessing follows primogeniture; a man blessed by such a father becomes the master of his brothers; such men they call "patriarchs." And they are not wrong in this—reality proves their belief true; for they commonly see that those men, whom the blessing of their fathers prefers to others, rule over their brothers and are endowed with the richness of the earth and the dew of heaven.

That law indicates by a well-known example that a eunuch is not worthy of a blessing. For since Jacob had the voice and hands of a eunuch, he was not Esau, and could not appear before his father without danger, otherwise his father would feel his bare neck with his hand, and, finding him to be without the hairy pelts, suppose that he wished to deceive him. And, enraged, his father would call down a curse instead of a blessing, whatever dishes he presented to him, and angrily reject him; and when he suffered rejection and lost hope, his face, incapable of blushing, would grow pale. And finally, he would not receive the blessing which he desired so much and for so long and sought with so great effort and such fervent longing (although it is not sought for its own sake, but rather, blind love of domination accompanies it, and whoever seeks it so fervently intends to do little good and wield great sway).

Heu, si subiectos habeat, correctio quorum
spectet ad ipsius examen! Quam male lapsis
de pastoris erit provisum conditione!
De lapsu carnis dico, cuius quia motus
190 hic spado non sentit, labentes despicit, unde
tale nihil passus passis non compatietur.
O utinam, quia non attendit onus sed honorem
in praelatura, numquam pertingat ad illam!
Quem tamen infauste Moyses si pontificaret,
195 veste videretur Aaron vultuque Maria.
        Talia monstra modo laudo, quia vivere possunt
femineoque carere toro; quamvisque solerem
felices solos coitu reputare potentes,
felices solos reputo cessare coactos.
200 Venerit unde mihi subito mutatio tanta,
discite vos, quos ferre iugum fastidit amoris!
        Unus erat toto Naturae vultus in orbe,
virginei floris decor et decus, unica sexus
gloria feminei, quae naturalibus et quae
205 gratuitis dotata bonis florebat eique
Fortunae bona non deerant adeo, quod in unam
tot bona personam concurrere non meminissem.
Tres credi poterant in ea certasse sorores,
muneribus Natura potens et Gratia larga
210 non exspectatis meritis Fortunaque nulli
conformis, largis sed avara et prodiga parcis,
quamvis detur in hac instantia virgine. Cui se
reddiderat praeter solitum multo meliorem
quam multis aliis, multis aliis meliori
215 largiflue sibi dans et opes et nobilitatem.
Cui Natura tamen dederat longe meliora,

Alas, if a eunuch should have subjects and their correction should look to his example, how poorly will provision be made for the sinners because of the condition of the shepherd! I speak of the sin of the flesh. Because this eu- 190 nuch does not feel its motions, he despises those who sin. For this reason, one who has never experienced these feelings will not feel compassion for those who have. Oh, were it only the case that he would never receive a prelature since he looks not to the burden but to the honor in it! Yet if Moses unfortunately were to make him a high priest, he would 195 look like Aaron in his dress and Miriam in his face.

But now I praise such monstrosities, because they can spend their life without a woman in their bed; and although I used to reckon fortunate only those capable of intercourse, now I reckon fortunate only those forced to be free of it. You, who are chafing at bearing the yoke of love, learn now 200 why such a great change suddenly came over me!

In all of Nature's realm there was but a single face, the charm and ornament of maidenly flower, the unique glory of the female sex, who so flourished, adorned with Nature's and 205 Grace's gifts, and on whom Fortune's favor was so richly bestowed that I could not recall so many good qualities ever coinciding in a single person. You could imagine three sisters had staged a contest in her: Nature, generous with her gifts; Grace, bountiful bestower of unanticipated merits; 210 and Fortune, conforming to no expectations, but tight fisted to the extravagant and lavish to the thrifty—although in this maiden she showed constancy. To her, Fortune had shown herself much better than to many others, contrary to her normal practice, generously giving both wealth and no- 215 bility to one who was better than many others, while Nature

corporis ac animi bona scilicet hinc, quia nulla
conferri poterat sibi moribus ingeniove.
Inde, quod in toto, prout aequore clauditur, orbe
220 non erat ulla suae similis praestantia formae,
non erat ulla suae similis dulcedo loquelae.
Quid, quod in omnibus his addebat Gratia tantum,
quod faceret semet ipsis meliora videri
singula, iudicium iustum vincente favore.
225 Certius et quamvis oculorum iudicium sit,
non tamen in lingua seu pectore sic favor ipse
vincebat sicut in forma; non aliorsum
sic apparebat victoria. Forma moveret
Hippolytum, si non oculos sibi tollere vellet.
230   Verum cur ad eam laudandam particulatim
descendisse velim? Cur ad praeconia cuique
debita membrorum modo describenda laborem?
Omnis eis minor est descriptio, singula lustres,
singula sunt meliora satis quam dicere possem.
235 Sed quoniam meminisse iuvat tot divitiarum
formosae dotis, modicum per singula libans
membra sigillatim discurro singula mirans,
ad quae lustrator oculus permittitur ire.
Singula contendunt se vincere, cum tamen unum
240 omnibus aspectum praesto, simul omnia summa
pace reformata et sopita lite quiescunt:
sic sibi respondent alterno cuncta nitore.
       Silva capillorum supereminet, atque rotundum
circumplexa caput clara praefulgurat ostro,
245 fulgori cuius radians color invidet auri.
Sed postquam dominam nutrita diu gravat, illam

had given her still better attributes, gifts of both body and mind, for no one could be compared with her in character or intelligence. Therefore, in the whole earth surrounded by the ocean, there was no supreme beauty like hers, and no sweetness of speech like hers. Furthermore, Grace added so much to all of these qualities that she made each and every thing seem even better than it was, so that her favor made an impartial judgment impossible. And although the judgment of the eyes is more definitive, nevertheless not even in speech or in heart was that favor so victorious as in her external appearance; in no other area was victory so apparent. Her appearance would have moved Hippolytus, unless he wished to blind himself.

Indeed, why would I want to work downward to praise her part by part? Why should I struggle now to describe the praises owed to each part? Every description falls short; should you have examined them individually, each one would be better than I could possibly say. But since I take pleasure in recounting the riches of the beauty with which she was endowed, touching lightly on each one, I'll survey her parts one at a time, admiring them one by one, wherever my roaming eye is permitted to go. Taken individually the parts would fight to outdo each other, but if I took a look at all of them as a whole, everything taken collectively would be at rest, with peace restored and their strife calmed: thus they all complemented each other with their varying beauties.

Uppermost was a forest of hair, encompassing her well-rounded head, with a brilliance that outshone purple and a radiant coloring that rivaled the splendor of gold. But after her hair had grown for so long that it began to weigh its

colligit in torquem sub quadam lege coercens;
hac a lege tamen remanent ad tempora quidam
exempti brevitate sua, crispidine rara
250   connexi, volitantque vago ludente reflexu.
Frons spatiosa, parum convexa; manus deus ambas
in qua plananda posuit, non sufficiente
alterutra manuum. Candorem lilia cuius
non vincunt, non aequat ebur, non florida cinnus.
255   Nigra supercilii sinuosaque linea cristae
exigui declivis utrimque superiacet inter
vicinos quodam lunato limite pacem
concilians, dum iure suo concedit utrique
uti, distinguens a fronte situs oculorum;
260   inter utrumque tamen, ubi fronti continuatur
nasus, tam naso quam fronte superciliisve
plus depressa parum discriminat area quaedam
nuda pilis, candore potens aequare ligustra.
    Subsidet his regio ridens et laeta, gemellos
265   quae speculatores fovet hospitio ciliorum;
intus pupillam vario cingente nigellam,
exhilarat circumgirata rotatio vultum.
Occultans oculos circumstat ibi seriatim
palpebra, ne laedat extrinseca causa superbos
270   ac indignantes, et semisphaeria nutu
claudit lascivo, qui munera spondet amoris.
Pure nec aut lacrimis oculorum ripa madescit.
Nasus in excessum nullum se transvehit, ut sit
longus vel curtus, aquilus simusve nec ullam
275   tractus in obliquum portendit proditionem.
Nec stillas cerebri naris cava pandit hiatu
nec libertatem negat halitui neque ricta

mistress down, she collected it into a ring, confining her hair
to its dominion; yet some hairs, exempt from this law be-
cause of their shortness, remained on her temple, gathered
in a loose curl, and floating about freely in a playful spiral. 250
Her brow was broad but not too rounded. God had to use
both his hands to smooth it—just one hand was not enough.
Lilies are no whiter than it was, ivory and the flowering
white thorn tree no match for it. The black and arched line 255
of her eyebrow lay over the crest of a slight slope on each
side, keeping the peace between two neighboring features
with a crescent-shaped boundary, as it allowed each to keep
its own domain, dividing the hollows of the eyes from the
brow. Yet between both, where the nose was connected to 260
the brow, a more sunken area was somewhat set off from the
nose, forehead, and eyebrows, an area without hair, and the
equal of the privet flower in whiteness.

Beneath these parts sat a region of laughter and joy, which 265
housed twin lookouts under the shelter of the eyelids. An
iris, contrasting in color, encircled her dark pupil, and its
lively circling motion conveyed happiness to her expression.
The eyelid, hiding the eyes, intermittently closed over them
so that no external cause might harm their proud and scorn-
ful gaze, and it enclosed the half spheres with a lascivious 270
wink, which promised the gifts of love. The rims of her eyes
were not moistened by pus or tears. Her nose did not extend
to any excess, being neither too long or too short, aquiline
or snub, nor did its length, in deviating from the straight, 275
indicate any infidelity. Her nostrils did not spread out drops
of her brain from their openings, and they neither prevented
free breathing, nor were they so gaping that they threatened

passibiles auras tristi fetore minatur.
At modicum consurgit apex hinc inde genarum
280 punica malorum vincens fragmenta colore.
Lilia mixta rosis in eo certare putares.
Conficiunt etenim niveus roseusque colorem
unum, sic tamen, ut rubeus vincatur ab albo.
In quibus et quaedam, domina ridente, creantur
285 fossiculae, tantum quae mansuetudinis addunt
in laeta facie, quod concessura videtur,
quicquid eam sibi conveniens persona rogaret.
Et modo caesaries modicas in seque retortas
contegit auriculas, modo castigatur ab illis.
290   Bucca brevis sola brevitate notanda, nisi tunc,
cum ridet; tunc namque statum redit ad mediocrem.
Labra tument modicum cerasorum invicta rubore
collectorum acri post imbrem sole secuto,
quae cum sint inversa parum, se velle parare
295 seque offerre videntur ad oscula suscipienda.
Sed domina ridente loquenteve seve cibante
intus cuiusdam spectabilis ordo catenae
clarior argento vivo se visibus offert,
dispositis ibi dentibus in serieque locatis
300 firmis, consertis, aequalibus atque minutis.
Terminus inferior faciei, mobile mentum,
in collem ad collum collatum colliculumque
ad labra se tollit, ad utrumque tamen moderate.
Collum tam planum quam plenum, non ibi nervi
305 corda riget, non vena tumet; cuius cutis omni
asperitate caret, nec foedat eam maculosa
menda, sed est nive candidior, nisi credulitatem
frangat hyperboleos laxata licentia tantam.

the susceptible breezes with an offensive stench. Next the top of the cheeks rose up a little on each side, surpassing pomegranate seeds in color. You would have thought that lilies mixed with roses were in competition there. For the snow white and the rose red produced a single color, yet in such a way that the red was overcome by the white. In these, also, some creases were created when the mistress laughed, which added so much mildness to her face when joyful that she seemed ready to concede whatever a person who met her approval should ask of her. And sometimes her hair concealed her modestly sized, flat-lying ears, sometimes it was held back by them.

Her mouth was small, and remarkable only for its smallness, except that, when she laughed, it returned to an average size. Her lips pouted a little, and were not surpassed by the bright red of cherries gathered when the sun follows after the rain; since they turned out slightly, they seemed to be readying and offering themselves to receive kisses. But when my mistress laughed or spoke or ate, the eye-catching line of a certain chain, brighter than quicksilver, offered itself to view inside her mouth, where her teeth were arrayed in rows, strong, close set, even, and small. The lower limit of her face, her mobile chin, rose in a hill toward the neck and in a mound toward the lips, yet gently in both directions. Her neck was as even as it was full—no tendon cords stiffened there, no veins bulged. The skin of her neck lacked any roughness, nor did a blemishing spot mar it—rather, it was whiter than snow, if the extended license of hyperbole does not shatter the believability of such a thing. Her enticing

280

285

290

295

300

305

Blanda manus facilem se praebet ad omnia, cuius
310 est digitus gracilis, plenus, tornatilis, aequus,
proque modo longus, vola lactea, lucidus unguis.
    Cetera sunt praeclusa mihi, tegit omnia vestis.
Divinare tamen licet et per visa gradatim
ad non visa venire, putando, quod haec meliora
315 sunt illis visis et quod captabiliora.
Sed coniectura cum sint mihi cognita sola,
sub quadam gaudent pertransiri brevitate.
Pectore compresso, surgente tumore gemello,
ubera conicio duo parvula, dura, recurva,
320 ac si complexu se velle premi fateantur
et complexuro se velle occurrere sponte.
Bracchia longa quidem, subtilia, mollia, plena.
Desuper acclives umeri rectique retrorsum.
Corpus procerum, pingues habitudine lumbi,
325 in strophio graciles, clunes humiles, satis amplae.
Mobilitas crurum curvato poplite, pesque
tam brevis, in medio sinuosus, rectus in ante,
prae cunctis perhibent partem pollere cupitam.
Et puto, quod nullus cultus nullusque paratus
330 aptior esset ei, quam si sine vestibus esset.
O utinam nudam videam, si tangere nudam
non est fas, saltemque semel, si non datur ultra!
Parva locutus sum, quia sufficientia verba
non sunt ad tantam speciem. Descriptio nulla
335 notificare potest, quantis se vellet amari
deliciis quantisve iocis se redderet aptam.
    Hauserat hanc oculus cupidus meus invidiosam
et collaturo suggesserat omnia cordi.
Cor nimis audacter coepit sperare, quod illam

hand made her adept at everything; each finger was slender, 310
full, well rounded, even, and the proper length; her palm was
milky white, and each fingernail was clear.

Her remaining parts were shut off to me—her garment
covered them all. Yet it is possible to speculate about them
and come little by little to what is unseen through what is
seen, by supposing that these parts are better than what is 315
seen and more captivating. But though they are known to
me only by conjecture, it is pleasing to recount them with a
certain brevity. When her chest was restrained, from the
twin rising swellings I deduced two slight breasts, firm and
pert, as if revealing that they wanted to be pressed in an em- 320
brace and would willingly offer themselves to one who em-
braced them. Her arms were certainly long, slender, soft,
and full. Her shoulders sloped down from above and were
flat on back. Her torso was elongated, her loins full by na-
ture but slender under her girdle, her buttocks small but 325
very shapely. The movement of her legs when the knee is
bent, and her foot—so slender, arched in the middle, and
straight in front—suggested that the desired part would ex-
cel all the rest. And I believe that no clothing and no adorn-
ment would have suited her better than to be without gar- 330
ments. Oh, if only I could see her naked, if it is not permitted
to touch her naked, just the once, if no more than once is al-
lowed! I have said little, because words do not suffice for so
wonderful an appearance. No description can make known 335
with how many charms she invited being loved, or for how
much pleasure she showed herself ready.

My lustful eye had devoured this enviable girl and had
urged my heart to offer everything. My heart too boldly

340 aut verbis aut muneribus convertere possem,
et praeter solitum cum verbis munera danda
disposui, si non oblata prius valuissent
verba, quibus totiens tot pectora sollicitaram.
Abdita paulatim scintillula crevit in ignem
345 immensum, totas iam possessura medullas.
Sed locus et tempus non concurrere loquendi,
praesertim, quia nimirum materque paterque
excubiis multis et sollicitudine multa
vallabant ipsam, ne subduci sibi posset,
350 blanditiis si forte levem concederet aurem.
Quid facturus eram? Quaerenda fuit mediatrix,
mutua verba loqui quae posset utrique vicissim
et facunda foret et suspicione careret,
ambos ut nullo mirante liceret adire.
355 Talia cum vigili cura meditarer apud me
totque revolvissem vetulas et saepe diuque
singula librassem lustrans urbem spatiosam,
occurrit tandem, quod erat paupercula quaedam
linguipotensque, meae vicina sororis (apud quam
360 saepe dabatur ei cibus intuitu pietatis)
et fuerat quondam dilectae sedula nutrix.
Hanc ratus esse mihi prae cunctis utiliorem
aggredior verbis, propono probabile thema,
plurima promitto, bene si celaverit, et, si
365 prodiderit, subiungo minas. Rationibus illa
se primum excusat ventura pericula pandens:
"Me miseram," dicit, "rem si sciret pater eius,
quid factura forem? Cuius mortis genus aut quas
exciperem poenas? Etiam tu forte negares
370 te iussisse mihi nec subsidium mihi ferres!

began to hope that I could persuade her with words or with 340
gifts, and contrary to my normal practice, I decided to give
gifts as well as words, in case the words previously offered,
with which I had seduced so many hearts so many times, did
not suffice. The hidden little spark grew gradually into a
huge fire that would soon take hold in all my bones. But a 345
time and a place for speaking never coincided, especially be-
cause, to be sure, both her mother and her father, with great
vigilance and much anxious concern, built a fortress around
her so that she could not be stolen away from them, if she 350
happened to lend a receptive ear to flatteries. What was I to
do? I had to seek out a female go-between, who could speak
an exchange of words for both of us in turn, and who was el-
oquent and without suspicion, so that she could come to
both of us without occasioning surprise.

When I was pondering such matters with wakeful care 355
and had given thought to so many old women and weighed
the merits of each frequently and for a long time, while
searching widely across the city, finally it occurred to me
that there was a certain poor but eloquent woman, a neigh-
bor of my sister (at whose house she was often given food 360
out of charity), who had once been the devoted nurse of my
beloved. Thinking that she would be more useful to me than
anyone else, I solicited her with words, I set before her a
worthy proposal, I promised her many things if she kept my
secret well, and I added threats if she should betray it. At 365
first, she found reasons to excuse herself, laying out the po-
tential dangers: "Woe is me," she said, "what would I do if
her father were to learn of the affair? What sort of death, or
what punishments would I receive? Even you would perhaps
deny that you had ordered me and wouldn't come to my aid! 370

Obsecro per superos, ne sollicitaveris ultra
me super his! In pace meam finire senectam
me, rogo, permittas. Magis eligo vivere tuta,
sufficiatque mihi paupertas haec mea paucis,
375 quos mihi concedunt fatalia pensa, diebus,
quam pro divitiis adeam cum sanguine manes.
Esto, quod evadam! Magis eligo vivere tuta,
quam metui tanto tua me promissio subdat!"
    Tunc ego, quanto plus reddebat difficilem se,
380 tanto spem per eam vincendi concipiebam
maiorem, tanto plus instandum fore ducens
et monstrans, quod res a patre sua sine culpa
sciri non poterat, nec enim se proderet ipsam
tam bona, tam prudens, tam circumspecta puella.
385 Attendi tandem, quod eam promissa movere
non poterant sine muneribus. Tunc exuo morem,
munera multiplico satagens promittere plura:
Sic urgebat amor, sic ad mea fata trahebar.
Ergo dare insolito dandi modus abfuit omnis.
390 Do capram vini, do bladum doque legumen,
do pernae partem, do peplum, do tunicam, do
palliolum, do pellicium, do subareos, do
tres species telae pro camisia facienda,
quarum quae melior, collum tegit atque lacertos,
395 pectus habet mediam, sed renes deteriorem,
parsque datur peior parti, quae cuncta lucratur.
    Mox testata deos furiis se devovet, optat
damna sibi, nisi vota fideliter exsequeretur.
Itque reditque frequens et narrat plurima primo:
400 cum quanta fuerit cautela nacta frequenter

I implore you, by the gods, do not trouble me any further about this matter! I ask you to let me finish out my old age in peace. I would rather live in safety—this poverty of mine should suffice for me, for the few days that the thread of life grants me—rather than for the sake of riches suffer blood-shed and join the company of the dead. Let me pass! I would rather live in safety than have your promise subject me to so much fear!"

Then, the more intractable she showed herself, so much greater was the hope I conceived of prevailing by her aid, thinking that I should insist all the more and demonstrating that the affair could not be discovered by the girl's father ex-cept by her fault, nor would such a good, wise, and cautious girl betray her. Finally I realized that promises couldn't move her without gifts. Then I put aside my usual custom and offered many gifts, eagerly promising more: so love urged me on, and so I was drawn to my fate. As a result I observed no moderation in giving because I was unaccus-tomed to giving: I gave a goatskin of wine, I gave grain, and I gave beans; I gave part of a pork leg, I gave a shawl, I gave a tunic, I gave a cloak, I gave a leather mantle, I gave sabots, I gave three kinds of cloth for making a smock, the best of which covers the neck and shoulders, while the chest gets the middle-grade one and the kidney area gets the inferior cloth, and so the worst portion is given to the part that earns everything.

Soon, after calling upon the gods, she cast her lot with the Furies and called down punishment on herself if her promises were not faithfully fulfilled. She repeatedly went back and forth, and at first told me how much she had done: how cautiously she often awaited an opportune hour, and

375

380

385

390

395

400

horam oportunam quotiensque retenta timore,
qualiter intrarit nihilominus, et modico post,
qualiter orsa loqui qualem praetendere causam
norit, cur spatio tanto non vidit alumnam
405 adque suum quo propositum descenderit ausu,
qualibus attulerint etiam me laudibus ambae.
Addit praeterea, qualem sit passa repulsam,
sed tamen urbane. Sic me miserum modo terret,
spem modo dat tenuem. Quodsi quando reprehendo:
410 "Tu sic debueras aut sic dixisse," fidem dat,
quod sic dixisset, testesque deos vocat omnes,
quod non mentitur. Quid credam, nescio; credi
cuncta necesse tamen; credo, quia credere oportet.
Sic me deducit verbis per tempora multa.
415 Fine suo res quaeque patet. Postquam vetularum
mendacissima me totiens ambagibus actum
iam non ulterius poterat producere, quodam
ingenio simulavit eam circumveniendam.
"O praecare meus," dixit, "fiducia vitae
420 summa meae, spes subsidii baculusque senectae,
perpendi, quod te super omnes diligat ista
virgo, sed nulla id posset ratione fateri.
Quare fraude pia—sed me miseram, miseram me!—
decipienda mihi est. Faciam, quod nocte notanda
425 lota caput comenda mihi retinebitur extra
maternos thalamos; cunctisque sopore sepultis
in camera parva, quae dextra est ingredienti,
qua dormire solent ancillae, ne pater eius
rumpat, ea thalamos introgrediente, soporem,
430 reclinare caput compellam. Tuque paratus
post nonam noctis tenebris nondum tenuatis

how often she was held back by fear, how she would nevertheless go in, and shortly after, how she began to speak, and knew what sort of excuse to make why she did not see her nursling for such a long time, and with what daring she came   405 to her purpose, as well as what sort of praises both of them said about me. Moreover, she added what sort of rejection she received, albeit courteously. In this way at one moment she alarmed my poor self, and at another moment gave slight hope. But if from time to time I scolded her: "You should   410 have said such and such," she swore that she did say those things, and called upon all the gods as witnesses that she was not lying. I did not know what I should believe; yet everything had to be believed—I believed because I had to believe. In this way, she led me on with words for a long time.

Eventually, everything was revealed. After that most deceitful of old women no longer could delude me with her   415 evasions, she pretended that the girl could be overcome by a certain trick. "Oh, my dear sir," she said, "the greatest bulwark of my life, my hope for aid and the staff of my old age, I   420 have come to the conclusion that this maiden loves you more than anyone, but in no way can she acknowledge it. For this reason, using a pious trick—woe is me, woe is me—I must deceive her! I will arrange that on an appointed night, when she has washed her face, I will keep her with me out-   425 side her mother's bedroom, and when everyone is buried in sleep, I will urge her to rest her head in a small room, on the right as you enter, in which the maids usually sleep, so that her father won't wake up when she enters the bedchamber. And you be ready and arrive after the ninth hour of the   430 night, when the shadows have not yet lightened. I will

advenies. Reseraro fores et mersero lumen
lampadis, ac tacite, paulatim cardine verso
sustentando quidem, ne perstrepat ingredieris.
435 In lecto nudam invenies, tunc impiger esto!
Si semel obtineas, frustrabere postea numquam!"
    Credulus et cupidus condictam praestolor aegre
noctem multa timens et mecum multa revolvens.
Ergo die facto, quo nox erat illa futura,
440 abluo me modicum, barbam pubemque recido
dansque brevi post meridiem mea membra sopori
praeparor insomnem noctem ducturus et inde
me cibo sorbilibus, me musto poto recenti.
Hinc, ne dormitem, me libris apto legendis,
445 providus ante tamen horologium moderandum
duxi, quo veniens fieret mihi certior hora.
    Quae simulac venit, candelae suffoco lumen,
incautus gradiens impingor in ostia, frontem
posti collido, foedatus sanguine fuso
450 turbor et offendor, offensus praecipito me
perque gradus scalae descendo non numeratos.
Tunc furiis me devoveo, furiis agitandum
me reputo; nec enim nisi raro sola venire
ista sinistra solent. Superos tamen invoco frustra,
455 multa vovens, favisse meis si sensero votis.
Vere non veniunt nisi raro sola sinistra:
Atria nam solitus servare rudis neque voti
conscius in sero male clauserat ostia portae
turbaratque seram; quae singula paene furenti

unlock the doors and extinguish the light of the lamp, and you silently then enter, gradually turning the hinge and taking care that it doesn't make a noise. You will find her in the bed, naked—then go to it! If you prevail once, you'll never be disappointed again!" 435

Unsuspecting and amorous, I waited impatiently for the appointed night, with many fears and many private thoughts. Consequently, when the day arrived which that night was to follow, I bathed myself a little and cut back the hairs of my beard and groin. By letting myself take a short nap in the afternoon, I prepared my body to spend a night without sleep, and then I fed myself broth and gave myself fresh grape juice to drink. After that, so that I would not fall asleep, I busied myself with reading books. However, to be safe, I resolved that the clock should be regulated beforehand, so that I should know for certain when the hour came. 440

445

As soon as the hour came, I snuffed out the light of the candle, and taking a step without sufficient care, I crashed into the door of my room, smashing my forehead on the doorpost. And now stained with my flowing blood, I was disoriented and injured. Already hurt, I then tripped head over heels and fell down the innumerable steps of my staircase. Then I cast my lot with the Furies, and reckoned that I must have been plagued by the Furies, for misfortunes only rarely come singly. Yet I called upon the gods in vain, promising to fulfill many vows, if I found that they had favored my prayers. But truly, misfortunes only rarely come singly: for the servant who usually attended to the entrance hall, inexperienced and unaware of my wish, had improperly closed the doors of the gate in the evening and had damaged the lock. Every one of these events to me in my frenzied state, 450

455

460 tam gravis auspicii fatalia signa fuerunt.
Iamque mei male compos eram strepitusque cavendi
cura mihi deerat, confringo fores et apertas
dimitto furtis exponens quicquid habebam.
Exeo, meque tot infortunia non revocabant.
465 Ad carae procedo domum, quam vecte remoto
sentio, si tacite faciam, mihi posse patere.
Incipio fieri laetus, lateraliter intrans
explorante manu cameram lectumque requiro.
En, humili strato quasi somno pressa iacebat.
470 Quanta, putas, interna meas dulcedo medullas
tunc demulceret! Quanto meus afficeretur
tunc animus desiderio, non est leve dictu.
Illico tollo moras, omnis damnosa videtur
quantumcumque brevis mora temporis, ocius ergo
475 abicio vestes, sed et acceleratio tanta
impedit accelerare meum, mora nascitur inde,
unde moram vitare volens sic accelerabam.
Abicio vestes subitoque praeoccupo nudam,
circumplexus eam, nec ei divertere quoquam
480 iam licet, omnis ei motus est forma negata.
Virginis artari sic vult pudor, et sibi parci,
si non parcatur, reputat. Cum virgine nostra
sic decuisset agi, si praesens ipsa fuisset;
a cupido Iove sic Semelem decuisset adiri;
485 *ipsaque erat Beroe* sic a Iove non adeunda.
Heu mihi, tanta meis regnans dulcedo medullis
quam modicum mansit! Repperi contraria votis,
vertitur in luctum citharae sonus inque stuporem
deliciarum spes, moritur fax ignis amoris.
490 Si quid erat, quod hepar ventoso turbine misso

was a sign of ill omen ordained by fate. And now that I had 460
lost my self-control and lost all concern about making noise,
I broke open the doors and left them open, exposing what-
ever I possessed to theft. I went out, and all my many mis-
fortunes did not deter me. I proceeded to the house of my 465
beloved, which I perceived was lying open to me, provided I
acted silently, since the door bar had been removed. My
spirits rose as I entered the bedroom, hugging the wall as
my hand found the way, and I searched for the bed.

Behold, she was lying in a humble cot, as if deep in sleep.
You may guess how great the inner joy was that then ca- 470
ressed my marrow! It is not easy to say how great the longing
was that then possessed my mind. Immediately I stopped
holding back. Any delay, however short, seemed a hardship.
And so I swiftly cast off my clothes, but so much hastiness 475
impeded my haste, and from it a delay arose with the result
that by wishing to avoid delay, I was actually increasing it. I
cast off my clothes and suddenly seized her naked body,
holding her in my embrace; now she cannot turn away in any
direction, every form of movement was denied her. In this 480
way, a maiden's modesty wishes to be compelled, and it
thinks itself spared, if it is not spared. It would have been
proper for things to be done in the same way with my
maiden, if she herself had been present; it would have befit-
ted Semele to be visited by lustful Jupiter in this way, *and just* 485
so Beroe herself ought not to have been visited by Jupiter.

Alas, how short a time such great pleasure stayed reign-
ing in my marrow! I obtained the opposite of my prayers,
the sound of the cithara was turned into a lament, my hope
for delights into stupefaction, the torch of my amorous fire
died out. Whatever it was that the liver, sending out a windy 490

fecerat arrectum, subito languetque caditque;
sopitur virtus, frigescunt omnia membra.
Credere quis posset, quod virgo quattuor implens
nuper olympiades adeo cito consenuisset!
495 Numquam tam modico rosa marcuit. *In nova formas
corpora mutatas* cecini, mirabiliorque
non reperitur ibi mutatio quam fuit ista,
scilicet, ut fuerit tam parvo tempore talis
taliter in talem vetulam mutata puella.
500 Heu, quam dissimiles sunt virginis artibus artus!
Accusant vetulam membrorum turba senilis,
collum nervosum, scapularum cuspis acuta,
saxosum pectus, laxatum pellibus uber,
—non uber, sed tam vacuum quam molle, velut sunt
505 bursae pastorum—venter sulcatus aratro,
arentes clunes macredine, crudaque crura
inflatumque genu vincens adamanta rigore:
Accusant vetulam membrorum marcida turba.
Concitus exsurgo; coepi firmare, quod illam
510 appeterem ferro, sed mens ad se revocavit
virgineam famam; quae scandala ne pateretur,
continui, quamvis omnis spes eius habendae
iam discessisset. Sic dextra quievit, amorque
extinctus vivum potuit superare dolorem.
515 Nec fuit hoc modicum, quod desperatus amavi,
immo probatio summa fuit, quod dignus amari
sum, qui sic possum iam desperatus amare.
Non tamen inveni, quae vellet amabilitati
respondere meae, sed non ideo minus isti,
520 quam non in culpa scieram, bonus esse volebam.

gust, had made erect, suddenly weakened and drooped; my vigor was put to sleep, my whole body became cold. Who could believe that a maiden who had just recently turned sixteen had so quickly grown old! Never has a rose shriveled in such a short time. I have sung *of forms changed into new bodies,* but no change is to be found there more amazing than this one was, that such a girl was so completely changed into such an old woman in so little time. 495

Alas, how dissimilar were her body parts from a maiden's! An aged retinue of body parts betrayed her as an old woman: her sinewy neck, the sharp tips of her shoulder blades, her rocky chest, her breasts sagging down from her hide—not full but as empty and flabby as shepherds' bags—her belly furrowed as if by a plow, buttocks dried up and skinny, rough legs, and swollen knee, stiffer than adamant. This withered retinue of body parts betrayed her as an old woman. Enraged, I got up; I began to declare that I would attack her with my sword, but I called to mind the maiden's reputation. So that she would not be exposed to scandal, I held back, although all hope of having her had already departed. Thus, my right hand desisted, and though my love was dead it was still able to suppress my live feelings of resentment. Nor was it insignificant that I loved hopelessly; on the contrary, it was the greatest indication that I am worthy of being loved, since I am now so capable of loving hopelessly. Nevertheless, I did not find any way she could recompense my friendship, but still for that reason I did not wish to be less kind to one whom I had not known to be at fault. 500 505 510 515 520

Expers consilii vix vestimenta resumo,
vestimenta resumo tamen; post meque recludo
portam, tam tristis quam laetus in ingrediendo.
Adque domum veniens vix atria claudere possum,
525 vix cameram; sine luce meo me reddo cubili.
Flebilis evolvo mihi quae vindicta placeret,
sed non invenio condignam: Si moriatur,
omnis poena levis, quam momentanea finit
mors; igitur vivat luitura diu scelus istud!
530 Sit mendica manum non inveniens miserantis,
estoque, si quid ei dabitur, modicumque malumque;
panem non comedat, nisi quem dederit putre granum,
non carnes, nisi de vetula sue sive leprosas,
non pisces, quos non denuntiet undique fetor;
535 nec vinum gustet, quin sit vel pingue vel acre!
Tussiat aeternum, iuncturas gutta fatiget,
febriat absque crisi, sitis insatiabilis assit,
assit frigus iners, sed et intolerabilis aestus;
si possint, sint ambo simul saltemve vicissim!
540 Fletus ei sit continuus lacrimaeque perennes,
singultus subiti, suspiria crebra frequenter,
oscitet halitibus distenta rigoribus atque
feteat eructatio, non emungere nares
possit, in os sanies descendat tota coryzae,
545 nec spuat hoc etiam, sed glutiat evomitura.
Nec vesica vel anus contineat vel urinam
vel stercus, sed continuo fluat ante retroque;
nam post tale nefas mala tot non posset habere,
quod mihi sufficiens posset vindicta videri.
550 Ecce, superveniens luctum dolor innovat, ecce,

At a loss what to do, I recovered my clothes with difficulty; nevertheless I did recover them, and I closed the door again behind me, as sad as I was happy when entering. Coming back to my home, I was hardly able to close the door to the entrance hall or the bedroom; without light, I returned 525 to my bed. Tearfully I pondered what revenge would please me but did not hit upon a suitable one. If she were to die, the whole punishment would be light, since a quick death would have brought it to an end. Therefore, may she live for a long time to pay for this crime! May she be a beggar, not 530 finding a charitable hand, and may whatever is given to her be meager and bad! May she not eat bread, unless it's made with rotten grain, or meat, unless it is leprous or from an old sow, or fish unless their stink announces them far and wide; may she not drink wine, unless it is dull and turned to vine- 535 gar! May she cough perpetually, may gout torment her joints, may her fever burn without breaking, may she have insatiable thirst, and may she suffer an immobilizing chill, but also intolerable heat—if possible, both at the same time, but at least in alternation! May her weeping be unending, and her 540 tears everlasting, her sobs sudden, her sighs frequent and numerous. May her mouth gape, distorted in stiff exhalations, and her belches stink. May she be unable to blow her nose, may all the snot from her nasal congestion descend into her mouth, and may she still not spit it out, but swallow 545 it and vomit it up. May neither her bladder nor her anus hold back urine or shit, but may she continuously be soaked in front and behind; for after such an offense, she could not have enough misfortunes for my revenge to seem sufficient to me.

Behold, the pain returned and renewed my grief, for 550

virgo datur taedis, longinquas nobilis illam
ad partes sponsus transducit; erat locus ille,
ad quem nulla mihi veniendi causa dabatur.
Necdum compereram sibi si mea sollicitudo
555   tam mordax innotuerat, nec iam mihi tempus
investigandi—tot erant his taedia taedis.
O quicumque meam tecum traducis amicam,
de thorace meo mihi cor traxisse videris!
Sed prohibere patrem non possum, quin, ubi malit,
560   sit iungenda, mea cum non intersit aperte.
Prae cunctis etenim secreto pertinet ad me,
cum iungi nequeat, quin me disiungat in ipso.
    At vero, postquam viginti circiter annos
cum sponso fuerat partuque effeta frequenti
565   et sua iam facies dispendia parturiendi
senserat, ecce, diem supremum claudere sponsum
Fata iubent. Placuit primogenito remanente
et pro dote sua procuratore relicto
ad patrios remeare Lares. Occuritur illi
570   omnibus a notis, consanguineis et amicis.
Praeveniens alios occurro longius illi
et brevibus verbis ex ordine singula pando.
Subridens dixit: "Memini certe satis horum,
excepto, quod anum te supposuisse putabam."
575   Me testante deos quod anum non supposuissem,
"Sed quid," ait, "meminisse iuvat modo talia? Numquid
iam sumus ambo senes quasi nec complexibus apti?"
Tunc instare volens multis venientibus illi
congavisuris vetor addere quae decuisset.
580   Quodam mane meos me forte revolvere libros
contigit; adque locum veniens, ubi dicitur illud,

behold, the maiden got married, and a noble spouse took her to a distant land, to a place where I had no cause to go. But I had not yet found out if my anxiety, so gnawing, had become known to her, nor did I have time to investigate— so painful were the nuptials. O whoever you are who took my beloved away with you, it's as though you ripped my heart from my chest! But I could not stop her father from having her married when he wanted, since she was not openly my concern. But secretly she belonged to me before anyone else, since she could not be joined to another without separating from me in doing so.

But truly, after she had been with her spouse for about twenty years and was worn out by frequent childbirth, and her figure had already felt the costs of bearing children, behold, the Fates command her husband to die. She decided to return to her paternal home, while her firstborn son remained behind, and she left an agent to see to her dowry. All of her acquaintances, relatives, and friends went to meet her. Arriving a while in advance of the others, I met her and laid out everything briefly from the beginning. She said, with a laugh, "I certainly remember all this very well, except that I thought that you had topped the old lady." When I swore to the gods that I had not topped the old lady, she said, "But what pleasure does it give to remember such things now? Just because we are now both old, are we no longer fit for sex?" Then, though wishing to follow up, I was prevented from making a suitable response because many people were coming up to welcome her.

One morning, I happened to be looking through my books, and when I came to the passage where it is written,

praecipue si flore caret et cetera, risi
perque fenestellam vidi dominam venientem
—a fortunatis prognostica multa videntur.

585 Praeteritura meas erat aedes saeptaque Solis,
monte Palatino laeva de parte relicto,
tendebat lauros tripodumque, oracula visens.
Occurri satagens offerre domestica, si quid
esset ibi placidum vel si divertere vellet

590 sub tectum nostrum modica recreanda quiete.
Subiunxit: "Non est modo tempus multa loquendi,
sed mediatricem sum provisura fidelem
ad te mittendam, cum se dabit inde facultas."
   Paulo post ad me facunda pediseca quaedam

595 mittitur et secum pretiosa iocalia defert
aurea cum gemmis miro fabrefacta paratu.
"Haec," inquit, "dominae sunt illius, suus ad quam
procurator heri pro nummis misit habendis;
sed quia tanta domi numerata pecunia non est,

600 ad mercatores praesentia pignora mittit.
Ast mihi compertae, quod te non oderit, istac
in mentem venit divertere; scire sed illam
nollem, quod per te venissem, neve putares,
quod te diligeret propter tua; sed modo sano

605 credas consilio. Laudo quod te penes ulli
si modo sunt nummi, retinere iocalia cures
et sibi mutuo des! Fingam, quod me repedantem
videris a mensis et quod mensas adeundi
quaesieris causam; qua comperta voluisti

610 sic sibi succurri. Sic cor furaberis eius;
pro certoque tene, quod sit tibi grata futura!"

especially if she has lost her flower, etc., I laughed, and through a little window I saw my mistress coming—the fortunate see many things that predict the future. Her intention was to 585 pass by my house and the precinct of the Sun, leaving behind the Palatine hill on the left side, and to head toward the laurels and tripod, to visit the oracles. I rushed to meet her eager to offer her my hospitality, if she could find any peace and quiet there or if she wanted to turn aside to re- 590 fresh herself with a short rest under my roof. She rejoined: "There is no time now to say very much, but I am about to get a faithful go-between to send to you when the opportunity presents itself."

Soon after, an eloquent serving woman was sent to me, and she carried with her precious golden jewels of marvel- 595 ous workmanship studded with gems. "These," she said, "belong to that lady. Yesterday, her agent sent them to be held in place of cash. But because there is not much cash on hand at home, she is sending them to merchants as tempo- 600 rary securities. However, it came into my mind, when I discovered that she does not hate you, to divert them here. But I would not want her to know that I have come your way, and you should not think that she loves you for your money; but now, trust in my sound plan. I recommend that if you 605 have any cash now in your house, you arrange to keep the jewels and give her cash in return for them. I will pretend that you saw me coming back from the moneylenders and that you asked my reason for going to the lenders, and when you learned why, you wished to help her in this way. And so 610 you will steal her heart; you can be sure that she will be grateful to you."

Erubui, si non facerem, loculosque sigillo
signavi plenos, retinere iocalia nolens.
Sic ubi quinque dies iam transivisse notassem,
615   nec de parte sua rediisset nuntius ad me,
"Esse potest," dixi, "cum sit res invidiosa
nummi, quod nummos non dixerit haec habuisse
sic a me, quia saepe locus committere furtum
suggerit, et vere locus est occasio furti.
620   Quod si commisit, ne deprendatur in illo,
dissuadebit ei, mecum ne quando loquatur,
ne quaeram, si salva pecunia venit ad ipsam.
Quodsi quaesiero, quid erit, si deneget illa?
Non habeo testes, nec erant testes adhibendi.
625   Debueram potius sua pignora detinuisse.
Tunc nihil excusasset eam, quin fassa fuisset,
cui dimisisset tot pignora, quae, nisi nummis
acceptis, non debuerat dimittere cuiquam.
Sed volui dominae mea sic exponere large
630   tam specie quam re, quod me censeret amandum.
O si paeniteat, quod ab initio mihi tantum
dura fuit, si paeniteat! Mihi sufficit immo
ultio nulla, nisi talis delectat amantes!"
Talia dicenti mecum se quaestio gratis
635   offert solvendam: Venit ecce pediseca ridens,
"O felix," dixit, "tua te precara salutat,
quodque tuum factum sit commendabile dicit,
plusque modus facto; grates tibi grata rependit.
Utque scias, quod te propter tua nolit habere,
640   sed tua propter te, refero sua pignora mecum.

I would have felt ashamed if I had not done it, and so I marked the full purses with a seal, but refused to keep the jewels. But when I observed that five days had already passed, and the messenger for her part had not returned to me, "It could be," I said to myself, "since money often causes trouble, that she has not told her mistress that she had received money from me in this way, because often the situation prompts a person to commit a theft, and truly this situation provides an opportunity for theft. If she committed a theft, so as not to be found out, she will dissuade her mistress from ever talking to me, so that I won't ask if the money came safely to her. But if I were to ask, what will happen if she denies it? I do not have witnesses, nor were there witnesses who could be summoned. I ought rather to have kept her collateral. That way, nothing would have absolved her from confessing to whom she had given such valuable collateral, which she would not have given to anyone, unless she had received money. But I wanted to offer my money to my mistress generously, in appearance as much as in fact, so that she would consider me worthy of love. Oh, if only she would regret that she was so harsh to me at the beginning, if only she would feel regret! No revenge suffices for me, other than the kind that delights lovers!"

While I was mulling over such things, the question unprompted provided its own solution. Behold, the serving woman approached, laughing, and said: "You lucky man, your dearest greets you, and says that she commends your deed, and the method even more than the deed; she gratefully thanks you. And so that you know that she doesn't want you just for your money, but rather your money because of you, I am bringing back her collateral with me. She

615

620

625

630

635

640

Optio, vult, tua sit, an sint mansura penes te
vel tecum referas veniens ipsa potiturus.
Quam cito nam poterit, pro certo credita reddet
proque modo facti vult reddere nobile faenus,
645 corporis optati faenus; iuvat istud amantes.
Tale decet nec tale potest exactio dici.
Hoc sero venies, sed tarde; ne modo quartus
addatur testis. Quartum non vult adhiberi,
nec possunt soli duo, si non tertius assit.
650 Unica sufficiam vobis servire duobus.
Te sibi seque tibi manus haec est una datura."
    His dictis abit, invito mihi pignora tradens.
In sero venio mecumque iocalia porto.
Nec retinere volo, quia, cum fuerint data, credam
655 extunc semper ei. Nam quae reperitur in uno
verax, credibilem se quantum ad plurima reddit,
et, nisi rupta fides sit per mendacia, durat.
Non quia non multi sint, qui modicum bene reddunt,
ut maiora sibi credantur, sed secus est hic,
660 namque datum semel hoc multis praeponderat unum.
Advenio, servatque fores ancilla parata,
mox introducit, mox lectum mittit in ipsum,
et quia me fallax alias deceperat, ipsam
attrecto manibus, respondent sufficienter
665 singula: frons, sedes oculi, nasus, labra, mentum;
sentio ridentem, ruo totus in oscula. Quid plus?
Nudus suscipior cum mansuetudine multa,

wants it to be your choice whether the jewels remain in your possession or whether you bring them back with you when you come to have your way with her. As quickly as she can, she will certainly pay back the loan, and for the manner of the deed she wishes to pay you high interest, the dividend of a desired body, a thing that pleases lovers. Such a thing is appropriate and cannot be called a 'tax.' Come to her this evening but late, so that no fourth person bears witness. She does not wish for a fourth person to be employed, nor can there be two alone, if a third is not at hand. I alone will be sufficient to assist the two of you. This is the only hand that will give you to her and her to you."

After this speech, she departed, leaving the collateral with me, though against my will. I came at a late hour and brought the jewels with me. I did not wish to keep them, because from then on I would always trust her, since she gave them to me. For, whoever is found to be trustworthy in one thing, renders herself believable in many others, and, unless this trust is broken through falsehoods, it endures. Not that there aren't many who pay back a small amount faithfully so that a greater amount will be entrusted to them. This was a different matter, for this one gift outweighed many. I approached, and the serving woman, who was watching the doors in preparation for my arrival, immediately led me in and immediately put me into that very same bed. Because a deceitful woman had misled me before, I felt her with my hands, and each part corresponded as it should: her brow, the position of her eyes, her nose, lips, and chin. I perceived that she was laughing, and I threw myself wholeheartedly entirely into kissing. What more can I say? Naked I was welcomed with much gentleness; I was completely

totus in antiqui delector amoris odore.
Quod fuerat, meminisse iuvat, quantique fuisset
670 integra, fracta docet. Numquam matrona totennis
praecipue post tot partus fuit aptior illa
nullaque munda magis fuit aut melioris odoris.
Quod superest, taceo; satis est dixisse, quod unum
venimus in lectum, quod uterque sategit utrique.
675 Qui cum pace receptus eram, cum pace recessi.
     Ecce, meis in visceribus nova rixa creatur:
lis gravis, ira furens, odium mortale, perennis
rancor, inhumanus strepitus, congressio dura,
quaestio difficilis, quam nulla solutio sedat!
680 Cum recolo tacitus trutinanteque mente revolvo,
quid fortuna mihi dedit et quid casus ademit,
evehor huc illuc: Fluitans hinc gaudeo multum,
quod super optato tam longo tempore vici.
Inde memor rursum quam tarde vicero tristor,
685 quod nullo reditura modo sit fracta senectus.
Auget laetitiam desiderium diuturnum,
auget tristitiam pigra desperatio, verum
ipsam laetitiam nec desperatio tollit,
nec desiderium valet evacuare dolorem.
690 Adiuto consorte suo constanter utroque
et tamen inter se non possunt pacificari.
Quae si concurrant, neutrum neutro superatur,
nec, si librentur, nutum facit ipsa statera.
     Quis doceat dominae grates sic solvere, quod nec
695 ingratus videar vel solvere largius aequo?
Haec est summa quidem, quod grates debeo mixtas:
Nec bona nec mala sint sibi longa, sed abbrevientur;

enchanted by the scent of an old love. I took pleasure in re-membering what she had been; although now broken, she taught how great she would have been intact. Never was a 670 matron of so many years, especially after so many child-births, a better lover than her, never was any more elegant or better smelling. I'll keep quiet about the rest; it is enough to say that we came together in one bed, and that each satisfied the other. I who had been received with peace withdrew 675 with peace.

Behold, new strife arose in my innards: a weighty dispute, raging anger, mortal hatred, perennial animosity, barbarous noise, harsh conflict, a difficult question which no solution could settle! When I contemplated in silence and weighed 680 in my mind what fortune had given me and what chance had taken away, I was carried now this way, now that. Wavering, on the one hand, I rejoiced greatly that I was victorious in gaining what I had desired for so long. Then again, on the other hand, mindful of how late was my victory, I grew sad because in no way shall a broken old age be made new again. 685 Daily longing enhanced the happiness, dull despair en-hanced the sadness; but despair did not take away the happi-ness, nor could the longing expel the grief. Though each was 690 constantly reinforced by its companion, still they could not make peace between themselves. If they fought each other, neither was overcome by the other, nor, if they were weighed against each other, did the scale itself tip.

Who could teach me how to give thanks to my mistress so that I neither seemed ungrateful nor appeared to be re- 695 paying her more generously than I ought? Indeed, this was the long and the short of it—that I owed her mixed thanks. May neither her successes nor her misfortunes be prolonged

si mala sint, placeant, quo si bona, displiceant, quo
non sic tristetur, quod sit penitus sine risu,
700 nec sic laetetur, quod sit penitus sine fletu.
Si sibi fiat honor, macula sine gloria non sit,
si vituperium, velox oblivio tollat,
si sit ei damnum, pro parte tamen relevetur,
si sit ei lucrum, pro parteque damnificetur,
705 si quando metuat, solacia concomitentur,
si sit consolata, metu non sit caritura.
Sed semper morbo careat; satis est sibi morbus
pessimus, irretinebiliter ruitura senectus.
Permixtas grates sic omnis amica meretur,
710 quae, nisi fiat anus, se non concedit amico;
et mea non habeat melius vel peius eisdem,
si sua culpa fuit. Sua culpa fuisse videtur,
cum memorem facti vetulae se confiteatur.
Nam facti vetulae nisi conscia primo fuisset,
715 non se post eius memorem confessa fuisset.
Nec tamen omnis anus est talibus annumeranda.
Semper erit iuvenis mihi, quam sic inveteravi.
Haec autem mecum quia non fuit inveterata
displicet atque placet. Placet obtinuisse, sed illi,
720 cui semper fuerit tam clara iuvencula, quod non
arrigit ad vetulam, non est leve continuare.
Attendas vetulam mecum non inveteratam.
Nam iuvenes mihi semper erunt, quas inveteravi,
nec minus annosam sum quaesiturus, eo quod
725 plus timeo, ne deterior foret illa priore,
(quam sperem melius facturam) praecipue cum

but rather shortened. If she experiences misfortunes, may they be pleasing, just as if she has successes, may they displease, so that she is not so sad that she is entirely without laughter, nor so happy that she is entirely without weeping. If she has honor, may her glory not be unblemished; if she is found to be at fault, may swift oblivion remove the memory of it. If she suffers loss, may it be partially repaid; if she earns a profit, may it be partially lost. If she is ever fearful, may solace attend her; if she is consoled, may she not be without fear. But may she always be free from disease; it's enough for her to suffer the worst disease of all, old age, unstoppably hastening onward. In the same way, every girlfriend deserves mixed thanks if she does not give herself to her lover until she is an old woman; mine too should not have it better or worse than the others, if the fault was hers. The fault seems to have been hers, since she admits that she remembered the old woman's deed. For if she had not been aware of the old woman's deed from the beginning, she would not have admitted that she remembered it afterward. Yet not every old woman should be reckoned to be like these. A woman whom I have grown old with will always be young to me. However, because this woman did not grow old with me, she gave both pleasure and displeasure. It was pleasing to have obtained her, but for one, to whom she was always so outstanding as a teenager that he didn't get aroused by her as an old woman, it was not easy to keep seeing her. You must understand that this old woman did not grow old with me. For women whom I have grown old with will always be young to me, and I am not about to seek one who is younger, because I am more afraid that she will be worse than the aforementioned one (whom I hoped would do better), especially since

nunc quam primo minus praesumeret esse potentem,
et dici posset: Vetulus iam desipit iste.

LIBER TERTIUS

Istae sunt causae, propter quas amodo nolo
vivere sicut eram solitus nec subdere collum
plus intendo iugo nervos carpentis amoris.
Sed quoniam non usque caret matura senectus
5 insidiis et adhuc temptatio plurima restat,
quid faciam? Repetamne iocos, quibus ante vacabam,
delicias, quibus utebar iuvenilibus annis?
Non repetam, quia tunc etiam non me relevabant
a carae cura, nec eis oblivio curae
10 talis inest; desiderium potius revocarent
et dici posset: Vetulus iam desipit iste.
     Sed scio, quid faciam. Studio complectar anhelo
lucem, quam mecum dixi prius esse reclusam;
lucem doctrinae, quae rerum sedula causas
15 rimatur, sublimis apex in philosophia;
lucem doctrinae, quae cum sit caelica, terras
non dedignatur, sed in exilio peregrinat
isto nobiscum solacia vera ministrans.
     Adiciamque iocos dociles mathesisque sequaces.
20 Sumptibus exiguis aliquatenus aedificabo
concernens ad materiam geometrica quaedam
sic abstracta quidem, quod non sine materia sint.
Algebraeque memor, qui ludus arithmeticorum,
admittam ludum, qui rithmimachia vocatur,
25 inveniam si discipulos, quia non nisi pauci

she will assume that I am less potent now than I first was, and it could be said of me, "Now that old man is acting foolishly."

Book Three

These are the reasons why from here on out I do not wish to live as I had been accustomed, nor do I intend to place my neck any longer under the yoke of a lover who tugs at my fetters. But since mature old age does not completely lack snares, and a great deal of temptation still remains, what am 5 I to do? Am I to revisit the games with which I formerly passed the time, the delights I enjoyed in my youthful years? I won't revisit them, because even then they did not relieve me of concern for my beloved nor do they bring forgetfulness of such cares; they might instead revive my desire, and 10 it could be said: "Now that old man is acting foolishly."

But I know what I should do. With unstinting diligence, I shall describe the light that I said to myself had been previously revealed; the light of doctrine that diligently probes the causes of things, the lofty summit of philosophy; the 15 light of doctrine that although it is heavenly, does not disdain the earth but wanders in exile here with us, administering true solace.

And I will turn my attention to games that are instructive and pursuant to mathematics. Once these simple things 20 have been established to some extent, I will construct, with regard to matter, certain geometrical things that are in fact abstracted, but they do not exist without matter. Mindful of algebra, which is an arithmetical game, I will allow the game called rithmomachia, provided that I find pupils, since there 25

sunt hodie, mathesim qui censuerint imitandam.
De cantu capiam partem, quam musica scribit,
adque creatoris laudem mea cantica vertam.
Ascendam in caelum, si demonstratio pennas
30   annuat, et cursus astrorum verificabo
instrumenta levans et scribam posteritati,
qualiter inveni loca singula tempore certo,
ut conferre queant, sicut fecere priores.
    Inde creatorem per res intendo creatas
35   venari et demum per rerum quaerere causas
causam intellectu cum transcendente supremam,
sciturus per eas, super omnia cui reverendum,
cui me devoveam perfecto corde diesque
consumpturus in his, quos nutu cuncta moventis
40   significatores velut instrumenta dederunt,
per quae prima quidem regit omnia causa, prout vult.
De quibus in maiore meo licet inveniatur
libro, quod dixi Platonica verba secutus:
Neu regio foret ulla suis animalibus orba,
45   *astra tenent caeleste solum formaeque deorum,*
non tamen hic, nisi quod certum est, volo dicere; quare
diffinire necessarium non est modo, cum non
constet, utrum vivant caelestia corpora necne,
affirmare quod est temerum incertumque negare.
50   Sed quocumque modo sint, certa indagine constat,
quod, quamvis diversus eis sit motus eantque
nunc celeri motu, nunc tardo, nunc retrocedant
et nunc directe, nunc aut septentrio sursum
efferat aut retrahat pars meridiana deorsum,
55   nunc grandem parvamve putes diametron habere,
compositus tamen est diversus motus eorum

are few today who reckon that mathematics should be studied. I will take the part from song that the art of music writes, and I will turn my songs toward praise of the creator. I will rise into the sky, if my proof grants me wings, and I will 30 verify the courses of the stars, raising my astronomical instruments, and I will write for posterity how I found particular places at a certain time, so that they can discuss them, just as their predecessors did.

Then I intend to seek the creator through creation and 35 eventually to seek, through the causes of things, the highest cause with its transcendent understanding, in order to know through these inquiries, above all, who should be worshiped, to whom I should devote myself with perfected heart. To that end, I will spend my days on those signifiers, which, by the will of the one who moves all things, people have as- 40 signed as the instruments through which indeed the first cause rules all, just as he wishes. One can read about these things in my greater book, where paraphrasing the words of Plato, I said: *And so that no region might lack its own animate beings, the stars and the forms of gods occupy the ground of heaven.* 45 Yet here I only want to say what is certain; therefore, it is not now requisite to decide, since it is not certain, whether heavenly bodies are alive or not, something that is presumptuous to confirm and unsafe to deny. But however it may be, 50 it is evident from reliable investigation that, although they have different movements and sometimes they move in quick motion, sometimes in slow, sometimes they go backward and sometimes forward, sometimes the pole star in the north bears them up or the southern region draws them downward, and sometimes you would think that their orbits 55 have a large or a small diameter—nonetheless, their diverse

motibus ex aequalibus orbicularibus in se
et numeris certis et certa lege moventur.
Hoc etiam constat, quod mundi motus obedit
60 hic elementaris, sicut longus docet usus,
motibus ipsorum. Nec contradicere possunt;
qui quaecumque minus noverunt despiciunt et
dentibus invidiae praesumunt dilaniare.
Prima per ipsa quidem regit omnia causa prout vult;
65 organa sunt primi, sunt instrumenta supremi,
cuius amicitias hic si mihi comparo, nulli
post mortem teneor obnoxius esse deorum.
　　Quicquid enim teneat de dis sententia prisca,
unicus est Deus et Dominus, cui di quoque parent.
70 Salva sit ipsorum patientia, salvaque si non
esse potest, nisi diffitear, quod sentio, saltem
non dedignentur, cum sint rationis amici,
si rationibus experiar, si discutiam, quid
credi conveniat super agnitione deorum—
75 utrum sint plures vel forte sit unus eorum,
qui di dicuntur, pater et deitatis origo.
Quod si sic, iam sunt virtutes particulares
et non di, nisi grammatices accomodet usus
hoc nomen "deus" ad virtutes significandas
80 omnes, quod potius deberet abusio dici.
Tunc idiomalis haec dici quaestio posset,
quae modici pretii reputatur apud sapientes.
At si non licet os in caelum ponere, certe
non possum cogi, quin credam, quod mihi dictat
85 mens, quae de caelo mihi credita dicitur esse.
Ergo loqui liceat de primo principio, quod

movement is composed of circular motions that are uniform in themselves, and they are moved according to definite numbers and definite rules. This is also evident: that the motion of the corporeal universe here is subject to the 60 movements of these heavenly bodies, as lengthy experience teaches, and no one can say otherwise. Those who do not understand anything despise such knowledge and presume to tear it apart with the teeth of their jealousy. But in fact, through these very movements the first cause rules all, just as it wishes; they are the implements of the first cause, they 65 are the instruments of the highest. If I win its friendship for myself here, then after death I am not held in subjection to any of the gods.

For whatever ancient opinion maintains about the gods there is a single God and Lord whom the other gods also obey. Let their forbearance be undiminished, and even if it 70 cannot be undiminished unless I deny what I perceive, at least let them not disdain me, since they are friends of reason, if I seek out through reason, if I scrutinize what is fit to be believed about the understanding of the gods, whether 75 there are many, or perhaps only one of those entities, which are called gods, the father and the origin of divinity. But if so, now they are particular powers and not gods, unless the term "god" allows the grammatical usage to signify all the powers, although this should rather be called an improper 80 usage. Then, this could be called a question of language, which is reckoned to be of little value among the wise. But if one is not allowed to speak about the heavens, certainly I cannot be compelled not to believe what my mind dictates to me since that very mind is said to have been granted to 85 me from heaven. Therefore, it should be permissible to

sic est principium, quod non est principiatum.
Et quaeratur, utrum sint plures principiantes,
exempli causa, sicut quidam posuerunt,
90 ut bona principiet alter, reliquus mala, vel sit
unicus amborum, diversimode licet, auctor.
Quocirca dico, quod causa sui nihil esse
principiumve potest, quin omnipotens etiam sit;
nec decet esse deum, divinum dummodo nomen
95 restringatur ad id, quod non est principiatum,
sicut praedixi. Quid enim iuvat esse deum, si
non est omnipotens, deitasque quid addit eidem,
omnipotentia si circumscribatur ab ipso?
At verum nihil est adeo proprium deitati
100 sicut posse, nec id dignum est deitate, nisi sit
perfectum. Quare, si non est omnipotens quis,
nec deus esse potest. Sequiturque, quod, omnipotentes
si non esse duo possunt, nec di duo possunt;
di quoque si plures, et plures omnipotentes.
105 Arguo sic igitur: Duo si sunt omnipotentes
ac per id equales, aut hic dependet ab illo
aut non. Nam si sic, bina omnipotentia non est;
si non, istius poterit contrarius esse
ille voluntati, sua, si velit, impediendo
110 facta vel illius econtra forsitan iste;
nam si non possit, iam non est omnipotens is,
si vero possit, alius non omnipotens est.
Sic igitur rebus independentibus a se
omnipotentatus non posset inesse duabus,
115 quare nec deitas. Tantum est igitur Deus unus,
strenuus, excelsus, super omnia glorificandus.
Hic Deus est virtus quaedam, quae transilit omnem

speak about the first beginning, which is the beginning be-
cause it was not itself begun. And it should be asked whether
there are multiple first agents—for example, as some have
maintained, that one originates the good, and the other the 90
bad—or if there is a single author of both, though in differ-
ent ways. Therefore, I say that nothing can be the cause or
the origin of itself without being omnipotent; nor can it
properly be a god, so long as the term "god" is confined to 95
that which was not begun, as I said above. For what good
does it do for there to be a god, if he is not omnipotent, and
what does divinity add to him, if omnipotence is excluded
from him? In truth, nothing is so proper to a deity as power,
and that power is not worthy of divinity, unless it is absolute. 100
For this reason, if someone is not omnipotent, he cannot be
a god. And it follows that, if two cannot be omnipotent,
then there cannot be two gods; likewise, if there are many
gods and many omnipotent beings.

Therefore I argue as follows: if there are two omnipotent 105
beings and in this respect equal, then either one is subordi-
nate to the other or not. For if so, there is no double omnip-
otence; if not, one could be opposed to the will of the other
by hindering, if it wishes, its actions, or perhaps vice versa. 110
For if one is unable to do so, then it is not omnipotent, but if
it is able, then the other is not omnipotent. So therefore,
omnipotence cannot be present in two entities independent
of each other, and so neither can divinity. Therefore, there 115
is only one God, vigorous, lofty, and, above all, worthy of
veneration.

This God is a power which surpasses every power, a

virtutem, virtus super omnem simplicitatem
simplex, a nostra sic cognitione remota
120 simplicitate sua, quod per se scibilis ipsam
non est a nobis, non quod de parte sua sit
defectus, sed nos hebetes sumus ad capiendum
esse rei vires nostras ita transgredientis.
Sed nec habet virtus haec, cum sit prima, prius se
125 per quod in ipsius veniatur cognitionem.
Quare non nisi per sua posteriora scietur,
quae sunt res omnes quas mundus continet in se,
nam mundum Deus ex nihilo mundanaque fecit
solus ab aeterno. Sed cum non posset apud se
130 tanta pati bonitas etiam quemcumque colorem
invidiae, voluit quibus esset largus habere.
Et primo duo materiam lucemque creavit,
ut, per quod fieret, hic mundus haberet, et ex quo.
Sed qui materiam vult informem meditari,
135 cogitur, ut sicut punctum meditetur eandem.
Nam quantum nihil esse potest et fine carere,
finitumque quod est et formam constat habere.
  Ergo materiae, quae se reddit meditanti
sub puncti specie, lux illa supervenit, et cum
140 sit manifestatrix, ad formam suscipiendam
aptat eam, quoniam per totum digerit illam,
igniculisque fovens partem diffundit in omnem,
motibus oppositis, faciens diametron ubique.
Cumque sit ambarum finita potentia, standi
145 terminus est positus, quo sistitur utraque virtus,
scilicet extendens extensaque sic, ut in illis
plus nec agente potest patiens nec agens patiente.
Commensurat eas eadem proportio, sicque

ON THE OLD WOMAN

power single beyond all singleness, so removed from our understanding in its singleness, that it is not knowable to us in its essence, not because it is deficient in some part, but because we are sluggish in understanding the essence of a being that so transcends our abilities. But this power, since it is first, does not have anything prior to itself by which we can come to an understanding of it. Therefore, it will be known only through its later acts, which are all the things that the world contains in itself, for God, alone from eternity, made the world and the things of the world from nothing. But since such great goodness would also be unable to suffer any nuance of envy, it wanted to have something to which it might be generous. First he created two things— matter and light—so that this world should have something by which and from which it was made. But whoever wishes to visualize formless matter is forced to visualize it as if it were a single point, for nothing can have magnitude and lack a limit, and what is finite must have form.

Therefore, that light intersects with matter, which may be visualized in the form of a point, and since it is an illuminator, it prepares it to take on form, since it pervades it in its entirety, and, spreading warmth with its fires, suffuses every part, by its opposing motions, causing an expansion in every direction. When the capacity of each of them reaches its limit, a static end point is established, where each power comes to a halt, namely the one causing expansion and the one being expanded, so that among them the passive one cannot be affected any more by the active or the active affect any more the passive. The same proportion delimits

crementi motu cessante reflectitur in se.
150 Hac fit sphaera via, tali distincta tenore,
ut pars interior sit densior, apta quieti,
in qua plus de materia, de luce minus sit,
pars sit et exterior subtilis et apta moveri,
in qua plus de luce, minus de materia sit.
155 Haec pars humanam speciem regit, illaque pascit.
     Porro pars sphaerae, medium quae possidet et quae
densior est alia, per quattuor est elementa
sic connexa sibi divisa, quod alterutrorum
vires oppositas medium commune maritat.
160 Inque novem caelos extrinseca dividitur pars,
quorum forma quasi tunicatim contineat se;
in quorum septem propiori parte planetae
septem discurrunt diversis motibus acti.
Horum sunt superi Saturnus, Iuppiter et Mars,
165 Sol medius, sub Sole Venus, praecepsque sub illa
Mercurius, terraeque propinquior infima Luna.
Stellas octavum caelum fixas habet uno
motu contentas, ut in his contrarietas sit
tanta, quod unicus est, ubi corpora plurima, motus,
170 et rursum motus, ubi corpora singula, multi.
     At nonum caelum, quantum ad nos ordine primum,
quantum ad naturam dictum quoque mobile primum,
nullum corpus habet, sed lux diffusa per ipsum,
quanto materiae radix removetur ab ipso,
175 tanto concerni potuit minus, ut fieret lux
illic visibilis; nec enim nisi materiatum
visibus offert se. Motu lux ista diurno
caelum, sic a materie radice remotum,

them both, and so it is turned back on itself once the motion that brings growth ceases. In this way, a sphere is created, divided in such a manner, that the inner part is denser and inclined to motionlessness and in it there is more matter and less light, while the outer part is thinner and inclined to movement, and in it there is more light and less matter. The latter part rules the human species, the former part nourishes it.

Moreover the part of the sphere that occupies the middle and that is denser than the rest is both connected to itself and divided by the four elements in such a way that the middle they share unites the opposing strengths of each. The outer part is divided into nine heavens, whose form is like concentric layers; in the part of these closer to the earth, seven planets roam, driven by seven different motions. The highest of these are Saturn, Jupiter, and Mars, the Sun is in the middle, Venus beneath the Sun, beneath Venus swift-moving Mercury, and nearer to the earth is the lowest, the Moon. The eighth heaven holds fixed stars united by a single motion, with the result that there is a very great contradiction among these heavenly bodies, because there is a single motion where there are multiple bodies, but on the other hand, many motions where there are single bodies.

But the ninth heaven, with respect to us the first in rank, but in respect to nature called the first thing to move, has no body, but light is diffused throughout it. To the degree that the essence of matter is removed from it, it is less subject to the intermingling necessary for light to become visible there; for only when blended with matter does it offer itself to sight. This light, by its daily motion, moves this heaven, so distant from the essence of matter, with such swift power

tam rapida virtute movet tantoque vigore
180   circumvolvit, ut et caelos secum trahat omnes
in se contentos, secum circumrotet omnes
nocte dieque semel et mundanum super axem.
Axis mundanus est linea, quae quia transit
per centrum mundi inque polo finitur utroque,
185   maior ea nulla est immotaque sola quiescit.
Sola quiescit, sed non est longissima sola.
Exclusa maiore potest aequalis haberi,
circulus omnis enim, qui dividit in duo sphaeram,
maximus est pariterque suus longissimus axis;
190   quorum qui supra mundi componitur axem,
cuius describit motum revolutio primum,
dicitur aequator et dicitur aequidialis.
Sed quia sunt multi motus praeter memoratum
his octo caelis, unus tamen est generalis
195   et super axem, qui mundi declinat ab axe
per quintam decimam, modico minus, et suus orbis
non est aequatore minor, qui dicitur orbis
signorum vel zodiacus; quantumque recedit
axis ab axe, suus declinat et orbis ab orbe;
200   caelorumque sub hoc motus describitur octo.
     Sed quia caelos hos motus vehementia primi
vincit nec possunt ipsum usque sequi, reputatur
ipsorum motus primo contrarius esse.
Non tamen est, sed id incurtatio visibus offert,
205   vincunturque magis, quanto magis inde remoti,
et qui tardior est, velocior esse videtur.
Nam lux illa movens virtus est immediate
a primo motore fluens in mobile primum
et movet ipsum sic, ut motor non moveatur,

and makes it revolve with such energy, that it drags with it   180
all of the other heavens contained within it and causes them
all to move in a circle with it once each day and night above
the world's axis. The world's axis is a line that, because it
passes through the center of the world and terminates at
each pole, none is greater than, and it alone rests unmoving.   185
It alone is at rest, but it is not alone in being the longest. Al-
though there is nothing greater, it can be considered to have
an equal, for every circle that divides a sphere in two has the
maximum diameter and is equal to its longest axis. Of these   190
circles, the one that is placed above the axis of the world,
whose revolution describes the first motion, is called the
equator and also the equinoctial. But while there are many
movements in these eight heavens in addition to the one
mentioned, there is yet one general movement above the   195
axis, which is tilted from the axis of the world by a bit less
than a fifteenth part and whose orbit is not less than the
equator. This is called the orbit of the signs, or the zodiac,
and however much its axis tilts from the world's axis, its or-
bit also tilts from the equator; and the motion of the eight   200
heavens is delineated beneath this.

But because the strength of the first motion surpasses
these heavens, and they cannot follow it all the way, it is
thought that their motion is in opposition to the first mo-
tion. However, it is not, but rather that failure to keep up
presents itself to sight, and the further they are from it, the   205
more they are surpassed, and the one that is slower seems to
be faster. For that moving light is power, flowing directly
from the prime mover into the first thing to move, and
he moves it in such a way, that the mover is not moved,

210 sed manet immotus. Licet illa necesse moveri
sit, quaecumque movent contactu, non tamen illa,
quae virtute movent, idcirco necesse moveri.
　　Amplius hoc caelum sic hac virtute movetur,
ut numquam totum mutare locum queat in se,
215 sed solae partes eius mutant loca quando
circumvolvuntur, quia motus is orbicularis,
cui nihil oppositum, semper durabilis ergo,
sese continuans in partem semper eandem
et circa medium, quia nec leve nec grave caelum est.
220 Ast elementorum levitas ubi vel gravitas est,
est motus rectus, quia, quod gravitate movetur,
ad medium trahitur et, quod levitate, recedit
a medio; quorum sunt oppositi sibi motus
ad loca tendentes diversa, quibus sibi nactis
225 quodlibet in propria regione quiescit eorum
inde nec extrahitur nisi per motum violentum.
　　Hae mundi partes, caelestis scilicet illa,
haec elementaris, mundo servire minori
non dedignantur. Mundus minor est homo, cuius
230 e caelo vita est et victus ab his elementis.
Sic dictus, quia sit mundi maioris ad instar
factus, converso licet ordine, nam quod in illo
grossius est iacet in medio, subtilius extra.
Hic vero latet interius subtile, velut sunt
235 cor, cerebrum nec non et hepar, dominantia membra;
testiculique, licet sint ex his, sunt tamen extra
ob generativam foris auxiliantis egentem.
Ista quidem vice caelorum funguntur in ipso;

but remains immobile. Although it is necessary for those 210
things that move by contact to be moved, nevertheless it is
not on that account necessary for those things that cause
motion through power to be moved.

Further this heaven is moved by this power in such a way
that it can never in its entirety change its position in respect
to itself, but only parts of it change their places in it when 215
they revolve, because that circular motion, that meets no
opposition, is therefore everlasting, always maintaining it-
self in the same part and around the middle, since heaven is
neither light nor heavy. But where there is lightness or 220
heaviness in the elements, there is straight motion, because
what is moved by heaviness is drawn toward the middle and
what is moved by lightness withdraws from the middle. The
motions of each are opposite each other and are directed to-
ward different locations, and when they have gotten there,
any one of them that has come to rest in its own region can- 225
not be pulled away from there except by violent motion.

These parts of the world, namely the heavenly and the el-
emental, do not scorn serving the lesser world. This lesser
world is man, whose life comes from heaven and whose sus- 230
tenance from these elements. He is so called, because he
was made in the image of the greater world, although in re-
verse configuration, for what is coarser in the greater world
lies in the middle, and what is finer on the outside. But in a
person, the fine material remains hidden on the inside, such
as the heart, the brain, and also the liver—the ruling organs; 235
and the testicles, although they are part of these, are none-
theless external because their generative function needs
the assistance of an opening. Indeed, these organs play the
role of the heavens in a person, and have been specifically

et quibus est servire datum specialiter istis,
240 scilicet arteriae, pulmo tracheaque cordi,
venae, fel et splen hepati, nervique cerebro
sensus et motus, et semen dantia vasa
testiculis, stomachusque cocus generalis eorum.
    Sol in corde manet et in arteriis dominatur
245 vivificans per eas totius corporis artus.
Mercurius patulam pulmonis habet regionem,
tracheam quoque vociferam linguamque loquacem.
Testiculos Venus et quae semen vasa ministrant
sortitur, sed hepar Iovis est stomachusque cibator.
250 Splen Saturnus habet, Mars fel, et Luna cerebrum.
Stellatum caelum nervos, sensus habet atque
nonum motivos, cuius rapit omnia motus.
Virtutes iterum potes assignare planetis,
et naturales in primis: Appetit ergo
255 Mercurius, retinet Saturnus, digerit autem
Iuppiter, expellit Mars, pascit Luna, nutrit Sol,
atque Venus generat. Post quas et sic animales:
Sentit Iuppiter, et Sol cogitat ac ratione
utitur, ac meminit Saturnus, Luna localem
260 exercet motum, discernit Mercurius, Mars
iram succendit, desiderium Venus auget.
    Compositos itidem dabis humores elementis:
Aera sanguis habet, habet ignem cholera, terram
melia, phlegmon aquam. Sed rursus homogeneorum
265 membrorum quaedam sunt horum danda quibusdam:
Ossa quidem terrestria sunt aqueaeque medullae,
aereae carnes, cutis ignea, cetera claudens
in se, sicut ibi tria circumplectitur ignis.
Distribuuntur item sic officialia membra:

assigned to people as their servants: the arteries, lungs, and 240
the windpipe to serve the heart; the veins, gall bladder, and
spleen, the liver; the nerves, sensation, and movement, the
brain; the vessels that give semen, the testicles; and the
stomach is the cook shared by them all.

The Sun dwells in the heart and reigns over the arteries,
giving life through them to the parts of the entire body. 245
Mercury holds wide sway over the lungs, as well as the voice-
bearing windpipe and the talkative tongue. Venus is allotted
the testicles and the vessels that supply semen, but the liver
is Jupiter's, as is the stomach that digests food. Saturn holds 250
the spleen, Mars the gallbladder, and the Moon the brain.
The starry heaven has the nerves, and the ninth heaven sen-
sation and movement, whose motion carries everything
along. Again, you can assign powers to the planets. First the
natural powers: consequently, Mercury desires, Saturn holds 255
in check, while Jupiter distributes, Mars expels, the Moon
feeds, the Sun nourishes, and Venus begets. After these, in
the same way there are the animal powers: Jupiter feels, the
Sun thinks and uses reason, while Saturn remembers, the
Moon exercises local motion, Mercury discerns, Mars in- 260
flames anger, and Venus increases desire.

Similarly, you can assign matching humors to the ele-
ments: blood has the qualities of air, yellow bile of fire;
black bile of earth; and phlegm of water. And again, certain
parts of the body can be assigned to certain elements 265
that are similar to them: the bones are like the earth, the
marrow is like the water, the flesh is like the air, while
the skin that encloses the rest within itself, just as fire sur-
rounds the other three elements in the cosmos, is like fire.
So also are the organs distributed according to function:

270 Arce manens caput in supera iuri datur ignis,
venter aquae, dorsum terrae, manuumque pedumque
ramos aer habet, cuius per inane vagantur.
Sic homo maioris est mundi factus ad instar,
sic homini totus maior mundus famulatur,
275 sic hominem caelique regunt elementaque pascunt.
    Sed specialius est caeli pars una dicata,
ut proprie per eam species humana regatur.
Nam quamvis homini totum caelum famuletur,
appropriata tamen est cuilibet ex elementis
280 quaedam pars caeli: Regionem Sol regit ignis
materiamque cometarum sublimat ad ipsam
subtilemque levat pro dando rore vaporem.
Inde minoribus est datus aer quinque planetis,
ad quorum motum mutatio temporis omnis
285 accidit et veniunt nix, grando, tonitrua, fulmen,
ventique et pluviae. Lunae sequitur mare motum
acceditque ad nos, quotiens ad meridianum
Luna venit, quotiens et ad horizonta, recedit,
fortius accedens, quotiens ascendit ad augem
290 orbis Luna sui. Cuius centrum quia distat
a centro mundi, nomen quoque traxit abinde
cuspidis egressae. Similique modo quotiens est
orbis in auge brevis, quem nominat ars epicyclum,
et quotiens utriusque simul conscendit in augem,
295 est, sicut plus esse potest, accessio fortis.
Tunc etiam pisces meliores sunt ad edendum,
praecipue, qui sunt in conchis degere nati.
In terra tandem stellae fixae dominantur,
ad numerum quarum datus est numerus specierum;
300 quae tamen ex stellis cui serviat ex speciebus,

dwelling at the highest summit, the head is assigned to the   270
domain of fire, the belly to that of water, and the back to
that of earth, while the branches of the hands and feet are
assigned to the air through whose void they wander. Thus,
man was made in the image of the greater world, and so the
whole of the greater world serves him; the heavens rule him   275
and the elements feed him.

But one part of heaven more particularly is dedicated to
governing the human species as its own. For although all of
heaven serves mankind, still a certain part of heaven has
been assigned to each of the elements: the Sun governs the   280
region of fire and elevates the material of comets toward it
and lifts up thin vapor for making dew. Next the air has been
assigned to the five lesser planets, at whose motion every
change of season happens, and snow, hail, thunder, light-   285
ning, wind, and rain come about. The sea follows the move-
ment of the Moon and comes toward us whenever the Moon
arrives at the meridian, and when it approaches the horizon,
the sea recedes, rising with greater strength whenever the
Moon ascends to the apogee of its orbit. Because the center   290
of its orbit is distant from the center of the earth, for this
reason it also has been called the distant center. And in a
similar manner, whenever its short orbit, which the art of
astronomy names the "epicycle," is at its apogee and when-
ever the orbit of both the sun and the moon reaches its apo-
gee at the same time, there is as strong a high tide as there   295
can be. At that time, too, the fish are better to eat, especially
those that were born to live in shells. Finally, the fixed stars
have dominion over earth, to whose number corresponds
the number of species; yet it is unknown which star serves   300

nescitur, sed homo regitur specialiter orbe
nono, qui caelos et continet et movet omnes.
Unde fit, ut, sicut stellarum motus obedit
et trahitur caeli, quod continet omnia, raptu,
305 sic dominatur homo cunctis aliis speciebus.
Sicut et in caelo lux est subtilior isto,
sic homo dignior est mentisque capacior altae.
Sicut et hoc caelum primus fovet immediate,
sic hominis speciem super omnia diligit idem.
310   Et cum de cunctis sit cura Deo speciebus,
de solis individuis huius speciei
cogitat, in quorum sunt cuncta creata favorem,
illis praecipue dans quandam nobilitatem,
vim speculativam, divini munus honoris,
315 per quod dignatus sibi nos est assimilari
infundendo creans ipsam infundensque creando.
Ac aliae vires animae cum commoriantur
omnes corporibus, se separat unica vis haec
corpore nec pereunte perit, quoniam licet ipsa
320 non sit ab aeterno, postquam tamen incipit esse,
durat in aeternum, cuius quia condiciones
aeternas quasdam inveniunt, sub tempore quasdam
dixerunt, quod eam factor lucis creat inter
tempus et aeternum confinem ambobus ad instar
325 horizontis, qui duo semispheria mundi,
visum scilicet a non viso, dividit aeque.
Separat autem se quoniam de corpore toto,
non habet organicam respondentem sibi partem.
Est igitur sine fine manens, ubi coeperit esse.
330   Horum mundorum nullo Deus iste iuvante
materiam potuit, scivit voluitque creare

which species, though man is specifically ruled by the ninth circle, which both contains and moves all of the heavens. For this reason, it happens that, just as the motion of the stars obeys and is drawn by the rapid movement of the heaven that contains everything, so man has dominion over all other species. And also just as light is finer in the ninth heaven, so man is of greater worth and more capable of lofty thought. Just as the prime mover nurtures this heaven directly, so he esteems the human species above all. 305

And though God cares for all species, he thinks only about individuals of this species, for whose advantage all things were created, giving them in particular a certain nobility, the ability to reason, the gift of divine honor, through which he deigned that we should be made similar to himself, creating that ability in the process of imparting it, and imparting it in the process of creating it. And while all the other abilities of the soul die with the body, this ability alone separates itself from the body and does not perish when the body perishes, since, though it does not exist from eternity, nonetheless, after it begins to exist, it endures forever, because philosophers find certain conditions of the soul eternal, and they have called certain others subject to time, since the maker of light creates the soul between time and eternity, akin to both, just like the horizon, which equally divides the two hemispheres of the universe, namely, the seen from the unseen. Moreover, as soon as the soul separates itself from the whole body, it does not have the physical part responding to it. Therefore, it remains in existence without end, once it has begun to exist. 310 315 320 325

This God was able, knew how, and wished to create the matter of these two worlds with no assistance, and to shape 330

ac ipsos de materia formare creata
maiori lucem infundens animamque minori,
et placuit sibi, quod tales essent duo mundi
335 quodque duae partes, quas mundus habet minor, essent,
haec finibilis, et semper durabilis illa,
et quod maiori motus essent duo mundo,
hic finibilis, et semper durabilis ille.
Non tamen univoce sumatur semper utrumque;
340 nam semper durant animae sine fine manentes,
sed motus cessare potest durasseque semper;
semper enim durat, quod tempore durat in omni
et motum tempusque sibi liquet esse coaeva,
nam nec motus erit sine tempore nec sine motu
345 tempus. Quae sicut coepisse simul potuerunt,
stare simul poterunt, cum terminus affuerit, quem
conditor imposuit, nec eum novit nisi solus
impositor. Sicutque fit, ut durante perenni
motu causatur perpes generatio, sic et
350 iste status causat vitam sine fine quietam,
ut, quod vixerat hic ad tempus in his elementis,
vivat in aeternum super orbes glorificatos
—de rationali dico, cui vita superstat.
    Statim ergo veniente statu fient nova cuncta,
355 schemate nam simili status innovat omnia, sicut
et motus generat. Caeli generatio moti
est effectus et eiusdem surrectio stantis.
Ad motum caelum finiti temporis esse
pertinet; ad stans atque quietum pertinet esse
360 aeternum fixumque manens et glorificatum.
Porro statum sequitur surrectio tam generalis,
quam praeter motum generaliter omnia stabunt.

them from created matter by infusing the greater with light and the lesser with soul, and it pleased him that the two worlds would be of this nature and that the lesser world would have two parts, the one finite, and the other always enduring; and that there would be two motions for the greater world, the one finite, and the other always enduring. Yet the similarity between the two should not be assumed to be absolute, for souls endure forever, remaining without end, but motion can cease and always endure. For something that always endures, endures in all of time, and motion and time are clearly coeval, for there will be no motion without time, and no time without motion. Just as these were able to begin at the same time, so they could stop at the same time, when the end arrives that the creator has imposed, an end that no one knows except the one who causes it. And just as it happens that perpetual generation is caused by the sustained continuation of motion, so also its stopping causes a life of unending restfulness, so that what had lived here temporarily in these elements lives for eternity above the exulted orbits—I speak of the rational part of the soul, whose life continues.

Therefore, all things will be made new at the moment when this stopping occurs, for this stopping renews everything with a similar design as before, just as it also produces motion. It has the effect of generating a moving heaven, as well as mobilizing it from a stationary position. For heaven to be of a fixed period of time pertains to motion, for it to be eternal, fixed, and glorified pertains to it being stationary and at rest. Furthermore, a mobilization follows upon its stopping as universal as will be the universal stillness of all

Ergo necessario nova fient omnia, caelum
sidera, mundus; et hic et corpora nostra resurgent.

365 "Si stet motus," ais, "sic est, sed stare necesse
non est; et quamvis sit naturale resolvi,
quod iunxit natura, tamen non vult Deus illud,
quod ratione bona iunctum fuit, usque resolvi;
unde fit, ut, quicquid natura solubile iunxit,

370 sanxierit bonitate sua divina voluntas."
Haec ais; haec et ego: Simul unica perficiendis
omnibus organicis non sufficit entelechia;
est animabus et hoc aliquid, quo dicitur una
quaelibet illarum, quo differt omnis ab omni.

375 Si vero motus non stet, generatio semper
continuabitur, et species humana creatas
infusasque novas animas sibi multiplicabit.
Separat autem se virtus animae speculatrix
propter eam causam, quam dixi; sic animarum

380 infinitus erit numerus. Natura sed istud
non patitur, nec stare potest quare neque primum.
Sic stabit motus, sic corpora nostra resurgent,
ad proprium corpus anima quacumque reversa.
Non quod Deucalion sit Pyrrha futura, sed illud

385 corpus idem numero, quod habebat, uterque resumet,
ut, quia pro meritis reddenda est gloria, poena
pro culpis, proprios actores quaeque sequatur.
Sic mutabit nos excelsi dextera solo
verbo (nam standum si iusserit, illico stabit),

390 non ut dissolvat, quae iuncta bona ratione
sunt, sed ut in melius commutans sanciat illa.

things without motion. So, inevitably, everything will become new—the heavens, the stars, the world; and this world and our bodies will rise again.

"This is the case if motion should stop," you say, "but it is not necessary for it to stop. And although it is natural for what nature has joined to be separated, nonetheless, God does not want something that has been joined with good reason ever to be separated; so it happens that whatever nature has joined in a separable union the divine will has consecrated with its own goodness." That is what you say, but I reply: a single entelechy is not capable of completing all organisms at the same time; souls also have something else, by which each of them is said to be unique, and by which every soul differs from every other. But if motion does not stop, generation will always continue, and the human species by itself will multiply the creation and animation of new souls. Moreover, power, the guardian of the soul, divides itself for the reason I have said above; and thus there will be an infinite number of souls. But Nature does not allow this, therefore she is able neither to stop nor to be the first thing. Thus, the motion of the universe will stop, and our bodies will rise again, when every soul has been returned to its own body. Not so that there will be a Deucalion and Pyrrha in the future, but rather, each will take up again that body which it had before, the same in number so that, because glory must be given in exchange for merits, and punishment for faults, each reward or punishment corresponds to an individual's actions. Thus, the right hand of the most high will change us by a single word (for if he orders something to stop, it will stop on the spot), not to separate what has been joined together with good reason, but to consecrate them by transforming them for the better.

Forte tuus tamen id non sustinet intellectus
ignis reliquias sic in melius renovari
posse, quod et memini dicens haec de Iove verba:
395 *Esse quoque in fatis reminiscitur affore tempus,*
quo mare, quo tellus correptaque regia caeli
ardeat et mundi moles operosa laboret.
Sed de hoc non est ius; is enim, qui primo creavit
omnia de nihilo, reparare potest ea multo
400 fortius ex aliquo, renovando modo meliori.
Hic Deus omnipotens est virtus illa suprema,
cui me devoveo, cui soli confiteor me
totum deberi, cui soli debeo grates
tam de gratuitis quam naturalibus et quam
405 fortunae donis. Isti me iudice soli
debetur reverentia, debetur famulatus.
Huius amicitias hic si mihi comparo, spero,
quod meliore gradu coram se stare iubebit.
Huius cultorem me repromitto futurum,
410 huius et—o utinam merear—*meminisse priusquam*
adveniant anni, quos dicam non placituros,
sol ut obumbretur et stellae lunaque solis
lumen, post pluviam redeant nubes iterato,
custodesque domus seu fortes commoveantur,
415 *quique vident per parva foramina, contenebrescant,*
filia carminis obsurdescat, surgere mane
quae solet ad vocem volucris, ducantque molentes
otia, formident timeantque excelsa viarum,
flore suo canescat amigdalus, imminuatur
420 *capparis, in lumbis impingueturque locusta,*
rumpatur funis argenteus, atque recurrat
aurea virga, super contrita sit hydria fontem,

Yet, perhaps your understanding does not grasp the idea that what is left over after a fire can be renewed for the better in this way, a concern I also mention when citing these words about Jupiter: *He also recollects that it is fated that there* 395 *would be a time when the sea, the land, and the palace of heaven would catch fire and burn, and the carefully constructed mass of the world would suffer.* But no universal principle requires this, for he who first created all things out of nothing can renew these things much more vigorously out of something, making them even better. This omnipotent God is that 400 highest power to whom I devote myself, to whom alone I confess that I am totally indebted, and to whom alone I owe thanks, both for the gifts of grace and for the gifts of nature and fortune. In my judgment, to him alone reverence is 405 owed, to him alone obedience. If I win his friendship for myself here, I hope that he will command me to stand before him somewhere better.

I promise that I will be his worshipper and be mindful of him—oh, may I merit it—*until the years come, which I predict* 410 *will bring no pleasure, when the sun and the stars, the moon and the light of the sun shall be darkened, and the clouds shall return again after the rain. The keepers of the house and strong men shall tremble, and those who look through windows shall be darkened.* 415 *The daughter of music shall grow deaf, she who is accustomed to rise up in the morning at the sound of the bird. The millers shall prolong their leisure, and they shall shun and fear the high places of the roads. The almond tree shall grow white with blossom, the caper bush shall waste away, and the locust shall grow fat in* 420 *its loins. The silver cord shall be broken, and the golden staff shall shrink back, and the pitcher shall be smashed at the fountain,*

cisternamque super confringatur rota, pulvis
in terram redeat, sed liber spiritus ipsum
425 *evolet ad Dominum, qui desursum dedit illum.*

Temporis illa dies finem faciet mihi vita
victuro meliore quidem, si reddidero me
gratum factori largitorique bonorum,
praecipue si serviero sibi, si bonitatem
430 ipsius summam dilexero corde tenaci
menteque perfecta, si glorificavero laude
neve creaturae cultus impendero dignos
maiestate sua seu reddendos sibi soli.
Sic igitur metuenda dies non est mihi mortis,
435 et, si non alias, ideo saltem, quia finem
exilio faciet mors: regibus exulibusque
communem patriam parat et communiter omnes
urbe sua recipit et nullos inde relegat.

Porro non penitus caret utilitate, quod ipsa
440 terminat exilium, quale est habitare sub arcto,
quale Getas inter, quia proximitate Getarum
deterius nihil esse potest, ubi vivere certe
non aliud reputo quam mortem continuare.
Quamvis esse malam mortem super omnia dicant,
445 non nihil est finire malum; mala sunt bona finem
impositura malis. Non semper vivere vellem,
si non concessum simul esset posse reverti.
Nam quoniam reditum mihi iam sperare negatum est,
opto mori; sed si mihi vivere forte liceret
450 in patria, gravior foret exspectatio mortis.

Nec me quorundam deterret opinio vana,
qui dicunt animas apud infernalia regna
exercere, quod hic exercuerant, quia verum

and the wheel broken at the cistern. The dust shall return into the
earth, but the spirit shall fly free to its Lord, who bestowed it from   425
above.

That day will mark the end of time for me, when I will
live in a better life—at least if I render myself acceptable to
the maker and bestower of good things, especially if I am
obedient to him, if I love his supreme goodness with a stead-   430
fast heart and a perfect mind, if I glorify him with praise and
do not expend on the created world the worship that befits
his majesty and should be rendered to him alone. Therefore,
I have no cause to fear the day of death, for this reason at   435
least, if for no other, because death will make an end of exile:
it provides a homeland common to kings and to exiles, re-
ceives all in common in its city, and banishes no one from it.

Further, death is not entirely without its benefit, in that
it ends exile, like that of living in the far north, and among   440
the Getae, for nothing can be worse than the vicinity of the
Getae, where I reckon that life is nothing other than a pro-
longed death. Although they say that death is the worst of
all evils, it is no small thing to put an end to evil; bad things   445
are good, if they put an end to evils. I would not want to live
forever, if at the same time the possibility of returning was
not allowed. For as soon as I am denied the hope of return, I
would prefer to die; but if, by chance, I were allowed to live
in my homeland, the expectation of death would be harder   450
to bear.

I am not deterred by the groundless opinion of certain
men who say that, in the infernal kingdoms, souls continue
at what had occupied them here, because if this were true, I

si foret hoc, non exilium fugerem moriendo.
455 Di melius! Quodsi dixisse redarguar illud,
non fuit hoc, quia sic sentirem, sed quia vulgo
cum loquerer, vulgi decreta tenere volebam.
Verior et potior sententia philosophorum,
illorum proprie, quos illa scientia dives
460 occupat astrorum, qui partem iudiciorum
exercent et principiorum reddere causas
sufficiunt varios effectus inde probantes.
    Hos apud invenies, quid significare planetis,
quid signis domibusve datum, quia circulus ipse
465 dividitur bimode per bis sex signa domosque;
haec divisio naturalis et haec situalis.
Diversasque trahunt vires ab utraque planetae;
qui cum sint septem, duo sunt ibi lumina magna,
estque planeta diurnus Sol nocturnaque Luna,
470 et rursus Sol masculus est et femina Luna,
Sol calidus siccus, et est umida frigida Luna.
Pertinet ad Solem virtus activa caloris;
pertinet ad Lunam passiva sed umiditatis.
Sicque potest dici Sol sponsus Lunaque sponsa,
475 ex quibus in mundo res omnis habet generari
humorem Luna praestanteque Sole calorem.
    Post Solis Lunaeque faces sunt lumina quinque
propter naturas totidem, quia sunt elementis
quattuor affines, commixta ex omnibus una:
480 Frigidus et siccus est Saturnus, calidusque
Mars est et siccus, et Iupiter est calidus sed
umidus, atque Venus est umida frigida, mixtus
Mercurius convertibilem se reddit ad omnes.
Rursus Saturnum dicunt Martemque malignos,

could not escape exile by dying. Heaven forbid! If I am ac- 455
cused of saying such a thing, it was not because I felt that
way, but because when I spoke to the common people, I
wished to keep to the opinions of the common people. Truer
and more powerful is the opinion of philosophers, particu-
larly those whom the rich study of the stars occupies, who 460
play the part of judges and are capable of declaring the
causes of the first principles by testing their different ef-
fects.

From them you will learn what the planets signify, and
what the signs and houses signify, because the orbit itself is 465
divided in two through the twelve signs and houses; the one
division pertains to nature, and the other to place. The plan-
ets draw different powers from each; though they are seven
in number, there are two great lights: the Sun, the diurnal
planet, and the Moon, the nocturnal one. Furthermore, the 470
Sun is masculine and the Moon is feminine; the Sun is hot
and dry, and the Moon moist and cold. The active power of
heat pertains to the Sun, while the passive power of mois-
ture pertains to the Moon. Thus, it can be said that the Sun
is the groom and the Moon is the bride, from which every- 475
thing in the world has to be produced, since the Moon pro-
vides moisture, the Sun, heat.

After the brightest lights of the Sun and the Moon are
five lights—a number in accord with nature, because four
are associated with the elements, and one is a combination
of all of them. Saturn is cold and dry, Mars is hot and dry, 480
and Jupiter is hot and moist, while Venus is moist and cold,
and the hybrid Mercury is capable of changing into them
all. Furthermore, they say that Saturn and Mars are malefic,

485 sed plus Saturnum, Martem minus, ex aliaque
parte Iovem Veneremque bonos, plus hunc, minus illam,
mixtum Mercurium ponunt in utroque vicissim.
　　Ex his principiis sunt inter cetera multa
conati domini stellarum reddere causam,
490 cur sit nona domus fidei vel religionis.
Nam cum Saturni sit circulus altior, inde
incipiunt primaeque domus venantur ab ipso
causas et proprietates, iterumque secundae
a Iove, qui succedit ei, similique deinceps
495 scemate per reliquos, donec sit septima Lunae.
Inde revertatur: Octava domus moderanda
Saturno, post nona Iovi. Nisi Iupiter ergo
significare fidem per praenarrata probetur,
nec poterit domui nonae praestare, quod ipsa
500 significare fidem possit vel religionem;
sed quod significet sic, per praedicta probetur.
　　Fortunas Iovis et Veneris praediximus esse,
maioremque Iovi dedimus Venerique minorem;
cumque duae vitae sint, praesens atque futura,
505 dignior illa quidem, quam sit praesens, ideo quod
plus valet aeternum quam quod pro tempore durat.
Propter id est Veneri data significatio supra
fortunas huius mundi, sit gratia verbo,
ludos et cantus, ornatus atque colores,
510 quodque per olfactum gustumve iuvat coitumque,
et concludendo breviter super omnia mundi
gaudia, quicquid in hac est delectabile vita.
Sicque Iovi cessit vitae fortuna futurae,
assertive quam nullus describere posset,
515 immo negative vult describi, quasi dicas

Saturn more so, and Mars less, and on the other hand, Jupi-   485
ter and Venus are benefic, the former more so and latter less,
while they assign the hybrid Mercury to each character in
turn.

From these first principles among many others, the au-
thorities on the stars have tried to declare the reason why   490
the ninth house is the house of faith and religion. For, since
the orbit of Saturn is higher, they begin from there and hunt
the causes and qualities of the first house from it, and those
of the second one from Jupiter, which follows Saturn, and
successively according to a similar scheme for the rest, up to   495
the seventh house of the Moon. Then the sequence is begun
again: the eighth house must be governed by Saturn, and af-
ter it the ninth by Jupiter. Therefore, unless Jupiter should
be shown to signify faith in the first place, it would not be
able to convey to the ninth house the ability to signify faith   500
and religion; but that it signifies this is demonstrated by the
aforesaid.

We said above that good fortunes are associated with Ju-
piter and Venus, and we assigned the greater fortune to Jupi-
ter and the lesser to Venus. Though there are two lives, the
present and the future, the latter life certainly is more wor-   505
thy than the present one, because the eternal life is worth
more than the one that lasts temporarily. For this reason,
Venus is said to signify the fortunes of this world, for exam-
ple, games and songs, decorations and colors, and the plea-   510
sures of smell, taste, and sex, and, to sum up briefly, all the
joys of the world, whatever is enjoyable in this life. In the
same way the fortune of the next life falls to Jupiter, some-
thing which no one could describe by positive statements.
On the contrary, it needs to be described negatively, as if you   515

"qua nihil est melius, nihil est iocundius usquam."
Quod cum non possit nisi religione fideque
quatenus acquiri, merito quoque Iuppiter illas
significat, merito domui nonae dedit illas.
520 Ex quibus ulterius venabimur, ut veniamus
in vitae saecli venturi cognitionem.
      Significare fidem Iovis est et religionem.
Ergo secundum quod complectitur ipse planetis
et fidei species debent diversificari.
525 Sicque fides sunt sex, sed non nisi quattuor usque
tempus ad hoc praesens latas invenimus esse.
Si complectatur Saturno Iuppiter, ex quo
Saturnus gravior est omnibus ipseque nulli
iungitur ex aliis, omnes iunguntur eidem,
530 esse fides debet, quae nullam confiteatur
ex aliis, omnes tamen inclinentur ad ipsam;
talis erat Iudea fides et talis adhuc est.
Si Marti, Chaldea fides creditur, apud quam
ignis adoratur, cui significatio Martis
535 concordat; sed si Soli, sequitur quod adorent
militiam caeli, cuius princeps quoque Sol est;
si Veneri, iam nostra fides convincitur esse,
in qua, si libeat, quodcumque licere putatur,
scripta licet super hoc nondum lex inveniatur.
540   Et quia quattuor has iam praecessisse videmus
et reliquas etiam praesumimus esse futuras
Lunae postremam legem fore conicientes,
vel quia post alios est circulus infimus eius,
vel quia Lunaris motus corruptio legem
545 omnem significat tolli debere per ipsam.
Foeda fides erit haec, quam rex in fine dierum

were to say, "nothing is better than this, nothing ever is more joyful." Since this cannot be acquired in any way except through religion and faith, Jupiter rightly signifies these things and rightly has given them to the ninth house. From 520 these things, we will pursue our inquiry further, so that we arrive at an understanding of the life in the age to come.

Jupiter signifies faith and religion. Therefore, the types of faith ought to be distinguished as well, according to which of the planets is in conjunction with Jupiter. And so there 525 are six faiths, but at the present time we have found that so far only four have come into being. If Jupiter should be in conjunction with Saturn, since Saturn is heavier than all and is joined to none of the rest, but all are joined to it, there 530 must be a faith that recognizes none of the rest, although all of them incline toward it. Just such a one was the Jewish faith, and it still is. If Jupiter should be in conjunction with Mars, the Chaldean faith will be understood; in it, fire is venerated, which is in harmony with the signification of Mars. But if Jupiter should be in conjunction with the Sun, 535 it follows that men revere the army of heaven, whose chief is the Sun. If Jupiter should be in conjunction with Venus, the existence of our faith is then demonstrated, in which, anything is considered permissible as long as it is pleasurable, although a written law about this is not yet to be found.

And since we now see that these four faiths have come 540 already, we also presume that the rest are yet to exist, conjecturing that the final law will be that of the Moon, either because its circle is the lowest after the others, or because the corruption of lunar motion signifies that every law is to 545 be abolished by it. This will be a vile faith, which in the end

sive potens aliquis violenter et absque colore
est inducturus, qui divinum sibi cultum
usurpare volens occidet et opprimet omnes
550 contradictores; nec tanta occisio tanto
tempore pro turpi causa praecesserit unquam,
sed durare parum poterit, quia Luna figurae,
motus et lucis est mutativa frequenter.
    Ante tamen legem Lunae lex Mercurialis
555 promulganda manet. Sed propter Mercurii tot
circuitus et tot inflexus atque reflexus
difficilis credi super omnes lex erit illa
et multum gravitatis habens multumque laboris,
obvia naturae supponens plurima sola
560 concipienda fide. Quare dubitatio multa
surget apud multos nodosaque quaestio multa.
Sed quia Mercurius scripturae est significator
et numeri, per quae lex omnis habet stabiliri,
et quia praecipue non, quae sunt temporis huius
565 mira, sed aeternae promittet commoda vitae,
tot defendetur subtilibus argumentis,
quod semper stabit in firma robore, donec
tollat eam Lunae lex ultima sicut et omnes
vel saltem suspendat eam, quia, rex ubi nequam
570 praedictus sublatus erit cessanteque foeda
lege sua, vel erit tunc consummatio motu
stante, vel ex aliis praedictis legibus unam
omnes assument, et forte probabiliorem;
nam quia decepti fuerint communiter omnes,
575 ad resipiscendum venient concorditer omnes.
    Tunc fiet legum collatio. Forte videtur,
quod non debebit praeferri, quae colit ignem

280

of days a king or someone powerful will introduce violently and undisguisedly—someone who, wishing to usurp divine worship for himself, will kill and oppress all who speak against him. Never before in so great a span of time will there have been so much killing for a foul purpose, but it will only be able to last for a short time, because the Moon is frequently changeable in its appearance, motion, and light. 550

Yet before the law of the Moon, the law of Mercury remains to be made known. But because of Mercury's frequent revolutions and frequent retrograde and prograde motions, this law will be more difficult to believe than all others, requiring much seriousness and exertion, since it supposes many things contrary to nature that can only be understood through faith. For this reason, much doubt and many a difficult question will arise among many scholars. But because Mercury represents writing and number, on which every law has to be founded, and especially because it will promise not the wonders of this life but rather the rewards of eternal life, it will be defended by so many subtle arguments that it will always stand firm in robust strength, until the final law of the Moon abolishes it, just like all the others, or at least suspends it. For when the aforesaid wicked king is removed, and his foul law comes to an end, either this will be the end of the world when the motion of the universe stops, or all people will accept a single law from the other aforementioned ones, and perhaps they will choose the more credible law. For, since all of them will have been deceived in common, all will come to their senses with one accord. 555 560 565 570 575

Then there will be a comparison of laws. Perhaps it seems that the one that honors fire or the army of heaven ought

vel quae militiam caeli, quia nulla creata
res est digna coli. Rursum Iudea fides et
580   nostra, creatorem solum licet esse colendum
edoceant, tamen aeternum nihil inde mereri
promittunt sed quae praesentis sunt bona vitae.
Ista voluptates promittit, et illa fluentem
terram lac et mel. Lex autem Mercurialis
585   dignior esse fide reputanda videtur eo quod
aeternae vitae bona promissura sit, ad quae
nemo venire potest nisi religione fideque,
quae Iovis in sortem cesserunt significantis,
sicut praedictum est, aeternae commoda vitae.
590   *Felix, qui* sectae *causas* praenosse futurae
posset venturus per eas in cognitionem
quis sibi vivendi modus aptior esset ad hoc, quod
inde mereretur aeternae gaudia vitae.
    Dicunt astrorum domini, quod in omnibus annis
595   viginti iunguntur Iuppiter et pater eius,
cumque duodecies in signis triplicitatis
unius iuncti fuerint, seu tredecies ut
accidit interdum, tandem mutatur eorum
ad succedentem coniunctio triplicitatem.
600   Quarum consuevit coniunctio maxima dici,
quae fit in initio puncti vernalis, et ipsa
post quasi nongentos et sexaginta fit annos
ipso Saturno bis sex decies revoluto
significans nunc diluvium, nunc aeris ignes,
605   nunc terrae motus, nunc annonae gravitates,
regnorumque vices permutat et imperiorum.
Ast alibi quae fit mutata triplicitate
consuevit dici maior coniunctio, sectam

not to be preferred, because no created thing is worthy of worship. Then again, the Jewish faith and our own, although 580 they teach that the creator alone should be worshipped, nonetheless do not promise that anything eternal may be earned from them but instead just the good things of the present life. Our faith promises pleasures, and the Jewish one promises a land flowing with milk and honey. However, the law of Mercury seems to be something that will be more 585 worthy of faith because it will promise the advantages of eternal life, which no one can attain except through religion and faith, both of which have fallen to the lot of Jupiter, who signifies, as was mentioned above, the rewards of eternal life. *A person would be lucky* indeed if he could know in ad- 590 vance *the causes* of this future sect and could learn thereby what mode of living would be more advantageous for him to earn the joys of eternal life.

Authorities on the stars say that every twenty years, Jupi- 595 ter and his father are in conjunction, and that after they have come together in the configuration of a single triplicity twelve times, or thirteen times as sometimes happens, at last their conjunction is changed to a successive triplicity. And of these, the conjunction which happens at the begin- 600 ning of the vernal equinox and occurs after about 960 years, after Saturn has revolved 120 times, is traditionally called the "greatest conjunction." Sometimes it signifies a flood, sometimes fiery skies, or earthquakes, or food shortages, 605 and it changes the fate of kingdoms and empires. But the conjunction which happens at other times when the triplic- ity changes is traditionally called "the greater conjunction,"

significans mutansque fidem per climata quaedam;
610 et fit post annos quasi quadraginta ducentos.
 Una quidem talis felici tempore nuper
Caesaris Augusti fuit anno bis duodeno
a regni novitate sui. Quae significavit
post annum sextum nasci debere prophetam
615 absque maris coitu de virgine. Cuius habetur
typus, ubi plus Mercurii vis multiplicatur,
cuius erit concors complexio primo futurae
sectae, nam nusquam de signis sic dominatur
Mercurius sicut in signo Virginis; illic
620 est eius domus, exaltatio triplicitasque
per totum signum nec non et terminus eius
in primis septem gradibus. Dictique prophetae
typus habetur ibi, quamvis sub aenigmate; namque
his in imaginibus, quae describuntur ab Indis
625 et Chaldeorum sapientibus ac Babylonis,
dicitur ex veterum scriptis ascendere prima
virginis in facie; prolixi virgo capilli,
munda quidem magnique animi magnique decoris,
pluris honestatis; et in ipsius manibus sunt
630 spicae suspensis, et vestimenta vetusta;
sede sedet strata, puerumque nutrit puero ius
ad comedendum dans. Puerumque Iesum vocat ipsum
gens quaedam, sedet et vir ibi sedem super ipsam.
Haec scripsit prior ille propheta Noe venerandus
635 et docuit primogenitus Sem filius eius.
Haec autem caeli pars ascendebat in hora,
qua cum Saturno Iovis est coniunctio facta
nuper significans sectam, quia triplicitatem
mutavere suam nec non etiam prope punctum

signifying a new sect and a change of faith through certain regions. This happens every 240 years or so. 610

Indeed, one of these conjunctions occurred recently in the happy era of Caesar Augustus, in the twenty-fourth year from the beginning of his reign. This signified that six years later, a prophet should be born of a virgin, without inter- 615 course with a man. A pattern of this kind is found whenever the strength of Mercury becomes greater, and that future sect will have a temperament in harmony with that power from the first, for never is Mercury so potent among the signs as in the sign of Virgo; there is its house, exaltation, 620 and triplicity throughout the entire sign, and likewise its term in the first seven degrees. And the characteristics of the foretold prophet are found there, although not openly; for among those images, which are described by the Indian, Chaldean, and Babylonian sages, the first is said in the writ- 625 ings of the ancients to ascend in the form of a virgin. This virgin has long hair, and she is elegant, with great courage and great beauty, and with a noble bearing; and in her raised hands are ears of grain, and her robes are ancient. She sits in 630 a covered chair, and she nurses a boy, giving the boy liquid to feed him. And a certain people calls this boy Jesus, and as a man he sits there on that same chair. The venerable prophet Noah wrote these things originally, and his firstborn son 635 Shem taught them. Moreover, this part of the sky was ascendant in the hour when the recent conjunction between Jupiter and Saturn happened, signifying a new sect, because they changed their triplicity, and, what is more, it was even close

640 veris, ubi fieri coniunctio maxima posset,
principio signi propior si forte fuisset.
Tunc et erant anni Grecorum quinque trecenti
atque novem menses cum ter sex paene diebus.
    Felix, cui plene coniunctio tanta pateret
645 tamque potens fidei praeclarae significatrix,
per quam venturae quaeruntur gaudia vitae,
per quam cognosci mores et vita prophetae
praedicti possunt scirique potest per eandem,
quod sine peccato vivet super omnia verax
650 et quod doctrinae sanae, quod clarificandus
portentis et prodigiis mirabilibusque
virtutum signis. Quae certe posse patrare
non est humanum, sed digna deo potius sunt;
forte nec est hominem fas ipsum dicere purum.
655   Nam super hoc puero sunt olim multa locuti
quidam, qui vitam ducebant spiritualem
utentes parce somno potuque ciboque,
sensibilique suus elongabatur ab omni
spiritus et domita se sursum carne levabat.
660 Sic intellectus intendebatur eorum
in tantum, quod eis praenosse futura dabatur,
vel per somnia vel vigilando cadebat eorum
in mentem, per eosque loqui Deus ipse volebat,
ac ideo tales appellavere prophetas.
665 Tales dixerunt, quod sic de virgine nasci
debeat unus homo simul et Deus et quod utramque
humanam atque dei sit naturas habiturus.
Sed via possibilis non est, haec clausa videtur
porta meis oculis, quia non intelligo plane.
670   Hoc unum novi, quod homo fieri deus unquam

to the vernal equinox when a greatest conjunction could 640
have happened, if it had been closer to the beginning of the
sign. According to the Greek calendar, this happened at 305
years, nine months, and almost eighteen days.

Blessed is he who understands so great a conjunction,
such a powerful signifier of an excellent faith, through which 645
the joys of the life to come are sought, through which the
character and life of the aforementioned prophet can be
learned, and through which one can know that above all he
will live truthful without sin, that his doctrines will be 650
sound, and that he will win renown by portents, prodigies,
and the miraculous signs of his powers. The ability to per-
form miracles is certainly not human, but instead befitting a
god; perhaps it is not right to call him purely human.

For long ago, certain men said many things about this 655
boy, men who led spiritual lives, sparingly partaking of sleep,
drink, and food, whose spirit was far removed from the sen-
sible world and raised above the flesh they had tamed. Thus, 660
their understanding was intensified to such an extent, that
they were granted foreknowledge of the future, which came
into their minds sometimes in dreams and sometimes while
they were awake; through them God himself wished to
speak, and for this reason they called such men prophets.
These prophets said that one was to be born of a virgin, at 665
the same time human and God, and that he would have two
natures, both human and divine. But this is a path that is not
possible, a door that seems closed to my eyes, since I do not
wholly comprehend.

I know this one thing, that no human could ever be a god, 670

non posset, nam quod ex tempore coeperit esse,
aeternum non esse potest, quia, si cariturum
fine sit idcirco, quod sit deus, amodo saltem
non sine principio poterit fore; sed quod utroque
675 non caret, aeternum non est. Etenim duo ponit,
et, quod ab aeterno duraverit hactenus, et, quod
duret in aeternum. Quare, quod condicionis
non est aeternae, fieri nequit amodo tale.
Si deus est, igitur aeternus: Nemo deus fit.
680 Hoc unum novi, sed nescio, si deus esse
vellet homo. Si vellet enim, cum summa voluntas
non habeat vel habere queat, quibus impediatur,
posset homo fieri carnemque assumere posset
ac unire sibi; sed qua ratione moveri
685 posset ad hoc, ego non video. Tamen undique venor,
undique perscrutor, si possem forte venire
in verisimilem veramve probabilitatem,
qualiter induci deus ad quid tale volendum
posset; certus enim sum, quod lex Mercurialis
690 plurima naturae contraria sit positura.
    Hoc unum video, quod, cum Deus (ut retrodixi)
caelestem motum providerit esse staturum,
et sibi de solis individuis speciei
cura sit humanae, vult forte viam meditari,
695 qua possint homines in fine resurgere mundi.
Quare vult individuum specialiter unum
inter eos fieri, quod naturaliter ambas
in se naturas habeat nostramque suamque
ex unaque mori rursumque resurgere possit
700 ex alia, cuius virtute resurgere possint
omnes post habitum per eum de morte triumphum.

for what began to exist in time cannot exist eternally, because, if to be infinite is what it means to be a god, then at least from that point he will not be able to exist without a beginning; but whatever does not lack both end points is 675 not eternal. As a matter of fact, it assumes the two: both that it will last from eternity to this point, and that it will endure for eternity. For this reason, what does not have an eternal nature cannot thenceforth become eternal. If someone is a god, he is necessarily eternal: no one becomes a god. I know only this, but I do not know if a god would wish to 680 be a human. For if he did wish it, and since there neither is nor could be anything by which the highest will could be impeded, he could become man and could take on flesh and unite it to himself; but I do not see a reason why he could be moved to do this. Yet I hunt everywhere, I investigate ev- 685 erywhere, if I could perhaps find a plausible or true probability, how a god could be induced to want such a thing. For I am certain that the law of Mercury is going to ordain much 690 that is contrary to nature.

I see only this, that, since God has provided that celestial motion will stop (as I said before), and since he is concerned only about individuals of the human species, perhaps he wishes to plan a way by which men can rise again at the end 695 of the world. For this reason, God wishes there to be one individual in particular among them that inherently has both natures in himself, both ours and his own, and because of the former can die and because of the latter can rise again, by whose power all will be able to rise again after the tri- 700 umph over death achieved through him. This would cer-

Hoc esset certe dilectio maxima, sed non
miror, si summus sit munera summa daturus.
Sed, licet iste foret homo verus, non tamen ipse
705 nasci deberet sicut communiter illi
nascuntur, qui sunt homines puri, quia tantum
ac talem, per quem foret incorruptio danda,
ex incorrupta quoque nasci matre deceret.
Haec sunt, quae cecinit Cumanae Musa Sibyllae
710 nuper in urbe sacra, quasi cuncta fides oculata
praedocuisset eam vel in aure sua sonuissent.
Confiteor, quod dicta fides quam plurima ponet
obvia naturae, sed adhuc ibi quaestio restat
difficilis, de qua surgit dubitatio maior;
715 nam de praedictis quidam dixere prophetis,
quod Deus est trinus et quod nihilominus unus.
Hoc autem tantum meus intellectus abhorret,
quod nec materiam se vertere possit ad istam,
non quia non multum desideret, ut sciat huius
720 dicti radicem, si radix est ibi, verum
semita nulla patet mihi, qua veniatur ad ipsam.
Non tamen hoc verbum soli dixere prophetae,
sed quidam de philosophis, qui pauca locuti
magna subesse suis voluerunt pondera dictis;
725 e quibus in medium veniat famosior unus.
    Inquit Aristotiles, Grecorum philosophorum
princeps et dominus verique perennis amicus:
"Res omnes sunt tres, numerus ternarius in re
qualibet existit; nec nos extraximus istum
730 a nobis numerum, sed eum natura docet nos.
Nam per eum numerum similes res dicimus omnes
esse creatori, per eum quoque nos adhibemus

tainly be an act of the greatest love, but I wouldn't be sur-
prised if the highest power would one day give the highest
of gifts. But, although he would be a true human, nonethe-
less he should not have to be born in the way that those who   705
are purely human are commonly born, because it would be-
fit so great a person and one, who was to bestow incorrupt-
ibility, also to be born of an uncorrupted mother. This is
what the Muse of the Cumaean Sibyl sang of recently in the   710
holy city, as if the testimony of an eyewitness had given her
foreknowledge of all things, or they had resounded in her
ear. I admit that the faith I speak of will ordain a great deal
that is contrary to nature, but there still remains a difficult
question, about which greater uncertainty arises; for some   715
of the aforesaid prophets have said that God is triple and
that he is nevertheless one. Now this my intellect so abhors
that it cannot turn its attention to this matter, not because
it does not greatly desire to know the basis of this state-   720
ment, if there is a basis, but because no path is open for me
to approach it. However, not only prophets have made this
statement, but also certain philosophers, who, by saying lit-
tle, wish to lend great weight to their words; of these let a   725
single very famous one come forward.

Aristotle, the chief and master of the Greek philoso-
phers, and an everlasting friend of truth, says: "All things are
three, and the ternary number exists in everything. We have
not worked out this number by ourselves, but rather, nature   730
teaches it to us. For we say that through this number, all
things are similar to the creator; and we employ this number

significare Deum, qui, quamvis sit Deus unus,
est tamen et trinus." Sic dixit, nescio cuius
735   doctrinae praecepta sequens aut nescio cuius
philosophi zelans vestigia sive prophetae.
Dixit, quod trinus, nec dixit, quomodo; solum
dixit, quod sic est, qui numquam credulitatis
incessisse via visus fuit, usus ubique
740   aut rationibus aut cogentibus argumentis.
Hic autem nulla fultus ratione, velut si
texeret historiam, solum sic esse canebat,
et quasi per calamum plumbi fortasse locutus
spiritus est per eum, vesanaque pectora verbum
745   evomuere novum, quod non conceperat ipse,
ac si nec super hoc omnino tacere valeret
nec, quod dicebat, plene cognoscere posset.
     In quo sic illo famoso deficiente
nec confundor ego, mihi si perfectio desit
750   ad cognoscendum quaedam, quibus inferior sum;
nilque verecundor contra me vera fateri.
Defectivus in hoc meus intellectus abundat
in multis aliis, nec enim mysteria tanta
pervia sunt nobis, quia quae proportio lucis
755   solis ad obtusos oculos vespertilionis,
haec et ad ingenium nostrum huius materiei.
Nec puto posse capi, nisi postquam venerit ille
de caelo, caeli plene secreta revolvens.
Tunc etenim credam, si tantum dixerit ipse,
760   et, quia dicturum dicunt, etiam modo credo.
Ipsum venturum iam diligo iamque paratus
credere doctrinae, quam dixerit esse sequendam,
cultoremque suum me repromitto futurum,

to signify God, who, although he is one God, is nonetheless also threefold." So he spoke, following the precepts of some doctrine or other or zealous to imitate some philosopher or prophet. He said that God is threefold, but he did not say how; he said only that it was so, and he was someone who never took the path of ready credulity, and always relied on reasons and cogent arguments. Here, however, supported by no reasoning, as if he was inventing a story, he would only intone that it was so. And perhaps the spirit spoke through him as if through a lead pipe, and his possessed heart spewed out this novel statement, which he had not conceived himself, as if he could neither wholly keep silent about this, nor fully understand what he was saying.

Since that renowned philosopher was so far from fully understanding this, I am not disconcerted if I lack a complete ability to understand matters that are beyond me; and I am not ashamed to admit the truth at my own expense. My intellect, though imperfect in this matter, abounds in many others, for such great mysteries are not accessible to us, because my intellect understands this matter to the same degree as the blind eyes of a bat see sunlight. I do not think it can be comprehended until after that one has come from heaven who will fully reveal the secrets of heaven. Then truly I will believe, if only he will speak, and because they say that he will speak, even now I believe. Already I love the one who is to come, and already I am prepared to believe the doctrine that he will say must be followed. I promise that I will be his worshipper as long as he summons me,

dum tamen ipse trahat, quia, si non traxerit, ipsi
765 nemo placere potest et ad ipsum nemo venire.
    Docturus tamen est, qua nos veniamus ad ipsum,
monstrabitque viam, quia, per quam venerit ad nos,
illa tenenda via est; illac nos ire necesse.
Et iam praecessit de quadam virgine, per quam
770 in mundum veniet. Nobis erit haec adeunda,
hanc mediatricem dabit humano generi rex,
largitor veniae nostraeque salutis amator.
    O virgo felix, o virgo significata
per stellas, ubi spica nitet! Quis det mihi tantum
775 vivere, quod possim laudum fore praeco tuarum!
Nam nisi tu perfecta fores, non eligeret te
hic Deus omnipotens, ut carnem sumeret ex te,
uniretque sibi nisi digna fores etiam, quod
filius ille tuus, postquam surrexerit et de
780 morte triumpharit, te vellet honorificare
te super exaltans caelosque locans super omnes
et sibi concathedrans. Ubi namque locaverit illam
electam carnis partem, quam sumpserit ex te,
et carnem, de qua fuerit sua sumpta, locabit.
785 Fas etenim non est, quod, postquam portio carnis
una tuae fuerit sic cum deitate levata,
reliquias alibi locet, ut sua deminuantur
munera circa te, dum, quod bene coeperit hac in
parte tui, non in te tota prosequeretur.
790 Nam contracta manus tanto est indigna datore,
perfectum perfecta decent. Absit, quod, apud quem
plena potestas est, illi det dona recisa,
quam vult sublimare creaturam super omnem.
Sed nec ad id quod sic praelata resurgat oportet

because, if he will not summon me, no one can please him 765
and no one can come to him.

Yet he will teach us how we are to come to him, and he
will show the way, because the way by which he comes to us
is the way that must be taken; we must go that way. And he
has already come from a certain virgin, through whom he 770
will come into the world. We must approach her. The king
who grants forgiveness and desires our salvation will give
this woman to the human race as an intermediary.

O blessed virgin, O Virgo signified by the stars, where
your ear of grain shines! May God allow me to live long
enough to be a herald of your praises! For unless you were 775
perfect, this omnipotent God would not have chosen you in
order to take flesh from you, and he would not have united
it to himself unless you were so worthy that your son, after
his resurrection and his triumph over death, would want to 780
honor you, raising you on high and placing you above all the
heavens, and enthroning you with him. For indeed in the
same location where he will place that part of flesh he chose
to take from you, he will also place the flesh from which his
own is taken. For it is not proper that, after a single portion 785
of your flesh has been elevated with divinity in this way, he
should set what remains aside, so that his gifts to you are di-
minished, in that what he began so well in this one part of
you, he would not follow through in your whole being. For 790
an ungenerous hand is unworthy of so great a giver; perfec-
tion befits perfection. It would not be fitting for one who
has full power to give limited gifts to a woman whom he
wishes to elevate above all creation. But with regard to the
resurrection of someone so favored, it is not necessary to

795 exspectare statum motus in fine dierum,
quando resurrecturi sunt generaliter omnes,
praesertim cum sit illi carni specialis
causa resurgendi, quae materialiter illam
de se producet carnem, quae primo resurget,
800 unde resurgendi vis propagabitur ad nos.
Nec fas est etiam, quod eatenus in minus alto
sistatur suus ordo gradu, quia, quam Deus ante
saecula donandam tanto praevidit honore,
non opus est, ut eam velit exaltare gradatim,
805 sed simul assumet simul et sibi concathedrabit.
Illic esto tui memorum memor, optima virgo,
illic cum fueris pro nobis tracta, trahendis
pro nobis te non pigeat suadere, quod ad se
nos trahat is per te, qui per te venerit ad nos,
810 maxima quem per te dilectio traxerit ad nos.
A nobis ipsi sit gloria laudis; ab ipso
gratia sit nobis et metae nescia vita!

De nemore

Lucus amoenus erat quem fons faciebat amoenum,
umbraque sole carens et pratum gramine plenum.
Dulce sonans rivus et blanda querela volucrum,
aura virensque solum commendabant mihi lucum,
5 dumque morarer ibi quoddam mirabile vidi,
quod volo narrare si vultis ad ista vacare:

wait for the stopping of motion at the end of days, when all 795
universally will be resurrected, especially since that flesh
will have a special cause for resurrection, since it will pro-
duce from itself in material form that flesh that will be the
first to be resurrected, and from it the power of resurrection 800
will be propagated to us. Also, it is not proper that her rank
up to that point should be given a lower status, because,
since God foresaw before creation that this woman was to
be bestowed with great honor, there is no need for him to
want to elevate her in stages, but rather, at the same time as 805
her assumption, he will enthrone her with himself. In that
place be mindful of one who is mindful of you, most excel-
lent virgin! When you have been summoned there on our
behalf, do not begrudge interceding for us to be summoned
too, so that he who came to us through you and whom the
greatest love summoned to us through you may summon us
to himself through you. May he have the glory of praise 810
from us; from him may we have grace and a life that knows
no end!

On the Grove

There was a pleasant grove, which a fountain made pleasant,
and shade from the sun, and a meadow full of grass. The
sweet sound of the stream and the charming plaints of the
birds, the air and the greenness of the ground recommended
the grove to me, and while I lingered there, I saw something 5
marvelous, which I want to tell, if you care to attend to it:

Veste nitens aurique tegens diademate crines,
pulchra decens largosque tenens Opulentia fines
venerat in silvam strepitu comitata suorum.
10 Venerat armorum dives sed egena virorum,
nam multi coiere viri sed corpore molles,
et viles, quos esse mares vel nomine nolles:
balsama crinis olens, facies medicata colore,
blanditiae dulces, vaga lumina, risus in ore.
15 Circulus aureus, anulus aureus, aurea vestis
et caput et digitos et mollia pectora vestit;
esse viros et barba probant et militis arma,
haec duo si demas muliebria pectora credas.
Descendunt dominamque suam posuere sub umbra,
20 et lavere manus vicini fontis in unda.
Picta tapeta petunt et florida carpitur herba,
erigitur solium. Sedit regina superba
a dextra levaque cubant Paris et Ganimedes
crinibus effusis in cervices muliebres.
25 Terra feras, aether volucres, misit mare pisces,
esuriens reperiret ibi quicquid voluisset.
Ponitur alma ceres et in albo mazere bacchus,
salmon et sturion in regia prandia natus.
Illic pavones, illic ponuntur olores,
30 illic perdices anatesque gruesque videres.
Dat capreos, dat apros, dat cervos silva, dat ursos,
omneque malorum genus et genus omne pirorum.
Dat flavos in fine favos maturaque mora,
cornaque non dura nec non et cerea pruna.
35 Bacchus in argento, bacchus rutilabat in auro,
et simplex bacchus et pigmentis medicatus.
Sed quid plus? Uno totum volo dicere verbo:

With glittering garments and her hair covered with a golden diadem, with great beauty and a vast fortune, Opulence came into the wood, accompanied by the din of her followers. She came, rich in arms, but with a dearth of men, for though many men assembled, they were delicate of body, and contemptible, so that you would deny that they were males even in name: locks smelling of balsam, a face colored with rouge, sweet blandishments, wandering eyes, a laughing mouth. Gold hoops adorned their heads, gold rings their fingers, and golden garments their soft chests; their beards and their military weapons proved that they were men, but if you'd subtracted these two aspects, you'd have believed that they were women at heart. They dismounted and situated their mistress in the shade, washing their hands in the waters of the nearby fountain. They fetched embroidered tapestries, picking flowers and erecting a throne. The proud queen took her seat, and to her left and right recline Paris and Ganymede with their hair flowing over their womanly necks.

The earth provided wild beasts, the air birds, and the sea fish; a hungry person could have found whatever he wished there. Nourishing bread was served, as well as wine in a white wooden bowl, and salmon and sturgeon destined for a regal luncheon. Here peacocks were served, here swans; here you could have seen partridges, ducks, and cranes. The forest provided wild goats, boar, deer, and bears, and every kind of apple and every kind of pear. For dessert it provided golden honeycombs and ripe mulberries, juicy cornel cherries and wax-colored plums. Wine glowed red in silver and gold vessels, both unmixed wine and wine flavored with spices. But why say more? I will just sum it up in a word: the

deliciis densa vix stabat eburnea mensa,
dum sitis atque fames potuque ciboque fugatae.
40   Discedunt pariter iam deliciis superatae,
Diogenem cernunt et cognoscunt venientem,
nil secum praeter baculum peramque ferentem;
quod non ipse gerit, sua nec fore nec bona credit.
Audet ei sacrum sitis exsiccare palatum,
45 dumque diu fessis saevissima saevit in extis
intrandique locum considerat altera pestis,
Philosophia suo fontem monstravit alumno
unde petebat aquas prendens Opulentia sacras.
Spectat aquas dulces, spectat sine sorde liquores
50 margine gramineo crystallo lucidiores.
Spectat ibi vasa pulcherrima, munda parata,
divitis imperio dominae pro fonte locata.
Sed quia naturae vir duxit pocula secum,
pocula luxuriae contemnere iudicat aequum.
55 Ergo manus ambas immergens fontis in undas
cum naturali coepit cupa recreari.
Dumque sonum fontis audit regina superba,
intonat in flatus erumpit in aspera verba:
      "Degener atque miser—et vero nomine pauper,
60 nam nec habes censum nec habes sub pectore sensum—
nonne vides vasa pulcherrima munda parata?
Cur ea dimittis? Cur in fontem tua mittis?
An non pincernas equites istosque videbas?
Cur non audacter potumque cibumque petebas?
65 Et color et macies et vestis et omnis egestas
ostendunt qualem sensum sub pectore gestas.
I, puer, et vina cum nectare mixta propina!
I cito, pincerna, fer ei preciosa falerna!"

ivory table was so thick with delicacies that it could scarcely
stand, while thirst and hunger were put to flight with drink
and food.

As they left the table together, now stuffed with delica- 40
cies, they caught sight of and recognized Diogenes coming,
bearing with him nothing but his staff and satchel; what he
didn't carry himself, he didn't believe to belong to him or be
of any value. Thirst dared to dry up his hallowed palate, and 45
while it raged fiercely for a long time in his exhausted in-
nards and another plague looked for a place to enter, Philos-
ophy showed her nursling the fountain from which grasping
Opulence was drawing the sacred waters. He saw the sweet
waters, he saw the unfouled liquids on the grassy verge, 50
more transparent than crystal. There he saw the loveliest
vessels, clean and standing ready, placed by the order of the
wealthy mistress in front of the fountain. But because the
man brought nature's goblets with him, he thought it right
to scorn the goblets of luxury. Therefore, sinking both hands 55
into the waters of the fountain, he began to refresh himself
with his natural cup. And when the haughty queen heard the
sound from the fountain, she thundered and snorted and
burst into harsh words:

"Lowly, miserable fellow—a pauper in the true sense, for 60
you neither have wealth nor have reason in your heart—
can't you see the loveliest vessels, clean and standing ready?
Why do you ignore them? Why do you put your own in the
fountain? Didn't you see the cupbearers and the knights
there? Why did you not boldly ask for drink and food? Your 65
complexion, leanness, clothing, and complete poverty show
the kind of feelings you have in your heart. Go, boy, and
pour him wine mixed with nectar! Go quickly, cupbearer,
and bring him the precious Falernian!"

Ille ferebat ei iacinthina plena liei.
70 Diogenes animo magnus sed corpore parvus
tunc licet iratus subrisit et est ita fatus:
    "Prodiga vastatrix et luxuriosa voratrix,
et mundanorum generalis causa malorum,
vere tu miseros et degeneres facis istos.
75 Nam genus humanum satis est ab origine clarum,
nec Natura parum dedit illi divitiarum.
Nobilitas hominis extat deitatis imago—
nobilitas hominis virtutum clara propago.
Nobilitas hominis humilem relevare iacentem.
80 Nobilitas hominis mentem frenare furentem.
Nobilitas hominis naturae iura tenere.
Nobilitas hominis nisi turpia nulla timere.
Adde quod erecta persona fuit sibi facta;
cetera prona vident terram sed homo videt astra.
85 Non est magna satis haec gloria nobilitatis,
non poteris magnos his aequiparare tyrannos.
    "Sed naturales illius opes referemus
ut quis sit dives quis pauper notificemus.
Dives hic est qui vivit quasi cras moriturus;
90 ditior est qui cum moritur mox est oriturus.
Dives hic est qui fortuitas res sub pede pressit;
ditior est qui nil metuit quia nil male gessit.
Dives hic est vere qui plus nihil optat habere
quam Natura dedit bona quantulacumque fuere.
95 Aspice cum nimis ubertas et opes dominantur
ordine quo segetes et vites amplificantur:
vitis amoena suis uvis sed non alienis,
spicis pulchra suis seges est sed non alienis,
laetaturque pilo vulpis sed non alieno.

The cupbearer brought him jacinth cups full of wine. Then Diogenes, great in spirit, though small in body, although angered, smiled and spoke as follows: 70

"Lavish destructress and self-indulgent devouress, the general cause of the world's evils, verily you make those you prey on miserable and degenerate. For the human race is 75 most noble from its earliest origin; and Nature gave it no small share of her riches. The nobility of man stands out as the image of the deity — the nobility of man is the shining progeny of virtues. It is the nobility of man to raise up the humble and prostrate. It is the nobility of man to rein in a 80 raging mind. It is the nobility of man to observe the laws of nature. It is the nobility of man to fear nothing but dishonor. Consider also that his person was made upright; the other creatures, head down, see the ground, but man sees the stars. But the earthly glory of this nobility is not very great; 85 you cannot equate great tyrants with these good men.

"But we will recount man's innate riches, so as to make known who is rich and who is poor. Rich is he who lives as if he will die tomorrow; richer is he who, when he dies, will soon thereafter rise. Rich is he who presses beneath his foot matters governed by chance; richer is he who fears nothing, 90 because he has done nothing wrong. Truly rich is he who desires to have nothing more than the possessions Nature has given him, however insignificant they are. Consider 95 in what manner the wheat and vines are enriched when great abundance and riches hold sway there: the vine gives pleasure with its own grapes but not those of another, the wheat is lovely in its own ears of grain but not in another's, and the fox rejoices in its own fur but not in another's.

100   Ergo solus homo nitet et tumet ex alieno.
Regnum, papatus, urbes, castella, ducatus,
renones, pelles, aurum, preciosa supellex:
nec tua sunt vere nec tecum nata fuere."
     Haec ubi finivit cibus et item potus abivit.
105   Turba stupens ascendit equos urbemque petivit.

De vino

Qui cupis esse bonus et vis dinoscere verum,
ut mortis somnum sic mordax effuge vinum.
Nulla febris maior hominum quam viteus humor,
immodice sumptus vincit mortale venenum.
5   Sanctius est igitur viroso et sanguine multum;
quantum vina nocent, non tantum vipera laedit.
Inde tremor membris, inde est oblivio mentis,
poplite progressus nutans, et visio fallax.
Surdescunt aures, balbutit denique lingua,
10   perdens eloquium profundit semilatratum.
Ebrie, dic mihi, vivis? Dic, an morte gravaris?
Pallidus ecce iaces demens; sine mente quiescis.
Aegra quies oculos letali pondere pressit.
Non bona nec mala tu non mollia nec dura sentis.
15   Hac tantum distas a fato sorte sepulti:
quod tenuis miseros suppungit anhelitus artus.

And so it is man alone who thrives on and takes pride in what belongs to another. Kingship, papacy, cities, castles, dukedoms, furs, leather garments, gold, expensive furnishings: these are neither truly yours, nor were they born with you."

When he finished his speech, the food and likewise the drink disappeared. The stunned throng mounted their horses and made for the city.

On Wine

If you desire to be good and wish to discern the truth, avoid the sting of wine like the sleep of death. There is no human fever greater than the juice of the vine; when consumed immoderately, it surpasses deadly poison. Therefore it is much more potent than even infected blood; wine does so much harm that even the viper's bite cannot equal it. From it comes trembling of the limbs, from it comes oblivion of the mind, a walk with shaking knees, and faltering vision. The ears grow deaf, then the tongue stutters, and losing its eloquence, it produces a half bark. Drunkard, tell me, do you live? Speak—or are you in the throes of death? Behold, you lie pale and senseless; you fall asleep unconscious. A troubled drowsiness has overcome your eyes with its deathlike weight. You can feel nothing—neither good nor bad, neither soft nor hard. You are different from the fate of a dead person only through this happenstance: the fact that shallow breathing racks your miserable limbs.

O mortalis homo, mortis reminiscere casus:
nil distas pecude, si tantum prospera carpis.
Omnia quae cernis, vanarum gaudia rerum,
20   umbra velut tenuis veloci fine recedunt.
Praecaveas, felix, cum te dinoscis et audis:
quassans praecipiti dissolvat turbine finis.
Dilige pauperiem, mortales effuge gazas,
nam reddunt cupidis post carnis dulcia flammas.
25   Porrige poscenti victum vel contege nudum,
et te post obitum sic talia facta beabunt.
Quamvis perspicuus auro gemmisque nitescas,
id solum temet post mortis fata beabit
quod bene, quod iuste, quod recte feceris ipse.
30   Praeterea stomachus, qui cum dapibus facit escas,
viscera crassa vehit, sed macra corda gerit.
Decrescit sensu, grandescit corporis auctu,
carnea fit moles membra caduca ferens,
gutturis aut rheuma fauces angustat obesas
35   et perdit liquidos vox male rauca sonos.
Marcescunt refluo sopitaque ossa tepore;
ambulat et stertit nec vigilare valet.
Qui cupit ergo suam doctrina crescere mentem
castiget ventrem; sic homo doctus erit.

O mortal man, remember the misfortune of death: you are no different from livestock, if you just seek out what is pleasurable. All that you see, the delights of meaningless things, fade like an insubstantial shadow at the swift onset of death. Take care, fortunate one, while you still have self-knowledge and hearing: death with its violent whirlwind may shatter and undo you. Love poverty, flee mortal riches, for after the sweets of the flesh they bring flames to the greedy. Offer nourishment to the suppliant and clothing to the naked, then after death such deeds will bless you in like fashion. Though you shine conspicuously with gold and gemstones, this alone will save you after the fate of death: your good, just, and virtuous deeds.

Furthermore, the stomach, which feeds on rich feasts, leads to a stuffed belly, but a meager soul. He dwindles in perception but grows in physical bulk, and becomes a fleshy mass bearing frail limbs, or a catarrh in his throat narrows its now-fattened passageway, and the voice, harshly grating, loses its pure tone. The bones grow frail as they lose their strength with the ebbing of bodily warmth; he snores when he walks and cannot keep awake. Therefore, he who wishes to increase his intelligence should discipline his stomach; in this way he will be a learned man.

De somnio

Nox erat et placido capiebam pectore somnum
    et gravior solito tum mihi somnus erat.
Tunc mea terrifici presserunt pectora visus
    et, mea quod moveant, haesito, visa malum.
5 Quattuor a quadris surgebant flabra columnis,
    grandine commixta perfida surgit hiems.
Ecce duae species stabant in nubibus altis
    et sibi conflictu proelia mira dabant.
Altera flagranti ridebat vulnera vultu,
10   altera crudeli fuderat ore minas.
Interdum celso vicere cacumine nubes,
    interdum terris alteritate iacent.
Heu mihi! Diversa facies diversaque vestis,
    non illis vultus, non color unus erat.
15 Altera flammigero lustrabat nubila vultu
    aurificisque caput texerat illa comis.
In manibus gravidas plures gestabat aristas,
    in pedibus violas, ebria saepe tamen.
Nescio si minio vel qualibet arte fucatus
20   virgineo rubeus haeserat ore color.
Pinguior (Hesperidum germanam credere posses)
    continuo risu gaudia magna dabat.
Hanc ergo tenui cupiebam tangere tactu,
    sed levis ad nubes illa volabat avis.
25 Altera continuo plorabat perfida luctu,
    obscena facie, corpore turpis erat.
Cui caput immensum, collum subtile iacebat,
    sordibus et squalidum pectus habebat iners,

On the Dream

It was night and I was sleeping peacefully, but then my sleep became deeper than normal. Then terrible visions weighed heavily upon my heart, and I am uncertain of the evil that my visions portend. Four gusts of wind rose up from four columns; a threatening storm arose, bringing with it hail. Behold, two figures were standing in the high clouds, and in their clash they produced a marvelous battle. One was laughing at her wounds with a blazing countenance, the other poured out threats from her ruthless mouth. Sometimes they overtopped the clouds in lofty height, sometimes instead they lay prostrate on the ground. Ah me! They differed in form and dress; they didn't share a single appearance or coloring.

One was illuminating the dark clouds with her fiery visage, her head covered with hair of gold. In her hands she bore many plump ears of grain, and on her feet violets, yet she was often drunk. A reddish hue remained on her virginal face—I do not know if it was colored with rouge or by some other means. The plumper of the two—you might think that she was the sister of the Hesperides—inspired great joy with her continual laughter. So I desired to touch her lightly, but she flew up to the clouds, as nimble as a bird. The other one, deceitful, cried continuously; she had a repulsive face and an unsightly body. She had an enormous head while her neck was slender, and in her idleness her breast was caked

longior et macies cunctos tenuaverat artus
30   stridebatque nimis dentibus atque minis.
Saevior in digitis ignem ferrumque tenebat,
      cuius ab ore ferus exit odor nimius.
Quas bona portabat, ferro caedebat aristas,
      tunc cito sic caesas igne coquebat eas.
35 Sed bona de truncis festinaque grana trahebat
      lucique immissa tergere saepe studet.
Saevior illa tamen spicas non caedere cessat,
      hoc opus, ille labor inter utramque manet.
Heu male! Tum subito visa est taetra vincere forma
40   succubuitque taetrae forma benigna deae.
Non potuit tantas species bona reddere spicas,
      quas non foeda sua caederet illa manu.
Illic conveniunt tamquam ad spectacula multi
      et pavidis oculis bella stupenda vident.
45 Vir tamen ex illis veniens de nubibus unus
      hic mihi comperta voce locutus ait:
"Quodvis ista monent, quae cernis visa, futurum,
      temporis instantis maxima damna vides.
Quattuor a quadris, quae surgunt flabra columnis,
50   Mors sunt, Ira, Metus et Gemitusque simul.
Haec sunt pestiferae coniuncta ferocia dextrae
      et se connexo saeva furore tenent.
Hanc, bene quam cernis spicis adsurgere densis,
      divitias species dissimulata tenet.
55 Hanc, male caedentem quam ferro cernis aristas,
      heu heu crudelis est mala forma famis.

with filth; prolonged emaciation had withered all of her limbs, and she ground her teeth with loud screeching threats. The fiercer of the two, she held a flame and a sword in her hands, and her mouth emitted an extremely unpleasant odor.

With the sword she cut off the ears of grain that the good one was carrying, then, quick as can be, she began to scorch in the flame those she had cut. But the good one hastened to remove the grain from the cut stalks, and repeatedly strove to free the grain that had been hurled into the fire. Yet the fiercer one did not stop cutting off the ears of grain, and each of them persisted in the same effort and toil. Alas, how terrible! Then suddenly the loathsome figure seemed to be victorious, and the kindly figure succumbed to the loathsome goddess. The good apparition was not able to restore so many ears of grain that the horrible one could not cut them down with her hand. Many gather round that place as if to see a show, and they watch the astounding warfare with terrified eyes.

Nevertheless, a man from this throng, coming down from the clouds, speaking with an authoritative voice, says to me: "Whatever these visions that you discern foretell will come to pass; you are looking at the gravest sufferings of a time that is imminent. The four gusts that rise up from four columns are Death, Anger, Fear, and Sorrow. These savage creatures are wielded by a hand that brings destruction, and they cruelly conspire with united rage. The benign apparition that you see rising up before you with dense ears of grain represents riches in disguise. The one that you see maliciously cutting off the ears of grain with a sword—alas—is the terrible figure of cruel hunger. Because the good figure

Quod bona succubuit, visa est mala vincere forma;
    praevalet hoc nostro tempore saeva fames."
Talia dum senior pavido mihi verba dedisset
60   tum mihi nec sensus, vox neque mens fuerat.
Hanc quoque dum saeva superatam sterneret ictu
    perculit et totam mandere dente parat;
dumque ferox comitem crudeli dente voraret,
    ructuat et putrido sulphure complet aer.
65 Hinc cito per totos ceciderunt corpora campos
    et iacet infesto sulphure magna cohors.
Exitus hic somni; tremor hinc ferus ossibus haesit
    deseruitque calor membra pavore mea.

De ventre

Concilium celebrant humani corporis artus
    inter se, de se plurima verba serunt.
Incidit in ventrem sermo, de ventre queruntur,
    quod gravis est dominus et nimis urget eos.
5 Tandem, rhetorico pingens sua verba colore,
    aggreditur fratres garrula lingua suos:
"Quis furor, o cives, quae tanta licentia ventris
    audeat in nobis ponere turpe iugum?
Turpe iugum certe, quando servus dominatur
10   et dominus servit; hic iubet, ille facit.
Certe nos servi turpes, digni cruce, cunctis
    ludibrium, miseri degeneresque sumus.

has surrendered, the bad one is seen to win; in this time of
ours fierce famine prevails."

While the old man spoke such words to me, I was terri-   60
fied and had neither feeling nor voice nor thought. Also,
once the savage figure had vanquished her defeated rival
with her fists, she knocked her over, and prepared to chew
up her whole body; and as the fierce one was devouring her
colleague with cruel teeth, she belched and filled the air
with putrid sulfur. Because of this bodies quickly fell   65
throughout all the fields and a great crowd lay dead from the
lethal sulfur. At this point, I woke up; immediately a terrible
trembling seized my bones, and in my terror the warmth left
my limbs.

On the Stomach

The parts of the human body hold a meeting among them-
selves, and they exchange many words about each other.
Discussion turns to the stomach; they complain about the
stomach, that he is a severe master and that he makes exces-
sive demands of them. At length, embellishing her words   5
with rhetorical flourish, the talkative tongue addresses her
brothers:

"What madness, my fellow citizens, what excessive bold-
ness of the stomach dares to place a vile yoke upon us? It is
certainly a vile yoke, when a slave is master and a master is   10
enslaved; the one commands, the other performs. Certainly,
we are foul slaves, worthy of the cross, a laughingstock to all,

Nam ventrem dominum nobis elegimus ipsi,
   omnia colligimus, quae sibi grata putat.
15 Nulla quies nobis: monet hunc, movet hunc, vocat illum:
   'Surge, piger, somnos excute, tolle moras.
Quaere cibos epulasque para vinumque propina,
   mensam pone: dies praeterit, hora subit.
Ecce duo veniunt hostes mortemque minantur:
20   inminet inde fames, inminet inde sitis.
Ergo deficiam, nisi subvenias mihi velox
   preveniasque famem preveniasque sitim.'
Sic me, sic alios pulsat lascivia ventris,
   et me plus aliis turgidus ille premit.
25 Me, quasi praeconem causarum, iurgia saepe
   exercere iubet parvaque dona sequi.
Et modo patronus, modo iudex et modo testis
   clamo, iura patrum contero, falsa loquor.
Sub specie veri curans inducere falsum
30   fallo, periuro praetereoque fidem.
Fasque nefasque simul equali pondere libro,
   per licitum pariter illicitumque vagor.
Si lateri vel pontificis vel praesulis adsto,
   tunc unguenta paro blanda, placere volens.
35 Ungo blanditiis, ut delicias sibi venter
   accumulet: voces distrahit ille meas.
Nonne manus nostrae ventri servire laborant?
   Nonne minas eius imperiumque timent?
Furantur, rapiunt, operantur, et omnia venter
40   suscipit, et sorbet omnia Scylla vorax.
Huic oculus servit, venatur, currit ubique,
   nuntiat haec domino, quae meliora videt.

miserable and degenerate. For we ourselves chose the stomach as our master, and we gather everything that he thinks pleasing for himself. We have no peace: he admonishes one of us, torments another, and summons yet another: 'Get up, laggard, shake off sleep, don't delay. Find food, prepare the dishes, pour the wine, and set the table: the day is passing, the hour draws near. Look, two enemies approach and threaten death: here hunger is imminent, and there thirst impends. So I will fail unless you quickly come to my aid, and prevent hunger and prevent thirst.'

"In this way the stomach's unrestrained behavior disturbs me, and disturbs others, but that swollen one oppresses me more than the others. It is I whom he often orders to voice his disputes like a crier of cases and to pursue small gifts. Now as advocate, now judge, and now as witness, I make a clamor, undermine ancestral rights, and speak falsehoods. Undertaking to represent falsehood in the guise of truth, I deceive, perjure myself, and disregard good faith. I weigh the legal and the illegal together with equal weight; I range equally through the licit and the illicit. If I stand at the side of a pontiff or a prelate, then I provide enticing balms, in my desire to please. I anoint with flatteries, so that the stomach may gather delicacies for himself: he commandeers my voice.

"Don't our hands strive to serve the stomach? Don't they fear his threats and authority? They plunder, grab, labor, and the stomach takes everything, he sucks in everything, a voracious Scylla. The eye serves him, hunts, and runs everywhere; he reports to his master the fine things that he sees.

Heu pedibus quantos induxit saepe labores,
    quos nimis affligit, quos sine lege premit.
45 Inde dolor nostri consumit corporis ossa,
    membra quatit, vires haurit aratque cutem.
Est ad servitium nobis studiosa voluntas,
    gratia nulla tamen: conqueror inde magis.
Nam cum servitio respondet gratia, multum
50   temperat—immo facit dulce laboris onus.
Huic vero cum multa damus, cum multa paramus,
    non cessat querulus dicere: 'Pauca datis.'
Si dederis hodie, nisi cras dederis, nisi rursum
    et rursum dederis, perdere prima potes.
55 Et si forte suis dicit: 'Satis est, satis illud,'
    post modicum tempus incipit esse parum.
Dicite, quis tantam possit satiare Charybdim?
    Dicite, quanta cupit, quis dare tanta potest?
Hoc etiam nostros auget cumulatque labores,
60   et gula nos nimium pessima saepe premit:
Illi gustus adest, hic portam servat, et iste
    vilis leno, procax garcio, scurra vagus.
Hi duo per mundi currunt elementa: quid aer,
    quid pariat tellus, quid freta, scire volunt.
65 Non volucris penna, non evadit fera cursu,
    non cetus caeco gurgite tutus erit.
Noverunt varios hi dispensare sapores,
    ut magis alliciant illiciantque cibis.
Gustus discernit quod transmittit gula, venter
70   abscondit; probat hic, haec rapit, ille capit.
O venter, quanto disturbas crimine mundum
    inmundumque facis, turpia quaeque movens!

Alas, how many tasks he has often imposed on the feet! He burdens them excessively, he oppresses them without limit. Because of this, grief consumes our body's bones, shakes the limbs, saps strength, and wrinkles the skin. Our disposition is devoted to servitude, yet there is no gratitude: therefore, I complain all the more. For when gratitude answers servitude, it greatly tempers it—indeed, it makes the burden of toil sweet. Truly, although we give him many things, although we furnish many things, he doesn't stop grumbling, saying: 'You don't give very much.'

"If you give today, unless you give tomorrow and give again and again, you can lose the first things you gave. And if by chance he says to his servants: 'Enough, that's enough,' after a little while it begins to be too little. Tell me, who could satisfy such a great Charybdis? Tell me, who can give as much as that stomach desires? Because of this he even increases and overloads our labors, and the terrible throat often greatly oppresses us: taste attends on him; the throat guards the gate, and taste is a vile pimp, shameless mercenary, and roving rake! These two scour the world's elements: what the air and earth and seas produce, they want to know. No bird can escape it by wing, nor any beast by running; no whale will be safe in its hidden depths. They know how to impart different flavors, in order to better attract and entice with foods. Taste discerns what the throat transmits, and the stomach stores it away: the first assays it, the second swallows it up, and the third takes it in.

"O stomach, with how much crime you trouble the world and make it foul by stirring up all that is ugly! Because of

Propter te fiunt homicidia, furta, rapinae,
    insidiae, strages, iurgia, bella, doli;
75 ad coetum currit monachus, miles gerit arma,
    quiris sectatur lucra, colonus arat.
Ex te virtutum casus mentisque ruina,
    membrorum pestes luxuriaeque lues.
Tu Nabuzardan, princeps dominusque cocorum,
80   namque tibi sero mane coquina strepit.
Tu follis tumidus, vas plenum sordibus, immo
    plenus fece locus—non locus, immo lacus!
Vos ergo fratres mecum discernite, qualis
    hic dominus; mecum cernite, quale iugum!
85 Turpe iugum credo, quando servus dominatur
    et dominus servit; hic iubet, ille facit.
Turpe iugum vere, quando ratione sepulta
    in nobis venter imperat; illa silet.
Vivere debemus, non ventri, sed rationi;
90   vir bonus hanc, non hunc, optat habere ducem.
Paulus ait: *Venter esce datur escaque ventri;*
    sunt duo iuncta sibi; perdet utrumque Deus.
Nos ergo pudeat tali servire patrono;
    gloria nostra per hunc nobilitasque perit.
95 Surgite, state, precor, animo pugnate virili!
    Magna parit nobis praemia pugna brevis!
Aeternum pereat, qui ventri serviat ultra;
    sit procul a nobis, qui sua regna feret.
Sit sine fine labor, sit naufragium sine portu,
100   continuus sit ei perpetuusque dolor!"
His socios animat verbis facundia linguae,
    et movet et munit et docet esse viros.

you, homicides, thefts, plundering, ambushes, carnage, strife, wars, and deceptions occur; the monk hastens to have 75 intercourse, the soldier bears arms, the townsman chases profit, the serf tills the land. From you comes the collapse of virtue, the ruin of the mind, the affliction of the body, and the plague of luxury. You are Nabuzardan, chief and master of cooks, for your kitchen rumbles in the late morning. You 80 are a swollen sack, a vessel full of filth, a place full of sludge— not a place but a pit! And so, brothers, recognize with me what sort of master this is; recognize with me what sort of yoke! I believe it is a degrading yoke when a slave is master, 85 and a master is enslaved; the one commands, the other performs. A degrading yoke indeed, when the stomach commands us and reason is suppressed; reason is silent. We ought to live not by the stomach, but by reason; a good man 90 chooses to have the latter, not the former, as his leader.

"Paul says: *The stomach is for food, and food is for the stomach; the two are joined together, and God will destroy them both.* Therefore, it is shameful for us to serve such a patron; because of him our glory and nobility come to nothing. Get 95 up, stand up—I beg you—fight with a manly spirit! A brief battle will beget great rewards for us. May anyone who continues to serve the stomach be lost for eternity; may anyone who endures the stomach's reign be shunned by us. May he have toil without end, shipwreck without a port, and con- 100 tinual and perpetual grief!"

With these words the tongue's eloquence inspires her comrades, excites them, emboldens them, and teaches them

Ergo simul iunctos confoederat una voluntas
    adstringitque sibi, quos ligat unus amor.
105 Indicunt ventri bellum iurantque quod eius
    vincula dissolvent discutientque iugum.
Sic statuunt et sic confirmant: foedere facto
    ventrem destituunt nec famulantur ei.
Iam pes, lingua, manus et cetera membra quiescunt:
110   pes negat ire, loqui lingua, iuvare manus.
Prima dies belli tranquillo tramite currit,
    nec quicquam poscit ille nec illa ferunt.
Altera ieiunum nescit compescere ventrem
    latrantemque gulam pacificare nequit.
115 Tertia consumptos macie vix sustinet artus,
    namque maligna nimis urget ubique fames.
Pes torpet, manus aegrotat, languet caput, ora
    pallent, suspirant pectora, lingua tacet.
Omnia turbantur cum corpore: nullus in illo
120   est vigor, aeger ibi luctus, ubique dolor.
Rursus post longos gemitus conamine multo
    vix hos balbutit languida lingua sonos:
"Quid facimus? Nil proficimus, magis et magis omnes
    deficimus, premimur comprimimurque fame.
125 A ventris rabie venit haec iniuria nobis,
    hoc eius nobis parturit ira malum.
Sentio grande malum, sed causa mali mihi clausa;
    quod nocet, ecce patet; cur nocet iste, latet.
Nunc igitur, fratres, vobis presentibus ipsum
130   conveniam, quaeram, quae sit origo mali."
Tunc se convertens ad ventrem lingua: "Quid," inquit,
    "tam male nos laedis? hic furor unde tibi?

to be men. And so, a single determination joins them in a confederation and the ties of a single devotion bind them to each other. They declare war on the stomach and swear that they will unloose his chains and shatter his yoke. This is their decision, this their resolution: when the pact has been made, they desert the stomach and do not serve him. Now the foot, the tongue, the hands, and the other limbs grow inactive: the foot refuses to move, the tongue to speak, the hands to help.

The first day of the war runs its course quietly: the stomach asks for nothing, and the other parts do not bring him anything. The next day cannot calm the fasting stomach and is unable to placate the roaring throat. The third barely sustains the limbs emaciated through scarcity, for malevolent hunger presses the assault hard and from all sides. The foot drags, the hand weakens, the head droops, the cheeks grow pale, the chest sighs, the tongue is silent. Every aspect of the body is thrown into confusion: there is no strength in it, but anxious sorrow and grief are everywhere.

Once more, after long sighs, and with great effort, the weak tongue barely stammers these sounds: "What are we doing? We make no progress, we all fail more and more, we are oppressed and repressed by hunger. This harm comes to us from the stomach's anger—his wrath gives birth to this affliction of ours. I feel the affliction strongly, but the affliction's cause is obscure to me: that he harms is clear to see; why he harms remains hidden. Now, therefore, brothers, I will meet with him in your presence and I will ask him what gives rise to this affliction."

Then, turning toward the stomach, the tongue says: "Why do you persecute us so cruelly? Where does this wrath

Respice, nonne tuos concives perdere curas?
    Quando vides casum, non relevare paras?
135 Hostis es in civis; haec recta fronte repugnant –
    iuncta sibi melius, civis amicus, erunt.
Te vacuum, plenum te, semper habebimus hostem?
    Semper erit nobis tristis uterque status?
Quando iaces plenus, nimia te mole gravari
140   clamas et tecum nos facis esse graves.
Quando iaces vacuus, quia te ieiunia laedunt,
    latras et querulus nos facis esse graves.
Ergo precor miserere tui, miserere tuorum,
    Ne tecum pereant, teque tuosque iuva.
145 Exponas, cur tu quereris vel quid tibi quaeris,
    et ne quaeso noce, sed facienda doce."
His verbis claudit sermones lingua, vicemque
    venter ei reddens incipit ista loqui:
"Audivi linguae strepitus et eos patienter
150   sustinui, fratres; laedimur inde parum.
Lingua quidem membrum modicum, sed molle, citoque
    labitur et loquitur saepius absque modo.
Nam de scintilla magnum movet et fovet ignem,
    in fornace sua fabricat arma doli.
155 Inde nimis nostros agitat discordia cives,
    nam pacem turbat et mihi tela iacit.
Me dominum, fratres, vobis ostendit et hostem,
    sed scio quod vobis servio, vosque colo.
Cum nos de massa rerum Natura vocavit
160   et nobis formam materiamque dedit,
iunxit in humano nos corpore, iunxit amico
    foedere nos semper iugiter unus amor.

of yours come from? Take a look around: aren't you seeking to destroy your fellow citizens? When you see misfortune, don't you resolve to relieve it? You are hostile to your citizens; now the body's parts are fighting back directly—joined together, my friend and fellow citizen, they will be better. Will you always be our enemy, whether full or empty? Will both conditions always be grievous for us? When you are full, you complain that you are burdened by too much weight, and make us be heavy with you, too. When you are empty, since hunger causes you to suffer, you bark and, grumbling, you make us out to be burdensome. Therefore, I beg you to take pity on yourself and your own, lest we perish with you; help yourself and your fellows. You should explain why you are grumbling, or what you seek for yourself; and I beg you not to do harm, but to teach us what should be done."

The tongue ends her speech with these words, and in turn, the stomach begins to speak these words in reply: "I have heard the tongue's rumblings and I have endured them patiently, brothers; we take little offense from them. Indeed, the tongue is a small organ, but a supple one—she trips along, and often speaks without moderation. For from a spark she is stirring and nourishing a great fire; in her own furnace she is fashioning the weapons of deception. From those actions dissension is violently rousing our citizens, for she is disturbing the peace and hurling missiles at me.

"She presents me to you, my brothers, as your overlord and enemy, but I know for a fact that I serve and protect you. When Nature called us forth from the bulk of matter and gave form and substance to us, she joined us in the human body, and a single love joined us in a friendly union once

Omnia praecepit fieri communia nobis
    omnibus, ut proprium nullus habere velit.
165 Omnibus officium distinxit, meque ministrum
    constituit vobis et dedit esse cocum.
Inde paro vobis escas, alimenta ministro,
    vitam conservo, pauca reservo mihi.
Vos date, suscipio; susceptum decoquo; coctum
170   distribuo vobis, fercula quaeque gero.
Si vos ingeritis, ego digero; quod nocet, illud
    egero; quod prodest, hoc quoque cuique gero.
Pauper sum servus—nil possum ponere vobis,
    si nihil offertis, nam mea bursa vacat.
175 Nec nimium curo, nec ego minimum mihi quaero;
    in medio positus opto tenere modum.
A nimio veniunt fastidia, crimina, morbus,
    crapula, luxuriae faex laterisque dolor.
A minimo veniunt infestae mortis imago,
180   frons tristis, facies pallida, laxa cutis.
A medio veniunt mens semper sobria, corpus
    robustum, felix vita, iocosa quies.
Ergo sibi caveat dives ne devoret ultra
    quam satis, et pauper curet habere parum.
185 Et vos, si sapitis, servate modum mihi dando:
    dispensator ero pro ratione dati.
Saepe mihi dabitis, quia vultis saepe cibari,
    namque per hoc vobis vita salusque datur.
Surgite, ne vobis inducat inertia somnum:
190   somno desidiae iudico turpe mori.
Turpiter occumbit, quem torpor vulnerat; ergo
    surgite, mors properat, sentio: vita fugit."

and for all. Nature directed that all things should be in common to all of us, so that none would wish to have anything of his own. It distinguished a role for everyone, and appointed 165 me as your servant, assigning me to be the cook. Hence I prepare foods for you, I supply your nourishment, I maintain your life, and I retain a little for myself. You give, and I receive; I digest what I receive; I distribute the concoction 170 to you, I serve each of the courses. If you ingest, I distribute; I discharge what is harmful, and I serve what is beneficial to each of you.

"I am a poor servant—I cannot provide anything for you if you offer me nothing, for my purse is empty. I neither care 175 too much for myself nor ask for too little; placed in the middle, I hope to maintain moderation. Excess produces loathing, crime, sickness, hangover, the impurity caused by luxury and pain in the side. Too little brings the specter of inimical death, a sad appearance, a pale face, and loose skin. 180 The middle ground offers an ever-sober mind, a healthy body, a happy life, and a pleasant repose. Therefore, the rich man should take care not to consume more than his fill, and the pauper should be concerned about having too little. You 185 too, if you are sensible, keep to a limit in giving to me: I will be the dispenser in proportion to the giving. You'll give to me often because you want to be fed often, since by these means life and health is given to you. Get up, so that idleness does not make you fall asleep: I think it loathsome to 190 die in the sleep of idleness. The man afflicted by sloth dies a shameful death; therefore, get up! Death approaches, I feel it: life is escaping."

Ventris ad has voces membrorum turba resumit
    vires, et rediens induit arma vigor.
195 Surgunt, officiis insistunt, debita solvunt,
    invigilant operi singula membra suo.
Quos socios vitae fecit Natura, laboris
    tunc omnes socios mutua cura facit.
Sic litem sepelit laeto concordia fine;
200   hoc quoque vult finem carmen habere suum.

Metamorphosis flaminis in gallum

Altera sed nostris res dictu horrenda sub annis
claruit et toto iam non incognita mundo.
Namque Iovi sacrum cum plenus numine flamen
Vestali praesente choro solemne parabat,
5 iamque erat et tenui praecinctus tempora vitta
ornatusque caput mitra, pendebat ad imum
byssus et in Tyrio radiabat splendidus ostro,
tum Venus irridens, "Talem te prima sacerdos
excipiat," dixit; "lateat sub veste pudoris
10 tectus amor. Nostrum tua per modulamina numen
gaudeat et dulcis nostra sit cantus in ara."
    Nec mora flamineas transfixit flamma medullas.
Uritur et dum assueta deo praeconia temptat
dicere, languentis animi vox querula vulnus
15 nuntiat insani repetito carmine amantis.
Sensit et ipsa deae templo praefecta sacerdos
iam tandem furiale malum, dumque ora canoris

The throng of body parts recover their strength at these words of the stomach, and the returning vigor takes up arms. They get up, persevere in their duties, pay what is due, and each part attends to his own task. All those whom Nature made comrades in life, mutual concern then makes comrades in work. So harmony puts strife to rest in a happy conclusion; this poem also wishes to have its end. 200

195

Metamorphosis of a Priest into a Rooster

Now in our time another story became famous, both terrible to tell and well known now all over the world. Once when a priest full of divine spirit in the presence of the choir of Vestals was preparing the solemn rite for Jupiter, and already had his temples encircled with a slender fillet and his head ornamented with the miter, while his priestly garment was hanging down to the ground, glowing splendidly with Tyrian purple, at that point Venus mockingly said: "Let the chief priestess welcome you as you are; may love lie concealed under the robe of chastity. Let my divinity rejoice in your melodies and let the song be sweet at my altar." 5

10

Without delay the flame pierced through the priest's marrow. He burned with love and while he was trying to speak the usual praise for the god, the plaintive voice of his languishing spirit proclaimed in repeated song the wound of the possessed lover. The priestess in charge of the temple of the goddess finally herself felt the intoxicating evil, and

15

327

miratur iocunda modis, dum cantibus amens
tollitur et tacito collustrat singula vultu,
20 se manibus furiosa ferit. Nunc fixa cohaeret
obtutu, nunc mota gradu titubante caducum
vix tolerat corpus. Qualis canit orgia mater!
Plena deo iam totus habet praecordia flamen.
Invitant oculi, renuit pudor. Ausa pudorem
25 aggreditur vincitque Venus. Tumefactus in illam
fertur et, oppressam ne rideat ulla sororum,
prodigus in cunctas promit sua munera flamen.
Mox quoque de tanta nullam sine crimine turba
dimisisse potest (Veneris sic dona redundant).
30   Iuppiter haud impune tamen sua sacra profanis
laesa videns, turpi coeuntes foedere templo
eripit. At crimen mutata veste pudendum
dissimulat plumaque tegit miseratus utrumque.
Vertice cristato flamen decoratus, amictu
35 splendidus irradiat, collo caudaque superbit.
Longior et vox alta manet quae dividat horas,
debita quaeque suo persolvat vota Tonanti.
Sacra sed in parvum luxu peccantia rostrum
ora cadunt abeuntque manus pedibusque sub uncis
40 clauduntur remanetque sacro pro flamine gallus.
Induitur plumas simul et vittata sacerdos
statque viro subiecta suo. Nec prisca recessit
corpore mutato virtus: incensa libido
regnat et in multas dispergitur illa sorores.

while she was admiring his sweet singing and tuneful melodies, while she was driven wild by the songs and was surveying with silent countenance his individual features, she frantically beat herself with her hands. Now motionless she kept her eyes fixed on him, now moving with stumbling step she barely stopped her body from falling. Such a mother sings of Bacchic orgies! The priest already had his heart completely full of the god. The eyes incited him, shame opposed. Bold Venus attacked and conquered shame. Swollen, the priest rushed into her, and, so that none of the sisters could laugh at her being forced, he lavishly bestowed his favors on them all. Soon he could not leave anyone fault-free out of so many (so abundant were the gifts of Venus).

Jupiter, however, did not look on without retaliation at his rites being violated by wickedness, and removed from the temple those who had had intercourse in scandalous union. But he concealed the shameful crime by changing their vestments and, out of pity, covered both with feathers. The priest shone resplendent in his mantle with a crest decorating his head; he prided himself on his neck and tail. His far-reaching and loud voice remained to distinguish the hours and to deliver the prayers owed to his Jupiter, the Thunderer. But his consecrated mouth, defiled by lust, contracted into a small beak and his hands disappeared and were enclosed in hooked feet, and he remained a rooster instead of a sacred priest. At the same time the garlanded priestess also was clothed in feathers and was subject to her husband. And though his body was changed, he did not suffer any loss of potency: his burning desire still reigns and is distributed among the many sisters.

De distributione mulierum

Rebus in humanis non est res altera talis:
  si fuerit totis pulchra puella modis,
haec facit ut placeat quam plures quaerere certant.
  Si perit haec, quid erit quod quis amare velit?
5 Non aurum, non gemma placet, rubra purpura pallet,
  vir quoque sordebit et sibi turpis erit.
Haec pretium rebus dat quas in honore tenemus,
  haec placet—e reliquis nulla suis meritis.
Felices, bellae quorum sunt forte puellae,
10 munere vel Veneris, quae dominatur eis.
Namque volens dignis illas sociare maritis
  et dare praeterea quod decorabit, ea
caelitus advenit, media testudine sedit
  alta sub templi, quod Numa fecit ei.
15 Mox passis portis intravit clericus omnis,
  et fecit laetam quisque salute deam.
Tunc inquit: "Pulchras, vos cleri, sumite nuptas"
  et coepit sponsam tradere cuique suam.
Quas cum tradebat, sic his dea praecipiebat:
20 "Semper vos clerus possit habere meus,
  et clerum, bellae, possitis amare, puellae.
  Femina dum fuerit, iussio semper erit."
Post haec Mercurii properant et Martis alumni
  ad Venerem pulchrum poscere coniugium.
25 "Has ego non aliis" inquit "copulabo maritis,
  quas statui clero semper habere meo."
Atque refragantes et ei mala cuncta voventes,
  iussit mundanum semper habere malum.

On the Distribution of Women

In human affairs there is no other matter quite like this one: if there is a girl who is beautiful in all ways, she makes herself pleasing, and many strive to win her. If she perishes, what will there be for anyone to love? Neither gold nor gemstones will be pleasing, a rich purple garment will fade, even a man will be held of no account and will think himself foul. She adds value to the things that we hold in esteem; she alone is pleasing—nothing else is pleasing from its own merits.

Fortunate are those men whose girls are beautiful by chance, or rather through the gift of Venus, who has dominion over them. For Venus, wishing to unite those girls with worthy husbands and to give them additionally something that would honor them, came down from heaven and sat under the high middle arch of the temple that Numa made for her. Soon after, when all the doors were opened, every cleric entered, and each made the goddess happy with his greeting. Then she said, "Choose beautiful brides, you clergy," and she began to deliver to each his own bride. When the goddess bestowed them, she instructed them in this way: "May my clergy always be able to possess you, and may you, pretty girls, be able to love the clergy. As long as there is womankind, this will always be my order." After this the pupils of Mercury and Mars hastened to Venus to beg for a beautiful bride. "I will not," she said, "couple these girls with other husbands; I have decided to keep these girls for my clergy." And as they resisted her and threatened all evils, she ordered them always to experience worldly evil.

Plebs etiam pullo quae semper operta cucullo
30   post laicos venit, munus idem petivit.
Dixit diva Venus: "Meruit connubia clerus,
    nam metuunt monachi foedera coniugii."
Tunc illi Graecum dixerunt "kyri' eleison,"
    et Venus: "Hoc verbum dicite perpetuum.
35 Venistis tardi, non do possitis amari,
    do vobis salsas semper habere fabas."
Cesserunt fratres, cum non dedit illa iugales;
    unde manent clausis collacrimantque locis.
Res fuerant Veneris sub numine mille puellis,
40   quas dotes fecit et tibi, clere, dedit.
Sic homo quisque suum retinet per saecula donum,
    clericus et laicus et monachus tacitus.
Clerus habet pulchras rerum quascumque figuras,
    et mala sunt laicis, "kyrie" dat monachis.

Contra mulieres

Femina, principium fraudis, deceptio prima,
Adam per fraudem vallis deiecit ad ima.
Femina, ne videat fraudis sibi tollere crimen,
ipsa dedit pomum, comedit et avida primum.
5 Femina, ne videat fraudis sibi tollere crimen,
"Comede" cum dixit "satis tibi fiet amoenum."
Femina causa fuit mortis nostrae generalis,
poena tamen sequitur cunctas hinc perpetualis.
Ut caput est colubris, caput est sic et mulieris,

Also the people who are always covered with a cowl came   30
after the laity, and sought the same gift. Divine Venus said:
"The clergy have won the right for marriages, but monks
fear marital bonds." Then they said in Greek *"kyrie eleison,"*
and Venus said: "Keep on speaking those words forever. You   35
are latecomers, and I do not grant that you may be loved.
Instead I grant that you'll always have salty beans." The
brothers gave way, when she did not give them spouses; and
so they remain in their cloisters and weep together. This was
the fortune of a thousand girls under the divine power of
Venus—girls whom she made into dowries and gave to you,   40
clergy. So each man retains his own gift through the ages,
clergy, laity, and the silent monk. The clergy have anything
with a beautiful figure, and the laypeople have suffering, and
she gave the *kyrie* to the monks.

Against Women

Woman, the origin of error and the first deception, cast
Adam, through her deceit, into the depths of the valley.
Woman, so as not to escape the crime of deceit, gave the
apple herself and greedily took the first bite. Woman, so as   5
not to escape the crime of deceit, then said, "Eat—it will be
very pleasant for you." Woman was the cause of our com-
mon death, but because of this, perpetual punishment pur-
sues all women. The head of a woman is like the head of a

10   nam sunt mendosae sanctis virisque odiosae.
      Ut coluber callidus, sic omnes sunt vitiosae.
      Credo lupum pecori servare fidem meliorem,
      femina quam cuique verum conservet amorem.
         Fraude tument omnes—nullam sine fraude videbis.
15   Diligit ecce duos vel tres vel quattuor una,
      omnes amat pariter, nulli servat sua iura.
      Dicit ecce primo: "Te solum diligo virum;
      alter erit nullus, qui iam me possit habere."
      Quilibet adveniens primo vix inde remoto . . .
20   Mille licet veniant, sic omnes decipiuntur,
      et quae decipiant quam plures inveniuntur.
      Ante quidem possent omnes stellae numerari,
      et formica brevis elephantis aequiperari,
      et levius poterit leo vermiculo superari,
25   et draco flammivomens musca poterit sanguinari,
      ursus et araneae filo bene concatenari
      quam possint fraudes mulierum dinumerari.
      Ergo reas vir noscat eas, sed reputet illas
      pestiferas ac mortiferas sciat esse favillas.
30   Adam plasmatur, Deus imperat, exanimatur:
      ne maneat solus vir, femina vivificatur.

De ludo scacchorum

Qui cupit egregium scacchorum noscere ludum,
    audiat; ut potui, carmine composui.
Versibus in paucis dicam tibi proelia litis:
    quattuor in tabula bis loca sunt varia.

snake, for they are false and hateful to holy men. Like a cun- 10
ning snake, they are all vicious. I believe a wolf is better at
being loyal to a flock than a woman is at preserving true love
for anyone.

All of them swell with deception—you won't see one who
is free from deceit. See how one woman loves two, three, or 15
four men; she loves all of them equally but keeps her prom-
ises to none. See how she tells the first one: "You're the only
man I love; there will be no other now who can have me."
Scarcely is the first one gone when another arriving . . . Even 20
if a thousand come, all of them are likewise deceived, and
just as many women are found to deceive them. Indeed, all
the stars could be counted, the tiny ant could equal the ele-
phant, the lion more easily be overcome by a grub, the 25
flame-spewing dragon be bloodied by a fly, and a bear be
chained down by a spider's thread before all the deceits of
women can be enumerated. Therefore, a man should recog-
nize that they are guilty, and consider them pestilential,
knowing that they are fatal embers. Adam is molded, God 30
commands, and Adam is put to sleep: so that man does not
remain alone, woman is brought to life.

On the Game of Chess

Anyone who wishes to know the excellent game of chess
should listen; I have composed a poem on the subject as
best I could. In a few verses, I will describe the moves of the
game to you: there are eight different positions on the

5   Albescit primus, rubet atque colore secundus,
     aut niger aut glaucus pingitur aut rubeus.
   In primo rochus committere bella minatur
     statque secundus eques ludicra iura tenens.
   Tertius alfinus custos regalis habetur;
10   quartus rex retinet; femina quinta sedet.
   Post illos procerum revocabitur ordo priorum;
     procedit peditum turba velox nimium.
   Stat pedes, et dextra rapit et de parte sinistra,
     quem sibi diversum cernit et oppositum.
15   Et si quando datur tabulae sibi tangere summa,
     reginae solitum praeripit officium.
   Vir factus mulier, regi ferus arbiter haeret,
     imperat et regnat, hinc capit, inde labat.
   Bella movent primi pedites, labuntur et ipsi,
20   et reliquis timidam dant moriendo viam.
   Per spatium tabulae rocho conceditur ire
     in qua parte velit, si nihil obstiterit.
   Maior maiores rapit et fallendo minores,
     saepius et minimis fallitur a sociis.
25   Belliger insignis, prudens, celer, aptus et armis
     currit eques rapidus, qua patet arte locus.
   Decipit insontes socios et fraude carentes
     terret et insequitur, hinc capit, hinc capitur.
   Alfinus trivius, cornuta fronte timendus,
30   ante, retro comites decipit invigiles.
   A dominis minimi, domini capiuntur ab imis,
     sic mixti procerum; turba perit peditum.

board. The first is white, and the next is red in color—al- 5
though it can be painted either black or gray or red. In the
first position, the rook threatens to engage in battle, and
second stands the knight, grasping the rules of the game.
Third is the *aufin,* considered the guardian of the king.
Fourth, the king holds back; his wife sits fifth. After these, 10
the order of the previous nobles follows in reverse; a throng
of very swift-moving pawns advances in front of them.

The pawn stands his ground and takes from the right and
the left sides what he sees opposite and opposed to himself.
And if ever he is allowed to reach the other end of the board, 15
he snatches the queen's accustomed role. The male is
changed into a female and as a fierce tactician shadows the
king, commanding and ruling, here capturing and there giv-
ing way. The pawns are the first to wage war; they them-
selves are toppled, but in dying, they give a perilous path to 20
the remaining pieces.

The rook is allowed to go throughout the board in any
place he pleases, as long as nothing obstructs him. A power-
ful piece himself, he seizes both greater and lesser pieces by
trickery, but often he is tricked by lesser fellow soldiers. Dis- 25
tinguished in waging war, prudent, fast, and skilled at arms,
the swift knight runs wherever skill opens up a space. He
ensnares innocent fellow soldiers, frightens and pursues
those who lack guile, here capturing, there being captured.
The *aufin* of the crossways inspires fear with his horned
head; he catches unsuspecting nobles from the front and 30
from behind.

The lesser pieces are captured by the powerful ones, and
the lordly pieces by the weaker—so the nobles are mixed
together; the throng of pawns perishes. The king remains

337

Rex manet incaptus subtracta coniuge solus;
    coniuge subtracta nil valet in tabula.
35 Saepius est mattus servorum turbine saeptus
    et mattum suffert, si via nulla patet.

Doctrina mensae

Mensae doctrinam da nobis discere, Christe,
    desursum donans optima dona bonis,
sunt quia nonnulli, qui peccant in comedendo
    nec bene cognoscunt, est ubi rusticitas.
5 Mandere nobiliter usu doceatur et arte:
    usus et ars docuit, quod sapit omnis homo.
Nasus purgetur bene mucilagine primum
    nec manus attingat postmodo nuda luem.
Postque manus siquidem sunt omni sorde lavandae,
10   et bene tergantur; sit lue nuda caro.
Inde locum sedeas, erus aedis quem tibi donat,
    ne dicat socio: "Tu loca sume prius!"
Est modus in mensa mensuraque semper habenda.
    Ne comedas nimium, quod tibi sit nocuum.
15 Immensus pastus malus est nimiumque nocivus;
    displicet et superis et fugat ipse viros.
Inde mali morbi nascuntur et inde dolores;
    prandia sunt semper haec fugienda nimis.
Dum stas in mensa, sis largus desque libenter
20   ex his, quae mandis — nam cito praetereunt.

uncaptured, alone once his consort is taken; when his consort is taken, there is nothing of any value left on the board. Often he is checked after being fenced in by a crowd of servants, and he is checkmated if no path of escape opens up. 35

The Rule of the Table

Grant that we may learn the rule of the table, O Christ, and from on high, give the finest gifts to good men, because there are some who sin when they eat, and do not know well what constitutes boorishness. How to chew politely should 5 be taught through experience and art: experience and art have taught what every man knows.

First, the nose should be well purged of snot, nor should a bare hand afterward touch the mucus. And after, the hands should accordingly be cleansed of all dirt, and wiped thor- 10 oughly; the flesh should be unsoiled. Then you should take the seat that the master of the house gives you, so that he does not say to your companion, "You take a seat first!" Moderation and restraint should always be maintained in table manners. You shouldn't eat too much, because it is harmful to you. A vast amount of food is evil and very injuri- 15 ous; it displeases the gods and chases men away. From this, terrible afflictions arise, and thence pains; these meals are much to be avoided. While you remain at the table, you should be generous and give liberally of whatever you are 20 eating—for things swiftly pass. You should not close your

Non tua claudatur ad vocem pauperis auris:
    nunc sere, quae plena postmodo falce metas.
Nec prave sectum socius stomachetur ad unguem,
    ante recidatur inde supervacuum.
25 Tu quoque suspensis aliis digitis tribus esto;
    non tibi deturpet os neque pectora ius.
Pauca sedens comedas, si vis urbanus haberi,
    nec socium fallas nec bona cuncta velis.
Non intingatur scutellae bis bolus idem,
30   praesertim socio si sociatus eris.
Non supra lancem dependeat os alicuius,
    atque super mensam nemo valens iaceat.
Qui tenet in mensa cubitum vel brachia tensa,
    non est urbanus corpore sive manu.
35 In mensa caveas, ne sternutatio fiat,
    ac post te spuere semper adesto memor.
Gausape non tergas nasum, sed margine vestis:
    cum porcis comedat, quisquis idem faciat.
Sextipides pulicesque truces inter comedentes
40   tangere non temptes, scalpere sive caput.
Os neque delectet te rodere more canino,
    nec nimio morsu faux tua turpis erit.
Non digitos lambat, quisquis vult esse facetus,
    altera non ora cernere saepe velit.
45 Oraque cum manibus rara pinguedine foedes.
    Alterius morsus enumerare cave!
Ac in parte tua comedas spectando cacumen,
    nec tibi dormitet iugiter una manus.
Semper avaritiam fugito luxumque voracem:
50   obvia sunt famae talia namque tuae.

ear to the voice of a pauper: sow now what you shall reap in
fullness with a scythe hereafter. Your companion should not
feel distaste at your poorly cut fingernail—cut away in ad-
vance anything that is superfluous. You should also keep   25
your three other fingers raised; let the gravy not befoul your
mouth or your breast.

   You should eat little while you sit, if you want to be con-
sidered urbane—don't cheat your companion and choose all
the good bits. The same morsel should not be dipped into
the serving dish twice, especially if you will be sharing with   30
your companion. No one's mouth should hang over the plat-
ter, and no one who is healthy should lie on the table. He
who keeps his elbow or his extended arms on the table is not
refined in body or hand.

   Take care that you do not sneeze on the table, and always   35
remember to spit behind yourself. You should not wipe your
nose on the tablecloth, but on the edge of your robe: who-
ever does this should eat with the pigs. Don't try to touch
six-footed insects or savage fleas or to scratch your head,   40
while dining in the presence of others. Do not delight in
gnawing a bone like a dog, nor let your jaws be distorted by
too great a bite. Whoever wishes to be elegant should not
lick his fingers, nor should he frequently stare at the faces of
the others. You should foul your mouth and hands with little   45
grease. Take care not to count another's bites! And for your
part, you should eat gazing upward, and one of your hands
should not constantly be idle. You should always avoid greed
and voracious excess, for these harm your reputation. No   50

Invidiam sortis praeponat nemo sodali,
    et comedens omnis turpia cuncta fuget.
Nunc doctrina stilum vult ad potus removere:
    inscius inde mea pulcrius arte bibat.
55 Labraque cum manibus tergas pinguedine primum
    et tibi mandante principe sume merum.
Est ergo binis manibus cratera tenenda,
    tangere non pollex dulcia vina velit.
Non infundantur hominis genorbada baccho,
60   temperet in vino se nimis omnis homo.
Restringatur aqua multa vis improba vini,
    crapula quod nulla possit obesse tibi.
Multa meri genera, caveas, ne sumere temptes —
    saepe duo faciunt, quod nequit unus homo.
65 Ore cibo tumido semper potare caveto,
    nec respirabis postea quando bibis.
Contineas oculos nec circum quaque revolvas,
    ac cratera super dicere verba cave!
Porrige cratera post hoc socioque rotando,
70   ne sua ponantur hic, ubi labra tua.

De nummo

In terra summus rex est hoc tempore nummus.
Nummum mirantur reges et ei famulantur.
Nummos venalis favet ordo pontificalis.
Nummus in abbatum cameris tenet principatum.
5 Nummum nigrorum veneratur turba priorum.

one should confront a fellow guest out of jealousy for his fortune, and in eating, everyone should put all unpleasantness aside.

Now the rule wishes to turn my stylus to the subject of drinking: in this way, one who is ignorant may drink with more refinement by my art. First you should wipe your lips 55 and hands free of grease, and when the host bids you, take the unmixed wine. The cup should then be grasped with both hands, but the thumb should not touch the sweet wine. A man's beard should not be moistened by wine; every man 60 should show great moderation in wine drinking. The destructive force of wine should be kept in check with a good amount of water, so that no hangover can do you harm. Take care not to try many types of unmixed wine—often just two make one man incapable. Never drink when your mouth is 65 stuffed with food, and you will not belch after you drink. You should control your eyes and not roll them in every direction, and take care not to have words over the cup! After this, offer the cup to your companion, turning it round so 70 that his lips are not placed where yours were.

On Money

The highest king on earth at this time is money. Kings admire money and are enslaved to it. The venal pontifical order loves its money. Money holds first place in the chambers of abbots. The throng of black priors worships money. 5

Nummus cunctorum iudex est consiliorum.
Nummus bella gerit, nec si vult pax sibi deerit.
Nummus agit lites dum vult deponere dites.
Erigit ad plenum de stercore nummus egenum.
10 Omnia nummus emit, vendit, donat, et data demit.
Nummus adulatur, nummus post blanda datur.
Nummus agit villas, struit urbes, destruit illas.
Nummus mentitur, nummus verax reperitur.
Nummus periuros miseros facit et perituros.
15 Nummus avarorum deus est, et spes cupidorum.
Nummus in errorem mulierem ducit amorem.
Nummus venales dominas facit imperiales.
Nummus raptores reddit fore nobiliores.
Nummus habet plures quam caelum sidera fures.
20 Nummus securus plantat quae vult habiturus.
Nummus iter caeli claudit, reseratque fideli.
Nummus donatus dat honorem pontificatus.
Nummus perverse secreta facit sua per se.
Nummus cum loquitur pauper tacet, ut bene scitur.
25 Nummus dolores reprimit relevatque dolores.
Nummus corda necat, sapientum lumina caecat.
Nummus ut est certum stultum facit esse disertum.
Nummus mendicos fictos acquirit amicos.
Nummus formosas vestes gerit et preciosas.
30 Nummus splendores dat vestes exteriores.
Nummus eos gestat lapides quos India prestat.
Nummus dulce putat et eum gens tota salutat.
Nummus et invadit et quae vult oppida tradit.
Nummus adoratur quia virtutes operatur.
35 Nummus habet servos quibus auget aeris acervos.
Nummus aegros sanat, secat, urget et aspera planat;

Money is the decider of all councils. Money wages war, nor, if it wants it, will fail to get peace. Money prompts disputes when it wants to get rid of the wealthy. Money raises the needy from filth to plenty. Money buys, sells, and gives everything, and, once given, takes everything back. Money flatters, money is given in return for flattery; money raises villas, builds cities, and demolishes them. Money lies but is judged to be truthful. Money makes perjurers miserable and causes them to perish. Money is the god of the greedy and the hope of the covetous. Money leads a woman's love into error. Money makes imperial mistresses venal. Money renders robbers into nobles. Money produces more thieves than the sky has stars. Money cultivates in full confidence, certain to attain its wishes. Money closes the path to heaven, and unlocks it for the faithful. The gift of money confers the honor of the papacy. Money perversely makes its own secrets by its own means. When money talks, the poor man is silent, as is well known. Money suppresses sadness, and also relieves it. Money corrupts the hearts and blinds the eyes of wise men. Money, it's for certain, makes a fool eloquent. Money accrues sponging, false friends. Money wears elegant and expensive clothes. Money gives sumptuous outer garments. Money shows off those gemstones that India provides. Money delights, and all people salute it. Money both invades and betrays any towns it wants. Money is adored because it cultivates strength. Money has servants, with whom it increases its heaps of coinage. Money heals the sick, cuts, presses down, and smooths out the rough; it makes the

vile facit carum, quod dulce est reddit amarum.
Nummus laudatos pisces comedit piperatos.
In nummi mensa sunt plurima fercula densa.
40 Francorum vinum nummus bibit atque marinum.
Et facit audire surdum, claudumque salire.
    De nummo quaedam maiora prioribus edam.
Vidi cantantem nummum missam celebrantem.
Nummus cantabat, nummus responsa parabat.
45 Vidi quod flebat, dum sermonem faciebat.
Et subridebat, populum cum decipiebat.
Nummus honoratur sine nummo nullus amatur.
Qui perdit nummos carnales perdit amicos.
    Quem gens infamat, nummus "Probus est homo" clamat.
50 Ergo patet cuique quod nummus regnat ubique.
Sed quia consumi poterit cito gloria, virtus,
ex hac esse schola non est sapientia sola.

De amore

Si quem forte iuvat subdi sapienter amori,
    sic amet incipiens, ut mea Musa docet.
Turpe scelus vitans nullus temptet monialem,
    quae se contemnens est sociata Deo.
5 Assimilatur ei iam femina nupta marito,
    quam maculare quidem creditur esse nefas.
Praeterea ganeis venali corpore foedis
    munera ni tribuat, nemo placere potest.

worthless precious, and what is sweet, it renders bitter. Money devours excellent fish seasoned with pepper. On money's tables are many courses served one after another. Money drinks French and coastal wine. And it makes the 40 deaf hear, and the lame leap to their feet.

I will tell some things about money even greater than what I've mentioned before. I have seen money singing as it celebrates the Mass. Money was singing, and money was preparing the responses. I saw that it wept as it was deliver- 45 ing a sermon. And it smiled even as it was deceiving the people. Money is respected; no one is loved without money. He who loses his money loses his carnal friends. Of the man whom people denounce, money proclaims, "He is a fine fellow!" Therefore it is apparent to everyone that money reigns 50 everywhere. But because glory and power can quickly wither away, it is not wisdom to be from this school alone.

On Love

If by chance someone wishes to submit himself to love in a sensible fashion, let the beginner love in the way that my Muse instructs. To avoid a repugnant crime, let no man make an attempt on a nun, who—scorning him—is married to God. A similar situation is a woman already wed to a 5 husband, whom it is certainly considered an offense to defile. Moreover, no one can please the foul wenches with their bodies for sale, unless he pays them money. If a whore

347

Si se supponit meretrix, non praestat amorem,
10   non amat id quod agit, sed petit id quod habes.
Sunt aliae multae mulieres lusibus aptae,
    virginis et viduae laudo vacantis opus.
Virginis amplexus durissima pectora mollit,
    maestitiam pellit, cor super astra levat.
15 Dulcis amor viduae mollit quoque corda superba,
    quae melius cunctis et sapienter amat.
Pulchra puella vacans dulcissima gaudia praestat,
    mollibus apta iocis, libera corda gerens.
Has iuvenile decus sapienter discat amare,
20   arte quidem nostra noscat amoris iter.
Providus imprimis oculis sibi quaerat amandam,
    eligat ex multis, quae placet una sibi.
Hanc firmis oculis ridentibus intueatur,
    ut, quia diligitur, dulcis amica sciat.
25 Sed virtutis opes, generatio, forma decora
    ante repensetur, ne nimis alta petat.
Diligat aequalem vel paulo se meliorem,
    nam cito saepe ruit, qui super astra volat.
Inde locum quaerat, quo semper amica moretur,
30   quove puella manet, retia tendat ibi.
Huc veniat ludens, cantet suspiria coram,
    quae si non novit, militet arte sua.
Hic temptet vires, hic dulcia verba loquatur,
    quod placet, hoc faciat, res velut ipsa dabit.
35 Huc tamen ut vadat, prodest occasio ficta,
    qua prius inventa cautius urit amor.
Diligit hunc mulier, qui caute novit amare,
    ne consanguinei singula facta sciant.

submits to someone, she does not offer love—she does not 10
love what she does but seeks what you have.

There are many other women suitable for sport: I praise
the pursuit of a virgin or an available widow. A virgin's em-
brace calms the sternest breast, drives away sorrow, lifts the
heart above the stars. The sweet love of a widow also softens 15
a proud heart—she loves better than all, and wisely. The
lovely, unattached girl offers the sweetest pleasures—she is
suitable for tender games and has an unconstrained heart.
Let those in the glory of youth learn to love such women
wisely; indeed, by our art let him learn the course of love. 20

First of all, let him shrewdly cast his gaze in search of
someone to love, and let him choose from many the one
who pleases him. Let him admire her with steady, laughing
eyes, so that his sweet friend may know that she is loved.
But beforehand let him consider the richness of her virtue, 25
her lineage, and her fine figure, so that he does not aim too
high. Let him love one who is his equal or slightly better
than him, for often he swiftly falls who flies up to the stars.
Then let him find out the place where his girlfriend tends to
spend her time, or where the girl stays, and let him set his 30
nets there. Let him go there playfully, let him sing his lover's
sighs in her presence, and if he is ignorant of such matters,
let him soldier on with his own skill. At one moment let him
try force, at another let him speak sweet words; let him do
what gives her pleasure, as the situation itself shows him.
Nevertheless, a fictitious pretext for his going there is useful 35
so that if such an excuse is found beforehand, his love may
be more discreet. A woman loves a man who knows how to
love discreetly, so that her relatives do not learn every single
detail.

349

Nuntia quaeratur, in qua confidat uterque,
40   quae narret caute, quicquid utrique placet.
Muneret hanc iuvenis, quod sit super haec studiosa,
     et plus quam tribuat, polliceatur ei.
Audit ut haec illam, dulcissima narret amori,
     incipiens caute talia verba loqui:
45   "O speciosa nimis, vultu fecunda sereno,
     te iuvenile decus laudet et optet amans.
Qui cunctos alios superat spectamine morum,
     colloquium tecum vellet habere rogans.
Utile quod nimis est vestro tractabit honori
50   et plus quam famulus subditus esse cupit.
Omnia postposuit, nisi te non diligit umquam,
     me tibi direxit, sum quia fida tibi."
Forsitan in primis dabit aspera verba puella,
     sed cito, quae prius est aspera, mollis erit.
55   Dulcia verba quidem tunc nuntia proferat illi,
     quodque petit iuvenis, comprobet esse bonum.
Hunc modo commendet, modo laudes conferat illi,
     sic alternatim laudet utrumque simul.
Quod si displiceat modo consentire puellae
60   ad iuvenem rediens singula facta ferat.
Hic non diffidat, studiosius immo laboret,
     nutibus et signis saepe loquatur ei.
Ach quotiens teneram, quae numquam novit amare,
     talibus ingeniis languidus urit amor.
65   Hanc blandimentis attemptet nuntia saepe,
     nec cito desistat, quando puella negat.
Femina, quod prohibet, cupit et vult saepe rogari,
     improbitas vincit pectora, frangit amor.

Let them find a go-between in whom each one can con-
fide, and who can discreetly tell each of them what the other   40
wants. Let the young man reward her, so that she is zealous
in these matters, and let him promise her more than he
gives. When the girl is listening to her, let her tell of the de-
lights of love, discreetly beginning to speak words such as
these:

"O most beautiful one, endowed with a radiant face, let   45
the glory of youth compliment you and as a lover desire you.
Let one who surpasses all others in the display of his charac-
ter desire to engage in conversation with you as a suitor. He
will discuss only what is advantageous to your honor, and he   50
wants to be more devoted to you than a servant. He has put
aside everything else and loves no one but you; he has sent
me to you because I am loyal to you."

Perhaps at first the girl will return harsh words, but
quickly she who was once harsh will become mild. Then in-   55
deed let the go-between offer sweet words to her, and let her
affirm that what the youth wants is good. Now let her com-
mend him, now let her offer praises to the girl, and by turns
in this way, let her praise both of them at the same time. But
if, at that moment, the girl does not want to consent, let the   60
go-between return to the youth and report every single de-
tail. Let him not despair; on the contrary, let him work more
diligently, let him speak often to her through nods and sig-
nals. Ah, how often does languishing love by such talents in-
flame the passions of a delicate girl, who has never experi-
enced love. Let the go-between frequently ply her with   65
compliments, and let her persist even if the girl refuses. A
woman wants what she denies and wants to be entreated of-
ten; stubborn effort conquers her heart, and love breaks it.

Ferrea congeries dirumpitur improbitate
70 et durum lapidem gutta cadendo cavat.
Sic multis precibus et longo temporis usu
 colloquium fieri sponte puella volet.
Pro quo secretus prius est locus inveniendus,
 ut, quod utrique placet, nuntia sola sciat.
75 Si tamen, ut plerumque solet, sit curia plena
 et mos est dominae, cui velit ipsa, loqui,
tunc illam iuvenis blando sermone salutet
 et propius maneat clamque loquatur ei:
"Stella serena nitens, facie rutilante decora,
80 ecce tuum famulum nunc patiare loqui.
Si tua nobilitas, probitas et forma decora
 laudetur velut est, par tibi nulla manet.
Tu superas cunctas forma praestante puellas
 et vincis Venerem, ni foret ipsa dea.
85 Aurea caesaries, tibi frons est, ut decet, alta,
 ridentes oculi, nigra supercilia.
Quando moves oculos, vario certamine pungor,
 gaudia corda movent, sed tamen urit amor.
Candidus et rutilans simul est color ipse genarum
90 exornat faciem nasus et inde places.
Labra tument modicum, roseo perfusa colore,
 quae mihi, si possem, iungere velle foret.
Ordine formati candent albedine dentes,
 omnibus est gratus risus in ore tuo.
95 Complacet et mentum, gula proxima plus nive candet,
 quam quotiens video, cor sine fine calet.
Haec mihi significat, quantum sint candida membra,
 quae tegis interius vestibus ipsa tuis.

A mass of iron is shattered by audacity, and a drop of water   70
hollows out a hard rock by its fall.

Thus, after many prayers and a long investment of time,
the girl will come to wish for a rendezvous to take place. For
this, first a secret spot must be found that is agreeable to
both of them and that only the go-between knows. If, how-   75
ever, as frequently happens, the scene is a crowded court,
and it is the custom of the mistress to speak to whomever
she wishes, then let the young man greet her with a seduc-
tive speech, and remain beside her and speak to her secretly:

"Bright shining star, with your beautifully radiant com-
plexion, here I am: allow your servant to speak now. If your   80
nobility, virtue, and beauty can be praised adequately, you
are without peer. You exceed all girls in beauty, and you
would surpass Venus, if she weren't a goddess. Your hair is   85
golden, your brow is high (as it should be), your eyes are
laughing, your eyebrows dark. When you move your eyes, I
am stung by a contest of opposites: joy moves my heart, but,
nonetheless, love burns. The color of your cheeks is both
white and ruddy; your nose is an adornment to your face,   90
and you are beautiful because of it. Your lips are just full
enough, imbued with a rosy color, which I would—if I
could—join to mine. Your teeth gleam white in a lovely
alignment, and the smile on your face is a pleasure to all.
Your chin is also attractive, and the throat next to it shines   95
whiter than snow; whenever I see it, my heart burns end-
lessly. These signify to me how white the parts are that you
conceal beneath your garments. A lovely nipple matches

Utraque conformat tua pectora pulchra papilla,
100   quas, velut ipse puto, clauderet una manus.
Hic status est rectus, gracilis, complexibus aptus,
    bracchia cum manibus laude probanda vigent.
Cetera membra quidem proprio funguntur honore
    et plus quam possum dicere pulchra manes.
105 Cum te non video, pereo cupioque videre;
    inspiciens morior, nam nimis urit amor.
Iam tibi sum famulus; tibi, si placet, exhibeo me
    et semper faciam, quae mihi sola iubes.
Si me conspicies vel me digneris amare,
110   gaudeo plus quam si quis mihi regna daret.
Deprecor hoc tantum: famulum fatearis amandum,
    ut per te vivat, vita salusque mea!"
Forsitan illa sagax haec verba superba loquatur,
    ut, quod mente cupit, per sua verba tegat:
115 "Stulta petis, iuvenis, frustra laudas mea membra,
    si sum pulchra satis, cur tibi cura mei?
Vade, recede cito, ganeam me forte putasti
    et numquam dicas haec mihi verba magis."
Tunc dicat iuvenis: "Cur me, dulcissima rerum,
120   morte perire facis? Iam tibi crimen erit.
Munera magna peto, tamen haec sunt digna favore;
    si me forsan amas, nil tibi quippe nocet."
Inquiet illa quidem: "Fateor, non horreo quemquam,
    teque libenter amo, non nisi plura petas."
125 Tunc caput inclinat grates hilares referendo
    et semper famulus spondeat esse suus.
Sed tamen, ut merito possit semper famulari,
    laudes condignas praestet ubique sibi.

each of your breasts, which, I think, a single hand could en- 100
close. Your posture is straight, slender, and perfect for em-
braces; your arms and hands are vigorous and deserve praise.
Indeed, the rest of your parts merit their own esteem, and
you are more beautiful than I can say.

"When I do not see you, I perish, and I long for your 105
sight; I die when I contemplate you, for my love burns so
fiercely. I am already your servant; if it so pleases you, I will
give myself to you and always do what you alone command
of me. If you should look at me or deign to love me, I will 110
rejoice more than if someone should give me kingdoms. I
pray for this alone: that you acknowledge your servant wor-
thy of love, so that he may live through you, my life and my
salvation!"

Perhaps the cunning girl may say haughty words such as
these in reply, in order to conceal through her words what
she desires in her heart: "Young man, you're seeking some- 115
thing foolish; you praise my parts in vain—why does it mat-
ter to you if I am very pretty? Go away, withdraw quickly—
perhaps you thought I was a cheap whore—and never speak
such words to me again."

Then let the young man reply: "Why, my sweetest, do you 120
condemn me to death? The fault will be entirely yours. I
seek great rewards, nevertheless these things are worthy of
favor; if you happen to love me, no harm will befall you."

Then she will say: "I admit that I do not fear anyone and
that I love you willingly, unless you seek more."

Then let him bow his head, give his glad thanks, and 125
promise always to be her servant. But nonetheless, so that
he can serve her always as she deserves, let him offer her fit-
ting praises on every occasion. Let him request gifts as a

Postulet in signum sic incipientis amoris
130   munera, quae firment inter utrumque fidem.
Oscula digna magis tunc approbet, ac tamen eius
    ponat in arbitrio, quae dare dona velit.
Munere suscepto quasi tutus in eius amore
    laetus discedat gratificando sibi.
135 Posthac sollicitus discat, quo tempore solam
    inveniat dominam forte vacante loco.
Quae si non poterit, sapienter nuntia curet,
    artibus ut trahat hanc ad loca tuta iocis.
Huc veniat iuvenis, facie gaudente salutans,
140   adiunctis precibus laudibus usque vocans;
sic quoque, cum loquitur vel femina laude movetur,
    leniter hanc tangat vestibus ipse super.
Non adeo mentem rigidam tenet ulla puella,
    ut, si tangatur, risus in ore vacet.
145 Si fugiat tactum, subridens hanc comitetur,
    vel digito coxas comprimat atque latus.
Sed tamen in cunctis placidus modus est adhibendus,
    nam sine mensura nil valet esse bonum.
Curet ut insolitam faciat gaudere puellam,
150   dulcius exorans oscula grata petat.
Spondeat et iuret, quod non petit amplius ipse,
    nam bene sufficiunt talia dona peti.
Si negat illa quidem dare talia dona minando,
    haec eadem precibus non minus ipse petat;
155 sed quia sic multas verecundia saepius angit,
    ut quoque coniugibus basia iusta negent,
iungere non timeat violenter bracchia collo,
    ut prompte rapiat, quae negat illa dare.

symbol of their nascent love, to confirm their mutual fidel- 130
ity. Then let him commend kisses as more worthy gifts, and
nonetheless let her judge what gifts she wishes to give.
When he has received his gift, let him depart happy, con-
gratulating himself, like one assured of her love.

Thereafter, let him be careful to find out when he can 135
come upon his mistress alone in a conveniently deserted
spot. If he can't do this, let the go-between cleverly arrange
to draw the girl to a place safe for fun and games. Let the
young man come here and greet her with a smiling face, con- 140
tinually addressing her with praise as well as entreaties; yet
also, when he is speaking or the woman is moved by his
praise, let him touch her gently on her garments. No girl has
such a steadfast mind that, if she is touched, she will fail to
laugh. If she recoils from his touch, let him smilingly draw 145
closer to her, and with his finger press her hips and her side.
But in all of this, a calm manner is to be employed, for with-
out moderation, nothing good can come. Let him take care
to make the inexperienced girl happy, and entreating her 150
even more sweetly, let him seek freely given kisses.

Let him promise and swear that he seeks nothing more,
for it is enough to seek rewards such as these. If she then re-
fuses to give such gifts and threatens him, let him continue
to ask for them with entreaties; but because modesty so of- 155
ten troubles many women, so that they deny rightful kisses
even to their husbands, let him not be afraid to throw his
arm around her neck forcefully in order to take summarily

357

Si sua labra tuo tandem coniunxerit ori,
160   tunc teneant longas basia pressa moras.
Mobilis interea stringat manus una papillas
    et femur et venter sentiet inde vicem.
Sic postquam fuerit ludens calefactus uterque,
    vestibus eiectis crura levare decet.
165 Vim faciat iuvenis, quamvis nimis illa repugnet,
    nam si desistat, mente puella dolet.
Expectat potius luctando femina vinci,
    quam velit, ut meretrix, crimina sponte pati.
A ganeis tantum coitus decet esse petendus,
170   quae se pro pretio vendere cuique solent.
Qui quaerit coitum, si vim post oscula differt,
    rusticus est, numquam dignus amare magis.
Arte mea si quis sibi consociabit amicam,
    vatis opem quaerat, qua foveatur amor.
175 Admoneat dominam iuvenis per dulcia verba,
    colloquium fieri saepius ipse roget.
Saepe superciliis vel nutu longius instet,
    si prope non audet voce sonante loqui.
Tempore, quo stomachus sit prosperitate refectus
180   spiritibus laetis, potibus atque cibis,
anxius hanc adeat, Veneris solacia quaerat,
    tunc etenim melius diligit omnis homo.
Taedia non faciat plus quam sit posse laborans,
    fastidita frequens esca iacere solet.
185 Diligat occulte, cum non sit vilis amica,
    sic est furtivus dulcior omnis amor.
Gaudia quae sumpsit, curet celare modestus
    nec nomen dominae publicet ipse palam.
Qui culpa propria placidam sibi perdit amicam,
190   perpetuo doleat rusticitate sua.

what she refuses to give. If she eventually joins her lips to yours, then keep her lips pressed against yours for a long time. Meanwhile let a stray hand grasp her breasts, and then feel her thigh and her belly in turn. After both are warmed up through play such as this, he should throw off her clothes and lift up her legs. Let the young man use force, though she put up quite a fight, for if he stops, the girl will lament in her heart. A woman expects to be subdued in a struggle, rather than wanting, like a whore, to submit to the crime willingly. Sex should only be asked for from wenches who are accustomed to sell themselves to anyone for a price. A man who wants sex but delays the use of force after kisses is a peasant, nevermore worthy to love.

If anyone gets himself a girlfriend by my art, let him seek the aid of a poet in order to nurture his love. Let the youth encourage his mistress with sweet words, and let him frequently ask for meetings with her. Let him often and long pursue her with winks and nods, if he does not dare to speak to her up close and aloud. At the time when his stomach is restored with fine fare, with good spirits, drink, and food, let him approach her solicitously and seek the solaces of Venus; at such a time, as a matter of fact, every man is better suited for love. Let him not make things tedious, working harder than he is able; too much food tends to become boring.

Let him take his pleasure secretly, since his girlfriend is not lowborn, for every love is sweeter in secret. Let him take care to modestly conceal the pleasures that he has enjoyed, and let him not openly publicize the name of his mistress. Whoever loses his compliant lover through his own fault, let him forever grieve for his boorishness.

160

165

170

175

180

185

190

De remedio amoris

Qui fuerit cupiens ab amica solvere colla,
    plenius e nostro carmine doctus erit.
Nosse decet primum, quantum sit femina turpis
    et quantum noceat fetidus eius amor.
5 Si fuerit pinguis, gravis est ut plumbea massa,
    mollitie lutea turgida membra tument;
quae cute sudanti velut est axungia porci
    lubrica, saepe facit taedia tacta semel.
Macra placere nequit, quia pungunt hispida membra
10   exteriusque patent ossa rigente cute;
arida ligna quidem cito consumuntur ab igne,
    urit et assumptus sic perit eius amor.
Longa placet nulli, nec habet sub pectore sensum,
    est fatuae mentis, nescia quid sit amor;
15 iumento similis numquam satiatur ab ullo,
    cum se supponit, vix sua membra plicat.
Si brevis est, forsan per singula membra superbit,
    uritur interius, voce superba furit;
nil valet eius amor, quia tamquam vipera laedit
20   nec bene sufficiunt parvula membra ioco.
Candida si fuerit, pallor suus inficit ipsam,
    frigida membra gerens nescit amore frui;
despicit haec omnes iuvenes sua corpora cernens,
    marmorea statua candidiora putat.
25 Sed cur nigra placet, quae tacto corpore tingit?
    Gaudia turpis amor nulla movere potest;

On the Remedy for Love

The man who wishes to free his neck from his girlfriend will be more fully instructed by our poem. First, he should recognize how ugly the woman is and how much harm her foul love can do.

If she is plump, she is heavy as a lump of lead, and her sallow, bloated body swells from inactivity. When her skin sweats, she is slippery like pig grease and frequently provokes disgust, though only touched once.

Nor can a skinny woman please, because her spiky body pricks, and her bones show through her taut skin; it is true dry wood is quickly consumed by fire; so love for her burns but, once taken up, dies.

A tall woman is pleasing to no one, nor does she have good sense in her heart; she is simpleminded and does not know what love is. Like a cow, she is never satisfied by anyone, and when she lies under you, she can scarcely bend her body.

If she is short, perhaps she takes pride in her individual features; she feels passion inside and rages with a haughty voice. Her love is worthless since it wounds like a viper, and her little body is not well suited to lovemaking.

Should she be ghostly white, her pallor discolors her; her body is cold and she doesn't know how to enjoy love. She despises all young men; looking at her own body, she finds it whiter than a marble statue.

And why should a black woman please, whose body stains when touched? Offensive love can arouse no joy. Like some-

inferno similis tenet haec fuliginis instar,
    nocte quidem nulli crura levare vetat.
Rubra venenosa cholera male sanguine fervet,
30   demonibus similis fallere docta fuit;
haec melancholico quia sanguine tardius ardet,
    ex multis vitiis callida peius amat.
A nostra iuvenis si quis vult arte doceri,
    talia pensando linquere debet eam.
35 Sed mediae formae mulier per talia numquam
    displicet, immo velut sit dea, sola placet;
haec fovet interius gaudenti corde medullas
    cumque dolore gravi solvitur eius amor.
Aestimet imprimis, quantum laedatur amando
40   et quae praeterea damna sequantur eum;
efficitur fatuus, qui sic amat, ut modus absit;
    negligit officium quilibet inde suum.
Saepe novum veteri mulier praeponit amico,
    saepius incestas unus et alter amat.
45 Decipitur iuvenis: non est tam pulchra puella,
    cuius amore gravi laesus ad ima ruit,
ut putat. Eius enim facies est picta colore,
    vestibus ornatur vilia membra bonis.
Nil bene cernit amor, videt omnia lumine caeco,
50   fallitur in multis anxietate sua.
Vadat ad hanc iuvenis ieiunus mane repente,
    dum iacet in somno nuda, soluta caput,
gaudia tunc sumat, donec fastidia sentit,
    quod vult, plus faciat, quam sibi velle fuit.

thing hellish, this woman bears a resemblance to soot; indeed, at night, she does not refuse to lift her legs for anyone.

The ruddy woman wickedly seethes with poisonous bile in her blood, and she has learned to deceive like demons. 30 This woman, cunning in many vices, because she feels passion more slowly on account of her melancholic blood, is a harmful lover. If any young man is ready to be instructed by our skill, he should think on these things and leave her.

But a woman with features midway between these never 35 displeases in any of these ways; on the contrary, she alone is pleasing, as if she were a goddess. She warms the innermost marrow with a glad heart, and the end of her love comes with great sadness.

Let the young man consider first how much he is being harmed by loving, and in addition the damages that will ac- 40 crue to him. He will make a fool of himself if he loves so much as to lack moderation; for that reason a person will neglect his duty. Often a woman prefers a new lover to an old one; even more often, both the new and the old lover are devoted to the same promiscuous woman. The young man is 45 deceived: the girl, for love of whom he has received serious hurts and been cast into disgrace, is not as pretty as he thinks; her face is painted with rouge, and her ugly body is beautified by fine garments. Love distinguishes nothing clearly, it looks upon everything with a blind eye, and in 50 many cases it is deceived by its own anxiety.

Let a young man go to her early in the morning before breakfast, while she lies naked in slumber, her hair unbound. Then let him take his pleasure until he becomes sated, and let him fulfill more of his desires than he wished to.

55 Post hoc inspiciat, quantum sint turpia membra,
     quae nulli placeant, si medicina vacet.
   Hac ita dimissa iam diligat ipse laborem
     marceat et corpus fortius arte sua,
   sit cibus et potus modicus, ieiunia prosunt,
60   nec petet hanc rursus, nec putet inde vicem.

De philomena alter liber

"Sum noctis socia, sum cantu dulcis, amoena;
  nomen in ambiguo sic philomena traho."
Insomnem philomena trahit per carmina noctem,
  nos dormire facit, se vigilare docet.
5 Dic, philomena, velis cur noctem vincere cantu?
  "Ne noceat donis vis inimica meis."
Dic age, nunc cantu poteris depellere pestem?
  "Aut possim aut nequeam, me vigilare iuvat."
Vox, philomena, tua cantus educere cogit,
10   inde tibi laudem rustica turba canit.
Vox, philomena, tua citharas et carmina vincit
  et superat miris musica flabra modis.
Vox, philomena, tua curarum semina tollit,
  et recreat blandis anxia cordia sonis.
15 Florea rura colis, herboso caespite gaudes,
  frondibus arboreis pignora multa foves.

After this, let him view how ugly her body is, which would   55
please no one, if it weren't for the makeup. Once he has dis-
missed the woman, let him then devote himself to hard
work and enfeeble his body more steadfastly by discipline.
Let his food and drink be modest—fasting is helpful. Let   60
him not seek her out again, or think of her either.

Another Poem on the Nightingale

"I am the companion of the night, I am pleasant and sweet
in song; I, a nightingale, in this way derive my name in ob-
scurity."

The nightingale spends a sleepless night in song, makes
us sleep, and teaches us that she is awake. Speak, nightin-   5
gale: why do you want to vanquish the night with song?

"So no hostile force will harm my gifts."

Come, tell me: can you now avert pestilence through
song?

"Whether I can or can't, it delights me to keep my
watch."

Your voice, nightingale, prompts the voicing of song, and   10
so the country folk sing praise for you. Your voice, nightin-
gale, vanquishes citharas and songs, and surpasses musical
piping with its wondrous sounds. Your voice, nightingale,
removes the seeds of worry and revives anxious hearts with
its alluring sounds. You nurture the flowering countryside,   15
you rejoice in grassy fields, you foster many offspring in the

Cantibus ecce tuis recrepant arbusta sonoris,
    consonat ipsa sonis frondea silva comis.
Iudice me cygnus et garrula cedit hirundo,
20   cedit et illustris psittacus ore tibi.
Dic igitur tremulos lingua vibrante susurros
    et suavi liquidum gutture pange melos.
Porrige dulcisonas attentis auribus escas;
    nolo tacere velis, nolo tacere velis.

De quadam vetula

Ista furore suo nunc se corrodit ab intra
    tristis anus, quae me suppositare rogat.
"Spes mea dulcis," ait, "velis hic si figere membrum,
    omnia quae mea sunt, spes mea dulcis, habe!"
5 Ast ego, qui lutum vidi scabiemque fluentes
    inguinis a fovea, talia verba movi:
"Si mihi—per nasum!—donares, marcida, montem,
    nolo tui membro vulva sit aula meo.
Intus vidi eadem vexilla trementia centum,
10   mucida fila, picem, stercora mille caprae
milleque vermiculos, ranarum milia lectos,
    saepe paludineis ut fore cernis aquis;
milleque sanguinei volventes stercora rivi
    inde fluunt, tandem est marcida vulva tibi."
15 Is ego non modicam subito stomachatus in iram
    surgo "Pedem" dicens "accipe, tristis anus!"

foliage of trees. Behold, the orchards echo with your tuneful songs, the forest itself with its leafy foliage resounds to your tones. In my judgment the swan and the talkative swallow are inferior to you in speech, as is the famous parrot. Speak, 20 therefore, with your tongue trilling quivering notes, and sing a clear tune from your sweet throat. Offer sweet-sounding treats to attentive ears; I don't want you to be silent, I don't want you to be silent.

On a Certain Old Woman

This pathetic old crone who asked me to lie with her in her mad desire was now wasting herself away. "My sweet hope," she said, "if you will thrust your member here, take, my sweet hope, everything that is mine!"

But once I saw the filth and mange flowing from the pit 5 of her groin, I responded like this: "If you, scrawny hag—what a stench!—were to give me a mountain, I still would not want your vagina to be a hall for my member. Within it I saw a hundred banners shaking, musty fibers, tar, the dung 10 of a thousand goats, and a thousand little worms and thousands of frogs gathered together, as you often see in swampy waters, and a thousand bloody streams carrying along dung flow from there, so rotten, in sum, is your vagina."

Suddenly fuming with unrestrained rage, I rose, saying, 15 "Take my foot, pathetic old hag!" And I thrust my foot into

Et sibi vulvali figo fetente caverna
   et statim retraho protinus inde pedem.
Heu, heu, pes mihi totus olet totusque liquoris
20   calceus uber erat, solvere abinde rui.
Sed fugio; mirum: tanta marcedine laxus
   calceus a putrido concidit ipse pede
et locus ille diu, quo concidit, ora propinquus
   foeda fuit nec pus cessit abinde pedi.
25 Quid facio? Fontem, quo numquam clarior alter,
   accurro et latici quam cito subdo pedem.
Ecce aliud monstrum: fons ille venustior ante
   omnibus, excellens perdidit inde decus,
namque ubi fontem compellavere propinqui
30   hactenus, est citra foeda vocata palus.
Mirandum ecce aliud: manibus, quibus omnia lavi
   foeda pedis, mensem perstitit ille sapor,
neque minus stetit ille pedi post inde recessum
   credere nec poteram stercora abesse mihi.
35 Unde ego iuravi nullo peramare vetustam
   tempore, quae talis fercla saporis habent,
sed solum teneris me cum gaudere puellis,
   ut quarum prodit lacteus ore sapor.
Et si nunc omnes vetulas peramare iuvaret
40   rugosas, nobis nulla placebit anus.
Sic stomachum saturavit anus, sic foeda palato
   fercla tulit nostro, quod sibi semper ero
ut vitulis et ipse lupus, velut anguibus alba
   ibis amica, velut demonis ipse deus.
45 Di geminent vermes vulva culoque propinquo
   delicium et merdae crescat in ore tuo!

the stinking cavern of her vagina and immediately pulled it back from there. Alas, alas, my foot stank all over and my shoe was completely full of fluid, and immediately I was in haste to untie it. But I rushed away—it was a miracle: my shoe, loosened by so much discharge, dropped from my stinking foot, and for a long time, the place near where it fell was a disgusting shore, and the pus was still covering my foot.

What did I do? I ran to a fountain (none was ever clearer), and quick as I could, I dipped my foot into the water. Behold, another wonder: that fountain, once more lovely than all others, at that moment lost its superior beauty; for what its neighbors had called a fountain before, ever since has been called a foul swamp. Behold, another marvel: on my hands, with which I washed all the foulness from my foot, that odor remained for a month, and after I left there it was no less persistent on my foot, so I could not believe that the excrement had actually left me.

From then on, I swore never to love an old woman who has such a smelly dish, but rather only to take pleasure in young girls, since their mouth breathes a milky scent. Now even if I wanted to love all wrinkled old women, no old woman would please me. The old woman so overfilled my stomach and served such a foul dish to my palate, that to her I will always be like a very wolf is to calves, like the beneficial white ibis to snakes, like a very god to devils. May the gods multiply the worms in your vagina and in its neighbor, your anus, and may your mouth take increasing pleasure in shit!

De rustico

Rure morans quid agam, respondi pauca, rogatus.
Mane Deum exoro, famulos post arvaque viso.
Inde lego Phoebumque cio Musamque lacesso.
Prandeo, poto, cano, ludo, lavo, ceno, quiesco,
5 rustice, lustrivage, capripes, cornute, bimembris,
canifer, rudigena, pernix, caudite, petulce,
saetiger, indocilis, agrestis, barbare, dure,
semicaper, pilose, sagax, periure, biformis,
silvicola, instabilis, saltator, perdite, mendax,
10 lubrice, ventisonax, inflator, stridule, anhele,
audax, brute, ferox, pellite, incondite, mute,
hirte, hirsute, biceps, niger, hispidissime, fallax!

De tribus puellis

Ibam forte via quadam nullo comitante,
    solus Amor mecum, qui solet esse, fuit.
Dumque meos versus facio meditorque puellam
    cui possum versus mittere quos facio,
5 ecce procul video quasi tres nymphas venientes
    e quibus, ut memini, longior una fuit.
Haec medium sortita locum currebat, et omnes
    currebant pariter, sed tamen illa magis;

On the Rustic

What am I to do when I'm staying in the countryside? I
have answered in a few words, since you ask. In the morning
I pray to God; afterward I go to see the servants and the
fields. Then I read and I summon Apollo and I excite my
Muse. I have breakfast, I drink, I sing, I play, I wash, I sup,
I sleep, you wandering-in-the-woods, goat-footed, horned,   5
half-beast, dog-master, rubbish-born, swift, tailed, frisky,
bristly, unteachable, wild, uncivilized, hardy, half-goat,
shaggy, shrewd, false, two-formed, forest-dwelling, change-
able, dancing, incorrigible, deceitful, slippery, braggart,   10
puffed-up-with-pride, harsh-sounding, panting, bold, irra-
tional, fierce, skin-clad, uncouth, dumb, rough, hirsute,
double-natured, black, hairiest, deceptive rustic!

On the Three Girls

As it happened, I was traveling without a companion on a
certain road; only Love was with me, as is usually the case.
And as I was composing my verses and thinking of the girl
to whom I might send the verses that I was composing, be-
hold: in the distance I saw three women like nymphs ap-   5
proaching, one of whom, as I recall, was particularly tall. She
was running between the other two; all of them were run-
ning, yet she was a little ahead. Now if she had happened to

sed si forte manu iaculum sumpsisset et arcum,
10   illa mihi certe visa Diana fuit.
Sic etenim solet illa feras agitare per altas
     silvas cumque suis currere virginibus.
Tunc ego nosse volens formas et nomen earum,
     incepi subito currere, post salio.
15 Ut vero propius accedens quamque notavi
     cum vidi vultus qui latuere prius,
sensi non nymphas, sed pulchras esse puellas,
     quales aequoreas vix reor esse deas;
vix Venerem, vix Iunonem, vix Pallada pulchram
20   istis virginibus assimilare queam.
Mox facies, mox caesaries, mox corpus earum,
     mox manus et digiti complacuere mihi,
namque Cupido suam nostro sub corde sagittam
     ardentesque faces fixerat ipse suas.
25 Lis erat inter eas, quae doctior esset earum
     cantu: nam cantu doctior una fuit.
Currebant igitur tres, ut sub iudice vero
     iudicii laudem de tribus una ferat.
Prima rosas, pomum tulit altera, tertia ramum,
30   quae tria virginibus saepe placere solent.
Est opere pretium describere de tribus unam,
     pulchrior haec etenim de tribus una fuit.
Huius erant vestes gemmis auroque micantes,
     at nitor in toto corpore maior erat.
35 Crinis erat flavus rutilo circumdatus auro,
     at crines auro plus placuere mihi.
Vernabant roseae circum caput inde coronae
     cum tamen absque rosis splendida tota foret;

take a bow and arrow in her hand, she certainly would have 10
looked to me like Diana. Just so indeed the goddess often
drives the beasts through the deep forests and runs with her
maidens.

Then, wishing to discover their appearance and names, I
suddenly began to run, then to sprint. Truly, as I grew closer, 15
I made out each one, and when I saw the faces that previ-
ously had been hidden, I realized that they were not
nymphs, but girls as beautiful as I can scarcely imagine the
goddesses of the sea are. I could scarcely compare Venus,
Juno, or beautiful Pallas with those maidens. At once their 20
faces, their hair, their bodies, their hands, and their fingers
took my fancy; for Cupid had pierced my heart with his bow
and burning torches. There was a contest between them 25
over which of them was more skilled in song, for one of
them was more skilled in song. And so the three were run-
ning, so that one of the three might win a glorious judgment
from an honest judge. The first brought roses, the second
fruit, the third a branch, three objects that usually please 30
maidens.

It is worthwhile to describe one of the three: for this one
of the three was especially beautiful. Her garments sparkled
with gemstones and gold, but the splendor of every part of
her body was greater still. Her blond hair was encircled with 35
ruddy gold, but her hair was more pleasing to me than gold.
Crowns of roses blossomed around her head, though even
without the roses she would have been utterly splendid; her

frons speciosa nimis, gula lactea, colla manusque
40   urebant animos, sed sine fine meos.
Non magis in caelo sunt lumina clara sereno,
    quam fuerant oculis lumina clara suis.
Utraque praeclaras gemmas tulit auris et aurum
    utraque non tanto pondere digna premi.
45 Forma papillarum nusquam parebat in illa,
    vel quod parva nimis vel quod stricta foret.
Ubera saepe suis zonis strinxere puellae,
    turgida namque nimis displicuere viris;
sed non inter eas est haec referenda puella,
50   ubera nempe satis parva fuere sibi.
Balteus insignis, gemmis stellatus et auro,
    cingebat dominae corpora grata meae.
Singula quid referam? Si singula quaeque referrem,
    non puto sufficerent, vix puto mille dies.
55 Si qua latent, meliora satis sunt omnibus illis,
    cum scio pro certo quod meliora latent.
Quid facerem? Non ausus eram prius os aperire,
    nos aperire tamen ora coegit amor,
cum dixi: "Salve, comitum regina tuarum,
60   femina sive dea digna salute mea.
Salventur pariter comites quae te comitantur,
    e quibus una magis tu mihi, virgo, places.
Quod si vos aliquae rapiunt ad iurgia causae,
    iudicio dirimam iurgia vestra meo.
65 Iudicium nostrum debetis iure subire,
    nam patet ingeniis ars bona quaeque meis.
. . .
    Nec non et cantus edocuere meos."

374

gorgeous face, her milky throat, her neck and her hands un- 40
ceasingly inflamed my heart. The stars in the clear sky are
no brighter than the bright light in her eyes. Each ear had
earrings of gold and sparkling gemstones, yet neither ear de-
served to be burdened with such weight. The shape of her 45
nipples was nowhere apparent, either because they were too
small or because they were bound. Girls often compress
breasts with girdles, for busts that are too full are displeas-
ing to men; but this girl should not be considered one of
that type; her breasts were without doubt small enough. An 50
extraordinary belt, glimmering with gold and gemstones,
girded the lovely body of my mistress. But why describe in-
dividual details? If I were to describe each aspect, I don't
think there are enough days, I think even a thousand days
would scarcely suffice. Whatever things are hidden are suffi- 55
ciently better than all others — since I know for certain that
better things are hidden.

What was I to do? I hadn't dared to open my mouth be-
fore, but love compelled me to open my mouth, so I said:
"Greetings, queen of your companions, worthy of my greet- 60
ing whether you are a woman or a goddess. Greetings like-
wise to the companions who accompany you, among all of
whom you, maiden, are most pleasing to me. Now if some
reason draws you into a quarrel, I will resolve your quarrel
with my judgment. By rights you ought to submit to my de- 65
cision, for I am thoroughly learned in all the liberal arts . . .
and they also taught me my songs."

Protinus, audito de cantu, prosiluerunt
70   et mox quaeque: "Meus arbiter" inquit "eris."
Conspicimus gratum florenti gramine pratum
    cum fuit in medio quercus et umbra loco.
Illic iudicium fieri placet: huc properamus,
    nam placuit nobis omnibus ille locus.
75 Hic in graminea primus tellure resedi
    praecepique suo quamque sedere loco.
Tunc quae virgo rosas portabat primo iubetur
    psallere; iussa prius psallere prima canit.
Illa canit fera bella Iovis, fera bella Gigantum
80   atque refert illos igne perisse Iovis.
Haec ubi finivit cantus, mox virgo secunda
    cuius ramus erat, cespite membra levat.
Constans in medio, Paridis referebat amores,
    haec sibi namque magis cantio nota fuit.
85 Vix sibi desierat, cum tandem tertia virgo,
    nam restabat adhuc tertia virgo, canit.
Utque suos fuerat circumdata flore capillos,
    obstitit atque manu quemque silere iubet.
Ipsa Iovem, teneros risus cantabat amoris,
90   qualiter Europam luserat ipse suam.
Vox sua grata fuit cunctis, mihi gratior uni;
    unus enim fueram qui sibi gratus eram.
Haec quotiens sonitum roseo fundebat ab ore,
    reddebant sonitum proxima saxa suum,
95 haud secus Ismariis in collibus Orpheus olim
    cantabat cythara cuncta movendo sua.
Sic quoque Sirenes quondam cecinisse feruntur,
    cum vellent Ithacas detinuisse rates;

Immediately, when they heard about my singing, they leaped up and at once each said: "You will be my judge." We noticed a pleasant meadow with lush grass, in the middle of which was a shady oak. There we decided to hold the hearing and we hastened to it, for that place was agreeable to all of us. On the grassy ground there I took a seat first, and I instructed each of them to take her own seat. Firstly I ordered the maiden who was carrying roses to sing a tune; ordered to sing first, first she sang. She sang of the fierce battles of Jupiter and of the giants, and she told of how they perished by Jupiter's fire. When she finished her song, immediately the second maiden, who had the branch, raised her body from the turf. Standing in the middle, she told of the loves of Paris, for this was a song that she knew better.

Scarcely had she finished when the third maiden—for the third maiden still remained—started singing. And when she had wreathed her hair with blossoms, she stood in front and with her hand ordered each of us to be silent. She sang of Jupiter, of his youthful mockeries of love, and of how he deceived his Europa. Her voice pleased everyone, but it was especially pleasant to me alone; for I was the only one who was pleasing to her. Whenever she poured forth song from her rosy mouth, the nearby rocks echoed her song, just as Orpheus once sang in the Ismarian hills, stirring all with his lyre. In this way also the Sirens are said to have sung once, when they wanted to delay the Ithacan ships; each one

cantu quaeque suo retinere parabat Ulixem,
100   non tamen astutum detinuere virum.
Quod si vox nostrae foret hinc audita puellae,
      sola licet cantu detinuisset eum.
Haec ubi finivit cantus vocemque repressit,
      laudavi cantus protinus ipse suos.
105 Utque meum per iudicium comites superaret,
      dixi: "Iudicio vincis cuncta meo;
voce tua comites devincis et arte canendi,
      nec tantum voce, sed simul et specie.
Ergo tibi geminae dentur cum laude coronae,
110   nam tecum victrix bina trophea refers."
Tunc, faciens geminas vario de flore coronas,
      imposui capiti praemia digna suo.
Illa quidem tacito delectabatur amore,
      sed doluere nimis eius honore duae.
115 Hinc ait: "O iuvenis, per quem mihi tanta paratur
      gloria, debentur praemia magna tibi.
Utque tuum meritum modo quale sit experiaris,
      atque probes nostrae foedus amicitiae,
ipse ores a me quodcumque placet tibi munus:
120   me tribuente feres quidquid habere voles.
Sed, ne fallacem me credas esse puellam
      at noscas verbis pondus inesse meis,
per sacra sceptra Iovis iurabo quae tibi dixi."
      . . .
125 "Munera pro meritis promittis maxima, virgo,"
      dixi, "pro meritis munera magna petam.
Nunc peto te, quaeso, cupio tibi consociari
      —tu mihi nempe places—si tibi forte placet.
Nullum me teste donum pretiosius est te;
130   te mihi si dederis praemia magna dabis.

intended to detain Ulysses with her song, yet they did not 100
hold back that sly man. If he had heard the voice of my girl,
she alone would have detained him with her song.

When she finished her song and checked her voice, I im-
mediately praised her singing. And since, in my judgment, 105
she surpassed her companions, I said: "You are the victor in
all respects, in my judgment; you exceed your companions
in voice and in skill at singing, and not just in voice, but also
in appearance. Therefore, with praise you should be awarded
two crowns, for in victory you are carrying off a double tro- 110
phy."

Then, making two crowns out of different flowers, I
placed the well-earned prize on her head. Indeed, she was
delighted by my love, as yet unvoiced, but the other two
were exceedingly pained by her honor. Then she said, "Oh 115
young man, because of whom I have won such glory, you too
ought to get great rewards. And for you to experience now
the extent of your merit and to confirm our pact of friend-
ship, you may request whatever reward you please from me:
whatever you want I will grant that you win. But, so that you 120
don't think that I am a deceitful girl, and so you know that
my words carry weight, I will swear by the sacred scepter of
Jove what I have said to you." . . .

"You promise the greatest rewards for my merits, 125
maiden," I said, "and for those merits I will ask for great re-
wards. Now I'm asking for you, please, I wish to be united
with you—for truly, you are pleasing to me—if perhaps that
is agreeable to you. I swear that no gift is more precious
than you; if you give yourself to me, you will be giving me a 130

Cum Venus ad Paridem, Pallas Iunoque venirent
    offerretque sibi munera quaeque sua,
cum sibi dona ferunt, elegit de tribus unum,
    scilicet ut pulchra virgo daretur ei,
135 sed si quid sciret pretiosius esse puella,
    non electa sibi pulchra puella foret.
Exemplo docet ergo suo quae dona petamus.
    Huius ad exemplum te, speciosa, peto,
hic qui non timuit Venerem preferre duabus,
140   cuius suscepit in pretium iuvenem.
At tu, quae per me superare duas meruisti,
    da mihi, quaeso, tua virginitate frui.
Sed si non tanto videor tibi munere dignus
    est dare quod salva virginitate potes.
145 Haec igitur, si non mihi vis dare cetera dona,
    res licet exterius acta iuvare potest."
Nec mora, virgo decens teneros faciens mihi risus,
    "Ne dubites," dixit, "noster amicus eris."
"Ne dubites," iterat, dubium me namque videbat,
150   "sola quidem soli iungar amore tibi.
Noster eris nostramque dabo tibi virginitatem,
    nam tibi servatur virginitatis honor.
Et ne spe dubia per tempora longa traharis
    hac in nocte tori munera pacta feres."
155 Dixerat atque monens; comites properantur abire,
    ad castrum celeres dirigit inde gradus.
Iam mare contingit Phoebus cum curribus altum,
    cum subiit thalamos nostra puella suos.
Non bene certus eram, quamvis iuraverat, ut me
160   lege tori vellet consociare sibi;

great prize. When Venus, Pallas, and Juno came to Paris and each offered her own gift to him, and when they were presenting their gifts, he chose one of the three, namely, that a beautiful maiden be given to him; but if he knew of anything 135 more precious than a girl, he would not have chosen a beautiful girl for himself. By his example he teaches us the sort of gifts we should ask for. Following his example, my beauty, I ask for you—he was not afraid to prefer Venus to the other two, and as his reward from her he received a young woman. 140 And you, who thanks to me won victory over the other two, allow me, please, to enjoy your virginity. But if I do not seem to you worthy of such a prize, there is something you can give with your virginity intact. Therefore if you do not wish 145 to give me the rest of your gifts, something you do on the outside can also give pleasure."

Without delay the lovely maiden, laughing gently, said to me, "Do not doubt that you will be my boyfriend." "Do not doubt," she repeated, for she saw that I was doubtful, "Be 150 sure, I alone will be joined to you alone in love. You will be mine, and I will give my virginity to you, for the honor of my virginity is reserved for you. And so that you are not strung along for a long time in dubious hope, on this night you will obtain the promised rewards of my bed."

She spoke these encouraging words; her companions has- 155 tened to depart, at which point she directed her swift steps toward a castle. Phoebus had already reached the high sea with his chariot when my girl entered her bedroom. I was not entirely sure, in spite of her promise, that she wished to 160 unite with me in the rite of the bed; but, wishing to test

sed temptare volens—neque iam temptare nocebat—
   temptavi tandem calliditate mea.
Nam sibi mentitus me velle domum remeare,
   dixi: "Virgo, mane, me decet ire, vale."
165 Protinus illa mihi gratissima basia praebens
    "Hic tibi nobiscum cena paretur," ait,
   "hic tibi sint nostri communia gaudia lecti,
    hic nos una Venus iungat et unus Amor.
Nox tenebrosa venit, totum nox occupat orbem,
170   nec nitet in caelo luna serena suo,
ianua nulla patet per quam possis remeare
   nec potes in tenebris solus abire domum.
Saepe solent etiam noctis simulacra nocere
   his qui nocte viam continuare solent.
175 Hinc nox, hinc et amor te conantur retinere:
    impedit ecce tuas utraque causa vias.
Tertia sum, quae te conor precibus retinere;
   tu modo non vanas fac, precor, esse preces.
Miror si tria, nox et amor et pulchra puella,
180   non poterunt unum te retinere virum.
Care, precor, remane: motus sensurus amoris
   atque faces, si non ferrea corda geris."
Annui tum nostrae precibus votisque puellae
   quodque sibi placuit, non mihi displicuit.
185 Iam bene cognovi quod me non despiciebat,
   nam si despiceret, non ita me peteret.
Cena parabatur, fumabant undique carnes,
   undique mensa suos ponitur ante toros.
   . . .
190   Et complent operam femina virque suam.

her—since it did no harm to test—then I tested her with my cunning. For, pretending to her that I wished to return home, I said, "Stay, my girl, it is proper for me to go—farewell."

At once offering me the sweetest kisses, she said: "You should stay and have dinner with me; you should share in the mutual joys of my bed; may only Venus and Cupid join us here. Dark night is coming, night is taking possession of the entire world, and the moon is not shining bright in the sky; no door is open through which you can go back, nor can you go home alone in the darkness. Often, too, phantoms of the night are in the habit of harming those who seek to go on a journey in the night. Therefore, both night and love are trying to keep you here: look, each reason hinders your departure. I am the third; I am trying to stop you with prayers; do not render my prayers vain, I beg you. I am amazed if the three—night, love, and a beautiful girl—aren't able to keep you here, who are just one man. My dear, I beseech you: stay—you will soon feel the fiery stirrings of love, if you do not have a heart of iron."

I then assented to the prayers and entreaties of my girl, and what pleased her was not displeasing to me. Now I knew for sure that she felt no scorn for me, for if she did feel scorn, she would not have entreated me in this way. Dinner was prepared, the smell of meat was everywhere, and a table was set from all directions in front of the bed.

. . . and the man and the woman complete their task. One

165

170

175

180

185

190

Hic dat aquam, fert hic epulas, hic pocula ponit,
    nititur officio quisque placere suo.
Sedimus ad cenam—fuerat quoque cena parata—
    at non cena mihi profuit ulla nimis;
195 nam quotiens oculos dominae vultusque videbam,
    igne calescebant corpora nostra gravi.
Hach! quotiens gemitus, quotiens suspiria traxi,
    cum risus vidi, quos dedit illa mihi.
Gaudia sunt risus, sed si volo vera fateri,
200   ille mihi risus causa doloris erat.
Tum doleo, tum non valeo corpus recreare
    deliciis quarum pars mea magna fuit

. . .

    Dixit, at in primis oscula pauca dedit:
205 "Care meus, comede quas nunc tibi porrigo coxas,
    ut tribuam coxas hac tibi nocte meas.
Grande tibi pretium do, nam mea crura ferendo
    praemia magna feres, si tamen illa feres."
Has ego suscepi, cum carnibus ossa comedi,
210   nam non ulla mihi dulcior esca fuit;
quod si forte cibos tribuisset deteriores,
    prodessent tali condicione mihi.
Hoc ubi laudavit dedit aurea pocula, sumpsi
    quaque prius biberat, hac ego parte bibi.
215 Sic cibus ac potus potuerunt me satiare,
    qui poterant minime me satiare prius.
Finierat cena; post cenam mensa levatur,
    virgo iubet lectum quemque parare suum;
at famuli Bacchum velut ebria turba canentes
220   nec sibi nec nobis composuere thoros,

gives water, another carries the dishes, a third places the cups; each strives to please in his own capacity. We sit down to dinner—the dinner had been prepared—but no dinner was much good to me; for whenever I saw the eyes and the 195 face of my mistress, my body grew hot with a fierce fire. Alas! How often I sighed, how often I drew a deep breath, when I saw her laughing at me. Her laughter was joyful, but if I am to speak the truth, her laughter caused me grief. I 200 grieve, and I do not have the strength to refresh my body with the delicacies, the greater part of which were served to me . . .

She spoke, but first gave me a few kisses: "My dear, eat 205 the hipbones that I'm offering you now, just as tonight I will give you my hipbones. I am giving you an excellent prize, for by lifting up my legs you'll be taking a great prize, if you do indeed take them." I took them up and chewed on the bones and the meat, for no dish was sweeter to me; even if she had 210 offered poorer foods, even in that case they would have done me good. She praised my action, then gave me golden drinking cups; I took them up and drank from the same side where she had drunk earlier. Thus was I satisfied with the 215 food and drink that previously had satisfied me little.

Dinner was over; after dinner, the table was cleared, and the maiden ordered someone to prepare her bed; but the servants, like a drunken mob, were singing of Bacchus and 220 had not prepared beds for themselves or for us, but stagger

sed vino somnoque graves ibant titubando,
    nec norat solium femina virque suum.
Accubat hic somno, faeno iacet alter in alto
    graminibus strato sternitur ille solo.
225 Ipse torum dominae petii domina comitante,
    ipsa petit solium me comitante suum.
Ferre duos iuvenes torus illic ille valebat;
    quem scio non tantum, nos tulit ille duos.
Hunc manus artificis mira sculpaverat arte,
230   namque deos illic pinxerat atque deas.
Jupiter hic stabat ridens fallensque puellas:
    has cycni specie decipit, has aquilae.
Hunc in tam variis habuit pictura figuris,
    ut vix ullus eum crederet esse deum.
235 Ex alia parte picti fuerant nimis arte
    in lecto nudi Marsque Venusque simul.
Illic Vulcanum tendentem retia vidi,
    ut simul in lecto prendere posset eos.
Mox quoque pertimui ne nos comprendere vellet,
240   tam bene picturae finxerat auctor eum.
Cumque satis risi, risit quoque nostra puella,
    sed magis hic risus conveniebat ei.
Quid moror? Incumbo tandem lecto pretioso
    atque tegunt artus pallia picta meos.
245 Denique virgo iubet thalamis exire puellas
    firmavitque seris ostia clausa suis.
Undique fulgebant auratae lampadis ignes,
    tamquam cum rutilis Sol foret intus equis.
Se facit haec nudam, voluit quoque nuda videri,
250   at non in tenera carne fuit macula.

along, heavy with wine and sleep, and man and woman alike didn't recognize their own chamber. One reclined in sleep, another lay in the deep hay, the third was stretched out on the floor strewn with grasses. I myself headed for the bed of the mistress, accompanied by the mistress; she headed for her own chamber, accompanied by me. 225

That bed there was strong enough to bear two youths; I did not know that it was of such size but it bore the two of us. The hand of an artisan of wondrous skill had crafted it, for on it he had depicted the gods and goddesses. Here stood Jupiter laughing and deceiving girls: some he ensnared in the guise of a swan, others in the guise of an eagle. The painting captured him in such different shapes that hardly anyone would believe that he was a god. In another part Mars and Venus were painted with great skill, naked together in bed. There I saw Vulcan stretching out his nets in order to catch them in bed together. In that moment I was even afraid that he wanted to ensnare us, so well had the creator of the painting depicted him. 230 235 240

And when I had laughed a good bit, my girl also laughed, but this laughter better suited her. Why do I delay? At last I lay down on the luxurious bed and embroidered sheets covered my limbs. Finally the maiden ordered the girls to leave the bedchamber and secured the closed doors with their bolts. On all sides the flames from a gilt lamp were glowing, as if the Sun were inside with his radiant team. She stripped naked, and also wanted to be seen naked, and there was not a flaw on her soft skin. Believe me now, lovers, if 245 250

Nunc mihi credatis, si credere vultis, amantes:
    membra fuere sibi candidiora nive,
nec nive quae tacta Phoebo fuerat liquefacta,
    sed nive quam nullus sol tepefecit adhuc.
255 Ah! Quales umeros et qualia brachia vidi;
    candida crura nimis non valuere minus.
Parva papilla fuit, fuit apta, fuit speciosa,
    si paulo rigida, non minus apta fuit.
Pectus erat planum, planus sub pectore venter,
260   formabat medium corpus utrumque latus.
Non referam, quamvis poteram meliora referre,
    illam cum vidi, sed tibi non referam.
Vix me continui, cum corpora nuda viderem,
    quin raperem cupida lactea membra manu.
265 Quid faciam? Nequeo spectare diutius illam
    nec tamen aspicere candida membra nimis.
Quanto magis specto, tanto magis igne calesco;
    res eadem nobis et nocet atque iuvat.
Utque mihi satis est caro candida visa diuque—
270   et merito fuerat aspicienda diu—
ingreditur tandem lectum properando manuque
    pallia picta levans corpora nostra tegit.
Protinus, adductis ad candida colla lacertis,
    incepi dominae basia pressa dare;
275 oscula mille dedi, totidem mihi reddidit illa,
    sunt data mille sibi, reddita mille mihi.
Illa suum nostro lateri latus associavit;
    gaudebam lateri conseruisse latus.
Ventre suo ventrem nostrum tunc illa premebat
280   quaerebatque modis mille placere mihi.

you want to believe: her body was whiter than snow, and not
snow that Phoebus's rays have melted, but snow that no sun
had yet softened. Oh, such upper arms and forearms did I   255
see! And her fine white legs were no less beautiful. Her nip-
ples were small, well proportioned, and lovely—if a little
firm, no less pleasing. Her chest was flat, the belly under her
chest was also flat, and her two flanks shaped her figure in   260
between. I will not tell—even though I could tell of even
better things when I saw her—but I will not tell you.

   I could scarcely stop myself, when I saw her naked body,
from desirously grabbing her milky-white body with my
hand. What could I do? I couldn't look at her any longer, yet   265
I couldn't look away from such a white body either. The
more I looked, the more I grew warm with fire; the same
thing both harmed me and pleased me. And when I had had
enough of the sight of her white flesh for a long time—and   270
she certainly deserved my long gaze—finally she jumped
into bed, and with her hand lifted the embroidered sheets
and covered our bodies.

   Immediately, embracing her white neck with my arms, I
began to give urgent kisses to my mistress; I gave a thousand   275
kisses, and she gave back as many to me, a thousand were
given to her, and she returned a thousand to me. She joined
her side to mine; I was glad to have my body entwined with
hers. Then she pressed her stomach to my stomach and   280
sought to please me in a thousand ways.

"Tu mihi velle tuum comple velociter," inquit,
    "nam nox atra fugit et redit ipsa dies."
Inde rogat dextram, dextram porreximus illi;
    sed mihi dans mammas: "Quid modo sentis?," ait.
285 Quas dum tenui, dicens ego taliter illi:
    "Sentio" respondi "munera grata mihi.
Munera iam teneo quae saepe tenere cupivi,
    et nimis optavi munera quae teneo."
Inde manus retrahens, palpabam crura tenella,
290   illa fuere mihi dulcia melle magis.
Mox dixi: "Non est ullum preciosius aurum.
    Non est in mundo res mihi commodior.
Dilexi vero nobis data crura columbae,
    sed quae nunc teneo diligo crura magis.
295 Ergo iungamus duo corpora, iuncta premamus,
    et peragant partes corpora nostra suas."
Quid faciam? Referam quae fecimus? Hic pudor obstat,
    ipsaque ne referam nostra puella vetat.
Finis restabat; sed utrum bene cesserat an non?
300   Omnia novit Amor, novit et ipsa Venus.

Consolatio ad Liviam

Visa diu felix, "mater" modo dicta "Neronum,"
    iam tibi dimidium nominis huius abest,
iam legis in Drusum miserabile, Livia, carmen,
    unum qui dicat iam tibi "mater" habes,
5 nec tua te pietas distendit amore duorum
    nec posito fili nomine dicis "uter?".

"Make haste to satisfy your desire with me," she said, "for dark night flees and the day itself is returning." Then she asked for my right hand, and I offered it to her, but she presented her breasts to me, saying, "What are you feeling now?" As I held them, speaking to her in this way: "I feel," I 285
replied, "that I have a pleasing gift. I am holding the gift that I often wished to hold, and have greatly desired the gifts that I now hold."

Then I drew back my hand and caressed her delicate legs—they were much sweeter to me than honey. Next I 290
said: "There is no gold more precious. There is nothing in the world more pleasing to me. It is true I enjoyed the pigeon's legs served to me, but I enjoy the legs I hold now even more. So let us join our two bodies, let us press them to- 295
gether, and let our bodies play their parts."

What shall I do? Shall I tell you what we did? Here modesty stands in the way, and my girl forbids me to tell. The end still remains to tell; but did it turn out well or not? Cupid knows all, and Venus herself knows, too. 300

A Poem of Consolation for Livia

For a long time you seemed lucky, and just recently you were called "mother of the Neros," but now half of that name has left you. Now you read a sad elegy on Drusus, and now you have only one who can call you "mother." Now your mater- 5
nal heart no longer swells with the love of two, nor at the mention of the name of your son do you say, "Which one?"

Et quisquam leges audet tibi dicere flendi?
   Et quisquam lacrimas temperat ore tuas?
Ei mihi, quam facile est (quamvis hoc contigit omnes)
10   alterius luctu fortia verba loqui!
Scilicet: "Exiguo percussa es fulminis ictu,
   fortior ut possis cladibus esse tuis."
Occidit exemplum iuvenis venerabile morum:
   maximus ille armis, maximus ille toga.
15 Ille modo eripuit latebrosas hostibus Alpes
   et titulum belli dux duce fratre tulit.
Ille genus Suevos acre indomitosque Sicambros
   contudit inque fugam barbara terga dedit
ignotumque tibi meruit, Romane, triumphum,
20   protulit in terras imperiumque novas.
Solvere vota Iovi fatorum ignara tuorum,
   mater, et armiferae solvere vota deae
Gradivumque patrem donis implere parabas
   et quoscumque coli est iusque piumque deos,
25 maternaque sacros agitabas mente triumphos,
   forsitan et curae iam tibi currus erat.
Funera pro sacris tibi sunt ducenda triumphis
   et tumulus Drusum pro Iovis arce manet.
Fingebas reducem praeceptaque mente fovebas
30   gaudia et ante oculos iam tibi victor erat:
"Iam veniet, iam me gratantem turba videbit,
   iam mihi pro Druso dona ferenda meo.
Obvia progrediar felixque per oppida dicar
   collaque et osque oculos illius ore premam.
35 Talis erit, sic occurret, sic oscula iunget,
   hoc mihi narrabit, sic prior ipsa loquar."

And is there anyone who dares to tell you the rules for mourning? Does anyone restrain the tears that wet your face? Alas, how easy it is (although this has touched everyone) to speak brave words for another's grief, words such as 10 these: "You have been hit by a feeble strike of lightning only to make you stronger from your misfortunes."

A young man is dead, a worthy moral example: he was the greatest in arms, and the greatest in the toga. Just recently 15 he cleared out our enemies from their Alpine lairs, and as commander—along with his brother—he won the glory of the war. He subdued the fierce Suevian tribe and the untamed Sicambri, he turned barbarian backs to flight, he earned for you, Roman, an unprecedented triumph, and ex- 20 tended your power over new lands.

Ignorant of your fate, mother, you were preparing to pay your vows to Jupiter, to pay your vows to the armed goddess, and to satisfy father Gradivus with gifts, along with all the other gods it is right and dutiful to honor; and you were 25 thinking too in your mother's mind of the sacred triumphs, and perhaps already you had your mind on the chariot. Now you must hold a funeral procession in place of sacred triumphs, and a mausoleum awaits Drusus instead of the citadel of Jupiter. You were imagining him returned and you were cherishing in your heart the joy you anticipated; al- 30 ready he was before your eyes as a victor:

"Soon he will come, soon the crowd will see me giving thanks, soon I must present gifts on behalf of my Drusus. I will go out to meet him and will be called fortunate in every town and I will kiss him on his neck, mouth, and eyes. Just 35 so will he be, so will he meet me, and so will he kiss me; this he will tell me, just so will I speak first."

Gaudia magna foves: spem pone, miserrima, falsam;
    desine de Druso laeta referre tuo.
Caesaris illud opus, voti pars altera vestri,
40   occidit: indignas, Livia, solve comas.
Quid tibi nunc mores prosunt actumque pudice
    omne aevum et tanto tam placuisse viro?
Quidque pudicitia tantum instituisse bonarum,
    ultima sit laudes inter ut illa tuas?
45 Quid, tenuisse animum contra sua saecula rectum,
    altius et vitiis exeruisse caput,
nec nocuisse ulli et fortunam habuisse nocendi,
    nec quemquam nervos extimuisse tuos,
nec vires errasse tuas campove forove
50   quamque licet citra constituisse domum?
Nempe per hos etiam Fortunae iniuria mores
    regnat, et incerta est hic quoque nixa rota;
hic quoque sentitur: ne quid non improba carpat
    saevit, et iniustum ius sibi ubique facit.
55 Scilicet immunis si luctus una fuisset
    Livia, Fortunae regna minora forent.
Quid si non habitu sic se gessisset in omni,
    ut sua non essent invidiosa bona?
Caesaris adde domum, quae certe, funeris expers,
60   debuit humanis altior esse malis.
Ille vigil, summa sacer ipse locatus in arce,
    res hominum ex tuto cernere dignus erat,
nec fleri ipse suis nec quemquam flere suorum
    nec, quae nos patimur vulgus, et ipse pati.

Great are the joys you are nurturing: poor woman, put
aside false hope; stop reporting good news about your Dru-
sus. That great work of Caesar's, half of those you pray for, is   40
dead: unbind, Livia, your undeserving hair. What good is
your character to you now, your whole life lived with
modesty, and the fact that you so greatly pleased so great a
man? And what good is it to have taught so many women
through your chastity that it ranks highest among your ac-
claims? What good is it to have kept your mind righteous in   45
spite of the times in which you lived, to have lifted your
head high above vice, to have harmed no one (though you
had the opportunity to harm), and to have no one fearing
your political power, to have never allowed your powers to
wander into the field or the forum, and to have managed   50
your household within the permitted bounds?

Undoubtedly, the unfairness of Fortune reigns even over
morals such as these, and here too her capricious wheel ad-
vances; here too her effect is felt: she shamelessly rages so
that nothing escapes her grasp, and everywhere she exer-
cises an unjust rule. Certainly if Livia alone had been ex-   55
empt from grief, the domain of Fortune now would be di-
minished. What if she had not conducted herself so well in
every role that enviable qualities were not her characteris-
tics?

Consider also the household of Caesar, which certainly
should have risen above human misfortunes, with the ex-   60
ception of death. He is our consecrated guardian, set on the
highest eminence. He deserved to watch over human affairs
in safety, and neither to be mourned himself by his family
nor to mourn for any of them, and not himself to suffer what

65 Vidimus erepta maerentem stirpe sororis:
  luctus, ut in Druso, publicus ille fuit;
condidit Agrippam quo te, Marcelle, sepulcro,
  et cepit generos iam locus ille duos;
vix posito Agrippa tumuli bene ianua clausa est:
70 percipit officium funeris, ecce, soror;
ecce, ter ante datis, iactura novissima, Drusus
  a magno lacrimas Caesare quartus habet.
Claudite iam, Parcae, nimium reserata sepulcra,
  claudite: plus iusto iam domus ista patet.
75 Cedis, et incassum tua nomina, Druse, levantur:
  ultima sit fati haec summa querela tui.
Iste potest implere dolor vel saecula tota
  et magni luctus obtinuisse locum.
Multi in te amissi nec tu, tot turba bonorum,
80 omnis cui virtus contigit, unus eras,
nec genetrice tua fecundior ulla parentum,
  tot bona per partus quae dedit una duos.
Heu, par illud ubi est totidem virtutibus aequum
  et concors pietas nec dubitatus amor?
85 Vidimus attonitum fraterna morte Neronem
  pallida promissa flere per ora coma
dissimilemque sui vultu profitente dolorem:
  ei mihi, quam toto luctus in ore fuit!
Tu tamen extremo moriturum tempore fratrem
90 vidisti, lacrimas vidit et ille tuas
affigique suis moriens tua pectora sensit
  et tenuit vultu lumina fixa tuo,
lumina caerulea iam iamque natantia morte,
  lumina fraternas iam subitura manus.

we common folk suffer. We have seen him mourning for the 65
stolen offspring of his sister. The mourning in that case, as
for Drusus, was shared by the public. He buried Agrippa in
your sepulcher, Marcellus, and then that place received his
two sons-in-law. Scarcely had Agrippa been laid to rest and
the doors of the mausoleum firmly closed, when, behold, 70
his sister receives the funeral rites. Behold, tears were shed
three times already and now Drusus, the most recent loss, is
the fourth who draws tears from mighty Caesar.

Fates, now close the sepulcher that has too often been
unlocked—close it: your house is open more often than is
just. You depart, Drusus, and in vain your titles are raised: 75
may this vehement lamentation of your fate be the last one.
Such sorrow can fill whole eras and express deep-felt grief.
Many men were lost in you, but you—a host of so many
good men—were not the only one endowed with every vir- 80
tue nor was any parent more fruitful than your mother, who
alone brought forth so much excellence in two births. Alas,
where is that pair, alike in so many virtues, where that like-
minded piety and love that was never doubted?

We have seen Tiberius dazed by his brother's death, 85
weeping with a pale face and uncut hair, and with a counte-
nance betraying a grief unusual for him: alas, how palpable
was the sorrow on his face! You at least saw your brother in
his final moments before death; he saw your tears, and as he 90
died he felt your chest pressed against his own, and kept his
eyes fixed on your face—his eyes, now almost swimming in
the darkness of death, eyes soon to come under his brother's
hand.

95 At miseranda parens suprema neque oscula pressit
      frigida nec fovit membra tremente sinu;
    non animam apposito fugientem excepit hiatu
      nec sparsit caesas per tua membra comas.
    Raptus es absenti, dum te fera bella morantur,
100   utilior patriae quam tibi, Druse, tuae.
    Liquitur, ut quondam zephyris et solibus ictae
      solvuntur tenerae vere tepente nives.
    Te queritur casusque malos irrisaque Fatis
      accusatque annos, ut diuturna, suos.
105 Talis in umbrosis, mitis nunc denique, silvis
      deflet Threicium Daulias ales Ityn!
    Alcyonum tales ventosa per aequora questus
      ad surdas tenui voce sonantur aquas!
    sic plumosa novis plangentes pectora pennis
110   Oeniden, subitae, concinuistis, aves!
    Sic flevit Clymene, sic et Clymeneides, alte
      cum iuvenis patriis excidit ictus equis!
    Congelat interdum lacrimas duratque tenetque
      suspensasque, oculis fortior, intus agit.
115 Erumpunt iterumque lavant gremiumque sinusque,
      effusae gravidis uberibusque genis.
    In vires abiit flendi mora: plenior unda
      defluit, exigua si qua retenta mora.
    Tandem ubi per lacrimas licuit, sed flebilis, orsa est
120   singultu medios impediente sonos:
    "Nate, brevis fructus, duplicis sors altera partus,
      gloria conspectae, nate, parentis, ubi es?

But the poor mother neither impressed her last kisses   95
nor kept the cold limbs warm against her trembling breast;
she did not catch the escaping life as she pressed her lips
close, nor did she cut her locks and scatter them over your
body. You were carried off in her absence, while harsh wars
were detaining you, more beneficial to your country, Dru-   100
sus, than to yourself. She melts away, as the snow softens and
melts when it is struck by the sun and the west wind in the
warmth of spring. She laments you and your terrible misfor-
tunes and the mockeries of Fate, and she blames her years
for her living too long.

Just so in the shady forests does the Daulian bird, gentle   105
at last, mourn the Thracian Itys! Such are the laments of the
halcyons that sound with reedy voice through the stormy
seas to the heedless waves! Even so, beating your feathery
breasts with new wings, did you (who had suddenly become   110
birds) sing of the son of Oeneus! So did Clymene weep, and
so did her daughters, when the stricken youth fell from his
father's chariot on high!

Sometimes Livia dries up her tears, checks them, and
holds them back; taking control of her eyes, she suppresses
them within. But they burst forth again and flood her lap   115
and bosom, pouring from her heavy and full cheeks. The de-
lay only augments the power of her weeping: the waves of
tears flow fuller, if even a brief postponement has held them
back. Finally, when she was able in the midst of her tears,
she began to speak in this sorrowful way, though her sobbing   120
interrupted her as she spoke:

"My son, too short-lived, half of the fate of my double
progeny, and glory of your distinguished mother, where are

Sed neque iam 'duplicis' nec iam 'sors altera partus:'
    gloria conspectae nunc quoque matris, ubi es?
125 Heu, modo tantus, ubi es? tumulo portaris et igni:
    haec sunt in reditus dona paranda tuos?
Sicine dignus eras oculis occurrere matris?
    Sic ego te reducem digna videre fui?
Caesaris uxori si talia dicere fas est,
130   iam dubito, magnos an rear esse deos.
Nam quid ego admisi? Quae non ego numina cultu,
    quos ego non potui demeruisse deos?
Hic pietatis honos? Artus amplector inanes:
    evocat hos ipsos flamma rogusque suos.
135 Tene ego sustineo positum scelerata videre?
    Tene meae poterunt ungere, nate, manus?
Nunc ego te infelix summum teneoque tuorque
    effingoque manus oraque ad ora fero?
Nunc primum aspiceris consul victorque parenti?
140   Sic mihi, sic miserae nomina tanta refers?
Quos primum vidi fasces, in funere vidi
    et vidi eversos indiciumque mali.
Quis credat? Matri lux haec carissima venit,
    qua natum in summo vidit honore suum?
145 Iamne ego non felix? Iam pars mihi rapta Neronum,
    materni celeber nomine Drusus avi?
Iamne meus non est nec me facit ille parentem?
    Iamne fui Drusi mater et ipse fuit?
Nec cum victorem referetur adesse Neronem,
150   dicere iam potero 'Maior an alter adest?'

you, my son? But no longer 'double' and no longer 'half of
the fate of my progeny': glory of that distinguished lady who
is still your mother, where are you? Alas, where are you, you   125
who were once so great? You are being carried to the tomb
and to flame: are these the gifts to be prepared for your re-
turn? Did you deserve to meet your mother's eyes in this
way? Did I deserve to see you thus returned? If it is proper
for the wife of Caesar to speak such things, now I doubt   130
whether I should think that the gods are great.

"For what have I done wrong? What divine powers, what
gods have I failed to win over with my veneration? Is this
the reward for piety? I embrace lifeless limbs: the flames of
the funeral pyre are claiming them for themselves. Can I   135
bear to see you placed there, accursed as I am? Will my
hands be able to anoint you, my son? Do I now, unfortunate
as I am, hold you and gaze upon you for the last time, gently
stroke your hands, and press my lips to yours? Is now the
first time that you are seen as consul and victor by your
mother? Is it in this way, in this way that you are bringing   140
back such great titles to me, miserable as I am? The fasces
that I have seen for the first time, I saw during your funeral,
and I saw them reversed, signaling misfortune.

"Who would believe it? Has this most precious day come
for your mother, in which she sees her son in the most ex-
alted position? Am I no longer fortunate? Has half of the   145
Neros been taken from me, Drusus, renowned for the name
of his maternal grandfather? Is he no longer mine; does he
no longer make me a parent? Wasn't I just recently the
mother of Drusus, and wasn't he alive? When it is reported
that victorious Nero draws near, I can no longer ask, 'Is it   150
the elder or the other that is here?'

Ultima contigimus: ius matris habemus ab uno,
    unius est munus, quod tamen orba negor.
Me miseram! Extimui frigusque per ossa cucurrit:
    nil ego iam possum certa vocare meum.
155 Hic meus, ecce, fuit: iubet hic de fratre vereri:
    omnia iam metuo: fortior ante fui.
Sospite te saltem moriar, Nero! Tu mea condas
    lumina et excipias hanc animam ore pio.
Atque utinam Drusi manus altera et altera fratris
160   formarent oculos comprimerentque meos.
Quod licet, hoc certe: tumulo ponemur in uno,
    Druse, neque ad veteres conditus ibis avos.
Miscebor cinerique cinis atque ossibus ossa:
    hanc lucem celeri turbine Parca neat."
165 Haec et plura refert. Lacrimae sua verba sequuntur
    oraque nequiquam per modo questa fluunt.
Quin etiam corpus matri vix vixque remissum
    exsequiis caruit, Livia, paene suis.
Quippe ducem arsuris exercitus omnis in armis,
170   inter quae periit, ponere certus erat;
abstulit invitis corpus venerabile frater
    et Drusum patriae, quod licuitve, dedit.
Funera ducuntur Romana per oppida Drusi,
    heu facinus, per quae victor iturus erat,
175 per quae deletis Raetorum venerat armis:
    ei mihi, quam dispar huic fuit illud iter!
Consul init fractis maerentem fascibus urbem?
    Quid faceret victus, sic ubi victor init?

"I have come to the end of the road: I have a mother's status from only one, and it is by the gift of one alone that I cannot be called childless. Woe is me! I am afraid, and a chill runs through my bones: there is nothing now that I can with certainty call my own. Behold, he was mine: he prompts me 155 to fear for his brother; now I fear everything: before I was stronger.

"May I at least die while you live, Tiberius! May you close my eyes, and may your pious lips receive my spirit. Yet if only both the hand of Drusus and the hand of his brother could together tend to closing my eyes. Let this at least be 160 done—it is certainly possible: that we will be placed in the same tomb, Drusus, and that once buried, you will not join your maternal ancestors. I will be intermingled with you, ashes with ashes and bones with bones: may Fate bring about that day with her swift spinning."

She says this and much more. Tears follow her words, and 165 flow in vain over the face that had just been lamenting. But still, O Livia, his body almost—almost—was not returned to his mother and nearly lacked its proper funeral rights. Indeed, the entire army was determined to have their leader cremated in the armor in which he perished, but his brother 170 took the venerable body away from them against their will, and gave Drusus (as far as he could) to the fatherland.

The funeral procession of Drusus proceeds through the Roman towns, through which he would have passed in triumph—a terrible thought—and through which he had come 175 after crushing Raetian arms: alas, how different was this journey to that one! Is a consul entering a mourning city with broken fasces? What should the conquered do, when the conqueror enters in this way? With sorrowful cries

Maesta domus plangore sonat, cui figere laetus
180   parta sua dominus voverat arma manu.
Urbs gemit et vultum miserabilis induit unum:
    gentibus adversis forma sit illa precor.
Incerti clauduntque domos trepidantque per urbem,
    hic illic pavidi clamque palamque dolent.
185 Iura silent mutaeque tacent sine vindice leges,
    aspicitur toto purpura nulla Foro.
Dique latent templis neque iniqua ad funera vultus
    praebent nec poscunt tura ferenda rogo:
obscuros delubra tenent; pudet ora colentum
190   aspicere invidiae, quam meruere, metu.
Atque aliquis de plebe pius pro paupere nato
    sustulerat timidas sidera ad alta manus,
iamque precaturus "Quid ego autem credulus" inquit
    "suscipiam in nullos irrita vota deos?
195 Livia non illos pro Druso tam pia movit:
    nos erimus magno maxima cura Iovi?"
Dixit, et iratus vota insuscepta reliquit
    duravitque animum destituitque preces.
Obvia turba ruit lacrimisque rigantibus ora
200   consulis erepti publica damna refert.
Omnibus idem oculi, par est concordia flendi:
    funeris exsequiis adsumus omnis eques,
omnis adest aetas, maerent iuvenesque senesque,
    Ausoniae matres Ausoniaeque nurus.
205 Auctorisque sui praefertur imagine maesta,
    quae victrix templis debita laurus erat.
Certat onus lecti generosa subire iuventus
    et studet officio sedula colla dare.

resounds the house in which its joyful master had vowed to
fix the arms he had gained with his own hand.   180

The city groans and in its pain adopts one common ex-
pression: I pray for that demeanor for our foes. In disarray,
they close up their houses and hurry in alarm through the
city; in each and every place they are fearful and grieve both
publicly and privately. The courts are silent and the laws, un-   185
enforced, are mute and quiet; no purple can be seen in the
whole of the Forum. The gods hide in their temples and nei-
ther show their faces at the iniquitous funeral rites nor ask
that incense be brought to the pyre: their shrines keep them
hidden; they are ashamed to look on the faces of their wor-
shippers, for fear of the hatred that they have earned.   190

Some pious common man had raised his timid hands to
the high stars on behalf of his poor son, and when just about
to make his prayer, says, "But why should I credulously raise
ineffectual vows to useless gods? Livia, despite her great   195
piety, did not move them on behalf of Drusus: will I be any
very great concern for mighty Jupiter?" He spoke, and in
anger left his vows unmade and hardened his heart and
abandoned his prayers.

The people rush forward, their faces wet with tears, and   200
tell of the public loss at the consul's death. The eyes of ev-
eryone are the same, all weep united as one: we knights are
all present at the funeral rites, every age is there, both young
and old men mourn, Ausonian matrons and Ausonian daugh-
ters. The laurel of victory that was owed to the temples was   205
carried in front with the sad image of its possessor himself.
Noble youths vie to take on themselves the burden of the
bier and strive to offer their necks eager for the duty.

Et voce et lacrimis laudasti, Caesar, alumnum,
210 tristia cum medius rumperet orsa dolor.
Tu letum optasti dis aversantibus omen
 par tibi, si sinerent te tua fata mori.
Sed tibi debetur caelum, te fulmine pollens
 accipiet cupidi regia magna Iovis.
215 Quod petiit, tulit ille, tibi ut sua facta placerent,
 magnaque laudatus praemia mortis habet.
Armataeque rogum celebrant de more cohortes:
 has pedes exsequias reddit equesque duci.
Te clamore vocant iterumque iterumque supremo,
220 at vox adversis collibus icta redit.
Ipse pater flavis Tiberinus adhorruit undis
 sustulit et medio nubilus amne caput.
Tum salice implexum muscoque et harundine crinem
 caeruleum magna legit ab ore manu
225 uberibusque oculis lacrimarum flumina misit:
 vix capit adiectas alveus altus aquas.
Iamque rogi flammas extinguere fluminis ictu
 corpus et intactum tollere certus erat
(sustentabat aquas cursusque inhibebat ad aequor,
230 ut posset toto proluere amne rogum),
sed Mavors, templo vicinus et accola campi,
 tot dixit siccis verba neque ipse genis:
"Quamquam amnes decet ira, tamen, Tiberine, quiescas:
 non tibi, non ullis vincere fata datur.
235 Iste meus periit, periit arma inter et enses
 et dux pro patria: funera causa levet!
Quod potui tribuisse, dedi: victoria parta est;
 auctor abit operis, sed tamen extat opus.

You also, Caesar, praised your foster son with voice and tears, though sorrow intervened to cut off your mournful words. You asked for a similar death for yourself—though the gods rejected the omen—if your fates would only allow you to die. But heaven is your due; the great palace of eager Jupiter, mighty in thunderbolt, will welcome you. He achieved what he sought, that his deeds should please you, and your praise is the great prize of his death. The armed cohorts also pay homage to the pyre, as is the custom: the infantry and the cavalry perform these rites for their leader. They call you with a final shout, then again and a third time, but their voice echoes back from the surrounding hills.

Father Tiber himself shuddered in his tawny waves and, mist-shrouded, from midstream raised his head. Then with his mighty hand he lifted from his face his cerulean hair tangled with willow, moss, and reed, and sent forth streams of tears from his overflowing eyes: the deep channel scarcely holds the added waters. He was already resolved to extinguish the flames on the pyre with the impact of his stream, and to take away the untouched body (he was holding back his waters and curbing their course toward the sea, so that he could flood the pyre with his whole river), but Mars, nearby in his temple and neighbor on the Campus Martius, spoke these words, with cheeks far from dry:

"Though anger is appropriate for rivers, yet, Tiber, keep your peace: neither you nor anyone else is allowed to conquer fate. He died as one of my own, he died amid arms and swords and as a commander, on behalf of his country: let the cause lighten his funeral rites! I have paid the tribute I could: victory has been accomplished; the author of the deed is gone, but the work remains. Once I tried to sway

Quondam ego tentavi Clothoque duasque sorores,
240   pollice quae certo pensa severa trahunt,
ut Remus Iliades et frater conditor urbis
    effugerent aliqua stagna profunda via.
De tribus una mihi 'Partem accipe, quae datur' inquit
    'muneris: ex istis, quod petis, alter erit.
245 Hic tibi, mox Veneri Caesar promissus uterque:
    hos debet solos Martia Roma deos.'
Sic cecinere deae, nec tu, Tiberine, repugna
    irrite nec flammas amne morare tuo
nec iuvenis positi supremos destrue honores.
250   Vade age et immissis labere pronus aquis."
Paret et in longum spatiosas explicat undas
    structaque pendenti pumice tecta subit.
Flamma diu cunctata caput contingere sanctum
    erravit posito lenta sub usque toro.
255 Tandem ubi complexa est silvas alimentaque sumpsit,
    aethera subiectis lambit et astra comis,
qualis in Herculeae colluxit collibus Oetae,
    cum sunt imposito membra cremata deo.
Uritur, heu, decor ille viri generosaque forma
260   et facilis vultus, uritur ille vigor
victricesque manus facundaque principis ora
    pectoraque, ingenii magna capaxque domus.
Spes quoque multorum flammis uruntur in isdem;
    iste rogus miserae viscera matris habet.
265 Facta ducis vivent operosaque gloria rerum:
    haec manet, haec avidos effugit una rogos.

Clotho and her two sisters, who draw out the dreadful   240
thread with unerring thumb, so that Remus from Trojan
stock and his brother, founder of the city, might in some way
escape the pools of the underworld. One of the three said to
me: 'Take the portion of the gift that is given to you: of
these, one will turn out as you seek. Romulus is promised to   245
you, and soon both Caesars will be promised to Venus:
Rome, city of Mars, is due only these as its gods.' So sang the
goddesses. You too, Tiber—do not fight back pointlessly, do
not hold back the flames with your river, and do not spoil
the final honors for the dead youth. Go on and glide back   250
down, giving free rein to your waters." Tiber obeys, unfolds
his ample waves along his length, and enters his house built
of hanging rock.

At last the flame, having long hesitated to touch the
sacred head, snaked its way slowly until it was beneath the
standing bier. Finally when it engulfed the wood and gained   255
nourishment, with its upward-shooting flames it licked the
sky and the stars, just as it glowed on the hills of Oeta, of
Herculean fame, when the limbs of the god who lay there
were cremated.

Alas, all are burned: his manly beauty, his noble form and   260
kindly visage; burned up too his strength, the victorious
hands and the eloquent mouth of a prince, and his breast,
the great and spacious home of his intellect. Also, the hopes
of many burn in those same flames; that pyre holds the fruit
of an unhappy mother's womb.

The achievements of the commander will live, as will the   265
hard-won glory of his deeds: this remains, this alone escapes

Pars erit historiae totoque legetur in aevo
seque opus ingeniis carminibusque dabit.
Stabis et in rostris tituli speciosus honore
270 causaque dicemur nos tibi, Druse, necis.
At tibi ius veniae superest, Germania, nullum:
postmodo tu poenas, barbare, morte dabis.
Aspiciam regum liventia colla catenis
duraque per saevas vincula nexa manus
275 et tandem trepidos vultus inque illa ferocum
invitis lacrimas decidere ora genis.
Spiritus ille minax et Drusi morte superbus
carnifici in maesto carcere dandus erit.
Consistam lentisque oculis laetusque videbo
280 tracta per obscenas corpora nuda vias.
Hunc Aurora diem spectacula tanta ferentem
quam primum croceis roscida portet equis!
Adice Ledaeos, concordia sidera, fratres
templaque Romano conspicienda Foro.
285 Quam parvo numeros implevit principis aevo
in patriam meritis occubuitque senex!
Nec sua conspiciet, miserum me!, munera Drusus
nec sua pro templi nomina fronte leget.
Saepe Nero illacrimans summissa voce loquetur,
290 "Cur adeo fratres, heu, sine fratre deos?"
Certus eras numquam nisi victor, Druse, reverti;
haec te debuerant tempora: victor eras.
Consule nos, duce nos, duce iam victore caremus:
invenit tota maeror in urbe locum.
295 At comitum squalent immissis ora capillis,
infelix, Druso sed pia turba suo.

the greedy pyres. He will be a part of history, read of in every age and will make himself a subject for the poems of talented men. And you will have a statue on the Rostra, decked out with the list of your honors, and we will be called the   270
cause of your death, Drusus.

But for you, Germania, no right of pardon remains: shortly you will be punished, barbarian, with death. I will see the bruised necks of kings in chains, harsh bonds tied on savage hands, faces that are finally fearful, and on the faces   275
of those ferocious men, tears falling on unwilling cheeks. That threatening spirit, exulting in the death of Drusus, must be handed over to the executioner in a gloomy cell. I will pause and with lingering eyes I will happily gaze at the   280
naked bodies dragged through the filthy roads. May dewy Aurora with her golden chariot bring the day that realizes so great a spectacle as soon as possible!

Consider also the Ledaean brothers, stars in close accord, and their temples, conspicuous in the Roman Forum. In   285
how short a lifetime he fulfilled the characteristics of a prince, yet, judged on his services to his country, he died an old man! But, woe is me! Drusus will not look upon his rewards, nor read his own name on the facade of the temple.

Often Tiberius, weeping, will say in a soft voice, "Why,   290
alas, do I approach the brother gods without my brother?" You were determined, Drusus, never to return except as a victor; these times were destined for you: you were victorious. We lost a consul, a general, and a general who is now victorious: in the entire city grief has found its home. But   295
the faces of his comrades are unkempt, their hair disheveled—a wretched band, but loyal to their Drusus. One of

Quorum aliquis tendens in te sua bracchia dixit:
    "Cur sine me, cur sic incomitatus abis?"
Quid referam de te, dignissima coniuge Druso
300   atque eadem Drusi digna parente nurus?
Par bene compositum: iuvenum fortissimus alter,
    altera tam forti mutua cura viro.
Femina tu princeps, tu filia Caesaris illi
    nec minor es magni coniuge visa Iovis.
305 Tu concessus amor, tu solus et ultimus illi,
    tu requies fesso grata laboris eras.
Te moriens per verba novissima questus abesse
    et mota in nomen frigida lingua tuum.
Infelix recipis non quem promiserat ipse
310   nec qui missus erat, nec tuus ille redit
nec tibi deletos poterit narrare Sicambros
    ensibus et Suevos terga dedisse suis
fluminaque et montes et nomina magna locorum
    et si quid miri vidit in orbe novo.
315 Frigidus ille tibi corpusque refertur inane
    quemque premat sine te, sternitur, ecce, torus.
Quo raperis laniata comas similisque furenti?
    Quo ruis? Attonita quid petis ora manu?
Hoc tulit Andromachen, cum vir religatus ad axes
320   terruit admissos sanguinolentus equos.
Hoc tulit Evadnen tunc, cum ferienda coruscis
    fulminibus Capaneus impavida ora dedit.
Quid mortem tibi maesta rogas amplexaque natos
    pignora de Druso sola relicta tenes

them, stretching out his arms to you, said: "Why do you leave without me, why do you leave thus, without companions?"

What shall I say of you, most worthy wife of Drusus and worthy daughter-in-law of Drusus's mother? A pair well suited: the one the bravest young man, the other dear to that brave man, as he was to her. You were first among women and daughter-in-law of Caesar, nor did you seem less than the wife of great Jupiter. You were Drusus's, freely given, his last and his only love, and you were for him a pleasing respite when he was exhausted from toil. As he died, with his last words he bemoaned your absence, and his cold tongue mouthed your name.

Unfortunate woman, you receive neither the man that he had promised would return nor the one who had been sent away. That husband of yours is not returning, and he will not be able to tell you about the decimated Sicambri or the Suevi who turned their backs to his sword, or of the rivers and mountains and the famous names of places, or of any other marvelous things he saw in unknown lands. He is brought back to you cold, a lifeless corpse, and behold, a couch is laid out for him to lie upon without you.

Where are you being borne off, tearing at your hair like a madwoman? Where are you rushing? Why do you frantically strike your face with your hand? Andromache endured this when her husband was bound all bloody to the axle, frightening the horses that had been given free rein. Evadne endured this, when Capaneus offered his fearless visage to be struck by the flashing thunderbolts.

Why in grief do you pray for your own death and, in embracing your children, hold close the only remaining pledges

300

305

310

315

320

325 et modo per somnos agitaris imagine falsa
teque tuo Drusum credis habere sinu
et subito temptasque manu sperasque receptum,
quaeris et in vacui parte priore tori?
Ille pio, si non temere haec creduntur, in arvo
330 inter honoratos excipietur avos—
magnaque maternis maioribus, aequa paternis
gloria—quadriiugis aureus ibit equis
regalique habitu curruque superbus eburno
fronde triumphali tempora vinctus erit.
335 Accipient iuvenem Germanica signa ferentem,
consulis imperio conspicuumque decus
gaudebuntque suae merito cognomine gentis,
quod solum domito victor ab hoste tulit.
Vix credent tantum rerum cepisse tot annos,
340 magna viri latum quaerere facta locum!
Haec ipsum sublime ferent, haec, optima mater,
debuerant luctus attenuare tuos!
Femina digna illis, quos aurea condidit aetas,
principibus natis, principe digna viro,
345 quid deceat Drusi matrem matremque Neronis
aspice, quo surgas, aspice, mane toro!
Non eadem vulgusque decent et lumina rerum:
est quod praecipuum debeat ista domus.
Imposuit te alto Fortuna locumque tueri
350 iussit honoratum: Livia, perfer onus!
Ad te oculos auresque trahis, tua facta notamus
nec vox missa potest principis ore tegi.

of Drusus? And now in your dreams are you troubled by a   325
false vision, and do you believe that you hold Drusus in your
embrace? Do you suddenly reach out with your hand and
hope that he is back again, do you look for him on the empty
couch in his old place?

He—if such beliefs are not foolish—will be received in   330
the fields of the pious among his honored ancestors and—a
great glory to his maternal forebears and equal in glory to
his paternal ones—he will go, shining in gold, in a four-horse
chariot, and in regal dress, on an ivory chariot, he will
proudly have his temples bound with the triumphal garland.
His ancestors will receive the young man who bears the   335
Germanic standards and the remarkable distinction of con-
sular command, and they will rejoice in the well-deserved
surname of their clan, the only spoils he took as victor from
the conquered enemy. They will scarcely believe that he un-
dertook so many activities in so few years and that the man's   340
great deeds require so much space.

These deeds will bear him on high; these deeds, best of
mothers, ought to have lessened your grief! Lady worthy
of the men that the golden age brought forth, worthy of
your princely sons, and worthy of your princely husband,
see what befits the mother of Drusus and the mother of Ti-   345
berius; see from what bed you rise in the morning! The same
behavior does not befit the common people and the leading
lights: your household is obligated to perform something
special. Fortune placed you on high and commanded you to
guard your honored station: Livia, bear this burden to the   350
end!

You draw eyes and ears to you, we take note of your deeds,
and utterances from the mouth of a ruler cannot be con-

Alta mane supraque tuos exsurge dolores
    infragilemque animum, quod potes, usque tene!
355 An melius per te virtutum exempla petemus,
    quam si Romanae principis edis opus?
Fata manent omnes, omnes exspectat avarus
    portitor et turbae vix satis una ratis.
Tendimus huc omnes, metam properamus ad unam,
360   omnia sub leges Mors vocat atra suas.
Ecce, necem intentant caelo terraeque fretoque
    casurumque triplex vaticinantur opus.
I nunc et rebus tanta impendente ruina
    in te solam oculos et tua damna refer!
365 Maximus ille quidem iuvenum spes publica vixit
    et qua natus erat gloria summa domus;
sed mortalis erat nec tu secura fuisti
    fortia progenie bella gerente tua.
Vita data est utenda, data est sine faenore nobis
370   mutua nec certa persolvenda die.
Fortuna arbitriis tempus dispensat iniquis:
    illa rapit iuvenes, sustinet illa senes,
quaque ruit, furibunda ruit totumque per orbem
    fulminat et caecis caeca triumphat equis.
375 Regna deae immitis parce irritare querendo,
    sollicitare animos parce potentis erae.
Quae tamen hoc uno tristis tibi tempore venit,
    saepe eadem rebus favit amica tuis,
nata quod alte es quodque es fetibus aucta duobus
380   quodque etiam magno consociata Iovi,
quod semper domito rediit tibi Caesar ab orbe
    gessit et invicta prospera bella manu,

cealed. Remain exalted, rise above your grief, and keep (as
you can) your spirit ever unbroken! Can we find better ex- 355
amples of virtues in you than when you perform the office of
a Roman empress? The Fates await all; that greedy ferryman
waits for everyone, and his one raft scarcely holds the crowd.
We are all bound for that place, we hurry to one goal—shad- 360
owy Death summons everything under its rule. Behold, men
threaten destruction on heaven, earth and sea, and they
prophesy that the threefold construction will collapse. So
go on then, with such ruin hanging over the world, bring our
eyes back to you alone and to your losses!

He was the greatest of young men and the hope of the 365
people while he lived, and the supreme glory of the house-
hold in which he was born; but he was mortal and you were
not free from fear while your son waged fierce wars. Life is
given to be used; it is lent to us without interest, but the day 370
is not certain when it is to be paid back. Fortune apportions
time in unequal allotments: she snatches away the young,
she keeps alive the elderly, and wherever she hastens, she
hastens in a frenzy, blazing throughout the whole world and
triumphing blindly with a sightless team of horses. Do not 375
trouble the domain of the cruel goddess by complaining, do
not disturb the spirit of that powerful mistress.

Yet she who has come to you this one time with ill dispo-
sition has often been friendly and has favored your affairs,
for you were born in a high position, you were blessed with
two sons, and you married into the line of great Jupiter; Cae- 380
sar always returned to you from conquering the world and
waged prosperous wars with unconquered might; the Neros

quod spes implerunt maternaque vota Nerones,
   quod pulsus totiens hostis utroque duce:
385 Rhenus et Alpinae valles et sanguine nigra
   decolor infecta testis Isarcus aqua,
Danuviusque rapax et Dacius orbe remoto
   Apulus (hinc hosti perbreve Pontus iter)
Armeniusque fugax et tandem Dalmata supplex
390   summaque dispersi per iuga Pannonii
et modo Germanus Romanis cognitus orbis.
   Aspice, quam meritis culpa sit una minor!
Adde, quod est absens functus nec cernere nati
   semineces oculos sustinuere tui.
395 Quique dolor menti lenissimus influit aegrae,
   accipere es luctus aure coacta tuos,
praevertitque metus per longa pericula luctum,
   tu quibus auditis anxia mentis eras.
Non ex praecipiti dolor in tua pectora venit,
400   sed per mollitos ante timore gradus.
Iuppiter ante dedit fati mala signa cruenti,
   flammifera petiit cum sua templa manu
Iunonisque gravis natae impavidaeque Minervae,
   sanctaque et immensi numinis icta domus.
405 Sidera quin etiam caelo fugisse feruntur,
   Lucifer et solitas destituisse vias:
Lucifer in toto nulli comparuit orbe
   et venit stella non praeeunte dies.
Sideris hoc obitus terris instare monebat
410   et mergi Stygia nobile lumen aqua.
At tu, qui superes maestae solacia matri,
   comprecor illi ipsi conspiciare senex

418

fulfilled their mother's hopes and prayers, since under either's command the enemy was so often routed: the Rhine 385
and the Alpine valleys bear witness and the discolored Isarcus whose water is stained with dark blood, the rapacious
Danube and the Apulian in his remote world of Dacia (from
here Pontus is but a short journey for the enemy), the Armenian apt to flee, and the Dalmatian, finally made suppliant,
the Pannonians scattered over mountain peaks, and the 390
German world just recently known to Romans. See how
trivial this single injury is compared to so many blessings!

Consider also that he died far away and that your eyes did
not have to suffer seeing your son's half-dead eyes. In a grief 395
that seeps ever so slowly into your troubled mind, you were
forced to receive sad tidings with your ears; your fear anticipated grief to come amid long perils; when you heard the
news of the perils, your mind was already anxious. Sadness
did not come into your heart abruptly, but gradually and al- 400
layed by fear. Jupiter gave in advance a terrible sign of bloody
fate, when he attacked his own temples with his fire-bearing
hand, as well as those of grave Juno and of his fearless daughter Minerva; even the sacred house of the all-powerful divinity was struck. The stars too are said to have fled from 405
the sky, and Lucifer to have abandoned his accustomed journey: Lucifer was nowhere to be seen in the entire world: day
dawned but no star preceded it. This gave warning that the
death of a star threatened the earth, and that a noble light 410
would be drowned in Stygian waters.

But you, who survive as a consolation to your mother, I
pray that you will be gazed upon by her still in your old age.

perque annos diuturnus eas fratrisque tuosque
    et vivat nato cum sene mater anus.
415 Eventura precor: deus excusare priora
    dum volet, a Druso cetera laeta dabit!
Tu tamen ausa potes tantum indulgere dolori,
    longius ut nolis (heu male fortis!) ali?
Vix etiam fueras paucas vitalis in horas,
420   obtulit invitae cum tibi Caesar opem
admovitque preces et ius immiscuit illis
    aridaque affusa guttura tinxit aqua.
Nec minor est nato servandae cura parentis:
    hic adhibet blandas, nec sine iure, preces.
425 Coniugis et nati meritum pervenit ad omnes,
    coniugis et nati, Livia, sospes ope es.
Supprime iam lacrimas: non est revocabilis istis,
    quem semel umbrifera navita lintre tulit.
Hectora tot fratres, tot deflevere sorores
430   et pater et coniunx Astyanaxque puer
et longaeva parens: tamen ille redemptus ad ignes
    nullaque per Stygias umbra renavit aquas.
Contigit hoc etiam Thetidi: populator Achilles
    Iliaca ambustis ossibus arva premit.
435 Illi caeruleum Panope matertera crinem
    solvit et immensas fletibus auxit aquas,
consortesque deae centum longaevaque magni
    Oceani coniunx Oceanusque pater
et Thetis ante omnes: sed nec Thetis ipsa neque omnes
440   mutarunt avidi tristia iura dei.
Prisca quid huc repeto? Marcellum Octavia flevit
    et flevit populo Caesar utrumque palam.

May you live as long as both your brother's age and your own combined, and may your aged mother live with her elderly son. I pray that these things will come to pass: since god will 415 want to atone for past actions, he will grant that everything else will be joyful after Drusus!

Yet you, Livia, have dared so to indulge your grief that (alas, misplaced courage!) you refuse to eat? You had barely a few hours left to live, when Caesar brought you relief against 420 your will, plied you with entreaties intermixed with reminders of your duties, and moistened your parched throat with drops of water. And his mother's survival was no less a concern for your son: he offered persuasive prayers, as was his duty. The merit of your husband and your son is known by 425 everyone: with the aid of your husband and son, Livia, you continue to live.

Refrain now from tears: he cannot be called back from those realms once the ferryman has carried him in his ghostly skiff. For Hector, all his brothers and his sisters wept, his father too, his wife, his son Astyanax, and his aged 430 mother: yet he was ransomed for the funeral pyre; no ghost swam back across the Stygian waters. A similar thing also befell Thetis: Achilles the destroyer weighs down the fields of Ilium with his charred bones. For him Panope, his mater- 435 nal aunt, loosened her cerulean hair and swelled the boundless waters with her tears, as did a hundred of her fellow goddesses, the aged wife of great Oceanus, father Oceanus, and Thetis above all: but neither Thetis herself nor all of them changed the cruel laws of the greedy god. 440

Why repeat old stories here? Octavia wept for Marcellus, and Caesar wept for both of them openly before the people.

Sed rigidum ius est et inevitabile Mortis,
    stant rata non ulla fila tenenda manu.
445 Ipse tibi emissus nebulosum in litus Averni,
    si liceat, forti verba tot ore sonet:
"Quid numeras annos? Vixi maturior annis:
    acta senem faciunt, haec numeranda tibi,
his aevum fuit implendum, non segnibus annis:
450   hostibus eveniat longa senecta meis.
Hoc atavi monuere tui proavique Nerones
    (fregerunt ambo Punica bella duces!),
hoc domus ista docet, per te mea, Caesaris alti;
    exitus hic, mater, debuit esse meus.
455 Nec meritis quicquam illustrat magis: adfuit illis,
    mater, honos; titulis nomina plena vides—
CONSUL ET IGNOTI VICTOR GERMANICUS
    ORBIS,
    CUI FUIT, HEU, MORTIS PUBLICA CAUSA,
    legor.
Cingor Apollinea victricia tempora lauro
460   et sensi exsequias funeris ipse mei,
decursusque virum notos mihi donaque regum
    cunctaque per titulos oppida lecta suos
et quo me officio portaverit illa iuventus,
    quae fuit ante meum tam generosa torum.
465 Denique laudari sacrato Caesaris ore
    emerui, lacrimas elicuique deo.
Et cuiquam miserandus ero? Iam comprime fletus,
    hoc ego qui flendi sum tibi causa rogo."
Haec sentit Drusus, si quid modo sentit in umbra
470   nec tu de tanto crede minora viro.

But Death's law is unbending and inevitable; the threads are fixed and can't be checked by any hand. He himself, if released onto the misty shore of Avernus, if it were permitted, would proclaim these words with brave mouth: 445

"Why do you count the years? I have lived to a riper age than my actual years: deeds make one old, these are what you should count; it is by these that a full life is lived, not by years spent in idleness: let a long senescence befall my enemies. Your ancestors gave this advice, as well as my 450 Neronian forefathers (both commanders vanquished Punic armies!); the household of exalted Caesar—which is mine through you—teaches this too; such a death, mother, was mine by right. Nor does anything add more luster to my merits; they have received their honor, mother; you see my 455 name replete with titles—I am read aloud as GERMANI-CUS, CONSUL AND CONQUEROR OF UN-KNOWN LANDS, WHOSE DEATH (ALAS!) WAS FOR THE PUBLIC GOOD. My victorious temples are wreathed in Apollo's laurel, and I have experienced the rites 460 of my own funeral: the processions of men, such a familiar sight to me, the gifts of kings, all the cities read on their placards, and the sense of duty with which those young men carried me, who stood so dignified before my pyre. Finally, I 465 have earned praise from the sacred mouth of Caesar, and I have drawn tears from a god. Must I then be an object of pity to anyone? Cease now your weeping, this I ask, I who am the cause of your tears."

This is how Drusus feels, if he feels anything at all in the shadows, nor should you believe any less of so great a man. 470

Est tibi, sitque precor, multorum filius instar
    parsque tui partus sit tibi salva prior;
est coniunx, tutela hominum, quo sospite vestram,
    Livia, funestam dedecet esse domum.

You have (and I pray that you will always have) a son who is an example to many, and may the elder half of your offspring remain safe for you. You have a husband, the guardian of mankind, and while he lives, Livia, it is unbecoming for your household to be mournful.

Abbreviations

Buecheler and Riese = F. Buecheler and A. Riese, eds., *Anthologia Latina, sive poesis Latinae supplementu,* 2 vols. (Leipzig, 1894–1926)

Lampe = G. H. W. Lampe, ed., *A Patristic Greek Lexicon* (Oxford, 1961)

Lewis and Short = C. T. Lewis and C. Short, eds., *A Latin Dictionary* (Oxford, 1958)

MGH = E. Duemmler, ed., *Monumenta Germaniae historica: Poetae Latinorum Medii Aevi,* vol. 1, *Poetae Latini Aevi Carolini* (Berlin, 1881)

Schaller and Könsgen = D. Schaller and E. Könsgen, eds., *Initia carminum Latinorum saeculo undecimo antiquiorum* (Göttingen, 1977)

Walther = H. Walther, *Initia carminum ac versuum Medii Aevi posterioris Latinorum,* Carmina Medii Aevi posterioris Latina 1 (Göttingen, 1959)

Note on the Texts

We have consulted a variety of sources and manuscripts in preparing this edition. Throughout, we have regularized the spelling to conform to the modern standard version of classical Latin orthography, and we have instituted punctuation and capitalization to accord with the English. Except in a few special cases, we have not recorded such changes. Below, poem by poem, we identify the primary editions and manuscripts that have informed this volume.

SUMMARIES OF THE BOOKS OF THE *AENEID*

Shackleton Bailey, *Anthologia Latina* 1.1.

QUATRAINS ON ALL OF VIRGIL'S WORKS

Shackleton Bailey, *Anthologia Latina* 1.1.

VERSES ON FISH AND WILD BEASTS

Richmond, *Halieutica*.

WORDS FOR PAN

This anonymous work of the early Middle Ages (from the fifth to the ninth centuries) is transmitted under Ovid's name in several manuscripts, usually with the title *In rus-*

ticum (Against a Country Bumpkin). Although most of these manuscripts date to the fifteenth century, one may be as early as the ninth century (Paris, Bibliothèque nationale lat. 8094 = P, with the heading "*Ovidius Naso in* Amatoria arte *de Pan pastore dicit*," ("Ovid speaks of the shepherd Pan in the *Ars amatoria*"). It is edited by Kölblinger ("*Versus Panos* und *De rustico*"), along with *De rustico*. We keep Kölblinger's title, but the text presented here reflects the readings found in P.

THE WALNUT TREE

This poem, along with the *Halieutica* (presented in this volume as *Verses on Fish and Wild Beasts*), is—in the view of some (as discussed in the Introduction)—possibly an authentic work by Ovid; if that were the case, the poem would not be a "true" pseudo-Ovidianum. More consider it pseudo-Ovidian, however, than truly Ovidian; hence its inclusion here. Although estimates of its date of composition are extremely varied, ranging from the time of Ovid himself to the High Middle Ages, it was certainly attributed to Ovid by the eleventh century (in Florence, Laurenziana, San Marco 23; and Oxford, Bodleian, Auct. F.2.14). The current standard edition is Lenz, *Nux*.

ON THE FLEA

This poem, along with *On the Wonders of the World,* was attributed to Ovid before the thirteenth century (Munk Olsen, *L'étude des auteurs classiques,* 160–62). It is also one of the most popular pseudo-Ovidian works, found in at least one hundred manuscripts from the late twelfth through fifteenth centuries. The earliest known manuscript is Linz,

Oberösterreichischer Landesbibliothek HS 329, fols. 143v–144r (L). The current standard edition is Lenz, "De pulice libellus."

ON THE CUCKOO

This poem, often ascribed to Alcuin (for example, in *MGH*, pp. 270–72), was attached to Ovid by the thirteenth century and circulates under his name in at least twenty-five manuscripts. Among the earliest pseudo-Ovidian manuscripts are Oxford, Bodleian, Auct. F.4.29 (O), and Frankfurt, Universitätsbibliothek, Barth. 110 (F). Also known as *Conflictus veris et hiemis,* it acquires the title *De cuculo (On the Cuckoo)* by the thirteenth century (as in O and F). The speakers are labeled in many manuscripts, usually as *Ver* and *Hiems* ("Spring" and "Winter," as in O and F), but later also as Daphnis and Palemon (as in Munich, Bayerische Staatsbibliothek, Clm 5594). Our text is based on the *MGH* edition, with modifications that reflect the early pseudo-Ovidian tradition as represented by O and F.

ON THE NIGHTINGALE

Klopsch, "Carmen de philomela."

ON THE WOLF

This poem, sometimes attributed to Marbod of Rennes (ca. 1035–1123), is attributed to Ovid in several manuscripts of the thirteenth century and later; among the earliest are Dijon, Bibliothèque municipale 497, and Gotha, Forschungsbibliothek, memb. II 120. By the fourteenth century, some pseudo-Ovidian manuscripts (for example, Munich, Bayerische Staatsbibliothek, Clm 11601 = M) insert eighty-four lines in the middle of the poem. The earlier/shorter and later/longer versions were published as *De lupo* and *Ovidius de lupo,* respectively, by Voigt, *Kleinere lateinische Denkmäler,* pp. 58 and following. Our text integrates both versions to reflect the version found in M and other fourteenth- and fifteenth-century manuscripts, although the shorter version of the poem also continued to circulate (for example, in Piacenza, Biblioteca Communale Passerini-Landi, Landi 116).

On the Wonders of the World

James, "Ovidius."

On Medicine for the Ears

Lenz, "Das Gedicht *De medicamine aurium.*"

On the Four Humors

Friedrich, "Das pseudo-ovidische Lehrgedicht 'De quatuor humoribus.'"

On the Lombard and the Snail

Bonacina, "De Lombardo et lumaca."

On the Lamb

This poem is known from a single thirteenth- or fourteenth-century manuscript (Vatican City, Biblioteca apostolica, Chisianus H VI 205, fol. 31r = V), where it follows the *Amores* and precedes *De anulo* (= *Amores* 2.15). The explicit attributes it to Ovid. To our knowledge, it has not been edited or published before.

On the Louse

This poem is known from a relatively small group of manuscripts, the earliest of which date to the late twelfth (Tours, Bibliothèque municipale, Turonensis 879) or thirteenth century (Berne Bürgerbibliothek, Bernensis 505 = B). The recent edition of Bretzigheimer, "Das Pseudo-Ovidianum 'De pediculo'" improves upon Lenz ("[P. Ovidii Nasonis] De pediculo libellus").

On the Crafty Messenger

This poem gained attribution to Ovid by the thirteenth century (London, British Library, Add. 49368). The standard edition is Rossetti, "De nuntio sagaci." Of the fourteen manuscripts considered by Rossetti, only three continue past line 293; Modena, Biblioteca Estense, lat. 157—not known to Rossetti—also includes the entire poem.

On the Old Woman

The standard edition is Klopsch, *De vetula*. Occasionally we have preferred the reading in Robathan, *"De vetula,"* but in all such cases we have noted the deviation from Klopsch's text. As we have done throughout the volume, we have changed the punctuation without reporting it, but we wish to note that we more frequently followed the punctuation in Robathan's text.

On the Grove

This poem is known from four pseudo-Ovidian manuscripts: Frankfurt, Universitätsbibliothek, Barth. 110 = F;

Berlin, Staatsbibliothek, Diez. B Sant. 1 = B; Munich, Baye-
rische Staatsbibliothek, Clm 17212 = M; and Vatican City,
Biblioteca apostolica, Vat. lat. 1602 = V. The poem is also
transmitted, without title or attribution, in a thirteenth-
century manuscript of Virgiliana and pseudo-Virgiliana (New
Haven, Beinecke MS 700 = N), where it is preceded by *On
the Rustic* (also without title or attribution). The earliest
manuscript is F, which also contains the longest version of
the poem (104 lines). It is explicitly attributed to Ovid in F
and B, but titled *On the Grove* in three manuscripts: as *De
nemore* in F, and *De luco* in B and V. We have used F as our
base text, corrected with the other manuscripts and with
the preliminary edition of Lenz ("Das pseudo-ovidische
Gedicht *De luco*").

On Wine

This poem—an amalgam of verses from three poems attrib-
uted to Eugene of Toledo—is attributed to Ovid in four
known manuscripts; the oldest of these is Frankfurt, Uni-
versitätsbibliothek, Barth. 110 (F). Lines 1 to 16 correspond
to Eugene's carmen 6 (*Contra ebrietatem*, hexameter); lines 17
to 29 correspond to carmen 2 (*Commonitio mortalitatis huma-
nae*, hexameter); and lines 30 to 39 correspond to carmen 7
(*Contra crapulam*, elegiac couplets); see Farmhouse Alberto,
Eugenii Toletani opera. Our text is based on F—in which the
poem is called *De vino (On Wine)* and *De Bac(c)ho (On Bac-
chus)*—and corrected with the other pseudo-Ovidian manu-
scripts: Leiden, University Library, VLO 20 = L *(De Bac[c]
ho);* Venice, Biblioteca nazionale Marciana, Lat. XII 55 = V

(De vino); and Basel, Universitätsbibliothek, F VIII 1 = B *(De Ba[cc]ho).*

ON THE DREAM

Bertini, "De sompnio."

ON THE STOMACH

This poem, sometimes attributed to John of Salisbury, became attached to Ovid by the fourteenth century (Darmstadt, Universitäts- und Landesbibliothek, 755). The standard edition is Lenz, "Das pseudo-ovidische Gedicht *De ventre.*"

METAMORPHOSIS OF A PRIEST INTO A ROOSTER

The standard edition is Anderson, "A New Pseudo-Ovidian Passage." The hand that added the story to the margin of a manuscript of the *Metamorphoses* introduced it with the following phrase: *Isti versus non habentur communiter sed fuerunt reperti in quodam Ovidio antiquissimo* ("These verses are not generally included but were discovered in a certain very old copy of Ovid"). Another hand specified precisely where this story should go, just after the tale of Baucis and Philemon (*Metamorphoses* 8.679–724), with these words: *Hic deficit metamorphosis flaminis in gallum. Et versus illi qui sunt in alio latere debentur hic esse.* ("Here is where the *Metamorphosis of a Priest into a Rooster* is missing. And those verses which are on the other side ought to be here.") We have taken the title for this poem from the latter note. For these quotations, see Anderson, "A New Pseudo-Ovidian Passage," 7–8.

On the Distribution of Women

This poem is known from a single manuscript of the late fourteenth century, Vatican City, Biblioteca apostolica, Vat. lat. 1602, where it follows *Amores* 1.10 (fol. 49r) and precedes *On the Crafty Messenger* (fol. 49v). Therefore, although it has no title, incipit, or explicit, we deem it Ovidian "by association," like *Against Women*. The most recent edition is Hinz, "Kann denn Liebe Sünde sein?"

Against Women

This poem is known from a single manuscript of the late fourteenth century, Vatican City, Biblioteca apostolica, Vat. lat. 1602 (V), where it follows *On the Crafty Messenger* (fol. 55r) and precedes *Ibis* (fol. 56r). We deem it therefore Ovidian "by association" (like *On the Distribution of Women,* which appears earlier in the manuscript), although it has no title, incipit or explicit, or marginal notes. F. W. Lenz published a preliminary edition of the poem ("Der fraufeindliche Ovid").

On the Game of Chess

This poem—also collected in the well-known *Carmina Burana* (Munich, Bayerische Staatsbibliothek, Clm 4660)—circulated widely under Ovid's name by the early fifteenth century; among the earliest pseudo-Ovidian manuscripts is Berlin, Staatsbibliothek, Diez. B Sant. 3 (B). Our text is based on Schumann and Bischoff's *Carmina Burana* edition, modified to reflect the pseudo-Ovidian tradition represented by B.

The Rule of the Table

Klein, "Anonymi 'Doctrina mense.'"

On Money

Variants of this poem—like *On the Game of Chess,* also collected in the *Carmina Burana* (no. 11 in Hilka and Schumann, *Carmina Burana,* vol. 1, pt. 1)—are attributed to Ovid in four known manuscripts of the fifteenth century. The two main pseudo-Ovidian strands identified by Hilka and Schumann are based on Vienna, Österreichische Nationalbibliothek 3123 = V *(eta),* and Schlägl, Stiftsbibliothek 106 Cpl. 58 = S *(gamma).* The *eta* and *gamma* strands differ mainly in their ordering of verses. Our text follows the *gamma* tradition and is based on the longest version (fifty-two lines) known from a manuscript that attributes the poem to Ovid, Piacenza, Biblioteca Communale Passerini-Landi, Landi 116 (P).

On Love and On the Remedy for Love

These two long excerpts from the twelfth-century *Facetus* of "Aurigena" circulated in various configurations (that is, separately or together, and completely or in fragments) under the name of Ovid by the fifteenth century. The standard edition is that of Thiel ("Mittellateinische Nachdichtungen"), who did not link the poems to the *Facetus.* Thiel's 'Pseudo-*Ars amatoria*' *(On Love)* corresponds to lines 131 to 320 of the *Facetus,* while his 'Pseudo-*Remedia amoris*' *(On the Remedy for Love)* corresponds to lines 321 to 349 and 354 to 384. Rather than follow the conventional twentieth-century titles for these poems, we have taken our titles from one of Thiel's fifteenth-century manuscripts (Magdeburg, Domgymnasium, Cod. 280 Bf 33). See Thiel, "Mittellateinische Nachdichtungen," 157–59. Thiel reports that some manuscripts refer to the poem(s) as "Ovid's [work] without a title" *(Ovidii de sine titulo),* which is of interest because Ovid's *Loves (Amores)*—

three books of love elegies—were often referred to as "without a title" (*de sine titulo*).

ANOTHER POEM ON THE NIGHTINGALE

This poem is usually attributed to Eugene of Toledo, most recently in Farmhouse Alberto, *Eugenii Toletani opera,* where it is presented as four poems (carmina 30–33). It is presented as a single text and attributed to Ovid in three fifteenth-century manuscripts: Piacenza, Biblioteca Communale Passerini-Landi, Landi 116 = P; Paris, Bibliothèque nationale, lat. 8429A = P_1; and Paris, Bibliothèque nationale, lat. 3343 = P_2. It has never before been edited as a pseudo-Ovidian work.

ON A CERTAIN OLD WOMAN

Klopsch, "Das pseudo-Ovidianum *De quadam vetula.*"

ON THE RUSTIC

A compilation of the *Words for Pan* (see above) with four verses of an anonymous late antique poem (Buecheler and Riese 26; *De rustico* in Kölblinger) came into circulation in the late eighth century or early ninth century, variously attributed to Martial, Cato, and Avienus. In four fifteenth-century manuscripts, the two poems were attributed to Horace (Leiden, University Library, BPL 11E; Vienna, Österreichische Nationalbibliothek 3123) or to Ovid (Munich, Bayerische Staatsbibliothek, Clm 5594 = M; Berlin, Staatsbibliothek, Lat. fol. 49 = B, with the title *De rustico*). In two other fifteenth-century manuscripts (Prague, Národní Knihovna České Republiky, XXIII F 106; Munich, Bayerische

Staatsbibliothek, Clm 454), the first part *(Words for Pan)* was attributed to Ovid (as *In rusticum*), while the second part *(On the Rustic)* was attributed to Horace. Our text is based on Kölblinger, edited to reflect the pseudo-Ovidian tradition represented by B, and M. Kölblinger does not cite the thirteenth-century manuscript (New Haven, Beinecke MS 700) in which the first seven lines of *On the Rustic* precede *On the Grove* (both without title or attribution).

ON THE THREE GIRLS

Pittaluga, "De tribus puellis."

A POEM OF CONSOLATION FOR LIVIA

Schoonhoven, *The Pseudo-Ovidian "Ad Liviam de morte Drusi."*

Notes to the Texts

Georgics   Bailey brackets the introductory quatrain, preferring to exclude it since
              it only appears in one of his manuscripts.

Aeneid 5.3 Acestae *codices*: Aceste<s> *Bailey*

VERSES ON FISH AND WILD BEASTS

1	*Richmond proposes a lacuna before the first line.*
44	auxiliique *Haupt*: auxilioque *Richmond. Richmond proposes a lacuna between* sui *and* morsu. *Alternate readings, where identified with a different editor, are quoted from Richmond's apparatus.*
46	in *Vollmer*: his *Richmond*
52	*Richmond brackets this line and maintains that it more properly belongs after line 65.*
56	*Richmond proposes a lacuna between lines 56 and 57.*
57	prodidit: †prodedit† *Richmond*
59	*Richmond proposes a lacuna between lines 59 and 60.*
73	conpescitque *K. Schenkl*: conspissatque *Richmond*
81	*Richmond proposes a lacuna between lines 81 and 82. He also supplies* omnis *as a line ending for a proposed line 81a.*
82	*Richmond proposes a lacuna between lines 82 and 83.*
85	*Richmond proposes a lacuna between lines 85 and 86.*
90	*Richmond proposes a lacuna between lines 90 and 91. He also supplies* nam *in a proposed line 90a.*
101	*Richmond proposes a lacuna between lines 101 and 102.*
122	*Richmond proposes a lacuna between lines 122 and 123.*
127–30	*The manuscript has blank space here; Richmond argues that it is "futile to endeavor to reconstruct the gap here" as others have done.*

WORDS FOR PAN

2   hirpigena *Kölblinger*: hyrpegena *P. From* hircigena *(Kölblinger: a hapax legomenon).*

8   hirce *spelled as* hirte *in Kölblinger—N.B. this line is hypermetric.*

THE WALNUT TREE

39   inducta: illustra *Lenz. But Lenz is uncertain of this reading, and, indeed, the adjective* illustris *does not exist elsewhere in classical Latin as a first/second declension adjective; the majority of manuscripts have* inducta.

47   nostris: nostri *Lenz*

179–80   *This couplet is bracketed by Lenz as an interpolation that appears erroneously in most manuscripts.*

ON THE FLEA

5   nigro: <.> *Lenz. Most manuscripts (including* L*) insert* nigro *here.*

20   *Lenz sets a crux between* fierem *and* ad. *The line scans if one permits the author to allow intervocalic* m *to make position at the caesura.*

ON THE CUCKOO

3   arborea pariter laetas *O MGH*: arboreas pariter laeta *F*

4   Daphnis *corrected from* Dafnis *O MGH*: Daphus *F*

6   succinctum *F*: succinctus *O MGH*

9   prius *F*: prior *O MGH*

12   silvis *F*: tectis *O MGH*

       ritu *F*: rutilo *O MGH*

13   serena *F*: severa *O MGH*

15   suevit *F*: suescit *O MGH*

17   Phoebo *O MGH*: Phoebus *F*

18   cuculum *corrected from* cuculus *F*

       cantantem voce *F*: crescentem luce *O MGH*

20–21   *these lines are reversed in O and MGH*

21   continuat . . . amicam *F*: congeminat . . . amatam *O MGH*

22   segnis *F*: tarda *O MGH*

cuculo *O MGH*: cuculi *F*

23 Corpore quae gravido *F*: Qui torpore gravi *O MGH*
dormit *F*: tectus *O MGH*

24 stulti pocula *O MGH*: stultam poculam *F*

28 Ore *O MGH*: Quique *F*

29 aedificatque domus placidas et navigat undas *O MGH*: aedificet-
que domos placidas ac incolat undas *F*

32 placeat gazas optatas semper habere *F*: placet optatas gazas nu-
merare per arcas *O MGH*

34 tarda Hiems *O MGH*: cum tarda *F*

35 gazas vel congregat ullas *O MGH*: et gazas congregat ullas *F*

36 aut *F*: vel *O MGH*
primo *F*: ante *O MGH*
laborant *O MGH*: laborent *F*

37 multi *F O*: illi *MGH*
tibi *F O*: mihi *MGH*

41 prece ulla pascere cantu *F*: per te tu pascere tantum *O MGH*

42 cuculus tibi quae venient alimonia praebet *F*: tibi qui veniet cu-
culus alimonia praestet *O MGH*

43 e *omitted in F*

44 *This line is in O and MGH but not in F.*

45 plura *O MGH*: plura modo *F*

46 veniat *O MGH*: veniet *F*

48 sint *O MGH*: sunt *F*

50 veniantque *O MGH*: venient *F*

51 Phoebum varia *F*: varia Phoebum *O MGH*

53 carissimus *F*: gratissimus *O MGH*

55 dulce decus cucule salve *F*: salve dulce decus cuculus *O MGH*

On the Wolf

65 *The added text of Voigt's version b. ("Ovidius de lupo") begins here.*

105 indicta: *this does not scan.*

123 capras *corrected from Voigt's* carpas

148 *The added text of Voigt's version b. ("Ovidius de lupo") ends after this
line.*

192   *Some pseudo-Ovidian manuscripts include additional closing lines, e.g.,* Nemo mellitis sit verbis credere mitis, / Nam si crediderit, decipiendus erit. *M*

On the Wonders of the World

40   Astomos: *James prints no label for this description.*
104   Puerpera plebeia: *James prints no label for this description.*
106   Leo: *James prints no label for this description.*
122   Lilybaeano: Lilibitano *James. In regularizing the spelling, this line has become unmetrical.*

On the Lamb

2   agnos: argnos *V*
3   Primus: primum *V*
        ballat: balat *V*
6   quarti: quartus *V*
9   Septimus: Septimum *V*
12   decimi: decemi *V*

On the Louse

4   cito cepit *is the reading of B, corrected from* modo cepit *in Lenz. Bretzigheimer (p. 348, n. 6) makes the case for* modo sensit.
8   secuta *Bretzigheimer*: secura *Lenz*

On the Crafty Messenger

99   afore: affore *Rossetti*
166   perirem *Rossetti*: periret *in the manuscripts*
359   tibi sensum: tibi censum *Rossetti*

On the Old Woman

Book 1

68   tactu: tacto *Klopsch*
264   sabulone: stabilone *Klopsch*
435   omnino *Robathan*: omnio *Klopsch*

Book 2

Book 3

ON THE GROVE

12   et *B M V Lenz*: ut *F*
19   Descendunt *B M V Lenz*: Discedunt *F*
24   in cervices muliebres *B M V Lenz*: et cervix est muliebris *F*
27   mazere *Lenz*: machere *F*
28   natus *N Lenz*: nactus *F*
31   capreos *B M V Lenz*: campos *F*
32–33 *Lenz reverses the order of these lines.*
34   cornaque non *B M V Lenz*: cornaque nunc *F*
       cerea *M*: cetera *or* ceresa *(barely legible in F)*
44   exsiccare *M Lenz*: exiccare *F*; exsicare *V*; excutare *B*
49–50 *Lenz places this rhyming couplet after line 48. In the manuscripts these
       are lines 50–51.*
78   *This line is in B and V but not in F.*
82   nisi *M V Lenz*: non *F*
83–86 *These lines are only found in F.*
84   terram *was initially omitted in F, but was added at the end of the line
       (in the right margin), with a linking symbol to show that it was to be
       inserted here.*
86   his *F*: hos *Lenz*
87   Sed naturales illius opes referemus *Lenz*: Sed nos non tales illis et
       opes referamus *F. There is great variation in this line in the manu-
       scripts.*
91–92 *These lines are only found in F.*
94   quantulacumque *B M V Lenz*: quantula cuncta *F*

443

95–100	*These lines are only found in F.*
95	et opes *supplied by Lenz; occurs in line 87 in F*
	dominantur *corrected from* dominatur *F*
96	amplificantur *Lenz: The last word of the line is illegible in F.*
102	pelles *B M Lenz*: pellex *F*
104	item: bene *Lenz*

On Wine

14	tu non mollia nec dura *V (scanning "dura" with a short "u")*: non molle ferum neque *F*
23	effuge *V M*: dilige *F*
34	*This line does not scan as a hexameter.*
39	*A closing couplet follows the explicit in two manuscripts:*
	Si bene dicta leges longevuo tempore deges / Nam tu vinoso potes obniti furioso. *F*
	Et benedicta lege longens tempore vives / Non tuo vinoso corpore sanus eris. *B*

On the Stomach

85–86	*Cf. lines 9–10. This couplet is in approximately half of the manuscripts consulted by Lenz.*
141–42	*140a–b in Lenz. These lines are omitted from four manuscripts consulted by Lenz, and transposed in another manuscript.*

On the Distribution of Women

14	alta sub *Lehmann*: sub alta *Hinz following the MS reading*
27	refragantes et ei *Lenz*: reverentes et hii *Hinz following the manuscript reading*
	voventes *Lenz*: ferentes *Hinz following the manuscript reading*
37	non *added by Hinz*
39	puellis *added by Hinz*

Against Women

4	comedit *V*: gustavit *Lenz*
9	*Lenz inserts line 14* (Fraude tument . . .) *after line 9*

444

10   sanctis *corrected from* santi⁵ *V*

          sanctis virisque *V*: sanctisque viris *Lenz*

11   Ut coluber callidus *V*: Callidus ut coluber *Lenz*

13   cuique *V*: cuiquam *Lenz*

16   amat *V*: at *Lenz*

17   ecce *V*: enim *Lenz*

          virum *V*: vere *Lenz*

19   *Lenz adds an ellipsis at the end of the line.*

21   quae (que) *Lenz*: qui *V*

25   sanguinari *V*: saginari *Lenz*

27   possint *Lenz*: possit *V*

On the Game of Chess

9   alfinus *many variants found in the manuscripts, including* alficus *and* alphicus

34   nil valet *B and other pseudo-Ovidian manuscripts*: rex manet *Carmina Burana*

On Money

51   virtus *P*: Nummi *S V*

On the Remedy for Love

47   ut: et *Thiel*

51   Vadat *corrected from* Vodat *in Thiel.*

Another Poem on the Nightingale

1   Sum *P₂*: Dum *P P₁*

         sum *P₂*: sint *P P₁*

2   traho *P₁*: amabo *P₂*; thoro *P (readings uncertain)*

8   aut nequeam *P₂*: nequeam *P P₁*

         iuvat *Corpus Christianorum Series Latina*: docet *P P₁ P₂*

9   educere *P₁ P₂*: edicere *P*

13   tollit *P P₁*: pellit *P₂*

15   gaudes *P P₂*: glandes *P₁*

19   garrula *P P₂*: causula *P₁*

21   igitur *P P₁*: ergo *P₂*

           susurros *corrected from* susuros *P*; susurre *P₁*; susurro *P₂*

22   suavi *P₂*: suave *P₁ (reading uncertain)*; liram *P*

           pange *P₁ P₂*: tange *P*

On the Rustic

2   exoro famulos post arvaque *M*: quorum famulosque post arva *B*

5   lustrivage *Kölblinger*: lustrifage *B M*

6   canifer *M*: conifer *B*

           rudigena *M*: irpignia *B, reading uncertain*

           caudite *M*: cantate *B, reading uncertain*

           petulce *M*: peculte *B*

9   silvicola *M*: silvicula *B*

10   stridule *M*: stridole *B*

11   ferox *B*: verox *M*

           pellite *Kölblinger*: pellete *B*; polite *M*

A Poem of Consolation for Livia

34   osque *most manuscripts*: usque *Schoonhoven (conjectured by Axelson)*

219   te *all manuscripts*: ter *conjectured by Schoonhoven*

Notes to the Translations

Pref.10   *I have placed myself in front of you through these prefaces*: This turns
out to be an elaborate joke—"Ovid" would not dare to put
himself before Virgil, but then he does so with these titular po-
ems. The Latin verb *praeponere* literally means "to place before"
but was also a standard way to say "to preface" or "to prefix" in
the literary sense. Note that the ten-line preface to the *Sum-
maries* is written in elegiac couplets, Ovid's more characteristic
meter, while the *Summaries* themselves are in hexameters.

1.1   *A man great in war and second to none in piety*: Most of the first
lines of these summaries echo the first lines of the book they
preface. An extreme case is the summary of Book 9, which
takes as its first line *Aeneid* 9.1 in its entirety. Of the others, a
common pattern is that two words are picked up (for example,
Book 2). Books 6 and 11 depart from this pattern, and the sum-
mary of Book 10 includes the first word of the book's second
line. Many of the other lines also contain quotations drawn
from their respective books. These are so frequent that the ef-
fect is almost like a Virgilian cento. Because of these cento-like
quotations from the works they summarize, we have departed
from the series's practice of displaying the extent of the cita-
tion by italicization in these summaries.

1.6   *Elissa*: Dido.

2.5   *black Hector*: The same adjective is used to describe the ghost of
Hector when he appears in Aeneas's dream at *Aeneid* 2.272. The
ghost of Hector is also depicted as black in skin color and garb

in the illustration of this scene in the ancient codex *Vergilius Vaticanus*.

11.title   *in an unequal fight*: The Trojan ally Arruns stalked Camilla on the battlefield, then killed her when she was opportunely distracted by her pursuit of Chloreus.

Quatrains on All of Virgil's Works

Preface

1–2   *in thoroughly taming the earth with vines and trees, flocks and bees*: That is, the contents of the four books of the *Georgics*.

Eclogues

1–2   As in the *Summaries of the Books of the* Aeneid, most of the lines in these quatrains incorporate cento-like verbatim quotations from their respective works. For this reason, we have departed from the series' practice of indicating quotation of classical sources with italicization. The first line refers to *Eclogues* 1, the second to *Eclogues* 2 (quoting *Eclogues* 2.1), the third to *Eclogues* 6.

3   *and he bound old Silenus*: The subject is left unexpressed in the Latin and could be taken to indicate Tityrus (the character indicated as the narrator of *Eclogue* 6 at *Eclogues* 6.4) or Virgil.

Georgics

Intro.1   *the gifts of Lyaeus*: The gifts of Dionysus (that is, wine). See also the Preface and Book 2.

Intro.2   *Hybla*: A town in Sicily renowned in antiquity for its honey.

Intro.4   *He interrupted the work and began his narration a second time*: A reference to *Georgics* 3.1–48.

1.1   *What makes for thriving crops*: Compare *Georgics* 1.1.

1.1–2   *what stars the farmer should watch*: Virgil lays out this topic in *Georgics* 1.204–58.

1.3   *the cultivation of different locations*: Compare *Georgics* 1.52.

2.1   *the cultivation of fields and the stars of the sky*: Here the first line of Book 2 of the *Georgics* is taken in its entirety.

2.4   *olive trees*: Georgics 2.420–57.

3.1   *you, Pales, and you, world-renowned shepherd*: Compare *Georgics* 3.1. Pales was the Roman deity of shepherds and flocks, celebrated in the Parilia festival. The other shepherd is Apollo. Of course, a Christian reader might well think of Christ.

4.1   *the kingdoms scented by air-given honey*: Bees were believed to collect their honey from the air. Compare *Georgics* 4.1.

4.2   *weaving with wax*: Compare *Georgics* 4.34.

4.3   *which blossoms are suitable*: Georgics 4.103–48.

4.4   *the gifts of the gods*: Compare *Georgics* 4.1.

Aeneid

1.1   *He sings of arms and the man*: Compare *Aeneid* 1.1.

1.3   *the hospitality of Dido*: Aeneid 1.561–85.

1.4   *how the queen, at the banquet, asks about his misfortunes*: Aeneid 1.725–56.

2.1   *Everyone fell silent*: Compare *Aeneid* 2.1.

     unspeakable: Compare *Aeneid* 2.2, 84, 132.

2.3   *the fall of Priam*: Aeneid 2.486–558.

2.4   *he carried his father away*: Aeneid 2.705–29.

3.1   *After . . . events in Asia*: Compare *Aeneid* 3.1.

3.2   *of your tomb, Polydorus*: Aeneid 3.19–68.

3.3   *Andromache*: Aeneid 3.294–355.

     Helenus: Aeneid 3.356–462.

     the Cyclopes with their huge bulk: Aeneid 3.655–91.

3.4   *the loss of his father*: Aeneid 3.692–718.

4.1   *But now the queen . . . fire*: Compare *Aeneid* 4.1.

4.2   *desires a hunt*: Aeneid 4.129–72.

     She herself is captured in the hunt: Compare *Aeneid* 4.69–73, where Dido is compared to a deer and Aeneas to a hunter.

4.3   *applies your torches, Hymen, to a funeral pyre*: Aeneid 4.450–503.

4.4   *the son of Anchises has followed the commands of fate*: Aeneid 4.393–449.

5.1   *Meanwhile Aeneas was now sailing*: Compare *Aeneid* 5.1.
5.2   *honoring the tomb . . . with funeral games*: Compare *Aeneid* 5.58.
5.3   *the ships were set on fire*: *Aeneid* 5.604–99.
        the walls of Acesta: *Aeneid* 5.746–61.
5.4   *Palinurus fell from his vessel in the middle of the sea*: *Aeneid* 5.835–71.
6.1   *Still mourning, eventually Aeneas puts in at the shore of Cumae*: Compare *Aeneid* 6.1–2.
6.3   *fallen Trojans as well as Greeks*: Compare *Aeneid* 6.477–534 and elsewhere.
6.4   *Anchises tells him of his offspring who will advance to the stars*: Compare *Aeneid* 6.752–885. For this use of "stars" in Virgil, compare *Aeneid* 1.259.
7.1   *You, Caieta, also gave your legend to those shores*: Compare *Aeneid* 7.1.
7.2   *Aeneas . . . enters Latium*: Compare *Aeneid* 7.1–191.
7.3   *seeking a treaty*: Compare *Aeneid* 7.192–285.
        Juno rages: Compare *Aeneid* 7.286–341.
7.4   *impels Turnus and the neighboring peoples into battle*: Compare *Aeneid* 7.601–817.
8.1   *Turnus gives the signal . . . generals*: Compare *Aeneid* 8.1–25.
8.3   *Aeneas approaches the walls of Pallenteum*: Compare *Aeneid* 8.66–183.
8.4   *Venus brings arms crafted by Vulcan*: Compare *Aeneid* 8.370–453, 585–625.
9.1   *While this was going on in a distant part*: Compare *Aeneid* 9.1.
9.1–2   *Cybele ordered the ships*: Compare *Aeneid* 9.77–122.
9.3   *The slaughter of Euryalus and Nisus*: Compare *Aeneid* 9.168–524.
9.4   *the deaths that Turnus caused*: Compare *Aeneid* 9.525–818.
10.1   *Meanwhile heaven is revealed*: Compare *Aeneid* 10.1.
        there is a council of the gods: Compare *Aeneid* 10.1–95.
10.2   *Soon Aeneas returns*: Compare *Aeneid* 10.118–62, 290–307.
        fierce Pallas is struck down: Compare *Aeneid* 10.426–509.
10.3–4 *the son of Venus made . . . death*: Compare *Aeneid* 10.755–908.
11.1–2 *In the meantime, Dawn . . . Mezentius*: Compare *Aeneid* 11.1–99.
11.3   *the envoys bringing back Diomedes's reply*: Compare *Aeneid* 11.225–95.
11.4   *Volscian Camilla*: Compare *Aeneid* 11.532–96, 648–835.

12.1   *Turnus, when he saw*: Compare *Aeneid* 12.1.

12.2   *challenged the son of Anchises*: Compare *Aeneid* 12.54–80.

12.3   *a truce that Juturna was preparing to break*: Compare *Aeneid* 12.113–60, 468–99.

12.4   *But nonetheless he dies in the fight*: Compare *Aeneid* 12.887–952.

VERSES ON FISH AND WILD BEASTS

1   *distributed weapons*: Compare *dedit arma* with *arma dedi* in Ovid, *Ars amatoria* 2.741 and 3.1.

11–14   *when the bait is eaten*: The scar enters the net heedlessly, then realizes the danger. Just inside the mouth of the trap are pointed rods *(radiis)* that would injure the eyes of a fish attempting to escape back through the entrance. Therefore, the scar uses its tail to dash against *(occurrere)* the wickerwork.

30   *damaging example*: Damaging, that is, from the perspective of the fisherman.

40   *is borne*: "The passive of *ferre* seems here, as often, to denote a rushing motion over which the subject has no deliberate control . . . We must assume that the poet's wish is to describe an instinctive reaction on the part of the fish" (Richmond, *Halieutica*, 45).

46   *anthias*: The exact identity of the *anthias* is unknown. The same uncertainty applies to many of the other species of fish in this poem. For possible guesses, see Richmond's *Halieutica*. Since the identifications are themselves contested, we have preferred to either leave the names as they appear in the Latin or, in the case of the many fish named after common land animals, we have translated with "-fish" as in "wolffish," likely a type of pike. This close connection between the terrestrial and aquatic portions of the poem is otherwise lost in English.

83   *Yet*: Richmond posits the lacuna marked with the preceding ellipsis: "these words [*nec tamen*] make it quite clear that there must be a lacuna before these lines which contained something that implied the fisherman should venture out on the high seas" (*Halieutica*, 68).

99   *a big delay to ships*: The name *remora* (in Latin, "a delay") comes

from this fish's association with delaying ships. This line is surely an etymological pun since the Greek name, *echenais,* similarly means "ship-detaining." Whether this is also a Latin pun depends on the date of the poem, since *remora* does not appear to have been used as a name for this fish in Latin until after the classical period. Pliny (*Historia Naturalis* 32.2) refers to the remora as a *parvus admodum pisciculus* (a tiny little fish) and similarly contrasts its size with its ability to delay the largest ships (also at *Historia Naturalis* 9.79). Pliny even relates a story that a remora at the battle of Actium interfered with Antony's ship, contributing to his defeat (*Historia Naturalis* 32.3).

102 *cercyrus*: Lewis and Short identify this merely as "a sea-fish." In this and other cases where the exact fish species is unknown (see *tragus, lamyrus,* and *chromis* below), we keep the Greek or Latin name.

Words for Pan

1 *goat-footed, horned, half-beast*: Pan is half man, half goat. Compare *biformis* ("two-formed," line 4), *biceps* ("double-natured," line 8), etc. Note that all of the adjectives in this poem are in the vocative.

2 *Cinyphian*: The Cinyps is a river in Libya. *Cinyphius* means, in general, Libyan or African.

The Walnut Tree

26 *a complaint worthy of Clytemnestra*: Clytemnestra was killed by her own son, Orestes.

44 *something for which he should fear*: For example, valuables that could be stolen.

73–86 Five different games are described here. The first (73–76) was played by placing three nuts on the ground with a fourth stacked on top. The player attempted to scatter these by throwing nuts at them. The second (77–78) represents a variation on the first in which a sloping board was used to roll the nuts into the stack. The third game (79–80) was the guessing game called *par impar,* that is, "evens and odds." The next (81–

84) was a game played by drawing on the ground with chalk a triangle that was divided by parallel horizontal lines. The player would roll the nut into the triangle and win as may nuts as it crossed lines—provided that the nut stayed within the bounds of the triangle. The last game (85–86) was simply played by attempting to throw nuts into a pot placed at some distance from the players.

81   *a heavenly constellation*: The constellation Triangulum.

82   *the fourth Greek letter*: Delta (Δ).

109   *Polydorus*: A son of Priam, entrusted to the care of Polymestor, king of the Thracian Chersonese; Polymestor killed him for the sake of the gold he had brought with him (Ovid, *Metamorphoses* 13.429–39; at greater length, Virgil, *Aeneid* 3.13–68).

109–10   *the treasure of a wicked wife*: Polynices bribed Eriphyle with the gift of a necklace to send her husband, Amphiaraus, to the war against Thebes, though she knew he would die; compare Virgil, *Aeneid* 6.445–46.

111   *The orchards of the Hesperian king*: The garden of the Hesperides held trees with golden fruit.

118   *the Icarian dog*: The Dog Star (Procyon, in Canis Minor), supposed to be Maera, the dog of Erigone, daughter of Icarius of Athens. Its appearance in the western hemisphere heralded the onset of summer.

145   *that god*: Caesar.

155   *mark the fingers with dark juice*: The outer husk that surrounds the shell of the walnut will stain skin dark brown. The color cannot be removed immediately with water and can last for several days.

166   *Pontic beaver*: The beaver was thought to escape hunters by biting off the object of their chase, his testicles, which secreted an oil used in midwifery; compare *On the Wonders of the World*, 77–78. "Pontic" may allude to Ovid's exile.

On the Flea

17   *nature*: Adding to the obscenity of the humor, the Latin *natura* can also denote the genitalia.

On the Cuckoo

4   *Young Daphnis . . . his elder Palaemon*: Shepherds, who make numerous appearances in classical Latin literature. Daphnis: Virgil, *Ecologues* 2, 5, and 7; Ovid, *Metamorphoses* 4.277. Palaemon: Virgil, *Ecologue* 3. The poem is thus firmly rooted in the pastoral genre from the beginning and continues with the theme of the singing contest.

5   *sing the praises of the cuckoo*: The subject of this poem is probably the common cuckoo *(Cuculus canorus)*. Its migration to Europe from its winter sojourn in Africa was a harbinger of spring (Pliny, *Historia Naturalis* 18.249).

6   *Spring also came, girded with a flowery garland*: In some manuscripts, the personified Spring is made masculine, although the noun is neuter in classical Latin.

17   *Apollo*: Both the god of song and the driver of the sun.

44   *together with Daphnis . . . shepherds*: This line is omitted in some manuscripts, probably because Daphnis does not speak and plays no role in the poem after being mentioned in line 4.

On the Nightingale

Compare Ovid, *Amores* 2.6 and Catullus, poems 2 and 3 for classical treatment of birds in elegiac and lyric poetry.

1–4   The first two couplets were set to music by Jacobus Gallus Carniolus (also known as Jacobus Handl) and published in his collection of Latin secular madrigals, *Harmoniarum moralium* (Prague, 1589–1596).

71–72 *May you thrive . . . with its hide*: This cryptic closing couplet is found in several late manuscripts (including many attributed to Ovid). The scribe seems to be addressing the poem itself, wishing it a long life by means of recopying on calfskin (vellum).

On the Wolf

3   *by force*: *Virtute,* that is, by "virtuous" or "respectable" methods, such as hunting.

54 *made a brother*: The Latin term used here, *converso,* suggests that the wolf is a "converse" or lay brother, the term for a monk admitted usually late in life and not a member of holy orders.

57 *If gifts of mutton dishes do not please you*: The *Rule of Saint Benedict* technically prohibited monks from eating the meat of quadrupeds unless a monk was in poor health (*Rule of Saint Benedict* 39). That this rule was regularly violated is a point of satire throughout the poem.

64 *once the wolf is hooded*: That is, once the wolf has received his monastic habit.

65 The additional text of Voigt's version b ("Ovidius de lupo," in Voigt, *Kleinere lateinische Denkmäler,* 62–71) begins with this line.

105–6 *the brothers were observing the appointed fasts*: That is, during Lent; hence the play on words (*lentus,* "idle") in line 107.

115 *A crab isn't that big. I think that's a donkey*: The joke, as often in this poem, hinges on the monastic prohibition against eating quadrupeds (see above, line 57). It would be acceptable for the wolf to eat a crab but not to eat a donkey.

131 *I am the guardian of their masters*: As the monastery's keyholder (*claviger,* line 94).

137 *dark cowl*: A possible hint that the wolf is in the Benedictine Order, whose members wore black cowls; see also line 152. However, since the wolf is probably to be considered a lay brother, whose dress was sometimes distinguished in color from that of the other monks, it is not possible to be certain.

148 The additional text of Voigt's version b ("Ovidius de lupo") ends after this line.

182 *cheese and beans*: The cheap, bland food traditionally prescribed for monastics; see *On the Distribution of Women* 36.

187 *healthy monk*: As noted above at line 57, only sick monks were technically allowed to eat meat.

188 *the holy rule of Basil*: The fourth-century theologian Basil of Caesarea, one of the founders of communal monasticism. The *Rule of Saint Benedict* describes the "Rule of our holy father Basil" (*Regula sancti patris nostri Basilii*) as one of the "tools of virtue for right-living and obedient monks" (*bene viventium et obedientium*

monachorum instrumenta virtutum, 73.5–6), and in fact the *Rule of Saint Basil* was a major source for the *Rule of Saint Benedict.*

190   *sometimes I am a monk, sometimes a canon*: That is, a secular canon (cleric) who does not live in common under a Rule and is thus not prohibited from eating meat.

On the Wonders of the World

1   *The tree snake*: The verses throughout are meant to accompany and describe a series of illustrations. The titles serve as captions for the images. M. R. James has traced nearly all of these descriptions to Solinus's *On the Wonders of the World* (James, "Ovidius," 289), but, naturally, most appear in Pliny's *Historia Naturalis* as well.

8   *tragopan*: The tragopan is a fabulous horned bird described by Solinus, *On the Wonders of the World* 30, as "greater in size than eagles."

9–10   For this characterization of a people living in ancient Albania, see Pliny, *Historia Naturalis* 7.12, and Solinus, *On the Wonders of the World* 15, but the detail of the change in hair color with age from white to dark has been borrowed from a tale about a people living in India (compare Solinus, *On the Wonders of the World* 52).

11   *amphisbaena*: A mythical snake with one head at each end of its body. It was sometimes depicted making a loop with its body so that its two heads were facing each other, as seems to be the case here. See Pliny, *Historia Naturalis* 8.85. This line is a close paraphrase of Lucan, *Pharsalia* 9.719.

12   *The great Macedonian*: Alexander the Great.

14   *Gymnosophist*: The Greek name for an ascetic sect of Indian philosophers. Pliny describes how the gymnosophists were said to stand on hot sands throughout the entire day, standing now on one foot and then on the other; see *Historia Naturalis* 7.22.

16   The Himantopods ("thong-foots") were said by Pliny to be an Ethiopian people whose feet resembled leather thongs and on which they walked in a serpentine fashion; see *Historia Naturalis* 5.46.

17   The Anthropophagi ("cannibals") are described in many places in Pliny's *Historia Naturalis*. At 7.12, for instance, they are described as drinking out of skull cups and using human scalps as bibs.

23   Pliny says that the leucrocota lived in Ethiopia and was the fastest animal, resembling a mixture of the parts of many different animals; see *Historia Naturalis* 8.72.

28   *their jaws are split to the ears*: Meaning that the bull's mouth extends around its head from ear to ear. See Solinus, *On the Wonders of the World* 52.

32–33   Ladas was "a runner of Alexander the Great, whose name became a proverb for swiftness" (Lewis and Short).

35   The source of the Nile was considered to be one of the great mysteries of the ancient world.

36   The Hippopods were a race described by Pliny as having human form except for their feet, which were shaped like the hooves of horses; see *Historia Naturalis* 4.95.

37   The rhinoceros, also known as the unicorn, is described by Isidore of Seville, *Etymologies* 12.2.12–13, as susceptible to capture only by a maiden.

40   The Astomi were a race described by Pliny as having no mouths and living off the scent of fruit alone; see *Historia Naturalis* 7.25.

48   The Cynocephali ("dog-headed" people) were thought to live in India. They appear in many ancient sources. Pliny describes them at *Historia Naturalis* 7.31.

50   *spice builder*: Isidore describes how the phoenix, after living for five hundred years, gathers spices to form a pyre for itself, which it ignites with the rays of the sun (*Etymologies* 12.7.22). No doubt the image originally associated with the caption here depicted the phoenix's fiery death (a common image). The word *sic* (in this way) likely points to this depiction. The phoenix was forever being reborn from the ashes, hence its life was "indivisible" even as it ended.

51   Pliny relates that the Bitiae were said to do great harm through the evil eye, but curiously they are said there to have a double pupil in just one eye (*Historia Naturalis* 7.17).

54–55   "Julius Caesar" in the title is incorrect. It should have read "Germanicus Caesar." Apis was a sacred bull worshiped as a god in Egypt. As James, "Ovidius," 293, notes, the descriptions in lines 54–55 correspond to Solinus, *On the Wonders of the World* 32: "Apis gives clear omens about the future; it is the best sign if he takes food from the hand of the one consulting him. Moreover, when he rejected the hand of Germanicus Caesar, he revealed approaching misfortune, and Caesar died shortly thereafter."

63   *conceived with the father's death*: The female viper was believed to kill the male viper during mating; she, in turn, was killed by her offspring during their birth (Pliny, *Historia Naturalis* 10.169–70; Isidore, *Etymologies* 12.4.10–11).

67–68   For this story about Caesar, see Pliny, *Historia Naturalis* 7.91.

71   *it cannot feed without drawing its legs backward*: Pliny makes a similar remark about the elk (*Historia Naturalis* 8.39): "Its upper lip is so extremely large, for which reason it is obliged to go backward when grazing; otherwise, by moving onward, the lip would get doubled up" (J. Bostock and H. T. Riley, trans., *The Natural History of Pliny* [London, 1855], 263).

72   As James points out, *bufomon* is probably a corruption of *ichneumon*. The enhydros, ichneumon, and suillus are all discussed consecutively in Isidore's *Etymologies* 12.2.36–37, and Isidore seems to treat the ichneumon and suillus, at least, as the same animal. Of the ichneumon, Isidore says that it can "tell whether food is healthy or poisonous by its smell."

73–74   Compare Lucan's very similar description of the seps snake at *Pharsalia* 9.723.

76   *medicine requires it unharmed*: The beaver's testicles were thought to have medicinal properties, so the animal was useful only if it still had them. See Isidore, *Etymologies* 12.2.21.

79   See the note above at lines 54–55.

85   The Sciapods ("shade-foots") had a single enormous foot. Pliny locates them in India and describes them at *Historia Naturalis* 7.23.

92–93   According to Pliny, the leontophone's flesh was so poisonous to lions that hunters would sprinkle ashes made from leontophones onto meat from other animals in order to deceive and so poison lions. Because of this practice, lions would try to kill any leontophones they came across but used only their claws so as to avoid ingesting their poisonous flesh (Pliny, *Historia Naturalis* 8.136).

94   Compare Pliny, *Historia Naturalis* 7.10.

101   The pegasus here is the pegasus bird, a bird with horse ears; compare Pliny, *Historia Naturalis* 10.136.

102–3   The Blemmyae were said to be an Ethiopian people whose face was on their chest (Pliny, *Historia Naturalis* 5.46).

104–5   *Secretly the pious daughter nurtures a deserving parent at her breast*: See Solinus, *On the Wonders of the World* 1 and Pliny, *Historia Naturalis* 7.121 for the legend of a lowborn Roman woman breastfeeding her imprisoned mother (or her father, in later tellings); the spot of the prison was consecrated to Pietas, with a temple built in 150 BCE.

110–11   Phanesians are described in just this manner by Pliny at *Historia Naturalis* 4.95.

112–14   Compare Ovid, *Metamorphoses* 14.483–511 for the transformation of the comrades of Diomedes into birds.

115–17   The dipsas was a kind of venomous snake (Lucan, *Pharsalia* 9.610).

118–19   For the effects of the prester's bite, see Lucan, *Pharsalia* 9.790 and following.

120–21   The Arimphaei were a Scythian tribe said to live on berries (Pliny, *Historia Naturalis* 6.34).

122–23   During the First Punic War, the implausible claim arose that Carthage and its fleet were visible from Lilybaeum in Sicily, 135 miles away (Pliny, *Historia Naturalis* 7.85; Strabo, *Geography* 6.2.1).

126   *this plunder*: That is, a horse. Griffins were said to carry off horses. See Isidore, *Etymologies* 12.2.17.

ON MEDICINE FOR THE EARS

In several manuscripts, these verses follow immediately after *On the Four Humors,* sometimes as part of the same poem and sometimes as a separate poem.

13   The second half of the poem switches from elegiac couplets to dactylic hexameter. This might suggest that the first half of the poem was intended to serve as a preface for a much larger collection of remedies, only one of which has remained.

14   *houseleek juice*: Lewis and Short define the *herba semperviva* as "houseleek," a genus of perennial succulent.

20   *outer ear*: *Auricula* refers to the external ear, or pinna.

22   This closing line is omitted from some manuscripts.

On the Four Humors

2   *Thamyras*: Apollo is regularly acknowledged in ancient and medieval texts as the founder of medicine, but we have been unable to find the source for the story about Thamyras. Isidore of Seville begins *De inventoribus medicinae* (*Etymologies* 4.3) with Apollo (*Medicinae autem artis auctor ac repertor apud Graecos*, "Moreover among the Greeks he was the originator and inventor of the art of medicine"), followed by Aesculapius and Hippocrates, but omits any mention of Thamyras. In antiquity, Thamyras was best known as a poet/musician who challenged the Muses to a contest and, once beaten, was deprived of his voice by Apollo. The story would have been especially well known to medieval readers through Statius's telling in *Thebaid* 4.182–86; however, this passage does not contain an episode that can be referred to this anecdote. It would not be unreasonable to speculate that "the crime against his daughter" was sexual in nature, and thus constituted incest, and "the faulty parts" were his genitals, but of course this would not involve his ears. One could imagine the ears as the faulty parts only if Thamyras heard and believed some slander about his daughter. All this is speculative; it is to be hoped that some text will be found that explains the background to this reference.

15–16   *He taught everyone that the human body has four humors*: In accordance with the prevailing "humoral theory" (the idea that physical health was connected with bodily fluids), many texts of the ancient *Corpus Hippocraticum* attribute conditions such as epilepsy and mental illness to an excess (or, more rarely, to a lack) of humors. The summary of humoral theory that follows in this poem closely echoes Isidore of Seville, *Etymologies* 4.5 (*De quattuor humoribus corporis*).

18–19   *Among these, blood . . . language*: These lines present condensed versions of Isidore's two etymologies for blood at *Etymologies* 4.5.4–6. According to Isidore, blood's Greek etymology comes from "being animated, sustained, and alive," while "blood is so called in Latin because it is sweet." The Latin etymology depends on the closeness in the sound of *sanguis* (blood) and *suavis* (sweet).

27   *frothy*: *Spuma* literally means "froth" or "foam" and was commonly applied to the bodily fluids associated with the humor phlegm, such as saliva and semen.

ON THE LOMBARD AND THE SNAIL

4   *snail*: The titular *lumaca,* an Italianization of the Latin *lymax.* In the medieval satirical tradition of "the world turned upside down," the snail shows the cowardly nature of its opponent, the Lombard. Though snails are generally timid and inoffensive, their slithering and horns give them a devilish appearance. It is possible that there is also a connection between this work and a fourteenth-century vogue for marginal illustrations of knights doing battle with snails. See L. Randall, "The Snail in Gothic Marginal Warfare," *Speculum* 37, no. 3 (1962): 358–67.

11   *shield . . . horns*: Parts of a soldier's armor (see Virgil, *Aeneid* 12.88–89, in which Turnus arms himself before his encounter with Aeneas). The "shield" is the snail's shell. *Cornua,* usually an animal's "horns," can also describe the protuberance from a helmet that holds the plume.

52   *let the lawyers come forward*: Reminiscent of a cue in ancient comedy introducing a scene change and anticipating the arrival of new characters. The final *veniant* also has a framing function, recalling the initial *venerat* of the first line.

On the Lamb

1   *Azzo*: Azzo of Bologna (d. ca. 1220), a jurist and glossator who
    wrote influential commentaries on the Justinianic *Corpus iuris
    civilis*. We can only guess at why Azzo is the target of the po-
    em's satire, though some of his stances and actions during his
    time in Bologna are suggestive. R. Witt describes an episode of
    around 1200 in which Azzo, perceiving the threat to jurispru-
    dence posed by grammarians, openly disagreed with Bernard
    Dorna, a former student who "had offered a solution to a vexed
    passage in the law by a series of proofs including citations not
    only from legal texts but also from Ovid"; *The Two Latin Cul-
    tures and the Foundation of Renaissance Humanism in Medieval It-
    aly* (Cambridge, 2012), 429. Furthermore, in the 1190s, he op-
    posed the students of Bologna forming a university with their
    own rectors, on the grounds that the *Authentica habita*—the
    foundational document of the medieval university—had given
    masters jurisdiction over their students and that the Justini-
    anic Code stipulated that only those who exercised a profes-
    sion could elect rectors or have civil and criminal jurisdiction
    (Witt, *Two Latin Cultures*, 365).

2   *twelve especially wondrous lambs*: The poem could be taken as par-
    odying an apocalyptic text in order to mock Azzo and his stu-
    dents (compare the seven angels of Revelation 8). However,
    there is also the possibility that this poem was written by Az-
    zo's students as a sort of inside joke about each of their per-
    sonal characteristics, since the first lines of the poem seem to
    indicate that this was presented to Azzo by his class. Further-
    more, the twelve lambs evoke the apostles of Christ (the "apos-
    tles of the Lamb," Revelation 21:14), surely a favorable com-
    parison.

9   *lights the ground on fire*: The long *o* in *solum* required by the meter
    could suggest that this word be interpreted as "only" rather
    than "ground," which would require a short *o*. However, we be-
    lieve that the word is best interpreted as the noun here and
    prefer to assume a false quantity, since the verb *incendit* expects
    an object in context.

On the Louse

5   *squished*: More literally, "struck" *(ictus)*.

11   *fellows*: Literally, the nits or louse's eggs *(lendes)*. One might say, "progeny." This is a very rare and learned term.

13–14   For a poem-ending epitaph couplet, see Ovid, *Amores* 2.6.61–62, the memorial verses for Corinna's parrot, or *Heroides* 2.147–48, the epitaph Phyllis imagines for herself. A more elaborate epitaph, for the poet himself and comprised of two couplets, occurs at *Tristia* 3.3.73–76. Compare also the epitaph for the gnat that concludes *The Gnat (Culex)* in the *Appendix Vergiliana*.

On the Crafty Messenger

3   *But I am called back to arms*: A quotation from *Remedia amoris* 282.

8   *so many Parises, so many Ganymedes*: The Trojan princes Paris and Ganymede emblematize males who desire women and men, respectively.

17   *Daphnis*: Erroneously for Daphne; Daphnis was a young man (as in Virgil's *Eclogues*). All the figures mentioned here are known from Ovid. The conceit of the speaker becomes apparent: not just mortal women but goddesses desire him.

19   *Lusty Diana*: The idea of a "lusty Diana" is humorous, as Diana is the chaste goddess par excellence; also humorous would be the "runaway Io" (line 19) if she had already been changed into a cow, as befalls her in Ovid's *Metamorphoses*.

77   *if it is the place for it*: That is, if the location where they are speaking would be appropriate for the more intimate and secret conversation that follows.

122   *were to be done*: In Latin, the same word *(actum)* can mean both "done" and "deed." When the girl says "deed" *(factum)* in line 123, she is repeating the last word spoken by the messenger. *Actum* and *factum,* both meaning "deed," are used interchangeably throughout this passage as the meter requires. The "deed" *(actum* and *factum)* describes the final stage of love, that is, sexual intercourse. For the five stages of love, see the note on line 252 below.

134   *I won't disturb your tracks*: That is, "I won't chase after you."

228   *Ulysses*: That is, an eloquent and persuasive man. The figure of Ulysses as a cunning weaver of deceits is common in classical Latin literature (including the *Metamorphoses*).

252   *A caress . . . done*: "Caress" *(tactus)* and "deed" *(actus)* are variants on two of the canonical five stages of love: seeing *(visus)*, talking *(colloquium)*, touching *(contactus)*, kissing *(basia)*, and the deed *(factum)*, that is, sex; see also lines 122 to 126.

263   *Mars wed Venus, and Vulcan loved her too*: It is possible that the girl's misunderstanding here is intended as humor. It is of course Vulcan who "wed" Venus in a legitimate sense; Mars was the adulterer—if such conventional morality applies to the gods at all.

301   *Tell, good sir, who you are, and where are you going?*: Speeches in epics not infrequently open with a series of questions of this nature; for example, Virgil, *Aeneid* 8.113, 9.781.

323   *I don't know the name*: The play on *nomen/nominis/omen* recalls the Latin proverb *nomen omen* (the name is an omen).

336   *Pallas*: The goddess of wisdom, here called upon to restore the speaker's senses.

353   *you pass among the temples of the gods*: In the hope that one of the gods would cure her?

358–59   *If he seeks a reward . . . your senses*: These lines may belong to another speaker. They do not appear in some manuscripts. It is impossible to render the play on words of *censum* (reward) and *sensum* (sense, senses) into English.

383   *Davus*: The name of the messenger is finally revealed; "Davus" is almost proverbial as the name of a crafty servant, and certainly of a comic slave, as in Plautus, Terence, Horace, and Persius.

On the Old Woman

Introduction

Leo: The "chief of notaries" *(protonotarios)*, formerly a clerk *(scriniarius*, or "keeper of the *scrinium*," the archive) and secretary *(a*

commentariis) of a member of the noble Vatatzes family, proba-
bly John III, emperor of Nicaea (r. 1222–1254).

king of Colchis . . . Dioscurias: The kingdom of Colchis is an area
of the eastern Black Sea coast corresponding to northwestern
Georgia. The ancient city of Dioscurias is today known as
Sukhumi. This city is on the opposite side of the Black Sea
from Tomis (in modern Romania) where the historical Ovid
was exiled. There are at least two possible and potentially com-
plementary explanations for this confusion. At *Tristia* 3.9.33–
34, Ovid etymologizes Tomis from the Greek *tomê* (cutting),
identifying it as the spot where Medea (from Colchis) cut up
her brother Absyrtus's body. Also, in the Middle Ages, Dioscu-
rias was known locally by its Georgian name, Tskhumi, which
may well have become confused with the similar sounding To-
mis in the western medieval Latin sources likely used by our
author.

the Armenians: The inhabitants of Colchis would have spoken
Georgian, not Armenian, although in antiquity Georgia (then
Colchis) and Armenia were neighbors just as they are today.

Leo's Preface

1   *raised in the Paelignian countryside*: That is, the Valle Peligna, the
plateau where Sulmona (Ovid's *Sulmo*) is located. Compare
Amores 3.15.3, where the same phrase appears *(Paeligni ruris
alumnus)*.

8–9   Despite the fact that many readers, including, perhaps, the au-
thor of *On a Certain Old Woman,* take the colorful figure of the
go-between who ends up playing the "bed trick" on the narra-
tor as the titular old woman, these lines suggest that the au-
thor may have meant the title to refer to the woman whom the
narrator lusted after when she was young and with whom he fi-
nally consummated his love when she was mature. It was this
later encounter that was the turning point that led to the
change of life referred to here.

14   *one of his authentic works*: In Latin, the word used is *authentim*.

The author here further emphasizes the Byzantine context by using a word that seems to derive from the Patristic Greek *authentimios*, "original" (Lampe, 264).

The Author's Preface

2–3   *hexameters . . . pentameters*: Only Ovid's *Metamorphoses* are in dactylic hexameters; the rest of his "authentic" works are in elegiac couplets (alternating hexameter and pentameter lines). Hexameters are the meter of epic (heroic verse), while elegiac couplets were often employed by Roman poets for themes relating to love. The argument is that Ovid must give up elegiac couplets for the meter of epic because he abandoned love. This reverses the famous sentiment of *Amores* 1.1, in which Ovid declares that he set out to write an epic but the god of love removed a foot from the second line, thereby transforming his poetry into elegiacs and necessarily changing his subject to love.

3   *no hero*: Strictly, the translation should be "no master" since *herorum* is from *(h)erus,* not *heros.* However, the sense requires that *heros* is meant because hexameter is the heroic meter. Emendation would be problematic since *heroum* (the correct genitive plural of *heros*) would not fit the meter. Marginal commentary in the earliest manuscript of this poem (Bibliothèque nationale lat. 16252) simply glosses *nullus herorum* as *nullus heroum* rather than emending, so we have done the same. It is hard to accept that the author committed a solecism given the commonness of the word in the classical authors; nevertheless, it is worth noting that this is the only place in the poem where either *heros* or *(h)erus* appears.

Book One

1–4   The work opens with a version of the old saying "can't live with 'em, can't live without 'em." A misogynistic tone is thus introduced from the beginning and will continue throughout the text.

29   *it is seemly only for girls to embellish that body part*: "Ovid" is arguing
      that only women should wear makeup, so he left his own face
      unadorned. Ovid also wrote a didactic poem on women's facial
      cosmetics *(De medicamine faciei femineae)*, so this casual com-
      ment could be taken as strengthening the identification of the
      author with Ovid.

32   *tear ducts or the orifices of each sense*: The first refers to the eyes, the
      second to the ears, mouth, and nose, together the organs of
      four of the five senses. Any one of these could produce un-
      sightly discharge from its opening.

41–43 The author seems to mean that every individual created through
      sexual reproduction is unique, even though sometimes one
      might resemble another.

53   *open space*: Here *campus* perhaps refers to an open courtyard
      strewn at one time of the year with rushes and at another with
      straw. Both materials were common floor coverings in the
      Middle Ages.

62–63 *honey's bride*: The wax can be used for tapers only after it has
      been "divorced" from its bride, the honey.

71–97 This passage is an ecphrasis in which the narrator describes the
      murals that covered his bedroom wall. He is simultaneously
      boasting about his former great wealth in having such an or-
      nately decorated bedroom and also about the educational value
      of the murals, which stimulated his intellect and imagination.

99   *where any girl*: That is to say, virgins, married women, and wid-
      ows. The narrator boasts elliptically in this passage that he has
      slept with all three.

130   *with her husband footing the bill*: Or perhaps, more literally, "with
      her husband bearing it."

149–58 This passage addresses the potential pitfalls of taking a married
      woman as a lover. The author explains that difficulties can arise
      from acknowledging a child as an heir and adds the androcen-
      tric warning that husbands are more jealous of a wife's lover
      than a wife is of a husband's lover. Most dangerous, however, is
      the fact that a husband would have every legal and social right
      to mutilate the lover if caught.

154   *moves him to wage just warfare*: Compare *Ars amatoria* 2.397

(*Laesa Venus iusta arma movet,* "an injured Venus incites just warfare").

178   *almshouse*: *Elemosina,* the common medieval form of *eleemosyna.*

206–11   Here a "positive law" (a human-made, or "arbitrary" law) is distinguished from "natural law" (an inherent right).

215   *able to know a lover*: "Know" (*cognoscere*) in the so-called "biblical sense" of the word.

233   *the tears of Venus*: The fluids produced by the orgasm of both male and female.

253   *With the advance of the seasons*: That is, in summer.

272   *flails about*: The Latin verb *iectigat* used here seems to be a coinage by the author and appears in Latin literature only here. Du Cange suggests the translation "he throws his limbs here and there" (*hac et illac membra disiicit*); *Glossarium mediae et infimae Latinitatis* (Paris, 1883–1887).

308   *squirrels*: *Cyrogrillos* (nominative *cyrogrillus*), a common medieval variant of *choerogryllus,* which in antiquity referred to a porcupine but more commonly in the Middle Ages referred to squirrels.

316–21   Compare Psalms 41:2 "As the hart panteth after the fountains of water, so my soul panteth after thee, O God."

334   *uselessly in the wild*: If a deer is shot with an arrow, it will likely not die right away. If the dogs cannot track it, it will die in the wilderness "uselessly," in that the hunters will not be able to eat it.

336–37   This argument makes use of the medieval legal language of double jeopardy—"not twice for the same thing" (*non bis in idem*).

339   *a seine*: That is, a dragnet, a fishing net that hangs vertically in the water, with its bottom edge held down by weights and its top edge held up by buoys.

352   *from foreign elements*: That is, air and earth, two of the four ancient elements. They are foreign in that the fish's native element is water.

405–60   The earliest known exposition of elementary probability. See Bellhouse, "*De Vetula,*" for analysis of this passage, along with a translation by Nancy Prior (134–36).

424–25   The table of numbers here as well as those that follow are situated exactly as these are—between the verses—in the manuscripts. They are integral to the text, making this work the only epic that we know of to include tables of numbers within the body of the poem, not in the margins.

495   *you won't find a single penny remaining*: That is, the author has exactly broken even.

496–529   A description of the "tables game" *(tabula)*, the ancient "race game" (a game with moves controlled by the roll of a dice) that was the ancestor of modern backgammon. See R. C. Bell, *Board and Table Games from Many Civilizations,* rev. ed. (New York, 1979), 34–36, for the history and rules of this game. As in modern backgammon, the goal is to move your checkers in a circular direction from your side of the board *(castra)* past the enemy's side of the board and ultimately to safety. The dice determine how many positions the checkers can move, but it is up to the player to decide which checkers to move and where: hence the need for skill.

497   *swift*: Although *pernix* in this context clearly carries its usual classical meaning of "swift," the additional medieval resonance of "pernicious" is probably also intended.

510–16   Just as in the modern game, a single checker may be captured by an opponent's checker if it lands on it, but if two or more checkers occupy the same space, they are safe and the opponent's checker cannot land there.

517–29   In modern backgammon, this strategy is called a "priming game." The goal is to position one's checkers so that a stack of two or more occupy consecutive positions on the board. This forms a barrier that an opponent cannot get past.

577–78   The author follows Alexander Neckam (*De naturis rerum* 2.184) in ascribing the origins of chess to Ulysses.

600   *aufin*: One of the usual English names for the bishop before the sixteenth century. It was itself derived via French from the usual Latin name for the bishop, *alphinus,* which had been borrowed in turn from the Arabic for elephant *(al fil)*.

       maiden: In modern parlance, the queen. In other medieval descriptions of chess, queen *(regina)* or lady *(dama)* is the more common designation for this piece (see Murray, *The History of Chess* [Oxford, 1913], 508), but note that in line 614, the maiden is described as "royal" *(regia)*. Nevertheless, there are no metrical reasons why *regina* could not have been employed if the poet had so desired.

601–11   The rules for premodern chess differ from those for modern (international) chess. Most important, in the earlier (Indo-Arabic) game described here, the queen could move only one square diagonally forward or backward, making it weaker than the rook and the knight. The bishop was also considerably more restricted than in modern chess, since it could move only two squares forward on the diagonal. See Murray, *History of Chess,* 507, for a summary of this passage and 224–26 for a summary of the premodern moves assigned to each piece.

614   *bishop:* The use of "bishop" *(episcopus)* to describe the *aufin* is quite unusual at this time and place. Most modern languages do not so name the piece for the clerical office. In the Middle Ages, the term bishop was commonly used only in Iceland, and although it may have originated in England, the word "bishop," describing the chess piece, is first documented in the sixteenth century (see Murray, *History of Chess,* 508).

631–35   Gambling on chess games became so prevalent in France that Louis IX issued an ordinance against it in 1254. Although this fact cannot be used to date the poem, it does suggest that around the middle of the thirteenth century (the traditional date of the poem's composition) this practice was quite common and frowned upon by more people than just our author. See M. G. A. Vale, *The Princely Court: Medieval Courts and Culture in North-West Europe, 1270–1380* (Oxford, 2007), 172.

637   *which I have said are appropriate for girls to know:* The author is referring to the *Ars amatoria* 3.353 and following, where Ovid instructs girls to learn to play board games and dice. That this is indeed the reference here is confirmed by the author's quotation from the first line of this passage: "I am ashamed to teach such unimportant things" *(Parva monere pudet; Ars amatoria* 3.353).

639–48   Brief descriptions of the board games alquerque (played with twelve pieces) and nine-men's morris (played with nine).

649–98   For the history and rules of rithmomachia, see A. E. Moyer, *The Philosophers' Game: Rithmomachia in Medieval and Renaissance Europe* (Ann Arbor, 2001). The terminology in this passage and indeed the very game itself reflect Boethian mathematics. The first row contains the "fathers." For the evens, this is 2, 4, 6, 8, and for the odds, 3, 5, 7, 9. The next row is the squares of each number. For example, the second row of the evens would be 4, 16, 36, 64. The third row is produced by adding together each "father" (or root) with its square. For the evens, this is 6, 20, 42, 72.

661   *superparticulars*: The Latin reads *supraparticulares* here, but this is for metrical reasons. The usual term is *superparticulares* and, indeed, it appears so in the table following line 687. Superparticulars are numbers in a proportion of $(x + 1):x$. In this case, x is the value of each of the "fathers." For instance, the first number in the first row of the evens is 2 (the "father"); the first number in the second, 4; the first number in the third, 6. The ratio of 6:4 may be reduced to 3:2 = $(2 + 1):2$.

662   *quotity*: A technical term here meaning essentially "numerical value."

687   *the following table*: The table which follows shows the starting layout of the pieces on each side of the board. The multiplexes, that is, the second row, are so called because these numbers are in a multiplex proportion to the first row $(x:1)$, where x is each number in the first row. In the manuscripts, the columns of numbers listed below "complete pyramid" and "pyramid truncated by three" both appear within triangles, which represent the pyramidal pieces (the kings).

689   *win approval*: The Latin word *placidam* is something of a pun here because it can mean both "peaceful" and "pleasing." The game is a battle, which can make itself both peaceful and pleasing.

698   *does not yet know the names of the horses*: This is a direct quotation from *Metamorphoses* 2.192. In context, this phrase refers to Phaethon, who is foolishly attempting to fly the chariot of the

NOTES TO THE TRANSLATIONS

sun across the sky even though he has no knowledge of how to control the horses. The extent of his ignorance is revealed by the fact that he does not even know the horses' names. The quotation thus signifies someone who does not know, on a fundamental level, what he is talking about.

699–728   This digression concerning the "modern" disregard for a liberal arts education in favor of more vocational pursuits such as law has much in common with other treatments of this theme from the first half of the thirteenth century. Most famously, Henri d'Andeli's *Battle of the Seven Arts* (ca. 1240) allegorically depicts the contemporary university curriculum as a battlefield, in which the forces of the arts, especially literary studies, are being defeated by the forces of dialectic and the applied sciences, such as medicine.

708   *physiognomists*: People trained in the art of physiognomy, a popular premodern theory that people's character traits could be judged from their outward appearance, especially their faces.

709   *which art*: That is, one of the seven liberal arts that compose the trivium and the quadrivium, major components of the medieval educational system. The trivium is made up of grammar, dialectic, and rhetoric. The quadrivium consists of arithmetic, geometry, astronomy, and music.

722–23   *four higher disciplines*: The quadrivium, generally considered to be more advanced areas of study, while the trivium was seen as foundational.

735   *mechanical arts*: The liberal arts are being distinguished from the mechanical arts, which we would call today vocational skills or trades.

736   *love of money*: The Latin word here *(philopecunia)* is a coinage by the author to make a learned wordplay with philosophy *(philosophia)*, which in Greek means "love of wisdom."

759–60   These lines play elaborately with Latin words that begin with the root *capt–*. In the first instance, "captives" *(captivis)*, a secondary meaning may be intended that relies on the Old French derivative *chaitif,* meaning "wretched." The verb *capto* (to capture) also has the secondary meaning of "to gain understanding of something." The sense of these lines may be: These wretches, who have harmed you, do not actually understand you and for this reason they ought to be harmed.

765   *the most bountiful maiden scorns the greedy*: Alchemy held the promise of creating gold and with it, vast wealth, but the author maintains that no one—or at least no one seeking only money—had yet succeeded in getting rich through alchemy.

783   *elevation*: The Latin word *anabathrum*, from Greek *anabathron*, appears just once in classical Latin, only in the plural and only at Juvenal's *Satires* 7.46. In Juvenal it refers to elevated tiers of benches, but the singular form in the Middle Ages could have the additional connotations of a platform or a pulpit.

802–3   The sentiment ironically reverses Ovid's in *Amores* 10.48 where he says that "sordid profit never has happy outcomes" *(non habet eventus sordida praeda bonos).*

815   *the game of "algebra and almucabola"*: This is a direct reference to the mathematical treatise titled *The Compendious Book on Calculation by Completion and Balancing (Al-kitab al-mukhtaṣar fi ḥisab al-gabr wa'l-muqabala)* written by Al-Khwarizmi in the ninth century. This was translated from Arabic into Latin in the twelfth century by Robert of Chester with the title *The Book of Algebra and Almucabola (Liber algebrae et almucabola).* Our author has essentially reproduced the Latin title but changed "book" *(liber)* to "game" *(ludus).* The "game" being referred to is algebra, using known quantities to solve for unknowns. Although the Latin text here reads *almucgrabalaeque* in the manuscripts and both critical editions, Du Cange argues that the reading should be *almucabalaeque (Glossaria mediae et infimae Latinitatis,* under "almucabala").

816–18   Al-Khwarizmi's book is indeed one of the most important works in the history of mathematics. Although it is a substantial treatise, our author probably means that it would take up more than a single book of the epic to explain its subject. Since the first book, treating the subject of games, is at its end, there is no room left for so involved a description of algebra as it would require.

473

Book Two

8–20   In this list of the different methods by which males become eu-
        nuchs, there may be a distant and if so ironic echo of Matthew
        19:12.

21–195 Throughout our author's discussion of eunuchs, a considerable
        amount of wordplay involves the grammatical gender of the
        Latin words. Most of these effects cannot be rendered in Eng-
        lish, since most English words lack gender. One especially
        noteworthy effect comes from the author continually shifting
        the implied gender of the subject when it refers to eunuchs.
        The participles, adjectives, and pronouns vary in specifying
        feminine, masculine, neuter, common (either masculine or
        feminine), and all gender (feminine, masculine, and neuter).
        We have attempted to translate with the implied gender of the
        pronoun in English where possible. Even though this might
        cause occasional confusion for the reader, the same effect ex-
        ists in the Latin and seems to have been an intentional effort
        on the part of the author to emphasize the alterity of the sub-
        ject. For discussion of this passage and its relationship to wider
        medieval perceptions of eunuchs, see Clark, "Culture Loves a
        Void." Writing about gender and sex roles through the lan-
        guage of grammatical instruction was especially popular in the
        late twelfth century. See Jan Ziolkowski, *Alan of Lille's Grammar
        of Sex: The Meaning of Grammar to a Twelfth-Century Intellectual*
        (Cambridge, 1985).

51   *why the ablative case so pleases and the dative displeases it*: The sug-
        gestion is that the eunuch prefers the passive to the active sex
        role.

59   *unique*: The Latin adjective *mirivocus* appears to be another coin-
        age by our author. The adjectives from which it was created,
        mirificus (marvelous) and *univocus* (having a single meaning),
        also appear in some manuscripts, as scribes struggled to under-
        stand this new word—a word coined to describe a situation for
        which the author alleged no word could suffice.

59–61   According to Porphyry's *Isagoge* ("Introduction") to Aristotle's

Categories, a species is defined by a genus and a difference *(differentia);* "substance" is the highest genus, with "thinking" and "extended" as its differences, and "body" as the species of "extended substance." According to the author, since a eunuch cannot reproduce ("apportion flesh"), he cannot create other individuals like himself and so constitute a species or a genus. Hence, no other individuals can be a member of his species or genus. In dialectic, the relationship between individual and species is expressed in terms of subject and predicate. For example, in the statement "Socrates is a man," Socrates is the individual (subject) and man is the species (predicate).

66   *a monstrosity demonstrable with a finger*: This may simply mean that the individual deserves to be pointed out "with a finger" as being abnormal, but there also may be a coded reference to passive homosexuality derived from Juvenal, *Satires* 9.133 *(qui digito scalpunt uno caput,* "everyone who scratches his head with one finger"). If so, it would be a clear indication that the author does not just mean "eunuchs" in this passage but homosexuals, though it is worth noting that nowhere in the poem is the more common medieval term *sodomita* (or any form related to it) to be found. (Of course, one might think Ovid would not have known Jewish scriptures, but this "Ovid" does: see 2.159–85 and 194–95, as well as 3.635–36.)

79   *he is aided by no virtue of dignity*: The pun depends on the fact that "dignity" can have the technical meaning of "axiom."

83   *he lacks an even number*: According to R. L. A. Clark, "he quite literally does not have a 'pair'"; see "Culture Loves a Void," 289.

85   *in the end there sounds the lyre of the ass*: This may be a very complex—and potentially even bilingual—pun. Latin *ānus* is in the crudest sense an "ass" or "asshole," (compare English "anus"); with the mention of a lyre, we have the proverbial donkey playing the lyre. But instead of *asinus,* the author might know the Greek *onos.* Jean Le Fèvre's fourteenth-century French translation of *On the Old Woman (La Vieille)* also has "ass" (Clark, "Culture Loves a Void," 289). Because the context is sexual intercourse, this may also be a reference to passive homosexuality.

91–92   *his empty sack*: Surely a reference to the scrotum, devoid of testicles. See J. N. Adams, *The Latin Sexual Vocabulary* (London, 1982), 75.

98   *nor does it deserve the name "temperament"*: The pun depends on the fact that the Latin words for "temperament" *(complexio)* and "sexual embrace" *(complexus)* are closely related.

99   *so called by antiphrasis*: Antiphrasis is a rhetorical term meaning the use of a word in a sense opposite to its proper meaning.

103   *envious malice*: Compare Ovid, *Remedia amoris* 389 *(rumpere, Livor edax*, "burst, greedy Malice").

137   *positive law*: That is, human-made law, as opposed to natural law (inherent rights conferred by God, nature, or reason).

140   *sacred rites*: Jean Le Fèvre has *destinées* (fates) for *fasti*. In medieval Latin, *fasti* could possibly also mean "haughtiness" or "pride" (Clark, "Culture Loves a Void," 292).

141   *the priest will be either masculine or feminine*: A pun on the fact that the Latin word for priest, *sacerdos*, is a common-gender word (either masculine or feminine). In Latin grammar, the word cannot be neuter (literally, "neither"); hence the author implies that a neutered priest poses an unsolvable grammatical problem in Latin.

154   *hit a nail with a nail*: An ancient proverb, usually phrased as "to drive out one nail with another" *(clavo clavum eicere)*. Cicero used this phrase to describe getting over an old love with a new one. See Cicero, *Tusculan Disputations* 4.75.

159   *a certain book, whose author*: The book is Genesis and the author, Moses. A medieval gloss on this passage relates the following tale: "Plato, when he read the book by Moses, is said to have said, 'I marvel how that philosopher supposes everything but proves nothing.'" The Latin text of the gloss is quoted by Robathan, *"De vetula*," 150.

161   *credulous people*: "The Jews and today the Christians," according to a scholium on this text quoted in Latin by Robathan, *"De vetula*," 150.

168–69   This is a close paraphrase of Genesis 27:28.

170–83   Compare Genesis 27:10–40.

202   *In all of Nature's realm . . . face*: This line is taken from Ovid's *Meta-morphoses* 1.6.

229   *Hippolytus*: A common trope for male chastity, because he rejected the advances of his mother-in-law, Phaedra.

231   *work downward*: According to medieval manuals of rhetoric, one must always begin a description of a person with the head and then describe the other body parts in order from the top downward. Such descriptions of the ideal female body are quite common set pieces in high medieval poems and treatises on how to write poetry. Our author's description bears special resemblance to the one found in John of Hauville's *Architrenius* 1.364–2.71.

275   *nor did its length . . . indicate any infidelity*: This seems to refer to the medieval practice of cutting off or mutilating a woman's nose if she has been found unfaithful to her husband. See T. Pearman, *Women and Disability in Medieval Literature* (New York, 2010), chapter 3.

276   *drops of her brain*: Galen held that the mucus discharged through the nose came from the brain.

392   *sabots*: *Subarei,* a kind of wooden shoe traditionally worn by women in this period.

395   *kidney area*: The author seems to suggest that it is ironic that the part of the female body that is most desired is generally covered by cloth of the lowest quality.

443   *fresh grape juice*: This was a typical remedy for enhancing male sexual performance. Compare Avicenna, *De renovendis nocumentis* (Venice, 1582), tract. 6, pp. 1099–2000. Under the heading *"On impotency,"* Avicenna writes, "Their liquids and broths should be mixed with wine. He should drink meat broth. . . . A portion of grape juice should be ground up with it and drunk." The Latin text is cited in Robathan, *"De vetula,"* 152.

445   *clock*: The clock described here might be an attempt by our author to evoke an imagined world of classical antiquity, but giant stationary "alarm clocks" did exist at this period, in the form of the water clocks used by some monasteries to mark the hours for prayers. For the history of clockmaking in the thir-

teenth and fourteenth centuries, see John North, *God's Clock-maker: Richard of Wallingford and the Invention of Time* (London, 2006).

481–82   The author seems to suggest here that the girl would desire sex but would want to be compelled so that she could not be perceived to be at fault for the loss of her virginity.

484–85   This refers to the story told at *Metamormophes* 3.273–315, in which Juno disguises herself as Semele's old nurse, Beroe, so that she can trick Semele into asking Jupiter, her lover, to reveal himself to her in his true form. Semele asks Jupiter to do this under oath, and when he reluctantly does so, she is burned to ash by his divine presence. The first half of line 485 quotes *Metamorphoses* 3.278.

488   *the sound of the cithara was turned into a lament*: Compare Job 30:31.

490   The liver was thought to be the organ responsible for sexual desire. Compare Joseph of Exeter's *Ylias* 4.199–207, where Helen's overactive liver is blamed for causing her to fall in love with Paris, thereby triggering the Trojan War.

495–96   *I have sung of forms changed into new bodies*: Compare *Metamorphoses* 1.1–2.

576   The lover's reply to "Ovid" paraphrases one of Virgil's most famous lines (*Aeneid* 1.203): "Perhaps it will be pleasing one day to remember these things" (*Forsan et haec olim meminisse iuvabit*). It is echoed again below, in verse 669.

582   *especially if she has lost her flower*: That is to say, is no longer a virgin. The quotation comes from Ovid's *Ars amatoria* 2.665, a passage where Ovid discusses the advantages to having sex with older women.

585–86   The first clear indication that the setting of the poem is Ovid's Augustan Rome. Ovid's home was on the Capitoline (*Tristia* 1.3.29–30). A medieval gloss on the text here reports the following: "The Palace of the Sun was the chapel of the greater palace. Whoever has been in Rome and has seen the palace of Ovid would know the way, and it seems that this mistress was standing facing the bridge which today is called the bridge of Bartholomew." According to Robathan, "this is the bridge

which connects the Isola Tiberina with the Forum Boarium";
see Robathan, *"De vetula,"* 153.

618–19   *often the situation prompts a person to commit a theft*: According to a
scholium, this was a common proverb; see Robathan, *"De vetula,"* 154.

645   In 1230, Louis IX passed legislation forbidding usury (charging
interest on loans) in France. The sentiment in this line (anachronistically) might be connected to this; the offer of sex as interest stays within the letter of the law.

Book Three

3   *tugs at my fetters*: The word *nervus* can signify both fetters and
also tendons and sensory nerves (the strings in "heartstrings").
The meaning, thus, could also be "tugs at my heartstrings." Either sense (or both) could be intended here.

12   Compare John of Hauville's *Architrenius* 1.321–23: "I know what I
should do: as an exile, I have to search the globe for Nature. I
will come to wherever she secretly hides her remote home."

13   *previously revealed*: See 1.90.

19   *instructive and pursuant to mathematics*: The course of instruction
outlined here and in the following lines follows the traditional
ordering of the quadrivium, beginning with simple mathematics, that is, arithmetic, and moving on to geometry, music, and
astronomy.

21–22   *certain geometrical things that are in fact abstracted, but they do not
exist without matter*: This passage refers to the Aristotelian description of mathematics, transmitted by Boethius, as a concept that cannot exist separately from or independently of matter. Although for Aristotle mathematics was classified as "not
abstract," by the twelfth century it was being labeled as "abstract," yet still necessarily tied to matter. It is this tension that
the author seems to be highlighting in these lines.

27   *the part from song that the art of music writes*: The contrast here is
between music performance and music theory, that is, the liberal art *musica*.

40   *signifiers*: The planets and constellations, specifically as inter-
preted in astrology.

42   *in my greater book*: Compare *Metamorphoes* 1.72–73; Plato, *Republic*
508. In the Middle Ages, the "greater Ovid" *(Ovidius maior)*
meant the *Metamorphoses*, while the "lesser Ovid" *(Ovidius mi-
nor)* referred to the other commonly read works of Ovid, in-
cluding the *Ars amatoria, Amores, Heroides,* and the like.

164–70   This ordering of the planets reflects the geocentric (or "Ptole-
maic") model of the universe.

188–89   *for every circle . . . is equal to its longest axis*: The diameter of a
sphere will always have the same length no matter how it is ori-
ented, whether measured longitudinally (the axis) or horizon-
tally (through the equatorial plane).

194   *one general movement*: The zodiac is a feature of an ecliptic celes-
tial coordinate system; that is, its constellations are visible in
the plane in which the earth orbits the sun.

195–96   The axis of the ecliptic plane is tilted in relation to the axis of
the earth. This angle, called the obliquity of the ecliptic, had
been relatively accurately calculated in antiquity and the Mid-
dle Ages as being a little more than 23 degrees which, as our
author puts it, is just a little less than one-fifteenth of 360 de-
grees (24°).

229   *This lesser world is man*: It was common at this period to view the
macrocosm (the universe) as a mirror of the microcosm (the
human body), and vice versa.

262–65   The four humors (blood, yellow bile, black bile, and phlegm)
had been associated with the four elements (earth, air, fire, and
water) since antiquity. See Isidore, *Etymologies* 4.5.

264   *black bile*: The Latin word *melia* here must be a syncopated form
of *melancholia* (black bile), as Robathan suggests in *"De vetula,"*
158.

268   *fire surrounds*: On the most general scale, the classical cosmos
could be divided into four concentric spheres with fire on the
outside, then air, water, and finally earth in the middle.

292   *distant center*: This refers to the eccentric, the point in space
about which the planets were thought to orbit. In the Ptole-
maic system, the orbits of the planets were believed to be cen-

tered not around the center of the earth but around a point somewhat distant from the earth. Compare the similar discussion of the eccentric at John of Hauville, *Architrenius* 9.97–98, where Nature explains that the "eccentric orbit with a distant center is not fixed on the middle of the world" *(circulus ecentris egressa cuspide mundum / non figit medium).*

293   *epicycle*: The planets (which also included the sun and the moon) were thought to not only orbit around the eccentric but also to have their own smaller orbits around an imaginary point in space that moved along the path of the eccentric orbit (also called the "deferent"). These smaller orbits were called "epicycles."

372   *entelechy*: The vital force of biological organisms.

384   *Deucalion and Pyrrha*: The myth of Deucalion and Pyrrha is told at *Metamorphoses* 1.313–415. In the classical tradition, these were the only two humans to survive the great flood and repopulate the earth by throwing stones over their shoulders that then turned into people. Medieval authors generally identified this flood as the biblical flood. The myth is only tangentially alluded to here, as the main point of the argument is that, after the end of the universe, souls will return to their original bodies—not to someone else's.

395–97   *He also recollects . . . would suffer*: Ovid, *Metamorphoses* 1.256–58.

411–25   This passage is a close paraphrase of Ecclesiastes 12:2–7.

438   *banishes no one from it*: The verb for "banishment" *(relegat)* here alludes to Ovid's specific punishment, *relegatio.*

439–43   Here the poet echoes sentiments found in Ovid's exile poetry (e.g., *Tristia* 3.10.11 and 4.1.67). The Getae were one of the peoples that inhabited the area of Pontus where Ovid was exiled. Ovid generally expressed his dislike for the people but did claim to have written a poem in praise of Augustus in the Getic language.

443   *life is nothing other than a prolonged death*: Compare *Tristia* 3.3.53–54.

455–57   As Robathan puts it, "The author tries to reconcile statements of the Ovid of the Augustan period with those of thirteenth-century astronomers and philosophers" (*"De vetula,"* 160).

489   *authorities on the stars*: The direct source for most of the astro-
      logical claims that follow is Abū Maʿshar's *Book of Religions and
      Dynasties (De magnis coniunctionibus)* and his *Greater Introduction
      to Astronomy (Liber introductorii maioris)*. From the *Book of Reli-
      gions and Dynasties* comes the characterization of the six reli-
      gions based on the great conjunctions. The idea that Jupiter
      and the ninth house can signify religion may be found in Abū
      Maʿshar as well as in other astrological texts. For further dis-
      cussion, see Burnett, "The Astrological Categorization of Reli-
      gions."

533   *the Chaldean faith*: Zoroastrianism or, more generally, pre-Islamic
      Iranian religions.

535–36 *men revere the army . . . the Sun*: Evidently, a reference to ancient
      Egyptian polytheism. Roger Bacon's wording in a similar dis-
      cussion is remarkably close here and sheds light on our author's
      meaning (and potentially identity; see Introduction, note 8).
      He says, "If Jupiter is in conjunction with the Sun, the signi-
      fication is Egyptian law, which requires the army of heaven,
      whose chief is the Sun, to be worshiped" *(Si Soli [Jupiter com-
      plectatur], signatur lex Egyptia, quae ponit coli militiam caeli, cuius
      princeps Sol est);* see Robathan, "De vetula," 161. The "army of
      heaven" *(militia caeli)* is commonly used to signify the zodiac.

537   *our faith*: Greco-Roman polytheism.

539   *a written law*: Roger Bacon quotes this line in his *Opus maius* and
      explains that it refers to Islam, in his view a form of paganism
      with a holy book, the Koran.

546   *a vile faith*: The future religion of the Antichrist, the last major
      religion to appear before the end of the world.

554–55 *before the law of the Moon . . . made known*: Christianity, which fol-
      lowed the four faiths of Saturn, Mars, the Sun, and Venus (lines
      525–39) and preceded the faith of the Moon (lines 540–53).
      Compare line 690.

590   *A person would be lucky . . . the causes*: Though the overlap is only
      of three words, so famous is Virgil, *Georgics* 2.490 ("Fortunate
      is he who can know the causes of things") that readers will hear
      the echo.

595   *Jupiter and his father are in conjunction*: Every twenty years there is

a "great conjunction" of Jupiter and Saturn. Approximately every 240 years there is a "greater conjunction" of these planets, and roughly every 960 years there is a "greatest conjunction."

596   *triplicity*: An astrological term referring to a group of three signs of the zodiac that share a single element. For example, the triplicity of fire included Aries, Leo, and Sagittarius; the triplicity of earth, Taurus, Virgo, and Capricorn.

611   *one of these conjunctions occurred recently*: This "greater conjunction" of Jupiter and Saturn was sometimes associated with the star of Bethlehem. From what follows, it might seem that Ovid is meant to be writing this poem roughly six years before the birth of Christ. However, Ovid's exile did not take place until 8 CE—a fact that may or may not have been known to our author. But see also the discussion of the dramatic date of the poem, below in the note to line 769.

618–22   Mercury is "domiciled" (that is, has its most powerful influence) in the constellation Virgo (the Virgin). In astrology, there are considered to be four "essential dignities," which are, in order of value, house (domicile), exaltation, triplicity, and term. The dignity of a planet is determined by what degree of the zodiac it occupies at the time of the astrological reading. When a planet occupies a degree corresponding to its essential dignities, it is more capable of bringing about what it signifies. Mercury's house, exaltation, and triplicity occur anywhere in Virgo, but its term is limited to just the first six degrees (seven, counting inclusively) of Virgo.

624–33   The description of the zodiac sign Virgo has been taken from Abū Maʿshar's *Greater Introduction to Astronomy (Liber introductorii maioris)*. The author cannot attribute the description to the Persian Islamic scholar without breaking the illusion of Ovidian authorship, since he lived in the ninth century CE.

671   *for what began to exist in time cannot exist eternally*: The author's argument is that for something to qualify as a god it is not enough for it to live forever, it also must have existed forever backward in time. Thus, a god cannot ever have been born (as the Greco-Roman gods were) but must always have existed.

709–10   In the Middle Ages, many believed that Virgil had heard the

Sibyl's prediction and in that way prophesied the birth of Christ in the fourth *Eclogue*.

726–47   Comparisons of the nature of the Holy Trinity to Aristotle's causes first appear among Latin theologians in the early twelfth century; the sources of these ideas remain unclear. See S. Fazzo and M. Zonta, "Aristotle's Theory of Causes and the Holy Trinity: New Evidence about the Chronology and Religion of Nicolaus 'of Damascus,'" *Laval théologique et philosophique* 64, no. 3 (2008): 681–90.

769   *he has already come from a certain virgin*: This is the literal meaning of the Latin, but we note that the word *praecessit* (come before) poses numerous problems of interpretation. Chief among these is the fact that, except for in this one phrase, the author is careful to describe the virgin birth as a future event that has not yet come to pass. Even in the second half of this very sentence, the future tense is used; it is an obvious logical conundrum that Christ cannot have both entered the world already and yet also be about to do so. Rather than emend away the difficulty, we have chosen to present the received text since neither Robathan nor Klopsch note disagreement in the manuscripts here. However, we do suspect scribal interference early in the transmission, and we propose the conjecture *praedixi* as one possible solution. In this case, the line could be translated as "And I have already spoken above about a certain virgin, etc." However, if the manuscript reading is accepted, it is easier to reconcile the dramatic date of the poem with Ovid's historical exile in 8 CE.

774   *ear of grain*: A reference to the description of the zodiac sign Virgo found in Abū Maʿshar and quoted at lines 624–33. The author is reinforcing the idea that the zodiac sign may be equated with the Virgin Mary.

ON THE GROVE

8   *Opulence*: The female personification of *opulentia* gives the poem its alternative title, *Conflictus Voluptatis et Diogenis (The Clash of*

Pleasure and Diogenes), in the manuscript Vatican City, Biblioteca apostolica, Vat. lat. 1602.

23   *Paris and Ganymede*: That is, the effeminate men described in lines 10–18. Both are mythological Trojan princes. Compare *On the Crafty Messenger* 8.

27   *in a white wooden bowl*: The word *mazer* (wooden bowl) is rare in poetry.

35–36   Compare this passage to the similar description of a banquet at *Waltharius* 300–301: *Aurea bissina tantum stant gausape vasa, / et pigmentatus crateras Bacchus adornat* (Only golden vessels stand on the linen tablecloth / and spiced wine adorns the cups).

40   *now stuffed*: In the Latin, Opulence and her followers are all described in the feminine *(superatae)*.

41   *Diogenes*: Diogenes of Sinope, also known as Diogenes the Cynic, the fourth-century BCE philosopher noted for his simple lifestyle and behavior.

47   *Philosophy showed her nursling*: Diogenes was one of the founders of Cynicism.

53   *nature's goblets*: That is, the hands. One of the goals of the Cynic was to live self-sufficiently in accordance with nature.

68   *Falernian*: One of the most renowned ancient Roman wines, mentioned numerous times by Horace. See Plutarch, *Vita Antonii* 59.4, for Antony's quip about Sarmentus, the *delicia* (favorite) of Octavian, drinking Falernian wine in Rome.

69   *jacinth cups*: Cups made out of jacinth, a precious stone that is a reddish-orange variety of zircon.

72   *devouress*: *Voratrix,* the rare feminine form of *vorator.*

84   Compare Ovid, *Metamorphoses* 1.84–86: *Pronaque cum spectent animalia cetera terram, / os homini sublime dedit, caelumque videre / iussit et erectos ad sidera tollere vultus* (And although the rest of the animals face downward and look at the earth, he gave an uplifted face to humans, and bade them look to heaven and raise their eyes to the stars).

86   *these good men*: An interlinear hand in manuscript F glosses *his* (these) with *bonis* (good men), so we have incorporated this helpful elaboration into our translation.

90   One of the fundamental principles of Cynicism was an indifference to the vicissitudes of life (the Greek *adiaphoria*).

ON WINE

10   *a half bark*: Semilatratus appears to be a *hapax legomenon*.

ON THE DREAM

1   *It was night*: Compare Ovid, *Amores* 3.5.1 (*Nox erat et somnus lassos submisit ocellos*, "It was night, and sleep weighed down my tired eyes"); Virgil *Aeneid* 4.522; Horace *Epodes* 15.1.

7   *two figures*: Allegorical female apparitions, one positive (*bona*, "the good one," line 33), one negative (*saevior*, "the crueler one," line 31). Ovid, *Amores* 3.1 also imagines a contest between two female figures, Elegy and Tragedy.

17–18   The positive figure is revealed in line 56 to be prosperity (*divitiae*), representing Ceres (grain), bread, flowers, and wine.

21   *the Hesperides*: The three nymphs who tended Juno's garden at the western edge of the world.

25–26   The negative figure is revealed in line 58 to be hunger (*fames*), representing death, scarcity, and poverty.

45   *a man*: An interpreter of the dream for the narrator. Compare Genesis 41, in which Joseph interprets Pharaoh's dream as a prophecy of prosperity followed by famine.

49   *The four gusts*: That is, the Four Horsemen of the Apocalypse (Revelation 6:1–8).

ON THE STOMACH

7   Compare Lucan, *Bellum civile,* 1.8.

33   *a pontiff or a prelate*: In an ecclesiastical register, these would translate as "pope" and "bishop."

40   *Scylla*: The mythological monster plaguing ships opposite Charybdis in the Strait of Messina; see Ovid, *Metamorphoses* 14.1–74.

57   *Charybdis*: The whirlpool Charybdis is perhaps a more fitting metaphor than Scylla (line 40) for a hungry stomach. Compare line 66.

76   *townsman*: In classical Latin, *Quiris* (pl. *Quirites*) more specifically refers to a Roman citizen. Compare Ovid, *Fasti* 2.475–80.

    serf: In classical Latin, *colonus* specifies a farmer of land owned by another.

79   *Nabuzardan*: Or Nebuzaradan, the commander of Nebuchadnezzar's guard who oversaw the destruction of the Temple and the deportation of the people of Judah (2 Kings 25:8 and following). The Septuagint translates his official title as "chief cook or butcher."

82   *not a place but a pit*: A pun in Latin since the word for place (*locus*) is distinguished from pit or lake (*lacus*) by a single vowel.

91   *The stomach is for food . . . them both*: 1 Corinthians 6:13.

METAMORPHOSIS OF A PRIEST INTO A ROOSTER

3   *priest*: Anderson ("A New Pseudo-Ovidian Passage") identifies the *flamen* specifically as the *flamen dialis* who oversaw the cult of Jupiter in Rome. Lebek ("Love in the Cloister"), however, posits a medieval rather than an antique context for the poem, and identifies the *flamen* as a bishop or an abbot—a conclusion supported by the miter (*mitra*) worn by the priest in line 6. In Lebek's reading, the Vestals in line 4 are nuns, the "priestess in charge" (*prima sacerdos, praefecta sacerdos*) seduced by the *flamen* is an abbess, and the "solemn service" (*sacrum,* line 3) is the Mass.

6   *miter*: According to Lebek, this ecclesiastical headgear did not come into use in Western Europe until the eleventh century, giving a *terminus post quem* for the composition of the poem.

7   *priestly garment*: Lebek identifies the *byssus* as the alb, a long white garment derived from the Roman *tunica* and worn as a liturgical vestment.

16   *goddess*: The Vestal Virgins were in charge of the Roman cult of Vesta. In keeping with his medieval reading of the poem, Lebek puts forward the Virgin Mary as a Christian counterpart to this goddess.

22   *mother*: Presumably, the priestess's title of mother superior or

abbess. Note the mention of "sisters" in line 44 to refer to the women under her authority.

23   *full of the god*: Anderson notes that one would expect this to be "goddess" *(dea)* since the only deity introduced in the poem is Venus, but he leaves it at that. Lebek suggests that we are perhaps meant to understand Cupid here. Another possibility, however, is that the poet hoped that this phrase would be noticed and that it might help persuade the reader that this is "genuine" Ovid. Seneca the Elder (*Suasoriae* 3.7) tells the story that Ovid was so enamored of this precise phrase *(plena deo)* in Virgil that he stole it to use in one of his own poems. Yet this phrase does not appear in any surviving work by either Virgil or Ovid. Servius also does use the phrase, in his comment on *Aeneid* 6.50.

40   *he remained a rooster*: A joke? Having lost his clerical appearance, the *flamen* remains what he always was: a lustful cock.

On the Distribution of Women

5   *Neither gold nor gemstones*: Gold and gems are often connected in Roman elegiac poetry: for example, Ovid, *Amores* 1.10.61; *Remedia amoris* 343–44; *Heroides* 5.143.

13–14   *sat under the high middle arch of the temple*: Compare Virgil, *Aeneid* 1.503–7, on Dido's temple of Juno in Carthage.

14   *Numa*: Rome's second king, the maker of its religious laws, and a civilizing influence on the city (Livy, *Ab urbe condita* 1.18–21).

15   *every cleric*: The English words "cleric" and "clerk" share a common etymological origin in the Latin *clericus,* which possessed shades of meaning common to both of its English descendants. The clerics being celebrated here would have been among the lower orders of the clergy, who fulfilled secretarial and other such duties. Crucially for the poem, their vows did not forbid them from marrying.

23   *the pupils of Mercury and Mars*: Merchants and soldiers, respectively; that is, the laity.

33   *kyrie eleison*: "Lord have mercy." A prayer in the Roman Rite Mass.

36   *salty beans*: That is, a cheap, dull food.

41   *So each man retains his own gift*: The "distributions" of Venus can
           be summarized thus (following Hinz, "Kann denn Liebe Sünde
           sein?"):

           Clergy (lines 15–22 and 39–40) → 1. beautiful girls.
           Laity (lines 23–28) → 1. no girls, 2. the evils of the world.
           Monks (lines 29–38) → 1. no girls, instead salty beans, 2. the
           Kyrie.

AGAINST WOMEN

2   Compare Genesis 3:1–13.

19   *when another arriving*: We believe (with Lenz) that both the gram-
           mar and the idea are incomplete here and that one or more
           lines is missing. Potentially, the grammar could be made whole
           by emending *adveniens* (arriving) to *adveniet* (arrives), but in our
           opinion the sense could not.

29   *fatal embers*: Because they kindle the fires of love in the bones of
           men, a common Latin metaphor for falling in love.

30   Compare Genesis 2:20–22.

ON THE GAME OF CHESS

4   *eight different positions*: The eight squares in each of the eight
           horizontal rows.

7   *In the first position*: The corners of the chessboard (1a, 8a).

8–10   Working in from each corner, the knight is placed second (1b
           and 8b); the *aufin*, third (1c and 8c); the king, fourth (1d and 8d);
           and the queen, fifth (1e and 8e). In modern chess, the queen is
           positioned fourth and the king fifth.

9   *aufin*: The bishop, in modern terminology. See the note to *On the
           Old Woman* 1.600.

10   *his wife*: The queen.

11   *After these, the order of the previous nobles follows in reverse*: Work-
           ing back out to the corner, the bishop (1f and 8f), knight (1g and
           8g), and rook (1h and 8h). All of the pieces except for the pawns
           are often referred to as "nobles" throughout the poem.

12   The pawns, in the rows in front of the other pieces (2 and 7), advance first, opening the path to the other pieces (compare lines 19–20).

13–14   A pawn may capture an opponent's piece on a square diagonally in front of it.

15–16   A description of "pawn promotion," by which a pawn becomes a queen once it reaches the opposite side of the board.

21–22   The rook can move any number of squares horizontally or vertically, but it may not leap over other pieces.

26   The knight moves in an *L*-shape (two squares vertically and one square horizontally, or two squares horizontally and one square vertically) and may leap over other pieces.

29   *The aufin of the crossways*: *Trivius* (literally, "of the three-way intersection") may loosely refer to the piece's leap into the "third" square. In medieval chess, the bishop could leap two squares along any diagonal and could jump over an intervening piece. In the modern game, the bishop can move any number of squares diagonally, in all four directions, but cannot jump.

The Rule of the Table

1   *Grant that we*: *Da nobis* is a common liturgical refrain, as, for example, in the Lord's Prayer (*panem nostrum quotidianum da nobis hodie,* "give us today our daily bread"). The early reference to Christ produced doubt among manuscript compilers about the poem's attribution to Ovid (for example, in El Escorial, Real Biblioteca T.II.1, and Munich, Bayerische Staatsbibliothek Clm 18910).

22   *sow now what you shall reap in fullness with a scythe hereafter*: A common biblical metaphor (for example, Galatians 6:7–10).

25   *other fingers*: "Other" than the thumb and the index finger.

32   *no one who is healthy should lie on the table*: Contrast the Roman practice of reclining while dining at the *triclinium*.

39   *six-footed insects*: Presumably, lice; body lice have six legs.

43   *Whoever wishes to be elegant*: Ovid was associated with urbanity and elegance (*facetus*); compare the pseudo-Ovidian *On Love* and *On the Remedy for Love,* actually excerpts from the anony-

mous twelfth- or thirteenth-century didactic poem known as the *Facetus moribus et vita.*

66   *belch*: The meaning is not entirely certain. It could also mean "you will not gasp after you drink."

On Money

5   *black priors*: Dominicans.

40   *coastal wine*: The meaning of this phrase *(vinum marinum)* is unclear.

51   *glory and power*: Some manuscripts substitute *Nummi* for *virtus* (the glory of money), which changes the poem's closing moral.

On Love

1   *If... someone*: Though the overlap is only a word and a letter, this opening *(Si quem)* would put any student of Ovid in mind of *Ars amatoria* 1.1, which begins *Si quis...*

12   *I praise the pursuit of ... an available widow*: Elliot observes that "this advice runs counter to the church's teaching that widows were to remain chaste" ("The *Facetus*," 56n6).

33   *soldier on*: Compare Ovid, *Amores* 1.9.1, *militat omnis amans* (every lover plays the soldier).

On the Remedy for Love

2   *will be more fully instructed by our poem*: The echoes are still of the opening couplet of the *Ars amatoria.* Here, *carmine doctus erit*; in Ovid, *carmine doctus amet* (1.2).

5–34   The list of women cataloged according to their perceived bodily deficiencies may well derive from *Ars amatoria* 3.263 and following, where Ovid advises women how to make up for the less-than-ideal appearance afflicting each. Examples are the short woman *(brevis,* 263), the skinny one *(nimium gracilis,* 267), the pale one *(pallida,* 269), and the darker one *(nigrior,* 270).

15   *Like a cow, she is never satisfied by anyone*: Elliott notes that "in medieval animal lore, the cow was considered particularly wanton and lascivious" ("The *Facetus*," 57n23).

NOTES TO THE TRANSLATIONS

25   *black woman*: The literal translation here. Though it is possible that this phrase could be interpreted as describing any woman of swarthy complexion, the rest of the description suggests a racially charged description of skin pigmentation. Thus, in addition to the other negative "–isms" associated with Ovid's name in the Middle Ages, we might also add racism.

Another Poem on the Nightingale

2   *derive my name in obscurity*: The meaning of *in ambiguo* is not entirely clear here, but it could refer to a riddle-like etymologizing of the name *philomena* (nightingale). Michael Roberts points out (personal communication) that *–omena* is an anagram of *amoena* ("pleasant," line 1) and nearly so with *nomen* ("name," line 2). Note that we have preserved the spelling of the manuscripts for *philomena,* which in classical Latin is *philomela.* This could also be a reference to the story of Philomela told at *Metamorphoses* 6.438–674.

On a Certain Old Woman

7   *what a stench*: Literally, "by my nose" *(per nasum)*. One wonders if either author or reader was thinking not merely of Ovid's cognomen "Naso" but of the explanation for that nickname circulating in some of the medieval biographies of the poet, namely, that it derived from his knack of "sniffing" out scandals and the like.

43   *like a very wolf is to calves*: In other words, he will attack her.

44   *beneficial ibis*: That is, beneficial to humans, since snakes were thought to fear the ibis. Pliny relates that the Egyptians invoked the ibis to ward off snakes (*Historia Naturalis* 10.75).

45   *multiply*: Literally, "double" *(geminent)*.

On the Rustic

3   *I summon Apollo and I excite my Muse*: That is, engage in musical and artistic pursuits.

5–12 *you wandering-in-the woods . . . rustic*: The transition to the text of *Words for Pan* is abrupt, as if the speaker of the first four lines suddenly directs a string of insults at his imagined interlocutor.

6 *dog-master, rubbish-born*: In the later manuscripts, the *Cinyphie* ("Cinyphian," referring to the Cinyps river in Libya) and *hirpigena* (goat-born) of *Words for Pan* become *canifer* (a rare word, meaning "dog keeper") and *rudigena* (a *hapax legomenon;* literally, "born of rubbish"?).

ON THE THREE GIRLS

1 *As it happened, I was traveling*: Compare Horace, *Satires* 1.9.1.

6 *particularly tall*: The detail that one of the nymphs is taller recalls *Aeneid* 1.496–502, where Dido is compared to the goddess Diana, who, in this simile, towers over the nymphs accompanying her. It is indeed Diana whom the poet soon reveals (line 10) he has in mind.

10 *Diana*: Diana's famed virginity no doubt is also being evoked in the comparison, since this girl turns out to be a virgin, a major element of the story.

19 The three goddesses named here are not coincidental. They are the same three who asked Paris to decide which of them was more beautiful. In the following lines, the judgment of Paris is evoked again when it becomes clear that the narrator is meant to judge which of the three maidens is best at poetry.

53 *why describe individual details*: Compare Ovid, *Amores* 1.5.23.

60 The uncertainty as to whether the beautiful woman met in the wild is human or divine is traditional; compare *Aeneid* 1.327–39.

90–92 The third maiden sings of the rapes of Jupiter, the stories that Arachne weaves into the tapestry with which she would compete with Athena (*Metamorphoses* 6.103–28). Arachne's artistry was flawless, but Athena, enraged, turned her into a spider.

95 *Ismarian hills*: That is, Thracian hills, because Orpheus was said to have been Thracian.

144 *virginity intact*: The Latin (*salva virginitate*) is encountered in reference to the Virgin Mary; to have the same phrase used here

to refer to other-than-vaginal intercourse makes for a quite out-
rageous joke.

157   *Phoebus had already reached the high sea*: Sunset.

205   *hipbones*: We are to think of a choice cut of meat (perhaps a "sir-
loin," to modern palates).

231–34   The bed is painted with one of the same topics that the winner
of the contest related in her song: the rapes of Jupiter, stories
of transformation that feature prominently in the *Metamorpho-
ses*. In the form of a swan, Jupiter raped Leda (*Metamorphoses*
6.110 and following); the most well-known rape by Jupiter in
the form of an eagle was Ganymede (*Metamorphoses* 10.152 and
following), a male, though the author uses the feminine gender
here. For this female gendering of a male beloved, a possi-
ble fifteenth-century parallel is François Villon's "Ballade des
dames du temps jadis"; many critics believe that one of the la-
dies, "Archipiada," is in fact a garbling of Socrates's male be-
loved, Alcibiades.

235–38   This story is told by Ovid at *Metamorphoses* 4.167–89.

239   *he wanted to ensnare us*: That is, Vulcan did.

293   *I enjoyed the pigeon's legs served to me*: At the dinner described above
(especially line 205).

A POEM OF CONSOLATION FOR LIVIA

1   *mother of the Neros*: Livia, the wife of the Roman emperor Augus-
tus, was the mother of Tiberius Claudius Nero (the future em-
peror Tiberius) and Nero Claudius Drusus Germanicus (the
subject of this poem, born Decimus Claudius Drusus) by her
first husband, also named Tiberius Claudius Nero. These Ne-
ros should not be confused with Drusus's great-grandson, the
emperor Nero.

2   *now half of that name has left you*: Drusus's death on the German
frontier, after a fall from his horse, in September of 9 BCE pro-
vides the clearest *terminus post quem* for the composition of this
poem.

6   *nor at the mention of the name of your son*: That is, "Nero" (see line 1
     and note).

14   Arms and the toga here represent military and civilian (political)
     life, respectively.

15   *Just recently he cleared out our enemies from their Alpine lairs*: Drusus
     and Tiberius campaigned against the Raeti in the Etsch and Ei-
     sack valleys in South Tyrol in 15 BCE.

17   *the fierce Suevian tribe and the untamed Sicambri*: Two of the Ger-
     man tribes that Drusus battled in his last years.

22   *armed goddess*: Minerva.

23   *Gradivus*: Mars Gradivus.

28   *mausoleum*: Drusus was buried in the Mausoleum of Augustus.

39   *That great work of Caesar's*: Drusus had been under Octavian/
     Augustus's tutelage since the death of his father in 33 BCE
     (Cassius Dio, *Historia Romana* 48.44.4–5).

49   *the field or the forum*: That is, public life, which was not a woman's
     domain. The following line indicates that Livia kept within the
     expected Roman female sphere and looked after her house-
     hold. Schoonhoven (*The Pseudo-Ovidian "Ad Liviam de morte
     Drusi,"* p. 100) notes that "field" *(campus)* specifically stands for
     the *comitia,* the assembly for electing magistrates, which was
     being held in the Campus Martius at the time of the dramatic
     date of the poem.

65   *the stolen offspring of his sister*: The next four lines refer to the
     deaths of Marcellus, son of Augustus's sister Octavia, in 23 BCE,
     and of Agrippa, Augustus's right-hand man, in 12 BCE. Marcel-
     lus and Agrippa were the first and second husbands, respec-
     tively, of Augustus's only daughter, Julia. All of these, like Dru-
     sus, were buried in the Mausoleum of Augustus.

70   *his sister receives the funeral rites*: Octavia had died in 11 BCE.

75   *You depart, Drusus, and in vain your titles are raised*: That is, his fu-
     neral procession departs and the titles—literally, "names" *(no-
     mina),* likely referring to the placards *(tituli)* inscribed with his
     honors—that should have been carried in his triumph are in-
     stead paraded for his funeral.

85   *Tiberius*: The future emperor, born Tiberius Claudius Nero, is referred to by his cognomen (Nero) here and throughout the poem. To avoid confusion with the much later emperor Nero, we have used the part of his name more commonly associated with him, Tiberius.

86   *uncut hair*: Letting one's hair grow out was a sign of mourning.

89–90   *You at least saw your brother in his final moments*: Augustus, who was waiting with Livia at Ticinum (Pavia) for the return of his stepsons from their respective campaigns, sent Tiberius ahead to retrieve Drusus after learning of his accident. Tiberius arrived at Drusus's camp in time to see his brother still alive.

94   *under his brother's hand*: Tiberius would be responsible for closing the eyes of his deceased brother.

106   *Daulian bird*: The next seven lines refer to episodes related in Ovid's *Metamorphoses,* beginning with the story of Procne, wife of Tereus, king of Thrace, who avenges the rape of her sister Philomela by killing her son Itys and serving him as a meal to her husband. When Tereus pursues the sisters to Daulis in Phocis, the gods turn Procne and Philomela into a swallow and a nightingale, respectively (*Metamorphoses* 6.424–674).

109   *beating your feathery breasts with new wings*: The sisters of Meleager, son of Oeneus, who were turned into guinea fowl (*meleagrides*) after his death (*Metamorphoses* 8.515–46).

112   *when the stricken youth fell*: Phaethon, son of Clymene and the Sun (Apollo) (*Metamorphoses* 1.750–2.400).

139   *consul and victor*: Drusus was *consul ordinarius* in 9 BCE, and so was entitled to have the fasces carried in front of him (see line 141).

140   *such great titles*: Literally, such great names (*nomina*), that is *consul* and *victor.* See also the note on line 75.

142   *reversed*: When the fasces were carried in a funeral procession, they were carried upside down.

146   *the name of his maternal grandfather*: Marcus Livius Drusus.

158   *may your pious lips receive my spirit*: For the idea of the life escaping through the open mouth and being received on the lips of a

loving friend or relative (also at line 97), see Ovid, *Ars amatoria* 3.745.

161 *we will be placed in the same tomb*: The Mausoleum of Augustus, intended for members of the *domus Caesaris* (the imperial family). This tomb already held Marcellus, Agrippa, and Octavia (lines 65–70).

162 *your maternal ancestors*: Literally, "old ancestors," but referring to Livia's birth family, which has been supplanted by the *domus Caesaris* (see line 161).

173 *through the Roman towns*: Tiberius oversaw the transport of Drusus's body across the Alps to Ticinum. There, Augustus and Livia joined the funeral procession to Rome.

175 *Raetian arms*: Drusus's victory over the Raeti, a confederation of Alpine tribes, in 15 BCE, for which he was awarded the *ornamenta praetoria*, or "praetorian insignia" (line 15; Velleius Paterculus, *Compendium of Roman History* 2.95.1–2; Cassius Dio, *Historia Romana* 54.22; and Horace, *Odes* 4.4.1–28 and 4.14.8–24).

177 *with broken fasces*: It would seem that Drusus merited not only having the fasces carried in his funeral procession (turned upside down, as was common for funerals; see lines 141–42) but also broken.

180 *with his own hand*: Drusus may well have held the honor of capturing the *spolia opima*, the weapons and armor of the opposing general taken as spoils by the Roman general after single combat with him. This was considered to be one of the highest honors in Roman society, one only rarely achieved.

202 *we knights*: A reference to the author's equestrian status. Perhaps coincidentally, Ovid was also a member of the equestrian order.

204 *Ausonian*: A poetic term for the peoples of Italy.

210 *your mournful words*: Augustus delivered one of Drusus's funeral orations in the Circus Flaminius (Cassius Dio, *Historia Romana* 55.12 and following; Tacitus, *Annals* 3.5.1; Suetonius, *Divus Claudius* 1.5). The poet does not mention Tiberius's *laudatio funebris* for his brother in the Forum Romanum.

217–20   The *decursio* consisted of a solemn march three times around the pyre (see Virgil, *Aeneid* 11.188). According to Suetonius, the army paid this honor to Drusus every year at his memorial (*Divus Claudius* 1.3). It was also customary to call out the deceased's name three times once the pyre was lit.

231   This quarrel scene between Mars and Tiber recalls Virgil's description of Marcellus's funeral (*Aeneid* 6.872–74), furthering the association between the two presumed heirs of Augustus, who suffered early deaths (Schoonhoven, *The Pseudo-Ovidian "Ad Liviam de morte Drusi,"* 22–23).

245   *both Caesars*: Julius Caesar and Augustus.

258   *the god*: Hercules.

269–70   The Rostra (speaker's platform) in the Forum was adorned with honorific statues. A list of the honors that a man had won was usually inscribed on the base of his statue.

270   *we will be called the cause of your death*: "We" means "all of us Romans," because the inscription would read something along the lines of "he died for his homeland."

283–84   *the Ledaean brothers . . . and their temples, conspicuous in the Roman Forum*: The temple of Castor and Pollux, which had been destroyed by fire in 14 BCE, was rededicated by Tiberius in his and Drusus's names in 6 CE—a possible *terminus post quem* for the composition of the poem (Suetonius, *Tiberius* 20; Cassius Dio, *Historia Romana* 55.27.4; Ovid, *Fasti* 1.707–8). Schoonhoven (*The Pseudo-Ovidian "Ad Liviam de morte Drusi,"* 17) notes that Tiberius also announced the repair of the temple of Concord in his and his brother's names in 7 BCE, the year of his German triumph; the actual rededication took place in 10 CE (see Cassius Dio, *Historia Romana* 55.8.1–2 and 56.25.1).

290   *brother gods*: Castor and Pollux. See previous note.

299   *wife of Drusus*: Antonia, daughter of Mark Antony and Octavia, and mother by Drusus of Germanicus and the emperor Claudius.

320   *frightening the horses that had been given free rein*: Compare Ovid, *Heroides* 1.36 (*hic lacer admissos terruit Hector equos,* "here muti-

lated Hector frightened the horses that had been given free rein").

322   *Capaneus*: One of the Seven against Thebes. He was killed by a thunderbolt when he was climbing the walls of Thebes and challenging Jupiter. Evadne was the wife of Capaneus who, out of devotion, threw herself on his funeral pyre.

329–42   This paragraph concludes the consolation addressed to Antonia.

337   *the well-deserved surname of their clan*: Drusus and his descendants received the cognomen "Germanicus" (Suetonius, *Divus Claudius* 1.3).

369   *Life is given … without interest*: A reference to Lucretius's famous line, *vitaque mancipio nulli datur, omnibus usu* (life is given to no one as property, but to all as a loan, *De rerum natura* 3.971).

386   *Isarcus*: The modern river Eisack (see lines 15 and 175).

387–88   *the Apulian*: Likely a Dacian tribe. There is known to have been a town called Apulum in the center of the Dacian mountains (in modern Romania); Dacia was bordered on the east by the Black Sea.

388   *Pontus is but a short journey*: This remark would seem to suggest Ovid in Pontus, whether as the author or the person one is to think of as the author.

389   *the Armenian apt to flee*: Relations between Rome and Persia were settled by negotiation in 20 BCE, after Tiberius had marched into Armenia and set up a client king of Rome.

391   *the German world just recently known to Romans*: Besides his campaigns with Drusus in the Alps, Tiberius advanced to the Danube in 12 BCE (see line 387), while Drusus fought in Germany. The allusions to Pannonia and Dalmatia in lines 389–90 may refer to these campaigns of Tiberius.

413–17   Drusus died when he was twenty-nine, and Tiberius was four years older. In fact, Tiberius, dying at the age of seventy-seven, did live well past the sum of their two ages at the time of Drusus's death (29 + 33 = 62). Livia also lived as old as predicted, since, dying at the age of eighty-seven, she most certainly lived long enough to see Tiberius as a *senex* (old man). Such accurate predictions could be taken as evidence that the poem was written significantly later than its dramatic date.

435   *Panope, his maternal aunt*: Lewis and Short cite *Panope matertera* in this line as from Albinovanus Pedo, the Augustan poet and contemporary of Ovid, because it was to Pedo that Scaliger attributed the *Poem of Consolation for Livia* in *Catalecta veterum poetarum* (Leiden, 1573).

452   *both commanders vanquished Punic armies*: Appius Claudius and Gaius Claudius Nero. The former began the invasion of Sicily and the First Punic War, and the latter fought in the battle of Metaurus in 207 BCE.

462   *all the cities read on their placards*: Placards *(tituli)* with the names of captured cities were carried in the triumphal procession.

Bibliography

Editions and Translations

Alton, E. H. "De nuntio sagaci." *Hermathena* 46 (1931): 61–79.

Anderson, W. S. "A New Pseudo-Ovidian Passage." *California Studies in Classical Antiquity* 7 (1974): 7–16.

Bertini, F. "Amores III 5 e l'elegia pseudoovidiana 'De sompnio.'" In *Aetates Ovidianae: Lettori di Ovidio dall'Antichità al Rinascimento,* edited by I. Gallo and L. Nicastri, 223–37. Naples, 1995.

Bonacina, M. "De Lombardo et lumaca." In *Commedie Latine del XII e XIII secolo,* vol. 4, edited by F. Bertini, 95–135. Genoa, 1983.

Bretzigheimer, G. "Das Pseudo-Ovidianum 'De pediculo': Eine facettenreiche Laus." *Mittellateinisches Jahrbuch* 47 (2012): 347–85.

Elliott, A. G. "The *Facetus:* Or, the Art of Courtly Living." *Allegorica* 2 (1977): 27–57.

Farmhouse Alberto, P. *Eugenii Toletani opera omnia.* Turnhout, 2005.

Friedrich, A. "Das pseudo-ovidische Lehrgedicht 'De quatuor humoribus' als Beispiel mythischer Medizinaitiologie und Humoraltopik." *Mittellateinisches Jahrbuch* 42 (2007): 401–29.

Hilka, A., and O. Schumann. *Carmina Burana.* Vol. 1, pt. 1, *Die moralisch-satirischen Dichtungen.* Heidelberg, 1930.

Hinz, V. "Kann denn Liebe Sünde sein? Kleriker im Gefolge der Venus beim mittelalterlichen Ovid." *Mittellateinsiches Jahrbuch* 41 (2006): 35–52.

James, M. R. "Ovidius de mirabilibus mundi." In *Essays and Studies Presented to William Ridgeway on His Sixtieth Birthday,* edited by E. C. Quiggin, 286–98. Cambridge, 1913.

Klein, H.-W. "Anonymi 'Doctrina mense.'" *Mittellateinisches Jahrbuch* 13 (1978): 184–200.

Klopsch, P. "Carmen de philomela." In *Literatur und Sprache im europäischen Mittelalter: Festschrift für Karl Langosch zum 70. Geburtstag,* edited by A. Önnerfors, J. Rathofer, and F. Wagner, 173–94. Darmstadt, 1973.

———. "Das pseudo-Ovidianum *De quadam vetula.*" *Orpheus* 8 (1961): 137–41.

———. *Pseudo-Ovidius "De vetula": Untersuchungen und Text.* Leiden and Cologne, 1967.

Kölblinger, G. "*Versus Panos* und *De rustico.*" *Mittellateinisches Jahrbuch* 8 (1973): 7–27.

Lebek, W. D. "Love in the Cloister: A Pseudo-Ovidian Metamorphosis (altera sed nostris eqs.)." *California Studies in Classical Antiquity* 11 (1978): 109–25.

Lehmann, P. *Pseudo-antike Literatur des Mittelalters.* Berlin and Leipzig, 1927.

Lenz, F. W. "Das Gedicht *De medicamine aurium.*" In *Ovidiana: Recherches sur Ovide,* edited by N. Herescu, 526–40. Paris, 1958.

———. "Das pseudo-ovidische Gedicht *De Lombardo et lumaca.*" *Maia* 9 (1957): 204–22.

———. "Das pseudo-ovidische Gedicht *De luco.*" *Orpheus* 8 (1961): 119–36.

———. "Das pseudo-ovidische Gedicht *De sompnio.*" *Mittellateinisches Jahrbuch* 5 (1968): 101–14.

———. "Das pseudo-ovidische Gedicht *De ventre.*" *Maia* 11 (1959): 169–211.

———. "[P. Ovidii Nasonis] De pediculo libellus." *Eranos* 53 (1955): 61–74.

———. "De pulice libellus." *Maia* 14 (1962): 299–333.

———. "Der frauenfeindliche Ovid." *Orpheus* 7, no. 2 (1960): 107–17.

———. *Halieutica, Fragmenta, Nux; Consolatio ad Liviam.* 2nd ed. Turin, 1956.

Pascal, C. *Poesia Latina medievale.* Catania, 1907.

Pittaluga, S. "De tribus puellis." In *Commedie Latine del XII e XIII secolo,* vol. 1, edited by F. Bertini, 279–333. Genoa, 1976.

Richmond, J. A. *The Halieutica, Ascribed to Ovid.* London, 1962.

Robathan, D. *The Pseudo-Ovidian "De vetula": Text, Introduction, and Notes.* Amsterdam, 1968.

Rossetti, G. "De nuntio sagaci." In *Commedie latine del XII e XIII secolo,* vol. 2, edited by F. Bertini, 11–128. Genoa, 1980.

Schoonhoven, H. *The Pseudo-Ovidian "Ad Liviam de morte Drusi" (Consolatio ad Liviam, Epicedium Drusi): A Critical Text with Introduction and Commentary.* Groningen, 1992.

Schumann, O., and B. Bischoff. *Carmina Burana.* Vol. 1, pt. 3, *Die Trink- und Spielerlieder, Die geistlichen Dramen, Nachträge.* Heidelberg, 1970.

Sedlmayer, H. S. "Beiträge zur Geschichte der Ovidstudien im Mittelalter." *Wiener Studien* 6 (1884): 142–58.

Shackleton Bailey, D. R. *Anthologia Latina.* Vol. 1, pt. 1. Stuttgart, 1982.

Thiel, E. J. "Mittellateinische Nachdichtungen von Ovids 'Ars amatoria' und 'Remedia amoris.'" *Mittellateinisches Jahrbuch* 5 (1968): 115–80.

Voce, S. *Il "De Lombardo et lumaca": Fonti e modelli.* Soveria Mannelli, 2011.

Voigt, E. *Kleinere lateinische Denkmäler der Thiersage aus dem 12. bis 14. Jahrhundert.* Strasbourg, 1878.

RELEVANT STUDIES

Baldwin, J. W. *The Language of Sex: Five Voices from Northern France Around 1200.* Chicago, 1994.

Bellhouse, D. R. "*De Vetula:* A Medieval Manuscript Containing Probability Calculations." *International Statistical Review* 68 (2000): 123–36.

Bischoff, B. "Eine mittelalterliche Ovid-Legende." *Historisches Jahrbuch* 71 (1952): 268–73.

Burnett, C. "The Astrological Categorization of Religions in Abū Maʿshar, the *De vetula* and Roger Bacon." In *Language of Religion, Language of the People: Medieval Judaism, Christianity and Islam,* edited by E. Bremer et al., 127–38. Munich, 2006.

Castillo, C. "La composión del *Conflictus veris et hiemis* atribuido a Alcuino." *Cuadernos de Filología Clásica* 5 (1973): 53–61.

Clark, J. G., F. T. Coulson, and K. L. McKinley, eds. *Ovid in the Middle Ages.* Cambridge, 2011.

Clark, R. L. A. "Culture Loves a Void: Eunuchry in *De Vetula* and Jean Le Fèvre's *La Vielle.*" In *Castration and Culture in the Middle Ages,* edited by L. Tracy, 280–94. Cambridge, 2013.

Dörrie, H. *Der Heroische Brief: Bestandsaufnahme, Geschichte, Kritik einer Humanistich-Barocken Literaturgattung.* Berlin, 1968.

Dronke, P. "A Note on Pamphilus." *Journal of the Warburg and Courtauld Institutes* 42 (1979): 225–30.

———. "Pseudo-Ovid, Facetus, and the Arts of Love." *Mittellateinisches Jahrbuch* 11 (1976): 126–31.

Fairclough, H. R., trans. *Aeneid, Books 7–12; Appendix Vergiliana.* Loeb Classical Library 64. Rev. ed. by G. P. Goold. Cambridge, MA, 2001.

Ghisalberti, F. "Medieval Biographies of Ovid." *Journal of the Warburg and Courtauld Institutes* 9 (1946): 10–59.

Hexter, R. J. *Ovid and Medieval Schooling: Studies in Medieval School Commentaries on Ovid's "Ars amatoria," "Epistulae ex Ponto" and "Epistulae Heroidum."* Munich, 1986.

———. "Ovid in Translation in Medieval Europe." In *Übersetzung, Translation, Traduction,* vol. 2, edited by H. Kittel et al., 1311–28. Berlin and New York, 2007.

Langosch, K. *Das "Registrum multorum auctorum" des Hugo von Trimberg: Untersuchungen und kommentierte Textausgabe.* Berlin, 1942.

Lenz, F. W. "Einführende Bemerkungen zu den Pseudo-Ovidiana." *Altertum* 5 (1959): 171–82.

———. "*Rescindit ferro:* Una variante inedita nel Paris. lat. 13043 [Pseudo-Ovidio, Arg. Aen. VII 8 Sh.]." *Sincronie* 4 (1997): 211–16.

Munk Olsen, B. *L'étude des auteurs classiques latins aux XIe et XIIe siècles.* Vol. 4, pt. 1, *La réception de la littérature classique: Travaux philologiques.* Paris, 2009.

Préaux, J. G. "Thierry de Saint-Trond, auteur du poème pseudo-ovidien 'De mirabilibus mundi.'" *Latomus* 6 (1947): 353–66.

Reeve, M. D. "Appendix Vergiliana." In *Texts and Transmission: A Survey of the Latin Classics,* edited by L. D. Reynolds, 437–40. Oxford, 1983.

Richmond, J. A. "Doubtful Works Ascribed to Ovid." In *Principat: Aufstieg und Niedergang der römischen Welt,* vol. 31, pt. 4, edited by W. Haase, 2744–83. Berlin and New York, 1981.

———. "Manuscript Traditions and the Transmission of Ovid's Works." In *Brill's Companion to Ovid,* edited by B. W. Boyd, 443–83. Leiden, 2002.

Schnell, R. "*Facetus,* Pseudo-*Ars amatoria* und die mittelhochdeutsche Minnedidaktik." *Zeitschrift für deutsches Altertum* 104 (1975): 244–47.

Smolak, K. "Zu Text und Interpretation der pseudo-ovidianischen Elegie *De sompnio.*" *Wiener Studien* 96 (1983): 189–209.

Stohlmann, J. "Zur anonymen Tischzucht 'Doctrina mense': Ein Nachtrag." *Mittellateinisches Jahrbuch* 14 (1979): 282–83.

Tarrant, R. J. "Pseudo-Ovid." In *Texts and Transmission: A Survey of the Latin Classics,* edited by L. D. Reynolds, 285–86. Oxford, 1983.

Thiel, E. J. "Beiträge zu den Ovid-Nachdichtungen 'Pseudo-*Ars amatoria*' und 'Pseudo-*Remedia amoris*.'" *Mittellateinisches Jahrbuch* 6 (1970): 132–48.

Tilliette, J.-Y. *Baudri de Bourgueil: Poèmes.* Vol. 1. Paris, 1998.

Ullman, B. L., ed. *Scriptorum illustrium Latinae linguae libri XVIII.* Rome, 1928.

Viarre, S. *La survie d'Ovide dans la littérature scientifique des XIIème et XIIIème siècles.* Poitiers, 1966.

Villani, L. "Le tre nuces dello Pseudo-Ovidio: Riflessioni sulla *Nux.*" *Materiali e discussioni per l'analisi dei testi classici* 73 (2014): 99–112.

——. "Paride, Ganimede e la fonte 'etica' del *lucus amoenus.*" In *Natura ed etologia dall'antichità al Rinascimento,* edited by S. Pittaluga, 67–76. Genoa, 2015.

——. "*Pseudo Ovidius imitator sui* (De luco 25–26 e De ventre 63–66): La fortuna della creazione (poetica)." In Κτῆμα ἐς αἰεί: *El texto como herramienta común para estudiar el pasado,* edited by N. Olaya Montero, M. Montoza Coca, A. Aguilera Felipe, and R. Gómez Guiu, 139–45. Oxford, 2015.

Walther, H. *Carmina misogynica: Frauenfeindliche Proverbien und Gedichte des lateinischen Mittelalters.* Rev. ed. by T. Klein. Stuttgart, 2015.

Winter, U. *Die europäischen Handschriften der Bibliothek Diez.* Vol. 1, *Die Manuscripta Dieziana B Santeniana.* Leipzig, 1986.

Ziolkowski, J. *Talking Animals: Medieval Latin Beast Poetry, 750–1150.* Philadelphia, 1993.

Index